☆, Prologue

"Boom", the door of open suddenly, and 1 flickered instantly.

Shang Yuetang walked in slowly, holding the sword upside down. There were several rips on the lotus silk Pipa collar, revealing most of her snow-white and tender chest. Her snow-white plum blossom silk shoes stepped on the soft carpet, leaving bloody footprints with every step. She stared straight at the golden couch in the heavily lit area.

Under the three-and-five colored glass lamps, the golden couch shone with a hazy luster, and on the winding dragon head on the armrest, there was a slender jade-like hand. He leaned on the couch diagonally, his lips slightly raised, "Yuetang is great."

The room is full of colored glaze, precious trees and fragrant flowers, but none of them can hide this slow smile.

Shang Yuetang stared at him blankly, her breathing becoming more and more rapid, her hands trembling slightly. This man, this man, finally belongs only to her! With a roar in her throat, she pounced straight on him.

The man burst into laughter and stretched his limbs, letting the woman gnaw on him crazily. His low panting voice was mixed with whispers, "Yuetang is injured... They are all dead... I only want Yueetang, okay..."

Shang Yuetang made a hoarse sound in her throat, murderous intent and desire surged, and her eyes were full of bloodshot. She killed her master, killed her uncle, killed so many people that the Wuya Mountain was covered in blood, and finally got him.

From the first moment she saw him, she knew that this man would eventually bring her to ruin.

The man smiled gently, his slightly upturned eyes were shockingly dark, and his slender hands slowly embraced the graceful body.

The sky is like a dome, with countless stars.

The breeze swirled up from the bottom of the cliff, mixed with the faint scent of flowers.

Two figures flew out from the top of the cliff, as graceful as a startled wild goose. The figures flashed on the six hundred and sixty stone steps leading to heaven, and stopped directly outside the hall.

One of them laughed softly, "Ye Zi, it is said that there are thirty-three mechanisms and prohibitions in the Paradise Palace, with countless visible and hidden guards, and the defense is unparalleled in the world. I think it's just like this." His voice was ethereal and mellow, with a touch of unintentional laziness, as if someone had inadvertently played the seven strings. The moonlight was like water, and there seemed to be a faint halo flowing around her. The wide veil was covered with large silver roses, and the soft silver lily skirt fluttered like a butterfly, almost flying in the wind. She took a step forward silently and stretched out her hand to push the door of the palace.

The person next to her had a cold temperament. He reached out to stop her and took her behind him. "There is a smell of blood in the air, be careful." He pushed gently and the door of the palace was ajar. The door slowly opened.

The bright moon and starlight instantly disappeared among the shining pearls.

There was a person lying on the couch, with a lazy posture and seductiveness to the core. Her face was covered with an exquisite golden mask, but the exposed eyes were brighter than pearls.

On the snow-white carpet, a naked woman was curled up, with a pile of black and purple blood under her body. In the splendid room, the beautiful woman on the couch and the naked corpse on the ground were really weird.

Ye Zi hid the rouge behind her, glanced coldly at the woman lying on the ground, and then slowly returned to the person opposite.

"Wang Shi?"

"......" Speechless, only the slanted

phoenix eyes narrowed slightly.

The two looked at each other coldly.

Yanzhi slowly walked out from behind Ye Zi, holding a light green pill in her hand, "Ye Zi, if you want to ask a question, the other person has to be able to speak."

Second Senior Brother's "Divine Drunk" is said to put people and animals to sleep within a hundred feet. Even if there is an exception, the person is just still conscious.

Ye Zi frowned, and stretched out her hand a little too late. Yan Zhi's figure flashed slightly, bypassing the female corpse in the middle, and stopped in front of the couch.

Yanzhi looked at the golden couch in front of her with admiration. It was made of pure gold and had simple lines, especially the two black gems on the dragon head, which were crystal clear and shining.

When she crushed the pill and sprinkled it into the man's nose, she was still sighing in her heart that the world was going downhill and any random mountaintop dared to set up the dragon throne.

"Do you like it?" A very low and charming voice, completely different from Ye Zi's cold voice. Yan Zhi had just started to think, when the musky scent came over her head, and her waist was tightly embraced, and she was pressed down by someone.

At the same time, the sword light appeared.

The sword lights up sixteen states.

The shining tip of the sword stopped at the man's neck, the sword intent had pierced through his skin, and blood oozed out.

Ye Zi's eyes were already burning with flames, and she said word by word: "Let her go!"

The man smiled softly, his thumb gently stroking Yanzhi's neck, and his left palm gently released force. The veil shattered into pieces.

His eyebrows, like distant mountains, were lightly furrowed, and his dark eyes contained a hint of anger, but he was not frightened or afraid.

The man was startled, and his eyes were slightly rippled. Just like the ice melting, the spring waves wrinkled, and the charming look that captivated everyone quickly faded away, and the slanted black eyes became dark and unpredictable.

The tip of the sword had advanced an inch, and the knuckles holding the sword had turned white. Ye Zi's anger gradually cooled down, and his words were like ice and snow, "Let her go!"

The man seemed unaware and just pressed his thumb down slightly, and Ye Zi's sword really stopped. His eyes were still staring at the person under him with interest. Seeing her staring back at him without flinching, her small earlobes turned pink, and there was actually a hint of joy in her eyes, "You are both charming and smiling, and you admire my graceful beauty." Every word seemed to be lingering in his throat, romantic and charming.

The male body was pressed against her body, and her breath was full of strong musk. Yanzhi's anger rose little by little. Glancing at Ye Zi's left hand beside her, she felt calm and faintly sweet. Stinky leaf, it turns out that you can be so nervous sometimes.

The man was staring at her intently, and when he saw her eyes moving slightly, showing anger or joy, he felt something in his heart, and his eyes slowly became cold and fierce. He suddenly leaned forward and bit her lips hard.

"Bang", the clothes behind him were grabbed by someone and thrown heavily against the wall. His body turned around, and before the force was relieved, the sword light with murderous aura had already chopped down.

Yanzhi touched her lips, feeling ashamed and annoyed. Ye Zi had lost her mind, and was killed by every sword. Although the man was good at martial arts, he was also hit by several swords. He was seen falling and rolling, but he always found a way to survive when there was no time to lose. However, even with such actions, he did not look ugly, and still maintained the laziness and elegance in his bones.

Watching coldly, he saw that his shoulders and thighs were hit by several swords, and his gorgeous purple clothes were torn to pieces. Thinking of the instructions of the second senior brother, he slowly counted one, two, three in his heart...

Although Ye Zi was furious, his hands became more and more steady. His sword was sharp and sharp, without revealing a single drop of water. Although his opponent had been forced to be clumsy, his eyes were still full of indignity and humiliation. The scarlet on his lips pierced his heart like a needle. Yanzhi, his princess. Anyone who humiliated her would be killed!

His mind was clear, and the Lu Gou in his hand was in tune with his mind, humming and vibrating. Man and sword became one, the sword was like a meteor, and man was like thunder.

...... ten!

A perfect sword, with an unstoppable killing intent. Seven parts lonely, three parts stunning.

The tip of the sword came straight to his eyes, but the man did not move. In fact, he had nowhere to retreat.

"Ye Zi, he can't die yet." The long sleeves of Liu Shui wrapped around the tip of the sword, and Yan Zhi's voice was a little muffled. "Let's go." I finally went down the mountain, but I didn't see any fun. Instead, I was taken advantage of by others. I was in a bad mood and missed my master.

Ye Zi did not move, her murderous aura remained unabated. The man panted for a while, looked at Yan Zhi, slowly stretched out his slender fingers, and touched his lips.

Ye Zi's pupils slowly shrank, "Get out of the way!"

"No, you can't kill him." Yanzhi stood in front of him and said hatefully, "At least, not today." Second Senior Brother usually loves her very much, and she can't make things difficult for her Senior Brother.

Ye Zi's eyes moved to her red lips with difficulty, and then slowly moved away. Murderous intent suddenly surged, and the hook flew out of his hand.

"Dong", the black hair fluttered, brushed past the cheek, and went three inches into the wall.

Ye Zi stared at him coldly, "My name is Ye Zi."

If you don't kill me today, you can do it tomorrow. On the road to the underworld, I won't let you be a confused ghost.

He took Yanzhi's hand and looked at her deeply. Then they walked slowly out of the palace.

The candlelight in the hall was dim and the room was in a mess. Only one person was left, his eyes were deep.

The moon sets in the west.

After a night of silence, Mount Langya suddenly became noisy.

"Your Highness Prince Ju!" "Your Highness Prince Ju has found it..."

The author has something to say: Dear friends, Liu Liu has opened a new pit! Come out and show your face!

☆、Wedding

　　In the 43rd year of Shengyuan, Prince Ju Huangfu Jue, who had been missing for half a year, returned to the palace.

Ruizong was seriously ill, and the crown prince Huangfu Hao was having an affair with a concubine in the harem while he was in the palace. Ruizong was furious, deposed the crown prince, and exiled him to Youzhou. The queen knelt in tears in front of the bed and asked to make the youngest son Huangfu Yu the heir. The upright officials in the court, led by the Imperial Censor Xiao Dingfang, tried their best to protect the fifth prince Huangfu Xiu.

Ruizong had 25 sons, 10 of whom were given the title of king. Only the third, fifth, and twelfth princes were highly valued in the imperial court. The three of them were busy trying to win over the court officials. For a time, Shengjing was in turmoil and a storm was about to come. Only the tenth prince, Huangfu Jue, who had just returned from a disaster, stayed at home and refused to see any guests.

In the spring of the 44th year of Shengyuan, Emperor Ruizong passed away. The Minister of the Central Secretariat Wang Shouren and General Yan Yanzi of Yunhui followed the imperial edict and passed the throne to Prince Ju Huangfu Jue.

Wang Shouren was the leader of the civil officials, and Yan Yanzi was a military god. Twenty thousand imperial guards blocked the four gates of the palace and guarded the Suzaku Avenue. They easily pushed the tenth prince, who was at home enjoying the moon and singing, to the Taiji Palace, and the other princes were useless.

In the same year, Emperor Suzong ascended the throne, changed the reign title to Jian'an, and issued a general amnesty.

Wang Shouren was conferred the title of Duke Zhenguo, and Yan Yanzi was conferred the title of Marquis Yan'an. The Wang and Yan families were the most powerful at the time.

In the second year of Jian'an, Wang Shouren and other old ministers jointly submitted a memorial, stating that the harem was vacant and requesting the establishment of a queen. The emperor hesitated for a long time and sighed, "Without Ning Yunshu, who can compare with him?"

The old officials were demoralized on the spot. Li Kongfang, the Minister of Rites, burst into tears and died admonishing that beauty was the downfall of the country and that a virtuous woman should be chosen as the empress.

The emperor was furious and left in anger. He wore a yellow robe and announced the decree that Li Kongfang was pedantic and stubborn and disrespected the emperor. He was to reflect on his mistakes behind closed doors from now on.

The next day, Wen Qingyu, the Minister of Taichang Temple, and Bai Shuting, the Vice Minister of Rites, paid a visit to the Marquis of Yan'an's mansion.

Twenty years ago, the wife of the Marquis's mansion, Ning Yunshu, was the most beautiful woman in the world. Today, the eldest daughter of the Marquis's mansion, Yan Wanzhao, is also well-known in the capital. After the Marquis's mansion has a hostess who can gallop on the battlefield, it is very likely that it will produce another queen who is the mother of the country and has great power in the harem.

Since then, the Yan'an Marquis Mansion has been bustling with people.

April 16th, the third year of Jian'an, is a good day for marriage and groundbreaking.

Ning Yunshu half leaned against the rectangular table with huanghuali wood inlaid with mother-of-pearl and ivory stones, staring blankly at his daughter in front of the mirror. When did such a snow-white and tender girl grow so big?

The palace maids never tired of applying rose honey milk and white jasmine fragrance on the palm-sized little face. The thin eyebrows curved into the temples, and the watery red was blurred in the corners of the eyes. There was even a hint of pink on each cheek.

Where are those red lips that are always pouting? Where are those eyes that are so bright that they make even the stars dim? Is the woman sitting in front of the mirror really her naughty and eccentric Rouge? Why does she feel so strange to her mother?

"Yun Shu, Yun Shu?" Princess Changning held her arm affectionately, with a knowing smile on her face, "On such a happy day, you are not allowed to cry. If our queen is upset and her makeup is blurred, it will cause trouble."

Ning Yunshu raised his hand to wipe his cheek, only to find that his face was covered with tears. He smiled gratefully at Changning, and pinched the red gold and jade droplet armor hard into his palm, forcing himself to calm down.

The woman in front of the mirror had stood up gracefully, with her hair tied up high. The hair hanging down from her temples was as thin as a cicada's wing. She looked at me calmly and indifferently, and asked softly, "Mom, do I look good?"

Finally, she couldn't help but whimpering softly, and quickly covered her lips with a handkerchief. She nodded desperately, "It looks good, it looks good..."

Chang Ning chuckled and patted her affectionately, "You... are not as good as our queen, who can really control the situation."

Yanzhi stretched out her arms, and the palace maid put on a red silk gown with five phoenixes embroidered in gold for her. A halo of light swirled in the room. She spread out her sleeves, leaned forward and bowed, "Mother, I am leaving." Her voice was low, but her words were very clear.

The golden hairpins, the white jade cassia twigs, these layers of pearls and jade seemed to hurt her eyes. She slowly stretched out her hand, and every word seemed to be far away from her, "Yanzhi, be diligent and hardworking, day and night... do not disobey."

Yanzhi held her arms tightly to stop her involuntary trembling, and bowed down firmly.

Mother, I bid you farewell, my last bow. From now on, there will be no more Yanzhi in the world, only Empress Yan, a walking corpse beside the emperor.

The sandalwood incense in the porcelain-carved mandarin duck incense burner was curling, and the palace maids in the room were all silent. Only a slender girl raised her hands to her eyebrows and bowed her head to the ground. Her gold-rimmed skirt sleeves were winding on the ground. Despite the prosperity and splendor, it was difficult to hide the infinite desolation.

When she stood up, Ning Yunshu was already in tears. Yanzhi looked at her deeply, loosened her hand, and nodded to the palace teaching nanny, "Let's go."

Nanny Lai had served the Empress Dowager for many years, but she had never seen her so calm and indifferent. She was surprised, but said respectfully, "Your Majesty, please."

Ning Yunshu hurriedly took two steps forward to chase after her. In a trance, his hand was tightly grasped by someone. As he watched the dazzling phoenix dress disappear behind the auspicious dragon and phoenix screen, he could only cry out from his throat, "Yanzhi——"

Yan Zhi walked very steadily. After passing the central hall, out of the main gate, and onto the phoenix sedan chair, Yan Yanzi personally lifted the curtain for her, with tears in her tiger eyes, full of guilt and love. She just lowered her eyes and sat upright, saying softly, "Father, please go back."

She couldn't see Yan Yanzi's body tremble, her face full of pain and helplessness. She also couldn't hear the deafening noise of music and celebrations.

This deep and shallow, omnipresent red has imprisoned her heart tightly. If the heart is dead, there will be no suffering and no pain.

The phoenix chariot stopped at Chengtian Gate.

The Shao music bell sounded.

Civil and military officials stood on the steps.

Huangfu Jue stood in front of the Taiji Hall, his black brocade dragon robe with colorful auspicious cloud patterns and nine red gold dragons shining brightly. He looked at the people who were climbing up the stairs step by step, his black eyes were deep and unfathomable.

"Long live the Emperor, and a thousand years to the Empress! Long live the Emperor, and a thousand years to the Empress!" All the officials congratulated in unison.

Yanzhi's eyebrows did not move, and she walked slowly up.

Huangfu Jue suddenly walked down a few steps and rushed to meet Yanzhi. He grabbed her hands that were folded in front of her abdomen, and the softness in his palms was cold and stiff.

Huangfu Jue raised the corner of his lips slightly, "Is the Queen cold?"

Yanzhi shook her head slowly, her eyes fixed on the pair of boots with two dragons playing with a pearl in front of her. She leaned down and said, "Long live the emperor."

Huangfu Jue held her hand tightly. Under the heavy jewelry, he could not see her eyes. He could only hear her voice, which was very soft and cold, without any girlish brightness.

He laughed suddenly, "Queen, please stand up." He pulled her and walked a few steps to the front of the palace. Facing the officials who were congratulating him, he said in a loud voice, "Everyone, please stand up."

At this moment, a red sun has just risen, the morning glow is spreading layer by layer, and the layers of colored glaze on the top of the roof are filled with thousands of rays of light, dazzling the eyes.

The author has something to say: The new book is weak, so don't dive in.

☆, Bridal Chamber

The wedding of the emperor and empress was naturally grand and complicated.

After receiving congratulations from all the officials, the group went to the Taimiao to pay homage to their ancestors, and then went to the harem to meet the empress dowager. By the time they settled down in the Weiyang Palace and everything was settled, it was already dark.

The candlelight flickers red.

Huangfu Jue took the jade cup with dragon pattern from the maid. The red wine in the cup looked like rouge. He shook the cup gently, his eyes dark, and the corners of his lips slowly curled up.

The red veil was draped over and over, and on the red quilt with dragon and phoenix patterns was peanuts and red dates. On it sat his bride.

This is his bridal chamber, the bridal chamber that every man has once in his life.

Yanzhi is very tiring.

When the small wine glass appeared in front of her, her stomach twitched and she wanted to retch.

She stretched her hand out from under the

heavy silk and sackcloth, and gripped the wine glass tightly to stop the trembling. The man's breath was very close, with a faint scent of ambergris.

Fingers and palms intertwined, necks and cups intertwined. As soon as she closed her eyes, the wine cup was at her lips. The aroma of wine was so strong, how many years had it been hidden? Daddy, the jar you buried under the osmanthus tree, the jar that had been there for seventeen years, was it also as mellow and red as a drop of blood in your daughter's heart?

Get drunk. When you are drunk you can forget. When you are drunk you can endure.

This glass of wine weighs a thousand pounds. Yanzhi opened her eyes and looked at Huangfu Jue with an almost angry look. His hand was pressing on her wrist.

At first sight... Huangfu Jue silently thought to himself, and was satisfied to see the anger in her eyes turn into astonishment. He frowned slightly and said in a gentle tone, "The wine is too strong, let's change it."

Fuquan, the attendant, quickly brought over some snacks and said, "Your Majesty, you haven't eaten for almost a day. Fill your stomach first." He took the wine glass swiftly and whispered a few words to the palace maid behind him.

Huangfu Jue saw that the crystal dragon and phoenix cake was exquisite and pleasing, so he picked up a piece and handed it to

Yanzhi's lips, looking at him with a smile. He was indeed...very handsome, but he was dazed for a moment, and his eyes returned to indifference.

In the west wing, Daddy looked at her eagerly. What did she say? Even if I were a fairy from heaven, if it wasn't what I wanted, what difference would there be between me and a beggar or a butcher!

The pain spread from the bottom of my heart. I turned my face away from his hand and said, "I am not hungry."

"Oh!" A warm breath blew against his ears, and his fingers seemed to brush across his cheeks inadvertently. "This outfit must be heavy, are you tired?" His black eyes casually swept over the palace servant standing beside him, "Help the master to wash and dress."

Hot water was delivered immediately.

Linglong brought over the silver basin with mandarin duck, heron and lotus patterns from the bottom of the water, knelt down in front of the bed, and said cautiously, "My lady, I will help you wash up."

Yanzhi took off her phoenix robe and crown, and only wore a red brocade inner garment, which made her look even thinner. She nodded lazily when she heard this.

Huangfu Jue was sitting at the table, with Fuquan wiping his face, but he strode over, dipped the snow-white silk scarf in water, tightened it, and sat down next to Yanzhi. Seeing her black eyes looking at him warily, he just smiled and said nothing. He half lifted her chin with his left hand and gently covered her face with a wet towel. Layers of gouache, eyebrows, eyes and red lips painted in fine brushwork, he was tired of such delicate and lifeless puppets. The subordinates resisted slightly, "Don't move!" Although their words were smiling, they also concealed an irresistible majesty. The snow-white silk scarf was immediately covered with black and red. Linglong bent over and handed over another piece. He wiped it carefully and attentively.

After a while, he threw away the wet wipes and slowly looked at her face.

Yanzhi's back was straight, her hands resting quietly on her knees, allowing him to look at her.

Huangfu Jue's smile slowly froze, his eyebrows slightly raised, as if smiling but not smiling, he slowly said: "The wedding is very busy, the Queen... is very haggard."

Linglong looked at her young lady, who had an indifferent expression, sitting still, but her face was extremely pale. She knew that she was just relying on her stubbornness to hold on. The emperor's tone was unpredictable. She gritted her teeth and knelt down, "Your Majesty, please forgive me. Your Majesty admires your face and is worried. She has not been able to sleep well for several nights, so she looks a little haggard."

"Oh?" Huangfu Jue looked at Linglong, "You are really eager to protect your master, and you are so eloquent." He leaned over to Yanzhi's ear and whispered to Yanyan, "Do you really admire me so much?"

He was satisfied to see her small earlobes quickly turn pink, and her cat-like black eyes were tinged with anger, and suddenly became angry. Seeing her dodge to the side, he was about to get close to her, but suddenly he saw Rui Bai, who was serving him, come in anxiously and whisper in Fuquan's ear. He couldn't help but smile coldly in his heart, it really couldn't be quiet. He sat up straight and just looked at them.

Fuquan motioned Ruibai to go down, and saw Huangfu Jue's slanted phoenix eyes staring at him quietly. He looked at Yanzhi again, and it was as if it was a clay sculpture or a stone sculpture. There was a thin layer of sweat on his forehead, and abnormality was a demon. He was just hesitating, and Huangfu Jue said lightly, "What's the matter?"

Fuquan did not dare to delay and cleared his throat, "Your Majesty, Wen Liangyuan fell into the water. The imperial physician said that Liangyuan is already two months pregnant and dare not use medicine. Concubine Xian came to ask for your Majesty's instructions."

Huangfu Jue has been on the throne for a year, but still has no children. This is related to the royal bloodline, so he can only disturb the emperor's wedding night.

Huangfu Jue was silent for a long while, then stood up from the bed.

Fuquan quickly took the black silk robe with a blue-white gold lining and was about to serve him, but Huangfu Jue took the topaz double-handled wine cup he had changed into and came to Yanzhi, "Let's drink the wedding wine and toast together, and fly together."

His fingers were long and beautiful, and his dark eyes were full of apology. Yanzhi took the wine glass without saying a word and drank it all. A light laugh came from her ear, with a hint of bitterness, "Have a good rest." She stood up and Fuquan helped her get dressed, then strode away.

Fuquan followed closely and instructed the eunuch in charge and the head palace maid to serve carefully.

As she listened to the footsteps gradually fading away, Yanzhi finally relaxed her tense heart. She felt her limbs ache and she felt weak. Her eyes went dark, and she fell to the ground amidst the splendid scene of flowers in full bloom and dragons and phoenixes singing together.

Huangfu Jue walked out of Weiyang Palace, but he was not in a hurry to leave. He just listened to the sound of stringed instruments floating on the water for a while in the Hui-shaped corridor. When he heard a slight commotion in Weiyang Palace, he raised his eyebrow slightly, "Fuquan?"

"I'm here." Fu Quan was already accustomed to his unpredictable moods, so he stood by with bated breath.

"What do you think of the Queen?"

"The Queen... has an ethereal appearance and a divine temperament." Although every word was carefully chosen, it was not entirely a compliment.

Fairy-like appearance, heavenly appearance? Huangfu Jue smiled coldly. Thinking of the white dress that fluttered like a butterfly, the slightly flowing eyes, the anger and joy, his heart was a little hot. The prey has been caught in the net, and he has plenty of patience to grind off the sharp claws and tame it slowly.

"Let Han Lan go to Weiyang Palace to check the Queen's pulse some other day." He had already seen that the girl was holding on, but he didn't understand why her physical condition was so poor.

"yes."

"Let's go and see who is so bold as to disturb my wedding night."

The coral carpet woven with gold thread was smooth and soft, and people walked on it without making any sound. Amber walked closer, but the person leaning against the window did not react. Her black hair fell diagonally like a waterfall, revealing a section of her snow-white neck.

With a low sigh, he gently closed the wisteria carved window. Amber's voice was somewhat reproachful, "Master, the night is getting cold, go to bed."

A pair of blurry eyes looked at her, wet, as if carrying the rain in the south of the Yangtze River, and his voice was soft and dreamy, murmuring: "Amber, I can't sleep. When I think of him marrying someone else, my heart hurts so much. I can't sleep, and I will only have nightmares if I sleep."

Amber was silent for a moment, "The Emperor has already left Weiyang Palace."

Her eyes suddenly lit up, and there was a hint of purity in her smile, "He went...he still abandoned her...Amber, they are all the same, right, right?" She asked anxiously, with a bit of caution.

Amber nodded affirmatively, "The master is the most important in the emperor's mind."

"Oh," she patted her chest with her delicate hands and smiled innocently, "Go to bed. You have to get up early tomorrow morning, and I want to be the most beautiful."

Her smile was pure and beautiful, as charming as a young girl. But Amber's heart trembled slightly, the word love can mislead people.

The author has something to say: ················It's so cold············Floating

☆, Concubines

The Weiyang Palace was in a mess.

The brocade shirt with peony and phoenix patterns, the pleated phoenix-tail skirt with long sleeves and trailing legs, the golden hairpins and ruyi hairpins were all scattered all over the floor.

The palace maids and eunuchs on the ground were silent.

Yanzhi had loose black hair and no makeup on her face. Her face was pale. She was leaning on a yellow pear wood dressing table, her chest still heaving.

Yiyue and Laixi were the heads of Weiyang Palace, and they were extremely anxious. The Queen was supposed to receive the congratulations from the concubines in the palace in the morning, but the Queen Mother sent someone to tell the Queen to move to Yanxi Palace.

The Emperor and Empress got married, and the Emperor threw the Empress alone into the bridal chamber, and did not return all night. Last night, the Empress fainted from anger, and everyone saw it. The Empress Dowager's behavior was unknown. They were all old people in the palace, and they had seen many tricks of jealousy among the concubines. The current Emperor was romantic and amorous, and it was obvious that he did not take the Empress seriously, so the Empress Dowager's position was very important at this time.

Unexpectedly, the Queen would get so angry at this time.

As expected, she is a young lady who has been raised in seclusion. She cannot bear any grievance. Lai Xi quietly winked at

Linglong. We can't let the queen do what she wants today. There are so many eyes watching us in the harem.

Linglong looked at her young lady with red eyes, sighed, and said to Yiyue and Laixi: "Sister, come on, father-in-law, you go get ready first, I will help the queen with her makeup."

Lai Xiyiyue breathed a sigh of relief, bowed and left with the people in the room.

Linglong picked up the things on the ground lightly, and then slowly knelt down in front of Yanzhi. Yanzhi looked straight at her, with a willful look in her eyes.

Linglong held her hand in her palm and said softly, "Miss, Linglong entered the mansion when she was eight years old. Madam used 100 taels to make my father sign a death contract and taught me music, chess, calligraphy and painting, just to keep you company. Linglong knows the pain in your heart. Linglong will not object to whatever you want to do. Wherever you want to go, Linglong will accompany you."

Her voice was soft and gentle, like the water in a stream just melting from the ice and snow, clear and pure, neither fast nor slow.

Yanzhi's eyes slowly calmed down, the sky was endless, "Linglong, I can't hold on any longer, please leave the palace and take good care of mother for me."

She was originally a free lark in the sky, escorted by the bravest eagle in the north.

She could do whatever she wanted and travel thousands of miles. Shanji had a predestined relationship with her, and she would take on the unfairness with her sword. She really couldn't be a canary in this palace, let alone dress up and talk cleverly to compete with thousands of women for a man.

I would rather die than be without liberty. Linglong's tears flowed slowly, "Wherever the young lady is, Linglong is there. Before the madam came to the palace, she only gave Linglong one word – delay. Miss, can you bear it a little longer, okay? The cup of daughter's red wine last night was prepared by the madam a long time ago. It's just that thinking that the young lady is drunk, some things... can be endured. For the madam, wiping out the young lady's pride with her own hands is more painful than cutting out her heart. But the emperor didn't stay overnight in Weiyang Palace," she raised her head, tears welling up in her eyelashes, "Miss, if you can get through this night, there is hope for everything. For the madam, for Master Zhishang, wait a little longer, okay?"

Can you wait a little longer? Can you? The best is to live alone with a green lamp, but it is worse than death. Yanzhi laughed softly. There will always be so much love that is the heaviest and most restrictive. It makes people unable to breathe and unable to break free.

As soon as the Queen's phoenix sedan arrived at the gate of Yanxi Palace, Eunuch Cui and Nanny Lai, who were waiting there, knelt down with a group of palace maids and eunuchs, and shouted, "Long live the Queen!"

Lai Xi was certain of this when he saw it. Eunuch Cui was the chief steward of the Yanxi Palace, a man who had the final say in the palace; Nanny Lai was an old lady who had served the empress dowager since she was a child, and even the emperor had to respectfully call her Nanny when he saw her. These two people directly represented the empress dowager's attitude.

After Yanzhi "stood up", Lai Xi hurriedly helped Eunuch Cui up, "Little Xizi greets Eunuch Cui," and quietly handed over a green jade ring from his wide sleeves, laughing softly, "This is a meeting gift from the Queen to Eunuch Cui."

Eunuch Cui narrowed his eyes into crescents, and he slowly straightened his sleeves and said in a low voice: "You are very lucky. Serve him well, this person is of extraordinary origin."

Yiyue also helped Nanny Lai up, and the group then gathered together and headed towards the main hall of Yanxi Palace.

The current Empress Dowager, Nalan Ruoshui, was the empress of Emperor Ruizong. She had been in charge of the harem for decades and was deeply respected by Emperor Ruizong. After Huangfu Jue ascended the throne, his mother died early, and Empress Nalan was promoted to a higher rank. Huangfu Jue also respected the Empress Dowager very much and would pay him respects every morning and evening.

As soon as Yanzhi entered the flower hall, all the maids in the room knelt down to greet her. A little girl with bright eyes and a smile lifted the red curtain of the East Warm Pavilion. Then a hearty laugh floated out, "Yanzhi is here, come in quickly. There is someone waiting here eagerly."

The room was filled with laughter, but no one could suppress that soft voice, "Sister talks about it all the time and keeps it in mind, how can I not be curious?"

As soon as she entered the east warm room, the heat hit her face. Several smiling eyes, some scrutinizing, some evaluating, Yanzhi only noticed a bunch of winter jasmine flowers in a phoenix-head plum vase on the yellow pear wood flower stand, with swaying branches and delicate yellow stamens.

It was not the first time that he had met the Queen Mother. When Ruizong was in power, he had brought her into the palace to meet her twice. Although he had not seen her for several years, she was still graceful and elegant except for the fine lines at the corners of her eyes.

The maid spread out the brocade cushion and was about to kneel down to pay her respects. The Queen Mother grabbed her and pulled her to her side, "You are a family, why are you going through all the trouble of formalities? Show them how you are as a queen mother!"

It was that soft voice again, "Sister is really lucky. The wife of Marquis of Yan'an is hard to find in the world. I didn't expect that our queen is even better. She is truly a figure in a painting, a fairy concubine."

The person who was speaking was the woman sitting on the high-backed mahogany chair on the left side of the kang. She was wearing a palace dress with a high bun and a huge oriental pearl hanging from her forehead. Her manners were reserved and her movements were elegant. Her eyes were full of affection and looked at me with a haze of smoke in them.

The Queen Mother smiled and patted Yanzhi's hand, "Your Majesty is so lucky. Yanzhi, this is Concubine Wang."

Concubine Wang, Wang Linbo. The most beloved concubine of the late emperor. The younger sister of the current Right Prime Minister Wang Shouren, and the biological mother of Princess Qingping.

Yanzhi then called out "Toffee".

The Queen Dowager bowed slightly. Her eyes flickered slightly. The maid behind her brought up a red sandalwood box filled with gold and painted. She touched her hair with her green jade fingers and held it against her cheek. "These things of mine were all given by the late emperor when he was alive. They won't please you young people. If your Majesty doesn't like them, keep them as a reward for others."

Yanzhi raised her eyes and smiled softly, "The things of the imperial concubine are naturally good." Linglong took the box and Yanzhi opened it casually. It was a gold filigree inlaid ruby with double phoenixes and kingfisher feathers. The ruby was deep red and shining. Yanzhi closed the box gently. She was the daughter of the Marquis of Yan'an, and her master loved to collect rare treasures from all over the world. Although this hairpin was precious, it was difficult because of its fine workmanship.

"Thank you, Toffee."

Concubine Wang smiled but said nothing. The Queen Mother had already grabbed her hand and smiled as she looked at the people on the right. "This is Concubine Chen and Concubine Xiao." Both Concubines lived with their sons in their fiefdoms and had come to the capital specifically for the emperor's wedding. They both stood up with a smile.

Yanzhi saw that although the two behaved in a low-key manner, they were calm and not flashy. They should be living a very comfortable life in their son's fiefdom. She also took the brocade box handed over by the two with a smile. Concubine Xiao gave a gold-threaded fragrant wood inlaid cicada jade pendant. Yanzhi was very happy.

She held it in her palm and asked the Queen Mother, "Mother... Queen, does it look good?"

She came from the house with a calm expression. Although she was wearing a deep red brocade, her skin looked even colder than the frost and snow, which made her look even colder. It made people feel that she was aloof and arrogant, and difficult to approach. At this moment, she smiled and had a dimple. Her expression was bright, charming and lovely, which was unique to girls.

The Queen Mother was startled, then looked at her lovingly, "It is indeed beautiful." Then she smiled and said, "This golden fragrant wood is a good thing. Wearing it can calm your mind and concentrate your spirit."

The Queen Mother supported her chin with her bare hand, her sleeves with gold-threaded cloud patterns slid down, and the green jade bracelet on her wrist made her skin almost transparent. She burst into laughter, "Sister, you only care about praising others. Is it for nothing that Yanzhi calls you mother?" She smiled lightly, but her tone was extremely sincere. The sunlight at dawn shone on her face, which was perfect without a single flaw.

The Queen Mother just looked at the rouge with a smile, "My Queen Mother never likes to mix rouge and powder, but this thing has been with her for many years." The palace maid next to her handed over a wooden box with a yellow silk bottom, and the Queen Mother picked up a long hairpin with a golden phoenix pattern from it, with a look of nostalgia in her eyes, "This is the hairpin that the late Emperor personally pinned on my wedding day when he was still the Crown Prince. My Queen Mother gives it to you. I hope that you and the Emperor will be like me and the late Emperor, respect each other, support each other, have many children and grandchildren, and protect our vast country."

She carefully tied the long hairpin to Yanzhi's thick hair, her eyes solemn. Yanzhi saw that the smile of Concubine Wang had solidified on her lips, her eyes were unusually bright, and she looked straight at her. Slowly, her eyes dimmed, but there was a kind of sadness that penetrated deep into her bones. Avoiding her gaze, covering her lips with her long sleeves, she took a sip of tea.

Yanzhi's heart gradually grew colder and colder. This stunningly beautiful woman still had her own pride. What could support this pride? Was it the jealousy that kept her awake all night, or the endless loneliness?

The bright-eyed girl who opened the curtain came into the room, chirping, "Old Buddha, the masters of all the palaces have arrived."

The Queen Mother took Yanzhi's hand and

stood up. "I was so busy talking to you sisters that I almost forgot the time. Now that you have met the person, I am going to take him away."

Concubine Xiao Chen stood up with a smile.

The Queen Mother waved her hand, supported Yanzhi's hand and walked out, "You guys do it, we'll have tea later."

The author has something to say: Well, dear friends, if you don't urge me to update, Liu Liu really has no pressure. Just whip me as much as you want...

☆、Having a Son (Part 1)

beat

Linde Hall in front of the Yanxi Palace.

The palace maids were all wearing short round-necked shirts embroidered with small sunflower flowers. They lowered their brows and eyes, served tea and water, and their movements were silent.

Huangfu Jue had just ascended the throne and did not hold a large-scale selection of concubines. He only appointed his concubine Zhang Yuerong as the virtuous concubine. When he appointed Wang Shouren's legitimate daughter Wang Yan as the virtuous concubine, two of the four concubines were still vacant. There were only three concubines. At this moment, all five of them gathered in the Linde Hall.

The fact that the concubines went to the

Yanxi Palace instead of the Weiyang Palace to pay homage to the empress is intriguing in itself. They were all very observant and knew that the emperor had left the empress alone in the bridal chamber.

Some were smiling, some were concentrating, some were drinking tea, and some were sitting quietly. All five of them chose to remain silent. In the palace, those who were the most popular usually died the fastest.

When Yanzhi helped the empress dowager out from behind the four-panel mahogany screen in the side hall, all five of them were stunned. There was no shortage of beauties in the harem, but such a beautiful and graceful person, as beautiful as snow and jade, was rare.

The five people stood up, put on their clothes, and knelt down gracefully, "Good luck to the Queen Mother, good luck to the Queen."

The Queen Mother saw Yan Zhi's expressionless face, and there was a hint of annoyance in her expression, so she couldn't help but sigh in her heart. She smiled and looked down, "Everyone get up." She turned her eyes to Concubine Xian and asked with concern, "How is Wen Liangyuan now?"

Xianfei Zhang Yuerong stood up and smiled gracefully, "Thanks to the Queen Mother's blessing, Liangyuan and the baby in her belly are fine."

"Amitabha, Amitabha!" The Queen Mother clasped her hands together in the air, looking relieved, "May our ancestors bless us. This is the Emperor's first child, plus the Empress's wedding, so our Huangfu family is having a double celebration." She moved sideways and took Yan Zhi's hand, "Queen, all the concubines with positions in this palace are here. From now on, I will hand over this harem to you. Remember to be impartial and fair, and treat everyone equally, so that our descendants will continue for thousands of years."

Yanzhi looked at the sincere and loving eyes in her eyes, felt heavy in her heart, and nodded gently.

The Queen Mother looked at her with mixed feelings. She was clearly an orchid in the deep valley, but she happened to be in a wealthy place, in the most noble imperial family. Yun Shu, the darkest place is the palace. What can I do to keep these crystal clear eyes?

She sighed inwardly, straightened her face, and glanced at Concubine Shu and Concubine Xian, "The most important thing in the harem is harmony. Seeing you so dignified and generous, I am very happy. Serve the emperor well, assist the queen, and do your duty as a concubine, and I will reward you handsomely."

She had been in charge of the harem for many years and had accumulated great power. This one look left the five people with lingering fears and they all agreed.

The Queen Mother patted Yanzhi's hand and said gently, "You young people can chat among yourselves. Wang Yan is also new here, so go to the garden with her. After the Emperor's morning court, go to Concubine Xian to see Wen Liangyuan. This is related to the heir to the throne, so we can't be careless."

Xian Fei had already stood up and said with a smile: "Don't worry, Queen Mother, I, an experienced and experienced concubine, will definitely lead the way."

"You——" The Queen Mother smiled with a hint of doting.

Yanzhi also slightly curved her lips, but the smile was too shallow, and before it reached her eyes, it was swallowed up by the calm inky blackness.

On Taiye Lake, the blue waves are endless and the floating light is golden. Although there are no lotus leaves reaching the sky, just this water can cleanse the dust in your heart.

"I'll just sit here for a while, you guys go by yourselves." Yanzhi picked up a piece of Taibai Lake stone that was leaning against the railing, sat down leisurely, picked a double-stamen crabapple, tore the petals casually, and teased the koi in the pond.

The virtuous concubine was startled, and she opened her mouth but said nothing. She smiled bitterly and ordered the maid to prepare a brocade hand warmer, tea and snacks.

Linglong helped Yanzhi put on the soft fur brocade cape. Seeing that her face was already slightly pale, she couldn't help but said worriedly, "Madam, it's cold by the lake, you can't sit down."

Yanzhi waved her hands and stared at the pond intently. Red carps were waving their heads, chasing after the delicate stamens.

Xianfei walked up to Shufei and saw that she was just looking at Yanzhi. She smiled and said, "The Queen likes quietness. Why don't you accompany me for a walk?"

Concubine Shu smiled gently and smoothed her hair that was messed up by the wind, "Don't bother me, sister. Yan'er also thinks the scenery of Taiye Lake is quite beautiful." After that, she walked leisurely into the small pavilion next to her.

A trace of anger flashed across Concubine Xian's delicate makeup. Seeing Concubine Xiang looking at her with a half-smile, she could only suppress her unhappiness and said with a forced smile, "Among the twelve scenic spots in Shangyuan, Taiye Lake is the best."

Concubine Xiang covered her lips with a handkerchief that was used to welcome the sun after the rain and giggled, "Empress Xianfei is right, Taiye Lake is indeed beautiful. I can look at it every day and never get tired of it." She swayed her slender waist and went to the pavilion with Concubine Qi.

Xiangpin's father was the governor of Henan Province, a high-ranking official. He had never taken Xianfei, who came from a humble background, seriously, but it was the first time that he had spoken so disrespectfully to her. Xianfei saw the two of them chatting and laughing with Shufei in the pavilion, and she felt her temples throbbing, and it took her a long time to suppress her panic. A cup of chrysanthemum tea was handed over, and the bright yellow petals slowly stretched in the water. It was Tianpin.

Xian Fei's heart was slightly moved, and she took it with a smile, "My sister is thoughtful."

Concubine Tian smiled, "You're welcome, sister." She looked at the lake quietly, her profile peaceful and sweet, "It's windy, it's still very cold in April."

As soon as Huangfu Jue came home from the morning court, Fuquan met him and announced the empress dowager's message, saying that the queen was waiting for him to go visit Wen Liangyuan together.

Huangfu Jue was helped by Rui Bai to wash his face. As the warm towel brushed across his neck, he sighed comfortably. Rui Bai bit her lower lip, her eyes watery. Huangfu Jue placed his hands on her waist, rubbing it slowly. After a while, he asked, "Did the Queen Mother Jiang summon you to the

Yanxi Palace in the morning?"
Fuquan lowered his eyebrows and closed his eyes, "Yes. There are also concubines and queens above the rank of concubine."
Huangfu Jue raised the corner of his lips. His mother was really kind-hearted. That's good. With both the red cop and the white cop, the show would be lively.
"how?"
"The Empress Dowager was very happy and gave the Golden Phoenix Hairpin bestowed by the late Emperor to the Empress. The three concubines also received gifts. The Empress especially liked the Golden Thread Fragrant Wood Jade Pendant given by Concubine Xiao."
"Hmm..." Rui Bai hummed softly. The man's big hand squeezed her perky buttocks hard.
"Where's the Queen Mother?"
"The Concubine Dowager gave the Queen a pair of green jadeite and phoenix hairpins, but the Queen... didn't seem to like it."
His long black eyes lit up, his wandering hands paused, and Huangfu Jue chuckled. He's busy making enemies for himself so soon, little beast, picking only the hardest bones to chew.
Pushing away the already emotional Rui Bai, he asked, "Where is the Queen now?"
Fuquan said without hesitation, "The Queen, along with Consort Shu, Consort Xian, Consort Tian, Consort Xiang, and Consort Qi, are feeding the fish in Taiye Lake."
Flowers bloom on the roadside, willows sway by the pond. However, no matter how strong

the spring is in Shangyuan, it cannot compare to the vivid beauty of the world.

Huangfu Jue saw Yanzhi sitting alone against a rock at a glance. The bright red dress made her skin look even whiter, and she looked pure and innocent. She was like a red plum blossom in the snow, with a red wine stain on her jade skin.

"Your Majesty!" Xiangpin was the first to see him, she was surprised and delighted. Xianfei and others gathered around and bowed down. Their eyes were full of affection and deep love.

Concubine Shu blushed as well, looking at him with eyes full of smiles. This was her husband. Last night he had sex with someone else, and she could only sit alone in the bridal chamber. Her heart was half hot and half cold. One day, she would become the woman who stood shoulder to shoulder with such a man.

The young girl in her twenties has intoxicating eyes, fresh and bright like the new dew on the lotus.

Huangfu Jue smiled, watching her stand up, and called her Your Majesty indifferently. Her cheeks were unnaturally flushed, her lips were pale, and the golden phoenix on her temples was about to fly. He smiled more gently and subtly. He took the hand of the person next to him and asked softly, "Why are your hands so cold?"

"Your Majesty... Your Majesty..." Concubine Shu was nervous, and her heart was pounding with joy. She could only raise her head secretly and glance at him quickly, her eyes full of joy and shyness, wanting to tell him something but not being able to.

Huangfu Jue smiled even more happily, and wrapped his slender fingers around her snow-white soft hair. He said to the person behind him lightly: "Let's go."

The author has something to say: If I work hard to update, can you please stop lurking me, woo woo woo

☆、Having a Son (Part 2)

Minghua Palace, where the virtuous concubine lived, is on the west side, separated by the Anxiang Shuying Building and Zhenqu Pavilion. Along the way, the rockery is simple and interesting, and the waterfall splashes lovely.

Huangfu Jue seemed to like Concubine Shu very much. He ignored the angry and resentful looks around him and took the beauty's hand. He told her stories about the scenery in detail along the way, whispering to her in a very intimate way.

Shufei's face was flushed, and her eyes were fixed on Huangfu Jue, not hiding her admiration at all. Xiangpin followed him angrily for a while, stomped her feet, turned around and walked back.

Yanzhi walked very slowly. Being isolated, she felt more at ease. Looking at the mountains and rocks, all of which were exquisitely crafted, she felt her troubled heart slightly relieved.

Linglong saw her steps getting slower and slower, and said worriedly, "Miss, let's go back to the palace." She was afraid of cold, and after being in the cold wind for a long time, her complexion became worse. She vaguely knew what she was planning, but was afraid that she would take advantage of her body.

Yanzhi put her hand in Linglong's, her breath was disordered. Looking at the bluestone steps spiraling up in front of her, she couldn't help shaking her head and smiling bitterly. It was just a passing moment before, but now it's really a sickly body full of worries.

He smiled at Linglong soothingly, his voice slightly hoarse, "Let them carry a sedan chair." This illness must be exposed to others. Since she couldn't throw a tantrum and make a scene in the bridal chamber, she had to endure the illness for a while.

Linglong's eyes turned red, and she finally gave the order. Yanzhi supported her hand, half leaned on her, and slightly closed her eyes. But after a moment, she opened her eyes again and straightened her body again.

Linglong was startled, and then she saw Concubine Xiang running towards her angrily, with Concubine Qi jogging behind her.

Ruiyue and Zhenyu, two young palace maids, flashed out from behind Yanzhi and stood in front of her alertly. They all stretched out their hands, "The Queen is here, Concubine Xiang, please stop."

Xiangpin stopped abruptly, bit her red lips with her pearly teeth, and froze for a moment before she bowed, "May the Queen be well."

Yanzhi looked at her quietly. Among the three concubines, Xiangpin was the most beautiful. Her eyebrows were green without dyeing, and her lips were red without painting. She wore a golden silk eight-treasure beaded bun and a soft silver light silk lily skirt. Especially her angry eyes, which were bright and beautiful.

The wind was a little chilly, and I couldn't help but cough lightly, "What's the matter, Concubine Xiang?"

Xiangpin felt sore in her heart when she thought about the way the emperor looked at Shufei just now. The emperor has always been romantic and passionate, but he has always treated everyone equally. Only today, only today, he looked at that vixen like that, his beautiful eyes were full of deep affection, and he just stared at her. Tears of grievance rushed into her eyes, and she could no longer care about many things, "Empress, you are in charge of the harem and educate the concubines. You should urge us sisters to abide by the etiquette and not do anything to defile the palace."

Yanzhi looked at her, wondering vaguely in her heart why the women in the palace were willing to humble themselves to this extent.

Linglong gently pulled her collar, and she woke up from her trance. Seeing Xiangpin's suspicious look, she gently lowered her eyes and said softly, "Why do you say that, Xiangpin?"

Her calmness made Xiangpin hesitate, but she didn't want to back down. She didn't believe that someone wasn't attracted to Huangfu Jue, and her eyes were filled with tears of grievance, "Empress, Concubine Shu, she, she and the Emperor, hugged each other, shameless!"

Looking at the face that was twisted by jealousy and hatred, Yan Zhi's eyes quickly flashed with pity, "Shameless, Your Majesty, or Concubine Shu?"

"Of course it's Concubine Shu."

Yanzhi smiled gently, and her eyes, as clear as ice and snow, suddenly melted and were tinged with a hint of loneliness. "Xiangpin, I am not the one the emperor wants to marry. You must know that, right?"

Concubine Xiang was stunned.

She knew it, and everyone in the harem knew it. The emperor was in love with Ning Yunshu, and he appointed Yan Wanzhao, the eldest daughter of the Marquis's mansion and the granddaughter of the Duke of Fuguo, as the empress. For some reason, one month before the ceremony, the empress suddenly changed to Yan Zhi, the biological daughter of Ning Yunshu, the successor of the Marquis of Yan'an. Everyone familiar with □□ knew that this was a huge scandal.

However, the overwhelming wealth of the royal family and the Marquis's mansion silenced everyone."

Yanzhi continued, "The emperor married me only for the sake of the emperor's reputation. I can't do anything, so I can't help you either."

Her words were too blunt, and Concubine Xiang's face turned from red to white. After a while, she straightened her back, her eyes already showing disdain and contempt. She bowed slightly, and her voice was already a little arrogant, "The Queen just thought Shunhua was talking nonsense just now, Shunhua will leave."

Yanzhi smiled slightly and covered her cough with her hand, "Xiangpin, there is no need to be so polite."

"Since the Queen is not in good health, she should return to Weiyang Palace as soon as possible to recuperate." Her soft lily skirt drew a proud arc as she walked step by step towards Concubine Qi who was chasing after her.

After she turned around, Yanzhi staggered slightly, and Linglong hurried forward. Yanzhi buried her head in her neck and almost murmured to herself, "Linglong, it's so uncomfortable."

It's so uncomfortable to live like this, wearing a mask and being disgustingly hypocritical from head to toe.

Linglong hugged her tightly, "It will be fine, it will be fine."

The sedan chair was brought in quickly. It was a red soft felt with a lotus pattern and gold and silver threads. Yanzhi leaned on it and felt that the gold and silver were shining with a cold light. The familiar chill gradually seeped out from her bones. It had been a long time since she had felt this way. She gritted her teeth secretly, waiting for the chill to hit her bones like a huge hammer, making them crackle.

Yanzhi, there will never be another person who will open his fur coat, put you closest to his heart, and wrap you tightly with his body temperature. There will never be another person, Yanzhi, you only have yourself.

The dazzling sunlight gradually turned white, and there seemed to be a whistling wind in my ears, carrying ice chips and hitting me on the head.

She ran desperately, and her boots got stuck in the snow. She fell flat on the ground. The fluffy snow was sharp and cold, like a steel needle that instantly pierced into her flesh and bone marrow. She couldn't get up, no matter what she did...

"Empress, Empress..." Who is it, calling softly in my ear, so anxious, so sad.

Yanzhi exhaled slowly, and her delicate face gradually became clear. She blinked lightly and forced a smile, "It's okay, I just took a nap."

Linglong stared at her without blinking,

her voice trembling unconsciously, "Madam, we have arrived at Minghua Palace."

Yanzhi helped her hand and got off the sedan chair. Concubine Xian was waiting at the side and stepped forward hastily, with a worried look on her face. "Empress, are you feeling unwell? Do you want me to change the imperial physician?"

Yanzhi looked at her steadily, her eyes as clear as glass. The smile on Concubine Xian's face was a little embarrassed.

Yanzhi smiled slightly, walked forward slowly, and said lazily: "It's okay, I didn't get enough rest yesterday."

Minghua Palace is not as grand as Weiyang Palace, but it is more exquisite. The two courtyards, with mountains, rocks, grass and trees, are all well-arranged and ingenious. Green radishes are green, bees and butterflies are busy. Yanzhi walked across the small bamboo arch bridge, listening to the gurgling of the stream below. I felt a little relieved. If it is like this in the future, I have a small enclosed courtyard and a piece of sky behind the courtyard wall. Listen to the rain when it is cloudy, enjoy the moon when it is sunny, plant a few phoenix trees, tie a small swing, and raise a few cats and dogs. Can I also seek the freedom and perfection of my soul?

Wen Liangyuan lived in the Cuilinglong Pavilion, a side hall of Minghua Palace. There were three rooms, two bright and one dark. As soon as she entered the bright room in the middle, a fragrant breeze blew in her face. Yanzhi suddenly felt dizzy, and she calmed herself down before stepping in.

The room was very neat, with red sandalwood furniture with hollowed-out landscapes and figures, and two ebony armchairs with seven scrolls in the middle. In front of the boxwood hanging screen with the Eight Immortals, there was an incense burner and a zither stand.

The owner of the room should be quite elegant, and Yanzhi looked at the ancient seven-stringed lyre on the stand - Shengde Yiyin, and felt very favored.

When the people in the room saw her coming in, they all stood up. Concubine Xian took a step forward and lifted the curtain of the compartment for her, "Your Majesty, Liang Yuan is inside."

There was no Huangfu Jue, Yanzhi glanced at him slightly. She paused, and when she stepped over the threshold, her bracelet and hairpin touched each other, making a crisp sound.

Huangfu Jue was sitting on a coral round chair in front of the window, holding a small teacup with broken jade patterns in his hand. His pair of black eyes glanced at him with a smile.

Yanzhi watched his smile fade away, and he slowly walked over, his fingers curled quietly. She knew she was nervous. This man had a strong presence. Although his every move was graceful and elegant, she could clearly feel the wildness hidden under his gentle appearance.

This is a tiger basking in the sun. It is very dangerous.

Huangfu Jue looked at her carefully, her pale face, her dark eyes, the roots were moved too thoroughly, and she was hurt after all. Only this look, still did not retreat, did not give in, did not avoid. He slightly raised the corners of his lips, his black eyes were gentle, but there was no warmth, "Since the queen is not feeling well, there is no need to get too close to Liangyuan, go back to Weiyang Palace to recuperate."

Yanzhi was startled. This was so cruel. She turned around, covered her sleeves and coughed a few times. She glanced at the person sitting on the bed. Her long black hair was half tied up, her eyebrows were light, and she looked pitiful. She was only wearing a moon-white shirt, her red lips were half open, and her expression was obviously surprised.

Her expression grew colder, she straightened her back proudly, bowed slowly, and spoke in a cold and pleasant voice, "I will take my leave."

When I turned around, I heard an anxious whisper, "Your Majesty!" followed by a few whispers of laughter.

He smiled coldly in his heart. Huangfu Jue

was really lucky. From the virtuous concubines to the good concubines, they were all stunningly beautiful without any rouge or powder. However, considering his appearance and wealth, it was no wonder that all the women here threw themselves at him.

Her steps became faster and faster, and others thought she was angry out of shame. The sky was getting darker and darker, and she had to rest well. She still had Linglong and her mother. She no longer had the energy to analyze why Huangfu Jue was so heartless, so heartless that he was almost considerate.

The author has something to say: I have to work hard, work hard...

☆、Please take the pulse

The moon is above the willow trees.

Eight-treasure glazed lanterns were hung high, and palace maids moved silently and orderly between the courtyards.

The room was decorated with silver and red, and it was as warm as day. Han Lan put down the golden thread hanging from his wrist and pondered for a long time.

Li Luo, who was standing by, saw that Han Lan's wolf-hair brush had barely touched the paper, but he was unable to put pen to paper. She couldn't help but ask anxiously, "Doctor Han, is the Majesty's illness in any way?"

Han Lan suddenly put down his pen, stood up, and said in a deep voice: "Miss, please tell me that Han Lan dares to observe, listen, ask and feel the patient."

Li Luo raised her eyebrows, "Doctor Han, you are not sure?"

Han Lan had been serving the Imperial Hospital for many years, and even the Queen Mother treated him with great courtesy. He had never been ridiculed by a young palace maid. However, the Queen's pulse was very strange, and he could not use medicine casually, so he had to be cautious. He had to lower his posture and said, "I do have some doubts."

Li Luo's almond-shaped eyes revealed a hint of disbelief, and her tone was quite cold, "Please sit down for a moment, Imperial Physician. I need to consult the Majesty."

She twisted her slender waist, passed the small screen, and disappeared among the layers of gauze.

Han Lan felt that everyone in Weiyang Palace was extremely unruly. She was a queen who was abandoned by the king, but she was so arrogant. He waited there angrily for a long time before Li Luo came back.

Li Luo smiled at Han Lan, and then said slowly: "Her Majesty's order: Imperial Physician Han is a master of medicine, and can decide life or death with a single stroke. Her Majesty only has a minor cold, so the Imperial Physician will prescribe the right medicine."

Han Lan was startled, his face turned from red to white, and finally walked to the rosewood desk with a serious face, and quickly wrote down the prescription. After carrying the medicine box, he couldn't help but turn back to Li Luo and said, "Your Majesty's pulse appears to be an attack of wind and cold, and the lung qi is not flowing, but in fact, the pulse is weak and slippery, and it seems that there is a hidden disease. I will come to take your pulse again tomorrow, please think twice."

Li Luo looked at him with a smile, and after he finished speaking, she bowed slightly, "Doctor Han, take care, I won't see you off."

Yanzhi half leaned on the mandarin duck-shaped peach-colored soft pillow, looking at the prescription left by Han Lan, and smiled slightly, "Han Lan learned from Medicine King Wei, so his medical skills are not in vain. Li Luo, remove one qian of ginger, add one spoonful of white peony root, and three lotus seeds."

Li Luo took the prescription neatly and asked, "Miss, what should we do if he insists on taking your pulse tomorrow?"

Yanzhi looked listless, "It doesn't matter. The most he could find out is that I have a chronic cold, lack of energy, and have neglected to take care of myself."

Li Luo looked at her, her lips were almost

the same color as Su Jin's clothes, and she felt a pang in her heart, so her voice became softer, "I told them to boil the medicine."

Yanzhi hummed, Li Luo gestured to Linglong, and quietly stepped back.

Linglong stuffed the dried cloves into a silver aromatherapy ball and tied it to the hook of the bed. She dripped a few drops of essence in her hand and slowly massaged Yanzhi's temple. Looking at the collarbone clearly visible under Yanzhi's clothes, she said distressedly: "Miss, you haven't had a good meal for so many days. The lady must be very heartbroken when she sees you."

Yanzhi half-closed her eyes, her brows slightly furrowed, and she felt drowsy, but her heart was always floating in the air. The wealth and prosperity in front of her, the golden carvings and silver carvings, seemed like a nightmare, as if she could open her eyes and return to the snow-capped top, and that person, looking at her with bright eyes.

The world is one big dream. Where and who will wake up?

Huangfu Jue sat behind a flat-top desk made of yellow pear wood and cypress, his dark jade eyes showing unpredictable emotions.

Han Lan was still kneeling and chattering, "The maids in the Queen's palace are very arrogant. Not only did they not let me take the Queen's pulse, they also ridiculed me. Your Majesty, my medical skills are shallow..."

"Bang!" The white marble lion paperweight on the desk fell to the ground and broke into pieces. Huangfu Jue raised his eyes slantingly and stared at Han Lan steadily. Besides his handsomeness, he also looked a bit cruel.

Han Lan closed his mouth tightly, still with a stern face.

Huangfu Jue walked around the desk in a few steps and came to Han Lan. He grabbed his collar with his right hand and lifted it up fiercely. "The queen is lacking in energy and blood, is she born weak?"

Huangfu Jue was calm even when he ascended the throne, and never lost his elegance in front of others. Han Lan looked at the emperor's face, which was so close to him, and his throat rolled a few times before he nodded with difficulty.

"Good, very good." Huangfu Jue smiled sinisterly. He threw him away and circled around in place.

Han Lan saw a few faint footprints on the swastika-patterned floor and knew that Huangfu Jue was really angry. Although he didn't know where the emperor's anger came from, he still cared about his life, so he quickly straightened his clothes and knelt silently beside him.

Huangfu Jue turned to him again and said, "From today on, you will be on duty in Weiyang Palace. If you need anything, go to the inner treasury to get it. I want a lively and energetic queen. If not..." He took the nine-dragon jade pendant on his waist, and his slender fingers closed and opened, leaving a fine dust on the ground.

Han Lan's heart trembled, and he knelt on the ground, "Your Majesty, I obey your order."

Huangfu Jue's face was gloomy and his eyes were narrowed.

It's been a long time since I've felt this way. It's like when I was a kid and I got my favorite doll back, only to find it had no arms or legs. I hate this feeling of being controlled by others. I hate it so much. Whatever he wants, he will definitely get it completely.

Yan Yanzi, how dare you be so smart!

Three days after the wedding of the Emperor and Empress, Huangfu Jue informed the harem that the Empress was unwell and was resting in Weiyang Palace, and the concubines were not allowed to disturb her. The affairs of the harem were still temporarily handled by Concubine Xian. Wen Liangyuan was pregnant and was promoted to Ronghua.

When the decree came, Yanzhi was scooping lotus seed soup with a small spoon. She was startled when she heard the words, but her hands did not stop moving.

Li Luo was happy to see her drink half a bowl of soup, "Miss, you don't have to worry now." The young lady didn't have to receive the emperor or meet the women in the harem. They closed the door and recuperated quietly.

Yanzhi seemed to be thinking, "Li Luo, do you find it strange?" She had only met Huangfu Jue three times, and each time was just a passing glance. But she felt that this man was unpredictable and his emotions were hard to tell.

The three times they met, each time he became colder than the last. Did he really dislike her, or was he doing it on purpose?

Li Luo thought for a moment, "Miss, are you talking about the emperor? It's really strange. Logically, a person like Miss should be tempted. Maybe it's for the eldest lady?" The eldest lady is well-known in the capital, and her popularity is even higher than Wang Yan. But she mysteriously disappeared before the wedding, so it's not surprising that the emperor would be angry. He's venting his anger on others.

Swallow, evening, and light, even today, these three words can still cause sharp pain when they are pronounced on the tongue.

What can you use to repay what you owe me?

Feeling annoyed, he pushed the dishes aside and said calmly, "Ask Li Luo to control the palace maids. No one is allowed to go in or out without permission."

Seeing her unhappy expression, Li Luo knew she had said something wrong, so she quickly smiled and said, "Miss, Han Lan is here again, waiting in the side hall."

Yanzhi stood up, her newly cut Yuehua brocade dress hanging loosely around her waist, and she looked tired, "Let him wait."

Lai Xi and Yi Yue received the order and strictly controlled their subordinates. The huge Weiyang Palace was suddenly deserted. However, some people could not be stopped. The Queen Mother's phoenix sedan stopped outside the main gate of Weiyang Palace in the afternoon.

The Queen Mother bit her hair on her forehead and looked at her pale face distressedly, "How could she be so sick out of nowhere?"

Yanzhi smiled and said, "It's just a cold. It's nothing serious. Your Majesty, please sit in the outer room. Be careful not to get sick."

The Queen Mother looked at her, leaning against the pillow in a sickly manner, with a dull look on her face, yet still showing a sense of elegance. She felt angry and pitied at the same time, and could not help but said angrily, "Silly child. Not to mention that you are now included in the Huangfu family's genealogy, even if I am friends with your mother, I am worthy of being half your mother. How can you deny it? Call me mother!"

Although her eyes were slightly annoyed, they were full of genuine love. Her hands were soft and warm. She worshipped Buddha all year round, and she had a faint scent of sandalwood on her body. Yanzhi looked at her, her eyes became slightly moist, and she opened her mouth and really murmured, "Mother."

The Queen Mother's heart softened, she patted her hands, and sighed, "Child, you have a long life, and you will encounter anything. There is no obstacle in this world that you cannot overcome. Take care of yourself, and if you have any grievances, your mother will take care of it for you."

Yanzhi hummed softly.

The Queen Mother looked at her and said slowly, "Your body and hair are given by your parents. If there is something wrong with your child, it will hurt your heart. Don't take advantage of your youth and ignore your health. Han Lan is with you, right? He is also an old man in the palace and his medical skills are trustworthy. Why are you leaving him alone in the side hall? Even if you are angry with the emperor, you can't treat him like that. Call him over and take your pulse, otherwise I won't agree."

She spoke so slowly, and I felt a long-lost warmth in my ears. Yanzhi smiled while chewing the tea, but she just listened and didn't refute.

Linglong immediately left the house and asked someone to call Han Lan.

Han Lan stared at the white wrist on the red pillow, holding his breath. He pressed the pulse with his index finger, and raised his middle and ring fingers slightly. He pressed for a long while, frowning. He then changed to pressing with three fingers, and relaxed his fingers after a little force. Then he stood up, bowed to the Queen Mother, and left the bedroom.

Seeing his solemn expression, the Queen Mother became anxious and quickly got up and followed him out.

"Doctor Han, how is the queen?"

Han Lan hesitated, "I am a stupid minister. The Queen's pulse is sometimes floating and sometimes sinking, slow and sluggish. The disease is caused by wind evil, and the Qi and blood are weak. But there seems to be cold poison in the lungs, which should be congenital."

The Queen Mother was startled and asked quickly, "Is there any way?"

Han Lan said in a deep voice: "It's not a one-day job."

"I will leave the queen to you. Please take whatever you need."

Han Lan smiled bitterly. The tone of the Empress Dowager and the Emperor was surprisingly consistent. It seemed that the Empress might not be about to be sent to the cold palace as people had rumored.

"I will follow the Queen Mother's orders!"

The author has something to say:
············Gone with the Wind············

☆、Stop the Sorrow

The weather is getting warmer and the

nights are getting longer.

Yanzhi's bedroom was facing a weeping crabapple tree. She could smell the strong fragrance of the flowers when she opened the window. Lying in bed every day, she knew very well that the tall branch had already bloomed fifty-one flowers.

Han Lan resides in the Weiyang Palace. Golden Blood Swallow, Changbai Old Ginseng... and other medicinal herbs that can kill people or revive bones are moved into the Weiyang Palace like water.

She had to recover from her cold gradually. Weiyang Palace was always very quiet. Sometimes the only sound one could hear in the three-story courtyard was the sound of dripping sand. The only visitor was the Queen Mother of Yanxi Palace. She would come every few days and always sigh, "Yanzhi, it's too quiet here. It's better for young people to be energetic."

Huangfu Jue never showed up.

The people in Weiyang Palace didn't like to go out, and it was difficult for outsiders to come in. They closed the door, and it became the only paradise in the palace.

"Miss, Miss!" Li Luo ran into the side hall excitedly.

Smoke rose from the gold-lacquered enamel eight-hole incense burner. An essay on Great Compassion was almost finished. When she shouted like that, Yanzhi's hand paused slightly, and the word "Lin" was written with ink that penetrated the back of the paper.

Linglong sighed with regret and glanced at Li Luo in reproach, "What a reckless person!"

Li Luo stuck out her tongue. She really did it on purpose. The young lady has been cultivating herself these days, and she is so quiet that she almost becomes an immortal. The exquisite little girl only knows how to accompany the young lady to practice calligraphy, just like a clay sculpture or a wooden model. She looked at Yan Zhi with sparkling eyes, "Young lady, you should go and have a look. Eunuch Fu has sent you a rare toy. The hair is so long," she exaggeratedly pointed with her hands, "and there is a tuft of red hair in the middle of the ear. So cute!"

Yanzhi took the pen and tapped her forehead lightly like lightning, then said with a smile, "More lovely than you?"

Li Luo was so angry that she jumped up and down, and hurriedly looked in the diamond-shaped mirror, muttering, "You keep bullying me!"

Having her interest ruined, Yanzhi simply threw down her pen and said, "Linglong, let's go and see what this rare thing is."

The weather was fine, and Yu Liu remained motionless. Linglong still put a plain silk dress with an ancient smoke pattern on her. Fuquan was waiting in the front yard. When he saw her, he smiled and knelt down to

greet her. "Your servant greets the Queen."
Yanzhi waved her hand and looked at the cage with gold and mother-of-pearl patterns at his feet. It turned out to be a foreign puppy - a small snow-white ball, only the size of two fists, with a small tuft of fiery red hair on its forehead. The black eyes looked at her moistly, and her heart softened all of a sudden.

She took it out of the cage, and the little guy was soft and squirming restlessly. She touched the red hair on its forehead, and unexpectedly, its pink little tongue wrapped around her finger.

Yanzhi couldn't help but smile.

Fuquan was watching her expression from the side, and quickly came up to her and said, "Your Majesty, this is a tribute from Turo. When the Queen Mother saw it, she said you liked it, so she specially ordered me to bring it to you."

Yanzhi held it and walked towards the house, saying lightly, "Reward."

Li Luo handed Fuquan two pure gold ingots with a smile. Fuquan's eyes narrowed into a line, "Thank you for the reward, Your Majesty!"

Yiyue sent Fuquan out of the Chuihua Gate, and when she came back she saw Li Luo standing in the corridor, waving at her with a smile.

She and Lai Xi both grew up in the palace, and came to serve in Weiyang Palace at the request of the higher-ups. Li Luo and Ling

Long were the queen's dowry, one in charge of the interior and the other of the exterior, and they acted flawlessly. Although she smiled and called her sister, Yi Yue did not dare to be arrogant in anything.

After taking a few quick steps, Yiyue arrived at the corridor, "Sister, does the Queen have any instructions?"

Li Luo shook her head and handed her the pickled plums in her handkerchief. "No, the queen got a treasure and can't pay attention to us for the time being. Sister, did you just send Eunuch De back?"

Yiyue nodded, but frowned at the plum she handed over, "Too sour, I don't want it."

Li Luo loved snacks the most, and she loved sour food, so she always carried a small purse of snacks with her wherever she went.

Li Luo picked one up herself, squinting her eyes to feel the sourness, "Sister, this Eunuch De must be someone of great rank, I see you and Brother Xi are very respectful to him."

Yiyue looked at her and said with a smile, "Eunuch De is the chief steward of the imperial palace. He serves in front of the emperor. He is our real boss."

Li Luo thought about it and burst out laughing, "Since she is the one who serves the emperor personally, she should be serving the emperor in Jiuzhou Qingyan Palace and handling government affairs. How could she be so idle as to run errands for the empress dowager?" The former dynasty has not been peaceful recently. The war in the Western Regions is difficult, and the emperor must be in a bad mood.

Yiyue smiled bitterly. Li Luo had always been careless about her words and deeds, and the Queen did not control her. She looked at Li Luo and her expression became serious, "Sister. I have been in the palace since I was a child, so my horizons are not narrow. Although this dog today is not particularly rare, but... the fact that I got the Queen's fate in this way should not be just a coincidence."

Li Luo's eyebrows curved, "It just fits the name of the queen. Eunuch De also said it was called 'Xue Li Hong', it should obviously be 'Rouge Snow'."

She was so loud and clear that Yi Yue was so anxious that she wanted to cover her mouth, "Little Ancestor, what are you talking about! No matter how much the Queen dotes on you, you can't lose your sense of propriety."

Li Luo looked at her with clear eyes, "Sister, the queen has a very good temper, she won't care about this. It's just that I have wronged you these days. The queen has a calm temper, and you have to take care of everything outside. I'm sure you have been neglected a lot."

Yiyue shook her head, "No, never. Your Majesty has already moved into the Eastern Palace and is the true master of this harem.

Who dares to show disdain to us?"

Her tone was light and calm, but it had an aura that could not be underestimated. Li Luo looked at her with admiration, rubbing her body. "I admire you so much, I admire you so much!"

The two laughed and joked for a while, and then a young palace maid asked for permission to move to the next month, and the Ministry of Internal Affairs sent them the pattern of summer clothes. The two stopped.

Yiyue walked towards the inner hall. There were heavy curtains, columns carved with coiled dragons, walls inlaid with gold and jade, and gold bricks with carved mountains, rocks, flowers and birds under her feet. It was much more luxurious than the Marquis's Mansion. Her steps became faster and faster, and her relaxed smile gradually faded.

Miss, if King Xiang wants to draw a circle around us as a prison, what should we do?

The courtyard of the Weiyang Palace was filled with water from the Taiye Pond, and with the help of a few strange stones, a small waterfall was created. There was a bluestone by the pond, which was warm and moist.

Ever since Yanzhi discovered it, he loved lying on it.

That day, she was lying there lazily. The sun was shining brightly, casting sparse shadows of flowers on her face. Snowball was chasing his tail in circles at her feet.

The petals of the crabapple tree swirled and fell lightly, sticking to her forehead. The corners of her lips were slightly raised, and there were faint dimples on her cheeks.

What did you dream about that made your sleeping face so peaceful and beautiful?

Huangfu Jue walked out from the shade of the tree step by step, his footsteps light and soundless. His slanted phoenix eyes roamed over the snow-white skin inch by inch.

Snowball growled uneasily.

"Who?" Yanzhi opened her eyes lazily, her voice still a little languid from sleep. The next moment her eyes became clear, and Snowball was lifted up by two fingers on his back, flopping around, baring his teeth and growling. "Give it to me!" He stood up hastily and stretched out his arms.

Huangfu Jue raised his lips slightly. Han Lan was not a waste. Her face was finally not as pale as a ghost. He handed the dog to her and put his hands behind his back casually. "The dog raised by the queen?"

When the little snowball returned to her arms, Yanzhi felt relieved and immediately realized that she had made a mistake. Her black eyes returned to indifference and she bowed softly, "Your Majesty, please wait a moment. I will come to meet you after I get dressed properly."

She was only wearing a long palace satin dress, and her hip-length black hair was tied up loosely with a magnolia jade hairpin, which made her look bright and beautiful. Huangfu Jue smiled slightly, took a step forward, and stood in front of her, speaking in a natural and intimate tone, "Queen, I am your husband. There is no need for formalities between husband and wife."

He was too close, and the wind carried not only the musk of the man, but also the faint scent of lilies. Yanzhi frowned slightly, and her face became even colder. "The emperor is the ruler of a country."

Huangfu Jue's smile faded, his eyes darkened, and he slowly said: "Can't the ruler of a country be the husband of someone else?"

Yanzhi's eyes contained a bit of sarcasm, but her tone remained calm, "The emperor is rich and powerful, and there are three thousand concubines in the harem. Naturally, my husband is all you."

Huangfu Jue looked at her, watching her lower her eyebrows and eyes, quietly keeping a distance from him, with dark eyes surging. Suddenly he leaned down, his cheek very close to hers, "Queen, are you blaming me for ignoring you on the night of our wedding?"

Yanzhi was startled, and her body reacted subconsciously. She tapped her heels, spun slightly, and moved to the left of Huangfu Jue. She immediately swayed, her sleeves covering half of her face, and she said softly, "Your Majesty, I am not feeling well, so I will take my leave first."

Huangfu Jue watched her turn around and walk towards the bedroom with light steps. Her body was light, but her feet were weak and frail.

His eyes darkened. His flying sleeves had already passed the green bamboos. He raised his voice lazily, "Yanzhi," and his flying figure seemed to pause, and his steps staggered slightly, "Zhishang is back."

Stop the sorrow? Stop the sorrow! Yan Zhi suddenly turned around, with a half-surprise and half-joy in her black eyes.

Zhishang, on the Lightning Horse, dressed in black, with flying black hair and warm and bright eyes. Yanzhi, when I come back, I will give you the feather on the head of the Nanzhao chief...

Zhishang is the most important man in her life besides Ye Zi.

Huangfu Jue raised his eyelids slightly and sighed with regret, "I am planning to hold a dinner party to welcome Zhishang. Unfortunately, the Queen is not feeling well and cannot attend."

Yanzhi's eyes lit up little by little, like a meteor streaking across the deep blue sky. Gently smoothing her messy hair, she smiled dignifiedly and reservedly, "It's fine for me, the royal family to entertain meritorious officials, how can there be no hostess?"

The author has something to say:

☆、Qujiang Banquet (Part 1)

Huangfu Jue watched her change from respectful to arrogant, and the corners of his mouth unconsciously lifted. He walked up to her with his hands behind his back, his black eyes smiling, and slowly stretched out his slender hand to her side, "It's windy, I'll take you in."

His fingers were slender and shiny, with clear lines on his palms, like Udumbara in the dark night, slowly stretching out.

Yanzhi's breathing stagnated. The fingers in her sleeves slowly curled up, and then forcedly spread out one by one.

Huangfu Jue looked at her with a smile.

The flowing cloud pattern gradually emerged, and a white hand of the same color as the robe hovered in mid-air.

Huangfu Jue curled the corner of his lips, turned over his palm, held her hand tightly, and walked in front.

Linglong just raised her head from the pile of cloth and was stunned.

Li Sizhen from the Sizhen Room came to decide on the style of the young lady's new summer clothes. She seemed very anxious, but she didn't want to mess around with the young lady's clothes. The two of them spent a lot of time and finally decided on the styles of two outer shirts and four skirts. Unexpectedly, as soon as she looked up, she saw the emperor holding the young lady's hand, walking through the palace gate one after the other.

She hurriedly sat up from her clothes, rushed in front of the two men, knelt down and saluted, "This servant greets the emperor."

Huangfu Jue did not stop and responded casually, "Get up." Yanzhi just kept a straight face without even raising his eyes. Linglong's heart sank as she watched Huangfu Jue holding Yanzhi's hand and walking towards the inner room. She was anxious but helpless.

Fuquan walked up to her and said angrily, "Linglong, what are you still standing there for? What time is it? Serve the food."

Linglong was startled, and glanced at Fuquan, who was already being served tea by a young eunuch. She glanced at the inner room, which was very quiet. She left the hall, looking back every few steps.

Fuquan shook his head and smiled bitterly. Silly girl, if the emperor is really determined to do something, who can stop him?

The lunch in Weiyang Palace was passed around very quickly, and Linglong placed it in the side hall Yuedi Yunju. She went outside the inner room and coughed softly, "Your Majesty, it's time to eat."

The inner room was silent.

Linglong gritted her teeth, lifted the curtain of the pavilion with flowing light and inlaid pearls, and said loudly, "Madam, lunch is ready, shall we serve it?"

Huangfu Jue smiled softly and got off the bed, "Like the master, like the maid." He did not show any displeasure at all, but rather a hint of doting.

Yanzhi leaned on the carved wooden chaise longue, holding the book at an angle, and hummed.

Huangfu Jue leaned over to take her book away, then leaned over to trap her on the couch, his black eyes sparkling and shimmering, "Yanzhi, you look like a snowball when you are so angry."

Yanzhi looked at him coldly. This man had just used a few candies to trick Xiao Xueqiu away from her arms, and the man and the dog were rolling happily on her bed. At this moment, he leaned over, smiling with bright eyebrows and eyes, and there seemed to be billions of stars in his black eyes.

The anger in her heart grew little by little. Why did he barge into her life so brazenly and manipulate her life at will?

Dark waves flow, and the room is full of ambiguity.

Linglong bowed and quietly stepped back, "Pah!" Moyu Zhouyu was caught by her belt and fell to the ground. Linglong immediately knelt down and kowtowed, her voice trembling, "This servant deserves death, this servant deserves death!"

Huangfu Jue stood up and glanced at her with a half-smile, "You are so clumsy. You really deserve to die."

"She is mine. If the emperor wants to punish her, punish me." Yanzhi sat down in front of the red sandalwood dressing table with dragon and phoenix carvings and took out her jade hairpin. "Come here and help me with my makeup."

The black hair hung down, and the room was hazy. Huangfu Jue's smile deepened, but he only looked deeply in the mirror. He took the book that Yanzhi had previously held in his hand and walked out of the house. When he passed Linglong who was bent over the ground, he took a look at Zhou Yu who was torn into pieces and smiled softly, "You should be glad that your young lady married the current emperor." □□Antiques cannot match the smile of a beauty.

Huangfu Jue drank three cups of wine before Yanzhi came out.

The woman has a bun with red gold and agate tassels, a peach blossom on her forehead, and a satin dress with a cloud pattern of gold and silver. She is a palace beauty, cold and beautiful.

Huangfu Jue's eyes flashed with surprise, and she was full of charm, whether she was lightly made up or heavily made up. Some women in the harem were more beautiful than her, some were more charming than her, but no one would walk on the edge of ice and fire like her. Her every move, every smile, every joy, every anger, every anger, every smile, was naturally charming.

He lazily shook the wine glass in his hand, "Yanzhi, have a drink with me."

Without the emperor and empress, there is no loneliness. Such a distance makes people feel dangerous.

Yanzhi looked at him and said calmly, "Your Majesty, my name is Yan, Wan, Luo."

Yanzhi, rouge, too intimate, too sweet to make people sick. Only leaves, only when these two words are gently spit out from the tip of his tongue, will there be the smell of grass after the wind and rain. Clean and sweet.

Huangfu Jue supported his chin with one hand, and curled his thin lips slightly, but Yanzhi could clearly see that his eyes were dark and dark, without a trace of smile. "Yan, Wan, Luo." The words were pronounced very lightly, with a special rhythm, which was very touching.

Yanzhi remained silent, raised the wine glass with both hands and drank it all.

The emperor was here, so the lunch was much more sumptuous than usual. Yanzhi ate attentively, taking one or two bites of each dish with her chopsticks, never repeating the same thing. Despite Huangfu Jue's burning gaze, she chewed and ate elegantly and without any restraint.

Huangfu Jue poured himself a drink, and the two of them went their own way. The atmosphere was subtle and strange.

Fuquan nodded at Linglong, who shook her head slightly. Young lady never needed to be served when eating, and she didn't know the emperor's preferences, so how could she pick up the dishes and rice?

Fuquan had no choice but to pick up a few dishes that Huangfu Jue usually liked, put them in front of him, and said softly: "Your Majesty, you have to meet the military minister at noon, so drink less."

Huangfu Jue smiled slightly and actually put down his wine glass. He motioned Fu Quan to serve the rice and started eating along with the previous dishes. He finished two bowls of Imperial Yellow Queen Mother rice before putting down his chopsticks.

Yanzhi had already rinsed her mouth and wiped her lips, then sat aside with tea.

Huangfu Jue walked up to her, his eyes were lazy and casual, and he suddenly bent his middle finger and flicked her forehead lightly. Yanzhi looked at him angrily, raised her eyebrows and smiled, with a hint of evil charm in her nobleness, and whispered: "Tomorrow night, Fuquan will come to pick you up."

The anger in Yanzhi's eyes was surging, but it was firmly restrained by reason. She wanted to see Zhishang, so she couldn't turn her face now.

As soon as Huangfu Jue stepped out of Yuedi Yunju, he heard a crisp "bang" from inside. Fuquan was startled and stole a glance at the emperor's face. Huangfu Jue's eyebrows just raised, and the corners of his mouth actually smiled slightly. With his hands behind his back, he continued to move forward calmly.

Fuquan smiled bitterly in his heart. He had followed the emperor for a long time and knew that he was moody and unpredictable. If someone else did this, I'm afraid the ancestral graves of the nine clans would have to be dug up and the corpses whipped. He really had to be very alert to serve in the Weiyang Palace.

The next evening, the emperor held a banquet at Qujiang Lake.

Qujiang Pond is connected to Taiye Lake, and the water flows around Penglai in the pond. A nine-curve corridor is built around the pond, and people walking on it feel as if they are in the sky.

The colorful Phoenix Palace lanterns were high on the eaves, and the lights were winding like ribbons. The blue water was sparkling, and the lights and the moon were reflected. The room was divided into eight screens, and a banquet of various flavors was prepared. The palace maids had their hair tied up in a bun, and their shoulders were covered with colorful light silk. Their clothes were light and thin, and the room was full of □□.

The virtuous concubine wore her hair in a flying bun with red gold phoenix tail agate tassels in her hair. She wore a cloud-like satin brocade dress with colorful flowers and flying butterflies. She looked round and charming.

She personally organized the dinner, so she arrived early and looked around.

Today's banquet is for the new nobles in the army. The eldest son of Marquis of Yan'an, Yan Zhishang, the grandson of Duke Fuguo, Li Kaitai, and the youngest son of Prince Huaiyang, Huangfu Qingcheng, are all young and successful people, and are descendants of noble families.

She dared not be careless and had to be there in person. She just sat down to rest for a while, but she felt uneasy. Some things are better left unfinished, but if you do them, there is no way back. The tea was brought to her mouth, but she stopped, "Liu Shang, go over there and keep an eye on it, I'm still worried."

"Yes, your majesty." Yun Ni knelt down and saluted, then quietly retreated.

Concubine Xian looked towards the center of the pond, where the Penglai Mountain Pavilion was hidden in the dark night, with shadows looming. She stared at it for a long time, with a mixed look of excitement, sadness, expectation, hesitation, etc.

The banquet was supposed to be held at 12:00 p.m., but before 12:00 p.m., the concubines had already arrived one after another.

Xiangpin and Qipin came hand in hand. They wore peacock-patterned clothes with blue clouds and continuous pearls, and plum blossom-patterned skirts that trailed the ground. One was charming and the other was elegant, and both were dressed up carefully. Just after the beginning of May, Xiangpin was already holding a newly cut silk fan in her hand, half covering her beautiful face, and smiling, "Your Majesty, you have worked hard. I heard that the Queen has just recovered. I am sure she will be very happy to see you working so hard."

The virtuous concubine looked at her and smiled slightly, her red gold and jadeite pearl armor gently brushing against her tassels, "This palace is destined to be a hard worker, and I can't compare to my sister who can cultivate her character."

Xiangpin smiled sweetly, "Shunhua is stupid, not as virtuous as the Majesty, and can't play music or chess. She can't please the Emperor, so she is naturally at peace. Shunhua just feels sorry for the Majesty, and has worked hard for half a year, but it's not as good as a single word from her pillow."

Xian Fei looked at her. Xiangpin was younger than her. Her skin was as white as cream under her delicate makeup. Her eyes were like mercury in a pool, shining with cold light. However, there were a few very thin bloodshot lines beside her black eyes. She pursed her lips slightly, looking calm, "It's better to have something to do than nothing. Otherwise, how can I pass the long night? I can't be like my sister, and stay up all night until my eyes bleed."

Xiangpin was startled, and her body

trembled slightly with anger. The Queen was under house arrest, and Huangfu Jue had been favoring Wang Yan recently. She hadn't seen the Queen for several days. She wanted to take the opportunity to tease Concubine Xian, but she never thought that this woman was a needle in a cotton ball, and every needle would draw blood. She sneered and pulled Qipin into the corridor.

The virtuous concubine sneered silently, with deep jealousy in her eyes. "Fool, you just have a good father." She has nothing, and it is because she has nothing, no backing, no support, and no heart, that she can be where she is today.

At 1:00 pm, Huangfu Jue arrived at Qujiang Lake with Yan Zhishang and others on time. Huangfu Jue wore a light robe with a loose belt, and only the hem and cuffs had golden dragon patterns. He had a noble aura without being flashy, and his demeanor was far superior to others. Yan Zhishang followed closely behind him, wearing a heavy purple robe, with white jade hair, handsome eyebrows and eyes, and a look of spirit, standing tall like a green bamboo after rain.

As soon as the two of them arrived, all the girls looked over at them. Although Li Kaitai and Huangfu Qingcheng were both handsome, they could not help but become foils.

Huangfu Jue sat in the main seat, glanced at the concubines, and without lingering for long, he turned to Huangfu Qingcheng, "Qingcheng, how do you think of my Nine-Curved Corridor?"

Huangfu Qingcheng stood up and laughed, "My Langye Villa is far inferior."

Huangfu Jue stroked his forehead and chuckled, "Qingcheng is too modest. Langye Villa ranks first among the famous gardens in the south of the Yangtze River. I will go to Langye during my holiday tour to the south."

Huangfu Qingcheng bowed to the ground and said, "My father and I have prepared the bed to welcome you respectfully."

The virtuous concubine came forward with a gentle and generous smile, "Your Majesty, I have made all the arrangements. When will the banquet begin?"

As soon as she finished speaking, she felt a cold gaze beside her. Although Yan Zhishang had a faint smile on his face, his eyes were already cold as a knife. Concubine Xian felt her heart was cold, and her smile was already stiff on her face. When she looked at Huangfu Jue, her eyes were a little aggrieved.

Huangfu Jue raised his eyebrow and was about to speak when the eunuch in charge of ceremonies shouted in a long voice: "The Queen has arrived..."

Yan Zhishang immediately withdrew his gaze, stood up and left.

Six pairs of palace maids stood in a row holding palace lanterns. Yanzhi held

Linglong's hand and walked up the stairs step by step.

The long sleeves and pleated phoenix tail skirt, the skirt belt is winding, and the lotus is blooming with every step. The phoenix-like bun is soaring into the sky, and the black hair is rolling, the beauty of the country is hard to describe.

Even though there are thousands of people, there is only one person. Yan Zhishang smiled deeply, leaned forward and knelt, "Your Majesty, I wish you good health and long life, and may you live a thousand years and a thousand thousand years."

The author has something to say: It's so cold, the ice is freezing...

☆、Qujiang Banquet (Part 2)

Still with that casual voice, still with those penetrating eyes, Yan Zhi held his arms and whispered in his ear: "Brother, do you want me to die two years earlier?"

妹妹，他最心爱的孪生妹妹，他没能看到她穿上喜服，亲手将她送上花轿，再将抢走妹妹的男人狠狠揍上几拳。他的妹妹，在他在南诏枕戈待命，拼死搏杀时，带上了凤冠，嫁进了大明宫，成了母仪天下的一国之母。

Yan Zhishang was smiling all the time, with a deep smile and bright eyes. He held Yan Zhi's hand and led her to the emperor's side step by step.

Huangfu Jue kept smiling at them. Yan Zhishang knelt on one knee and said, "I forgot about my feelings for a moment and lost my manners. Your Majesty, please forgive me."

Huangfu Jue chuckled, "The royal family also values kinship, go ahead."

Yanzhi sat beside him and turned her head slightly, "Am I late?" Her eyelashes fluttered like a cicada's wings and there was a hint of pretended confusion in her expression.

Huangfu Jue's eyes were dark and dark, and no emotion could be seen. He looked at her for a long while before smiling and saying, "It's not too late if you come."

Yan Zhi smiled and took the jade pot in her own hand, filling Huangfu Jue's cup with wine. She turned to the virtuous concubine standing silently beside her, glanced at her, and showed her white teeth, "Serve the food, I'm very hungry."

Concubine Xian was startled, and immediately looked at Huangfu Jue, but found that he didn't pay any attention to her at all. She tapped the table with her five fingers, and her eyes were only focused on Yanzhi.

The silk handkerchief was kneaded into the palm of his hand unconsciously, and he still had a smile on his face. With a light clap of his hands, the palace maids entered one after another with silver plates on their heads.

She retreated quietly, glancing at the throne from the corner of her eyes as she turned around.

Yanzhi leaned back in the chair, the white jade pendant on her ear swayed slightly, and the smile in her eyes was like dewdrops on the lotus, flowing drop by drop.

Smoke gradually rose above the water and faint music could be heard from the lake. The dancer wore only a red silk bellyband and loose trousers. She grasped her waist, cast a glance and danced boldly and passionately.

Huangfu Jue loved vocal music, and there were hundreds of musicians in the Changyin Pavilion in the palace. He also sneered at the distinction between men and women, and usually did not avoid concubines when entertaining important officials. What's more, after being invited to a banquet by the emperor, he would go home with several more beauties.

At the dinner, there were many scenes of dancers seducing young officials.

Yan Zhishang had already drunk several cups, his face was slightly red, and his fierceness was gone, making him look more handsome. A dancer threw her sleeves and came to him. Her eyes slanted up, her waist bent back, and she actually picked up the wine pot with her red lips and slowly poured the wine into the white jade cup. She then held the white jade cup with her pearly teeth and gently brought it to Yan Zhishang's lips.

Huangfu Qingcheng and others burst into

laughter.

Yan Zhishang smiled slightly, opened his mouth, and took a sip of the wine. The dancer blushed, her eyes were charming, she spread her arms and spun lightly, and returned to the team. Her eyes were full of affection, always following Yan Zhishang.

Li Kaitai placed a bowl next to Yan Zhishang with a clang and said with a smile, "You, boy, kill people faster than others, and you are more popular with women than others. Come, let's compete in drinking capacity," he raised his thumb, "and see who is the best."

Yan Zhishang grinned slowly, "What's the prize?"

Li Kaitai rolled up his sleeves and said, "As for that beauty just now, whoever stands there will ask the emperor for her."

The seats of the concubines were all covered with screens, and only Yanzhi sat high in the main seat, lazily watching the situation below. Seeing that Li Kaitai openly used the dancer as a bet, he snorted coldly and said in a clear voice, "Zhishang, where is my gift?"

Her voice was clear and melodious, but it silenced the music in the room. The whole room was silent. Only two people did not change their expressions. Huangfu Jue poured wine by himself, and Yan Zhishang smiled helplessly.

He took the bundle from the attendant, held it up with both hands, and walked to the front of the emperor. "I use this zither to congratulate the emperor and the empress on their wedding. I wish our country will prosper for generations and the country will be peaceful and the people will be safe."

He untied the purple forge and found it was indeed a guqin.

The zither is of Fuxi style, made of cedar wood, with white jade pegs and a vermilion lacquer body. The belly of the body has cracks, and the bottom of the zither looks like a dragon.

Yanzhi's smile gradually deepened and then froze in her eyes.

In Zhou Dynasty, there was an ancient zither, and the phoenix cried in the sky.

Yanzhi, I'll find it and use it as a betrothal gift, okay?

He looked at her, his eyes bright as if a fire was burning, cautious and full of anticipation.

Okay? Okay?

A smile appeared on her lips. She held the zither on her knees and gently brushed the strings with her fingers. "Okay." She looked up at Yan Zhishang again, "I like it very much."

Yan Zhishang looked at her deeply, saw the strange look in her eyes, saw the weak smile on her lips, and slowly said, "Sister, this zither has not appeared in the world for a hundred years. Zhishang is honored, can I hear you play a song again?"

He spoke slowly. Her eyes flashed from panic to pleading, and then slowly calmed down. He finally finished speaking word by word.

Yan Zhibi closed her eyes and uttered from the depths of her throat, "Okay. What song do you want to listen to, brother?"

"I ask for a song of 'Phoenix Seeking the Phoenix' for my emperor."

The phoenix is coming, and the four seas are looking for it. Yanzhi looked at him straight, with sharp pain in her eyes. Zhishang, how can you bear to hurt me like this?

Wash your hands with clean water and wipe each finger with a silk handkerchief.

Yanzhi, for those who play the piano, must be genuine, pure, and natural.

With her bare hands raised lightly, the notes Gong, Shang, Jiao, Zheng and Yu begin to play. Hundreds of flowers bloom, hundreds of birds sing, and the phoenix flies.

Yanzhi, you are the master's most proud disciple. In the world today, the zither is the best and the doctor is the second. In the art of zither, the master cannot beat you.

The sound of the zither lingers, the phoenix sings, I toss and turn, thinking about it day and night.

Snowland has nothing to do with the royal family, Yanzhi wants to return all that she has learned to her master. If she doesn't save herself, she won't save others.

The sound of the zither is high-pitched, and hundreds of birds congratulate. The phoenix and the crane sing in harmony, and go hand in hand.

"Pa pa" Huangfu Jue clapped his hands slowly, startling the chirping of birds in the room. The people present realized that they had been infatuated without realizing it. "Good piano, good music, just for the Queen's love, I should make it clear. Zhishang, you drink this cup with me."

Yan Zhishang turned his gaze away from Yan Zhi and met Huangfu Jue's deep eyes, "Your Majesty, I am very grateful."

A person came from behind the eight screens, stood there gracefully, and smiled before she spoke. "The Queen's piano playing has reached perfection. I have shed tears without realizing it. Your Majesty, can I perform a dance to make everyone laugh?"

Huangfu Jue smiled and looked at her slowly, "I knew that my beloved concubine was good at calligraphy and painting, but I didn't know that she was also good at music. That's right."

"Your Majesty," Concubine Shu hesitated, her expression showing a hint of anticipation, "Once the Queen starts playing the zither, I'm afraid no one dares to accompany me. I dare to ask the Queen to play another song."

The room was silent again. The concubine danced in the hall and specifically asked the queen to accompany her. It was indeed a naked provocation. Huangfu Qingcheng and Li Kaitai were both busy eating, but Yan Zhishang cast his eyes on Yanzhi.

Yanzhi was polishing the zither, carefully wiping the strings with a white silk handkerchief, and seemed not to hear what Concubine Shu said.

Huangfu Jue said "hmm" nonchalantly, and turned his head slightly towards Yanzhi, "What do you think, Queen?"

The rouge had already reached the fifth string, and her fingers slid across it. With a buzz, the string broke at the root. She locked up at Huangfu Jue, her eyes wet and a little bewildered, "The string is broken." She looked at Yan Zhishang again and said softly, "Brother, I'm sorry."

When his eyes met hers, Yan Zhishang felt a great pain in his heart. Suddenly, Huangfu Jue laughed out loud, "That's a good ending. This sound should be the last!"

Yanzhi stood up holding the zither and bowed to Huangfu Jue, "Your Majesty, I am tired and will take my leave first."

Huangfu Jue smiled and nodded, "Go ahead, let Fuquan accompany you."

Huangfu Qingcheng and the others were all startled and stood up hurriedly, "Your subjects respectfully send off the Queen."

Yan Zhi smiled coldly, her gaze lingering on Yan Zhishang for a moment, and then she said slowly: "The night is still long, everyone enjoy yourself." She walked lightly, holding the zither and walking straight in front of Concubine Shu.

The author has something to say: Liu Liu works very hard, so she should be encouraged!

☆、The Lotus Man

She walked very fast, but her shoulders did not move at all, and her skirt fluttered like a rose in full bloom. In just a moment, she disappeared around the corner of the corridor.

As soon as her figure disappeared, everyone couldn't help but breathe a sigh of relief, and their eyes towards Concubine Shu were somewhat complicated.

Concubine Shu was standing alone in the hall. She must have come prepared today. The sleeves of her embroidered hibiscus flower were very wide, and she wore a brocade belt with two lotus flowers. Her pleated skirt was very complicated. Her black hair was tied up high, revealing a snow-white neck. She looked like a lotus floating on the water, fresh and graceful. But at this moment, her face was very pale, her back was straight, and her black eyes were staring straight at Huangfu Jue.

The virtuous concubine smiled and pulled her hand, "Sister, please go back to your seat. Are you still worried that you won't have the chance to dance for the emperor?"

Concubine Shu was pulled by her for a few

steps, and suddenly turned back to look at Huangfu Jue. There were tears in her eyes, sadness, disappointment, ugliness, expectation and other emotions, all mixed together, like the wind blowing the green duckweed, a mess, but more pitiful.

Huangfu Jue smiled slightly and whitened his finger at her.

Shufei immediately broke into a smile, shook off Xianfei's hand, and walked a few steps to Huangfu Jue. She looked at the empty seat next to Huangfu Jue and hesitated. Huangfu Jue stretched out his long arm and pulled her onto his knees. She screamed in surprise, and her face flushed instantly. Her whole body was filled with his hot breath, and she tried to break free but her hands and feet were weak.

Huangfu Jue smiled softly in her ear and said, "How about just sitting here?"

She bit her lower lip and glanced at him sideways, seeming to be happy but not happy, and also angry but still angry. She knew that the concubines below were already looking at her with swords and sabers, but she couldn't bear to say a word "no".

She began to cultivate her virtues and appearance at the age of five, and was completely trained by her family according to the standards of a concubine. Among the famous ladies in the capital, only Wang Yan could be compared with her. When she learned that the position of empress had fallen to someone else, she gritted her teeth in secret for many nights. Unexpectedly, her opponent turned out to be the unknown second daughter of the Yan family. Yanzhi's beauty is indeed amazing, but she is like a cold jade Guanyin. My mother had long said that men should be worshipped like fathers and cared for like sons. A woman who is too reserved will not be loved by men. As expected, for a month, the emperor stayed in her Zichen Palace almost every night, but confined the queen to Weiyang Palace.

She knew that she had become the public enemy of the entire harem, but she was secretly happy in her heart. She thought that with the emperor's favor and the support of her family, as long as she conceived a child, she would be able to ascend the throne paved by the phoenix.

When Yanzhi appeared tonight, her heart was in a panic. Her bright eyes were charming, and she was angry and happy, as if she had suddenly been enlightened by a master, and her whole person was incredibly lively. That night, she was childish, willful, and disregarded etiquette, but the emperor tolerated it. Her hands could actually play such a piano sound, and her self-conceitedness of being unparalleled in piano and chess was a huge joke.

She was afraid, she was greedy for this man. She was greedy for his looks, his body, his smile, his gentleness. Because of the obsession, she was afraid.

She was not afraid of being humiliated or being laughed at by others. She was only afraid that the man behind her was unpredictable.

Huangfu Jue held her in his arms and fed her with wine. Concubine Xian smiled and left, looking calm. She had been with this man for too long and knew that the woman he played with was just a plaything.

Huangfu Qingcheng and the others rolled up their sleeves and started playing drinking games.

There was still singing and dancing in the hall, but I wondered how many people actually appreciated it.

The water surface was gradually covered with mist, and from the mist came dots of white light, which had quietly approached the corridor without anyone noticing. There were hundreds of lotuses with thousands of petals floating on the waves, and the lotus cores were all candlelight, reflecting the crystal petals. Among them was a large lotus, and the petals actually opened one after another. There was a faint singing voice, and everyone unconsciously put down their wine glasses and listened attentively.

"Recalling the plum blossoms I went to Xizhou, I picked plum blossoms and sent them to Jiangbei. My shirt is as red as an apricot, and my temples are as red as crow chicks. Where is Xizhou? I paddle across the bridge with two oars."

The singing voice was light and graceful,

ethereal and vague. As the lotus petals opened, it gradually became clearer.

"Under the tree is the door, and the green hairpin is visible in the door. The man who opens the door does not come, so I go out to pick red lotus."

Thousands of candles surround a slowly opening white lotus, and in the lotus's heart a young girl dances gracefully. The dance moves gracefully, and the song sings clearly, "I miss my lover, but he is not here. I look up at the flying geese. The geese fly all over the western continent, and I see my lover going up to the brothel. The building is too high to see him, and I can't see him anymore. I'm on the railing all day long."

The moon was at the zenith, and the stars were shining brightly. It seemed as if the sky had turned upside down, and the fairy had been banished to the human world. Huangfu Jue seemed to be staring at her in a trance, and his hands had already loosened the delicate body in his arms. Concubine Shu was pale, and just stared at him in a daze.

The dance has stopped, the singing has faded. "The sea dreams long and deep, I am sad because of you. The sea dreams long and deep, I am sad because of you."

The lotus petals closed quietly again, and the person in the lotus stood in the middle, with bright eyes and white teeth, kneeling gracefully.

Huangfu Jue stared at it intently, his expression somewhat dazed. Seeing the lotus petals closing and gradually going away, he stretched out his right hand as if to keep it.

Concubine Shu's heart slowly sank. She saw the smug smile on Concubine Xian's lips and heard a sigh behind her. She could only hug him tightly, put on a bright face, and said with resentment, "Your Majesty, is she as pretty as me?"

Huangfu Jue looked at her, his eyes were a little confused, and gradually cleared up. He pinched her chin and said, "Yan'er is naturally beautiful, and others can't compare to her."

He smiled slowly and looked at everyone at the table, "A beautiful scene and a good time cannot be wasted. You have heard the best music and watched the best dance. Now go away."

The cloisonné enamel lotus mirror shows the beauty in the mirror with a serious look.

The extremely fine Daizi snails make the distant mountain eyebrows look extremely long, and the rouge made from peach blossoms is slowly highlighted. The black hair is loosely tied sideways, with only a platycodon and crabapple on the temples. The long skirt with peony and phoenix patterns is gently spun, and the room is full of spring.

She sighed softly, with a hint of sadness in her eyes, "Amber, am I old?"

Amber carefully arranged the silk ribbon around her waist and said with a smile, "Master, you are naturally not old. How many people in the palace can compare to your appearance?"

"Where is the queen?" she asked, eagerly probing Amber's face.

Amber looked at her tenderly, "In Amber's heart, the master is the most beautiful."

She smiled contentedly and murmured, "Amber, you are so kind." Her jade arms wrapped around her neck like vines, and she breathed in her ears, "Amber, Concubine Shu makes me very angry."

Amber's eyes gradually became blurred, and her breathing became heavy. "The concubine won't be able to enjoy her glory for long, and you can't do anything about it."

The slender jade hand slowly reached into her clothes, and the red lips murmured, "I don't care, the emperor hasn't come to see me for a long time. Anyone who entangles him must die. The virtuous concubine also. The lotus-picking girl actually created another lotus-picking girl..."

"My queen... Amber will help you... All those who hurt you... will all die..."

The author has something to say: Oh my God, please drop a brick and hit me to death, woooooo

☆、Night visit

Someone, Yanzhi, was suddenly awakened from

a half-asleep state.

Colorful porcelain candlesticks were burning in the distance, emitting only dim light. Huangfu Jue, wearing a thin satin dress, was leaning against the head of her bed. When she opened her eyes, the corners of her lips slowly opened, and her white teeth sparkled.

Yan Zhi was startled, and she sat up with her quilt in her arms, her eyes cold, "How did you get in?" She was in a bad mood tonight, and she kicked Linglong Liluo out. Even if there was no one guarding the house, were the hundreds of people outside the house dead?

Huangfu Jue smiled slightly, his eyes tilted up, as if he had drunk a lot of wine, his eyes were misty and watery. He was not wearing an outer robe, and the collar of his inner garment was open, revealing his smooth and flat chest.

"Shh." He gently tapped Yanzhi's lips with his slender index finger. He lowered his voice and said seriously, "Keep your voice down. I sneaked in."

He was very close to her, and the sweet and clear aroma of Biluo's wine filled her body. His index finger touched her lips, but he didn't move away, instead he gently rubbed them. Her eyebrows were furrowed, and without thinking, she patted him with her backhand.

Huangfu Jue smiled softly, grabbed her hands, and leaned down.

The silk was as smooth as water. Huangfu Jue held her tightly in his arms, and looked at her quietly with his long, deep eyes. His eyes flickered, as if he was neither drunk nor awake.

Yanzhi was forced to interlock her fingers with his. She struggled for a few times but could not move. Although his figure was suspended above her, his eyes were full of peach blossoms, and he must be lustful and ready to make a move. She felt ashamed and angry, and her eyes instantly turned cold. She looked at him coldly and said, "As the king of a country, do you also want to break into the house and pick flowers?"

Huangfu Jue tilted his head slightly, a strand of black hair slid down his cheek. He looked confused, innocent and charming, "Yanzhi, isn't this my palace? Aren't you my queen?"

Huangfu Jue lost his sharpness that penetrated people's hearts during the day, and was lazy and exhausted, but Yanzhi felt a chill down her spine. Just like a cat, it elegantly teases a mouse with its claws, and it may pounce with its sharp teeth at any time. Yanzhi slowly exhaled, trying to remain calm, "Get up first, I have something to tell you."

Huangfu Jue slowly shook his head, his eyes fixed on the bright red of her tightly pursed face, which was the most gorgeous color of the peach blossoms on the branches in March. His voice was so low that it sounded like a sigh, "Yanzhi, you smell so good."

"Don't call me Yanzhi!" Seeing his face getting closer and closer, she couldn't bear it anymore and struggled hard.

Huangfu Jue groaned as if she had kicked him somewhere, and then the man's warm body tightly covered her. Yanzhi only had time to turn her head, and the wet lips and tongue fell on her earlobe.

The delicate body below was very stiff and trembling slightly. Huangfu Jue bit the white jade earlobe in revenge, blew gently into the small ear, and murmured: "Yanzhi, you were not so cold to me just now."

Just now in the hall, she had exchanged glances with him, showing affection, how could she turn her back on him after taking advantage of him? He quietly looked around, marveling at the amazing elasticity of her skin. After a month, she seemed to have adapted well. Should I eat or not? He uttered a sound of pain.

Yanzhi's black hair was scattered on the soft pillow with golden and white patterns, and her eyes were as bright as lacquer because of anger. The big hand between her waist and abdomen was slowly groping, she closed her eyes and opened her mouth to shout, "Come... um..." The slippery lips and tongue, with a hot and aggressive breath, pressed up, tossing and turning, attacking the city. She didn't think about it, and bit down hard with her teeth.

Her lips were blocked savagely, and her mouth was filled with a thick smell of blood. The invader did not flinch, insisting on wreaking havoc in her softness inch by inch.

"Pa!" A crisp slapping sound.

Slowly licking the blood at the corner of his lips, Huangfu Jue narrowed his eyes, his pupils constricted, and stared at her coldly.

Yan Zhi's chest rose and fell violently, but her eyes glared at him fiercely. Since she chose to enter the palace, she knew this day would come, but she never thought about having both. What the Yan family wanted was just a chance to breathe. She could sacrifice her family's freedom, but she would not sacrifice her pride.

After a silent confrontation, Huangfu Jue suddenly relaxed. With a slight curl of his lips, he glanced at her and whispered, "Looking towards the southeast, a song of phoenix seeking phoenix. I never knew Yanzhi could play the piano so well." He suddenly put his hand on her slightly heaving chest, and his tone suddenly turned cold, "The person in your heart is annoying."

Yanzhi was startled, he had already left, standing on the ground, tidying up his clothes. With his back to her, he said slowly: "Yanzhi, even if it is a mistake for you to enter the palace, I want it to be a beautiful mistake."

The tone was very calm, but it showed the naked dominance of an emperor. As soon as the words fell, the man climbed out the window and left calmly.

Yanzhi watched him disappear, and her body suddenly lost strength. She slumped down onto the bed, and the contempt and hatred in her eyes were suddenly drained away. She felt as if she was in an abyss, in endless darkness. She could only keep falling, falling...

Linglong tiptoed towards the large rosewood carved bed. A figure was vaguely visible on the bed with rose-colored auspicious cloud patterns, still lying soundly.

"Miss, it's noon, it's time to get up." Linglong called softly.

There was silence in the tent.

"Miss, Miss?" Linglong called again. Ever since Huangfu Jue suddenly appeared the day before yesterday, no one in Weiyang Palace informed him, and she and Li Luo were not around, the young lady was angry. It has been two days, and she ignored them all. She went to the banquet last night, excited, and came back with a gloomy look. After coming back, she sat for half the night holding a zither. Today she didn't get up again, and she was already very nervous.

"Get out!" The hollow aromatherapy ball that was calm and focused was thrown out from behind the heavy curtains.

Linglong was startled, watching the aromatherapy ball rolling towards her, with fine scented powder scattered all over the floor, and her eyes immediately turned red. She knelt quietly on the floor without saying a word.

"Linglong," Yanzhi's voice sounded after a while. She was no longer as irritable as before, but very tired. "Tell mother that my brother's old injuries have not healed yet. Let him rest in the mansion for a few days."

"Miss..." Linglong hesitated to speak. Miss and the young master have had a good relationship since childhood. Why did she feel so sad after meeting the young master last night?

"Linglong, I'm sorry, I'm just too tired, please let me sleep a little longer. If anyone wants to see me, stop them."

Linglong smiled bitterly, "Miss, the emperor's newly appointed Lian Liangyuan has been waiting for an hour." When she heard that the queen was ill and there was no need to greet her, she burst into tears and choked up. If the queen was ill, she should greet her in front of the bed and serve her.

Yanzhi was silent for a moment before she asked coldly, "Why does she insist on seeing me?" Huangfu Jue had already issued an edict to entrust all matters concerning the harem to Concubine Xian, and the Weiyang Palace had long been deserted.

"A new concubine needs to pay her respects to the queen after her first night of being favored by the queen." Linglong chose her words carefully.

The first night, last night? Was it her after having sex in someone else's bed, or was it someone else's bed after leaving her? Yanzhi felt a blockage in her chest, and wanted to vomit. She just frowned and said, "Let her leave, and flush the floor with water."

Lian Pingting, the daughter of a criminal minister newly recruited by Changyin Pavilion, danced to impress the emperor, and was promoted to Liangyuan after enjoying his pleasure for one night. She lived up to her name, like a lotus in the water, which bloomed brightly even when it was lowered to the dust. Many women in the harem secretly envied and cursed her heartbreakingly. Hearing about the farce in Weiyang Palace in the morning, they all turned into gloating sneers.

Lian Liangyuan was turned away by the queen, and even the gate where she had stayed was washed back and forth three times with water from the Taiye Lake.

"Haha," Xiangpin laughed so hard that her body shook with laughter, and her red jade drop earrings fluttered against her cheeks. "Sister, our Jade Guanyin is really a wonderful person! Xiao Shunzi came back and said that Lian Liangyuan's little face is as yellow as a dry leaf in autumn!"

Concubine Qi pursed her lips and smiled. Seeing that she was laughing so hard that tears came out of the corners of her eyes, she took the teapot with the sea water cloud dragon pattern and slowly poured a cup of tea, "Stop laughing now, or you'll get a stitch in the side."

Xiangpin let out a long sigh, wiped her eyes with a handkerchief, picked up the tea bowl, and put it down angrily, "Zhang Yuerong, this bitch, can't win the emperor's favor, but she prefers to use such despicable means."

Concubine Qi looked at her worriedly, "Sister, she has the power to rule over the six palaces after all, so it's better not to confront her head-on."

Xiangpin smiled coldly, "Don't worry, I don't care about Zhang Yuerong's tricks. As long as the Yan family doesn't fall, she can only be a rat that hides from the light. As long as Yan Wanluo is in the harem, she will feel like a thorn in her throat. I don't need to do anything, the fox's tail will be exposed sooner or later."

Concubine Qi was collecting water to make tea, her movements were graceful and complicated, and the mist made her beautiful face hazy. Concubine Xiang looked at her and sighed, "Yunxi, you will suffer if you are always so indifferent."

Concubine Qi smiled, took a deep breath of tea, and said calmly, "You are not a fish, how can you know the joy of fish?"

Xiangpin smiled at her, and suddenly there was a sense of loss in her eyes, "Sometimes

I envy you, and sometimes I resent you – why did Dad insist on sending me to the palace? If I hadn't met him, I might have lived a happy life." Her hands slowly stroked her belly, "Yunxi, I want a child. If I have a child, I won't be unable to sleep every night."

Concubine Qi was silent. Having a child was their best destiny. But it was the pain of all the women in the harem. No woman had ever been pregnant before, and they even secretly suspected that the emperor was infertile. Wen Ruyu's pregnancy was like a thunderbolt out of nowhere, frightening people and disturbing the original peace of the harem.

She stretched out her hand, covered Qipin's hand, and said slowly: "Sister, don't worry. My father asked for a prescription from the Shatian Ancient Temple. I will have someone give it to you later. If Wen Liangyuan can do it, you can do it too."

Xiangpin didn't say anything, her eyes gradually became colder. Although she had only been in the palace for a year, she had seen many ways for the concubines to compete for favor. Wen Ruyu's pregnancy had already caused a stir, and the harem could no longer remain calm.

Wen Liangyuan can do it, she should be able to do it, and all the women the emperor has favored can do it. So why has none of these possibilities become reality?

Yanzhi stayed in bed all day, and the three

meals were brought back as they came. Linglong and Liluo were so worried that they looked at each other in tears. They slept on the floor outside the bedroom and stayed up all night. After a careful discussion, Liluo went back to the Marquis' Mansion after dawn and tried to get the lady to come to the palace.

Unexpectedly, Yanzhi called out after the hour of Mao. She looked quite calm, and let Li Luo neatly tie her hair into a bun, put on some light makeup, and drink a bowl of green stalk porridge before telling her to leave.

Linglong and Liluo were both stunned. This was the first time Yanzhi had asked to go out since she entered the palace. The two exchanged glances, Linglong was busy preparing clothes, and Liluo pretended to be happy and clapped her hands, "Miss, I heard from the palace people that there is a sea of kapok flowers in Langye Pavilion in Shangyuan Ten Sceneries. Why don't we prepare some food and go there for lunch?"

Yanzhi glanced at her calmly, then glanced out the window. It was not yet 7:00 p.m., and the red sun had just jumped out of the horizon. Li Luo touched her nose and smiled awkwardly.

Linglong brought two coats, one was the moon-white fine-grained gauze coat that Yanzhi usually liked to wear, and the other was a pink and brocade lotus silk coat. Yanzhi took a look and pointed to the one behind.

Linglong helped her get dressed and asked softly, "Where do you want to go, Miss?"

"Go to the Queen Mother and pay your respects." Since I had already attended the banquet, I couldn't pretend to be sick. It didn't matter to others, but the Queen Mother had to go and see her.

Before leaving, Yanzhi asked Yiyue to serve her. Although Linglong remained silent, Li Luo looked at her eagerly. Yanzhi glanced at her. He snorted coldly, "Don't go anywhere, stay at home, keep an eye on your subordinates, and let them know that there can only be one master."

Li Luo immediately perked up and answered crisply, "Yes." She had long wanted to arrange the staffing of Weiyang Palace, but it was the young lady who had been holding her back. A few days ago, she followed the chef in the imperial kitchen to learn how to make soup, and when she came back, she heard that the young lady had been caught off guard by the emperor. She was furious, and now that there was an amnesty order, she immediately summoned people in a hurry.

Linglong was thoughtful. The young lady had changed her mind, and should have given up the idea of forcing the emperor to depose the queen. In any case, having fighting spirit was a good thing.

The scenery of Shangyuan is really beautiful, with nature hidden in every step and the work of nature everywhere. When

Emperor Jing was in power, Shangyuan only had five scenes. One year after Huangfu Jue took the throne, he doubled the size. The architecture is a blend of local customs, with small bridges and flowing water, as well as strange peaks and valleys.

Yanzhi sat in the sedan chair, holding Snowball in her arms, and did not feel bored along the way.

The sedan chair suddenly slowed down, Zhenyu ran to Yiyue and whispered something. Yiyue frowned, thought for a moment, and said to Yanzhi with a smile: "Your Highness, it's still early, why don't we go around Langye Pavilion and then go to Yanxi Palace?"

Yanzhi held a piece of candy in her hand, making Snowball jump to get it. She didn't change her expression when she heard the words, and only said three words, "Go forward."

Yiyue smiled bitterly. When the queen was traveling, others should have avoided her. But the three women in front of her, Concubine Wang, Concubine Zhang, and Wen Liangyuan who was pregnant with a dragon seed, were all a drama. Looking at Yanzhi who was holding the puppy with wrinkled nose, she suddenly felt a heavy responsibility on her shoulders. Queen, please show mercy.

The author has something to say: Very diligent, very hard-working, Liu Liu wants to spend money...

☆、Negotiation

After walking a few dozen steps forward, Yanzhi saw them. Beside the road was a rockery made of white stones from Taihu Lake. Next to the rockery was a jade willow with twisted branches and emerald green branches. Concubine Wang, Concubine Xian, and Wen Liangyuan stood beside the jade willow with smiles on their faces.

Seeing her carriage stop, Concubine Xian and Wen Liangyuan bowed and paid their respects.

Yanzhi gently stroked Snowball's long fur with both hands, leaned against the backrest of the Pisces satin flower, and said lightly: "Get up."

Her eyes swept across Concubine Xian, but stayed on Wen Liangyuan for a moment.

Wen Liangyuan smiled, took another step forward, bowed deeply, and said in a gentle and soft voice, "Ruyu apologizes to Your Majesty. The last time the Queen came to visit, Ruyu was unable to pay her respects. Please forgive me, Your Majesty." Her movements were slow, her posture was graceful, and she looked elegant.

Yanzhi looked at her and said lazily, "It's my health that's not good. It has nothing to do with you." He ignored her and looked at Wang Linbo, raising his eyebrows slightly, "The Concubine looks refreshed today. I'm going to the Queen Mother. Would you like to come with me?"

Wang Linbo held the sleeves of his cloud-colored silk gown with his bare hands. There were only a few blazing pomegranates on his temples. He smiled slightly, his eyes fixed with affection, and said lazily, "It's a bad coincidence today. I'm about to go to Qingping's place. I'll chat with the queen another day."

Yanzhi let out a long "oh" and shrunk back onto the backrest. Her eyes dropped, and her fingers carelessly twirled the silver filigree amethyst ring, "Yiyue, let's go."

Yiyue replied respectfully, "Yes, Queen."

The palace maids carrying the sedan chair walked in unison, their hands steady and swift. In a moment, the double-carried sedan chair disappeared behind the red pillars of the corridor.

The concubine looked ahead, and the corners of her lips curled slightly, "The education of the Marquis's family is indeed extraordinary."

The virtuous concubine smiled coldly, "Don't worry about it, Concubine Dowager. She can boss the emperor around."

Her eyes moved, as if she was smiling, "She is really an ignorant child. But, she has a good father. Marquis Yan'an has made great military achievements, and she also has the ability to be arrogant."

Concubine Xian shook her head, her face darkening, "Not only that, the Empress

Dowager and the Emperor are both her support. Although the Emperor has not yet consummated his marriage with her, it is because her body is not doing well. She usually eats and wears the best. Concubine Dowager, have you noticed the clothes she is wearing? That is a tribute from Jiangnan, a horse of hundreds of colors, with only shadows of flowers in the dark and colorful butterflies flying in the bright. Ten embroiderers spent three years to get such a horse. Although I am temporarily in charge of the harem, I only got a list, and the Sizhenfang directly sent the clothes to the Weiyang Palace. The snow lion in the Queen's arms is also a tribute from Turo, and Fuquan sent it personally." She sighed, with a heavy heart, "The Queen is so domineering, if she becomes the most favored in the harem in the future, I'm afraid everyone's life will be difficult."

Glancing at her, Wang Linbo said calmly, "Xian Fei has always been sensible. Why are you so talkative today?"

Xian Fei paused, looking embarrassed, "Yuerong knew that the Concubine Dowager was fair, so she spoke her mind unconsciously."

"I am only the concubine of the late emperor, and the current empress dowager is your real mother-in-law. If you have anything in your heart, you can go and tell her." Wang Linbo's thin eyebrows were already a little annoyed, and his eyes swept over Wen Liangyuan with a hint of disgust, "Liangyuan is pregnant, it is really not suitable for her to walk around, if you have nothing to do, go back to Cui Linglong Pavilion to rest."

Wen Liangyuan was startled, a trace of grievance flashed across her eyes, but she still responded in a gentle voice, "Yes."

Wang Linbo put his hand on the arm that the young eunuch offered to him, and looked at Concubine Xian meaningfully, "Concubine Xian is the same age as the emperor, right? There are fine lines at the corners of her eyes. Women, it is better to spend less time on these things." After saying this, without waiting for her to speak, he supported the young eunuch's hand and walked away gracefully.

Xian Fei kept looking at her back. She was in her thirties, but still graceful and elegant, as graceful as the willows by the lake. She pursed her lips, and a deep sneer gradually emerged from the depths of her eyes.

When she turned back, there was a hint of embarrassment and loss in her eyes, and she forced a smile, "Ruyu, can you still walk? The imperial physician said that you have a poor appetite, and taking a walk can increase your appetite."

Wen Liangyuan gave her a grateful smile and said softly, "Sister, I'm fine. I suddenly feel very hungry. Let's go back to the palace."

Xianfei nodded quickly, "It's good that you're hungry, Ruyu, the child is the most important, we will go back immediately."

After saying this, without the help of the palace maids and eunuchs beside him, he personally supported Wen Ruyu and slowly returned to Minghua Palace.

Yanzhi was in a good mood all the way. When they entered the Yanxi Palace, Chenxiang, who was beside the Queen Mother, smiled and said "Yo", and wanted to take the snowball from her arms, "Queen, please put it here first."

Yanzhi was startled, then asked suspiciously, "Does the queen mother not like puppies?"

Chen Xiang shook her head. "The Queen Mother likes quietness, and the Yanxi Palace has never kept small animals."

Yanzhi looked at Snowball's big eyes and felt upset. Since the Queen Mother didn't like cats and dogs, Snowball couldn't have been sent by her. Snowball was carried away by Chenxiang, whimpering softly. She was reluctant to let him go, and she subconsciously reached out her hand, but she felt confused.

Yanzhi, even if your entering the palace was a mistake, I want it to be a beautiful mistake.

His words were like a spell, echoing in her ears word by word. It was so chaotic. Ever since she put on the phoenix crown and got into the bridal sedan, her life had been a mess.

She was upset and her face was gloomy. When she entered the inner hall, she saw Fuquan standing outside the curtain of the warm room with his brows lowered. When he saw her, he immediately bowed politely and said, "Your servant greets the Queen."

Yanzhi stopped, glared at him coldly, and turned back. He was here, so Huangfu Jue was also here. After last night, the person she least wanted to see was this man.

The door curtain of the warm room was lifted, and a maid wearing a dark red shirt with a pattern of five blessings holding longevity came out.

As soon as she saw Yanzhi, she immediately knelt down to greet him, and said with a smile: "The Queen Mother was still talking about you today, and it's a coincidence that the Queen is here."

Yanzhi had no choice but to let her get up first. Nanny Lai smiled happily and did not ask why Yanzhi wanted to go back. She took her hand and led her to the warm room. "The queen is finally well again. The queen mother does not have to nag about her several times a day."

Huangfu Jue was indeed here, sitting on the hardwood table inlaid with mother-of-pearl with the empress dowager on either side, his black eyes under the nine-dragon white jade crown glaring at her with a half-smile. The Queen Mother smiled and took her hand, letting her sit beside her. "My child, you are finally well. The Emperor has just arrived, too. Oh, did you make an appointment?" Seeing that she looked gloomy and didn't even look up, she asked in surprise, "What's wrong? Is there someone else who is irritating you?"

Huangfu Jue chuckled and said jokingly, "Mother, the whole city knows that you have married a domineering daughter-in-law. Who dares to bully her?"

"Nonsense!" The Queen Mother deliberately put on a serious face, "Yanzhi is the most well-behaved. If anyone dares to say anything bad about you, I will use my dragon-headed cane to beat him."

Yanzhi half leaned beside her, eyes on her nose, nose on her heart, and only hummed softly.

"Yanzhi, this is the yacon the emperor just brought. Look at it, it looks like a flower. I have lived for most of my life and have never seen one. Would you like to try one?"

"Not thirsty."

"Madame Lai's specialty, the Thousand Layer Golden Nut Pastry?"

"Not hungry."

......

The Queen Mother was finally speechless. One of the two people looked indifferent, and the other was confused. No matter how slow she was, she couldn't survive this muddy situation. She simply waved her hand and said, "I remember now. Alang said he wanted to come to see me and asked me to look after the marriage with her mistress. I won't keep you here. You two can just go together."

The Alang mentioned by the Queen Mother is the sister of the late emperor, the aunt of Huangfu Jue, Princess Zhaoyang. Her youngest son is also a famous playboy in the capital, he is already 23 years old, but the position of the first wife has always been vacant.

Huangfu Jue smiled slightly and said casually: "Since my aunt is coming, my mother will discuss it carefully with her. It just so happens that the Marquis of Yan'an also asked me to arrange a marriage for his family's Zhishang. If there is a good candidate, please keep an eye out for me."

As he spoke, he stood up, standing against the light, his brows drooping, "Is the Queen leaving?"

Yanzhi looked at him, her cold eyes silently ignited with blazing flames, a strange blend of ice and fire, absolutely dazzling. She slowly said, "Your Majesty, I will accompany you."

To the south of the Yanxi Palace, exotic flowers and plants are planted everywhere, and winding paths are paved with white jade from Nanshan Mountain. There is a pavilion among the flowers and trees, named Hua'e Xianghui Pavilion.

The palace maids brought tea and cakes in a continuous stream, then quietly left.

Yan Zhi folded her hands on her knees, stared at Huangfu Jue with clear eyes, and slowly spoke, "Your Majesty, Wanluo told me the truth today. I did have someone I loved before entering the palace. If Yan Wanzhao hadn't run away secretly, it wouldn't have been my turn to enter the palace to serve you."

The future queen eloped with someone before her wedding, and the person she eloped with was the twelfth prince, Huangfu Yu. She spoke of this scandal, which would have implicated the entire family, in such a calm manner.

Huangfu Jue gently fiddled with the tea leaves while holding the Momei purple clay tea lid, with a cold look on his face, "The Queen is reminding me that you are also going to cuckold me?"

Yanzhi shook her head. "Since I have entered the palace, I have cut off my worldly ties. But Wanluo is lazy and rebellious, so she won't be able to stay in the position of Empress for long."

Huangfu Jue put down the teacup, staring at her coldly with murderous eyes.

Her brother's happiness was in the hands of others, so Yan Zhi could only continue to speak patiently: "The emperor is magnanimous. Although he will not pursue the Yan family's crime of deceiving the emperor, the Yan family should also know shame and retreat. Daddy is old, and I hope the emperor can let him go home and think about his life. Wan Luo doesn't want anything else, just worshiping Buddha by the green lamp is enough."

Huangfu Jue's eyes slowly moved around her, his fingers tapping the tabletop, "When the birds are gone, the good bows are put away; when the cunning rabbit dies, the running dogs are cooked. Queen, are you worried that I am not tolerant enough, and have already paved a way out for my family?"

Yanzhi's face was already tired, and her fingers subconsciously fiddled with the jade buttons on her lapel. "Wanluo has no other intentions, but just wants his family to be safe and happy. The Yan family is already in a prosperous situation. If we marry into a wealthy family again, the family members will surely become arrogant. Rather than inviting disaster in the future, it is better to retreat now."

Huangfu Jue laughed out of anger, his tone becoming softer and softer, "In the final analysis, the Queen just doesn't want me to grant her a marriage. Yanzhi, are you afraid that Yan Zhishang will be like you, unlovable?"

His eyeliner is very long, and he usually looks affectionate even when he's not smiling. But when he glances at me at the side, he's like the chilly surface of a lake in spring, which has just thawed and is gorgeously cold.

Yanzhi's heart trembled, and she just met his gaze quietly.

Huangfu Jue reached out his hand and grabbed her chin like lightning, leaning forward to meet her, barely within a fingertip. The corners of his lips curled up, but the smile didn't reach his eyes, "I, don't, agree. You and I have worshiped the heavens, offered sacrifices to our ancestors, and entered the royal family genealogy. In life, you are mine, and in death, you must be buried with me."

Yanzhi did not struggle, but with a hint of mockery in her eyes, she said softly, "Is it interesting to force it?"

Huangfu Jue narrowed his eyes, leaned forward, and whispered in her ear, "Don't worry, between men and women, it's only fun if both of you are willing."

Yanzhi's face turned red. In terms of shamelessness, she was definitely no match for him, so she simply kept silent.

Huangfu Jue let her go, his eyes moved around her face, and then he spoke: "If you are not feeling well, don't let your mind wander. The Yan family is a loyal family, I will never treat them unfairly. You can choose the one you like from what Marquis Yan'an asked. Zhi Shang has asked to go to the Western Regions, and I promised him that if he can conquer Tiele within two years, I will grant him one request."

He paused, stood with his hands behind his back, and the golden dragon on his dark purple robe seemed to be flying into the sky. Suddenly, he grinned, his eyes and eyebrows were full of elegance, and the light around him dimmed, "So, you don't have to despair."

Yanzhi sat there for a long while, feeling irritated and nauseous. When he stepped down the marble steps with auspicious grass patterns, Fang Youyou said, "Why must it be me?" It happened that the breeze blew by, and the golden bells on the eaves jingled. She thought he didn't hear it. She was very unwilling in her heart. The carved railings and painted pavilions, the jade buildings, were interwoven into a dense spider web. The more she struggled, the more she wanted to flap her wings, the deeper she sank. Her mind was clear, but her hands and feet could not move.

Huangfu Jue paused, "There has never been anyone else."

The author has something to say: The collection has grown a lot, I am secretly happy, thank you all, thank you for your messages, thank you for your flowers...

☆, Free

The carved railings and painted pavilions, the jade buildings and terraces, were interwoven into a dense spider web. The more she struggled, the more she wanted to flap her wings, the deeper she sank. Her mind was clear, but her hands and feet could not move.

Huangfu Jue paused, "There has never been anyone else."

At 1:00 p.m., Lady Marquis of Yan'an set off for Weiyang Palace in accordance with the Empress's oral instructions.

The early summer sun was shining brightly, the windows with gilded and pastel cloud patterns were open, and the fresh air of water mixed with the faint fragrance of flowers poured into the house.

Yanzhi was waiting for her mother in the hall. The waiting time was always painful. She looked out the door several times during the time it took to drink a cup of tea. She couldn't tell whether she was feeling anxious or expectant, and her palms were already sweaty.

Li Luo knew what she was thinking and went outside to greet her early.

Because she was going to see her mother, she changed into a cloud-patterned silk shirt with hundreds of butterflies embroidered on it, and a colorful silk skirt with brocade patterns. She combed her hair into a bun and inserted a cloud-curled pearl hairpin in her temples. Linglong thought she looked pale, so she put on some rouge from Tianqiao Pavilion. If it weren't for her worried eyes, she would be as charming as a lotus in clear water.

As soon as Ning Yunshu came in, Yanzhi stood up suddenly. She was wearing the attire of a first-rank imperial edict, with numerous pearl hairpins and sparkling pearls, but her face only looked as pale as paper. There was no servant with her, and no sign of Li Luo. She just walked into the hall alone and quietly. Her dark eyes were dazed, as if she had a thousand thoughts on her mind.

"Mother, what's wrong with you?" Yanzhi hurried forward. Before she could get close, she stopped in a daze. There was suddenly a fragrance in the air. It was like orchid but not orchid, like musk but not musk.

Yanzhi felt her heartbeat was out of control, and she had to suppress it to prevent herself from shouting.

Master!

There will never be the same fragrance again in heaven or on earth.

When she was ten years old, she had just finished her medical studies and became fascinated with making incense. She melted the black ice crystals from the snowy mountains, melted the heart of thousand-year-old lotus seeds, and took the essence of ninety-nine and eighty-one kinds of exotic herbs from the snowy land to make this incense. It was a birthday gift for him.

From that day on, wherever there was a master, there would be the fragrance of orchid and musk.

"Master," she murmured softly, her eyes immediately misty, and she turned around in a circle, "Master..."

The peaceful wind suddenly became violent,

and a small vortex formed in the house. Before Linglong could scream, her eyes rolled up and she fell down. "Bang, bang, bang" all the windows on all sides closed, and a white shadow appeared out of thin air, gradually becoming clearer.

She wears a feathered robe with wide sleeves, fluttering black hair, and has eyes that are weathered and lonely, as if she has witnessed the changes in human affairs over thousands of years.

Yanzhi choked softly and ran straight over. Bai Zizai looked at her, his eyes flashing, his sleeves fluttering without wind. Ning Yunshu hurriedly called out, "Brother, don't..." Before she finished speaking, Yanzhi felt as if she had hit a hurricane or tsunami, with hundreds of forces pressing down on her. She took a few steps back, and a fishy and sweet taste rose up her throat. She was stunned for a moment, looking at Bai Zizai with aggrieved eyes, "Master..."

Bai Zi was stunned for a moment, and in an instant his eyes were filled with rage. With a flash of his body, he had already grabbed Yan Zhi's wrist. He thrust his middle finger forward, his expression changed drastically, and he shouted in a low voice, "Evil creature!"

"Master..." Yanzhi hugged his waist tightly, and suddenly she had a place to vent all the sadness and pain in her heart, and she burst into tears, "You... bullied me... you hit me..."

When she was three years old, Bai Zizai took her back to the Snow Region and she would only return home in the summer. To her, the Snow Region was more like her real home. Her master was the closest to her, a teacher, a father, a friend, and a friend.

Bai Zizai stood with his hands behind his back, looking up at the sky, letting her act coquettishly in his arms. Suddenly, there was a clear whistle, and the whistle was silent. Suddenly, fine cracks appeared on the set of cloisonné porcelain in the room. One turned into ten, ten turned into a hundred, and in the blink of an eye, it became a pile of fine powder.

In the Jiuzhou Qingyan Palace, Huangfu Jue was painting with a brush, and a man in black was standing next to him holding a sword.

The man in black's ears suddenly moved, "Here it comes." The voice was monotonous, like the collision of metal.

Huangfu Jue put one hand behind his back, still writing, and said calmly, "How is it?"

The light in the room was very good, but it could not illuminate the area around the man in black. His face seemed to be shrouded in mist, and it was unclear. He was silent for a moment, and then he spoke, "He seems to have entered the realm of heaven and man, and the law of freedom has reached perfection."

Huangfu Jue stopped writing and carefully examined his handwriting. "Ten years ago, you could still hold out ten moves from him. What about now?"

There was another moment of silence, and then the voice became more harsh, "...three moves."

Huangfu Jue was startled, then he burst into laughter, and he laughed very happily, "Let Yewu and the others withdraw. No matter how many people there are, they will only be cannon fodder."

After Bai Ziyi roared, his eyes looked at Ning Yunshu with anger like the Yellow River. After a quick investigation, he knew that Yanzhi had no true energy in her body and her martial arts were all wasted. He had no wife or children, and he favored Yanzhi among his four disciples. He really wanted the stars but not the moon. Seeing Yanzhi crying out of breath, he was extremely angry and hurt.

Ning Yunshu ignored his anger and stared at Yanzhi with a pair of eyes. She staggered slightly and fell into the rose-backed chair with carved huanghuali wood. She was extremely sad. Her daughter had never shed a tear in front of her. She realized at this moment that the embrace her only daughter needed when she was most vulnerable was not hers.

A tear slowly slid down from the corner of her eye. Yanzhi, I'm sorry for you.

She was originally very beautiful, but now

she looked sad and pitiful. Bai Zizai looked at her, thinking of her standing under the magnolia flowers in a red dress, and pouted her red lips. "Brother, from now on, you can't bully me anymore. Whatever I say is right. Otherwise, I will only play with Qingsongzi."

In the blink of an eye, twenty years had passed. He sighed inwardly, and his expression slowly slowed down. The little girl's eyebrows were still furrowed, and her virginity was still intact. It was not too late for him to come.

He stroked Yanzhi's back, and the Qi ran through her body, dissolving the blood clots. Seeing Yanzhi sobbing and wiping her snot and tears on his clothes, he frowned and said, "It's so ugly, stop crying. Change your clothes and follow me back to the Snow Region."

Yanzhi grabbed his collar and raised her little face. Her eyes were swollen like walnuts. "Master, why are you here? Didn't you say that people from the Snow Region are not allowed to get involved with the royal family for life?"

Bai Zizai's handsome face was slightly distorted, "When did I interfere in the royal family's affairs?" The first of the Ten Commandments for the Snow Region disciples is that if you join the royal family and interfere in the change of dynasties, you will die!

Yanzhi burst into tears again, "But I am

the queen now. If you don't come earlier or later, I have already given up my martial arts and married the emperor. How can you take me away?"

Bai Zizai was so angry at her that his hands and feet became weak. He raised his hands high but couldn't bring them down.

Ning Yunshu's cold voice suddenly sounded, "Brother, please go. There are many masters in the palace, and they must have discovered your whereabouts. Even if I risk my life, I will protect Yanzhi."

Bai Zizai's gaze seemed to have a body, and the sword energy slashed at him fiercely, and every word he said was tinged with ice and snow, "You protect her well? How? Sell her by pound and get your husband a promotion?"

Ning Yunshu stared at him blankly, and smiled bitterly after a long while, "Brother, is Yunshu so despicable in your heart? On the day Wanzhao ran away secretly, the chief steward in front of the emperor immediately brought the old maids in the palace to visit Wanzhao at home. Zhishang was far away in Nanzhao, and Yan Ziren was discussing matters in front of the emperor. I found out that the person who took Wanzhao away secretly was the twelfth prince, and went directly to the Yanxi Palace. Even with the empress dowager's plea, the emperor was still furious. The Yan family has more than a hundred people, and they are all at the emperor's whim.

Brother, what do you want Yunshu to do?"

Yanzhi sniffed and pulled Bai Zizai's sleeve, "Master, don't be angry. Huangfu Jue is more handsome than you, and he is also very generous. I like him very much."

Bai Zi was furious. He flicked his sleeves and pushed her hand away. "If you want to stay here, don't call me Master!" His face was stern but his voice was gentle. He had already achieved a state of freedom. Even when Ning Yunshu wanted to leave with Yan Yanzi, he had never been so hesitant.

Yanzhi's eyes were red again. She knelt on the ground and kowtowed three times in a proper manner. "I am an unfilial disciple, but Master, girls will always get married. Even if Yanzhi is not by your side, you will always be Yanzhi's most beloved master."

Bai Zizai looked at her, his eyes slowly turning cold. Disappointment, sadness and heartache all turned into terrifying murderous intent. He snorted coldly and his figure slowly blurred.

Yanzhi watched him slowly disappear, her eyes suddenly losing their spirit, like a flower in full bloom being blown off a branch by the wind. She shrank to the ground, hugged her knees, and hummed a ballad in a low voice.

My baby, don't cry, there is another flower house on the other side of the river.

The chicken is grabbing firewood, the dog is making a fire, and the kitten is cooking with a smile on his face.

......

The snake bites its tail to make steamed buns, and the baby falls asleep after hearing it.

The author has something to say: Two updates, wow, Liu Liu broke the record, is there any reward?

☆、Assassination

Huangfu Jue put the written words aside. There were already several pieces of paper on Ziyu's desk. He put the pen on the Doucai lotus-patterned washbasin and stretched his hands and feet.

The man in black held a sword in his hand, leaning against the Panlong Pillar, and seemed to have entered a state of meditation. The sunlight in the room was just right, and a small insect with light green wings flew in following the sunlight. When it was half a meter away from Xiu Ji, it seemed to encounter an invisible barrier, and its wings flapped slower and slower, slowly stopped, and fell to the ground.

Huangfu Jue's eyes followed it all the time, and he sighed with regret, "Xiu Ji, do you have any unfulfilled wishes?"

The monotonous voice was as calm as water, "If I hear the truth in the morning, I can die in the evening."

"It's really boring." Huangfu Jue laughed

sarcastically and took out a lotus from the glazed cloisonné vase on the cabinet. The flower was about to bloom, pink and red. He shook it gently, and fine drops of water dripped down. He slowly raised the corners of his lips.

Yanzhi, you probably cried like this, too. With your neck raised high, big tears flowed from under your tightly closed eyes, just like this, flowing over your pink skin. For the last time, I allow you to cry for another man, for the last time.

The light in the room dimmed, as if a dark cloud had just passed over the sun, and Xiu Ji's eyes suddenly opened.

The wind blew in, and the wind in June was icy and biting. Huangfu Jue narrowed his eyes slightly, watching the half-branch lotus in his hand slowly bloom. The three petals, from pink to white, swayed in the wind, but in just a moment they were covered with heavy frost, like an ice sculpture.

Snowflakes are flying all over the sky.

Xiu Ji slowly drew his sword from its sheath, his voice cautious and careful, "Who are you?"

The snowflakes are getting denser and denser. I can't see where they come from or where they go. I can only smell the cool fragrance in the air.

Xiu Ji's pupils constricted and his eyes were as sharp as a sword.

Huangfu Jue put the half lotus in his hand

back into the cloisonné bottle and examined it carefully. After hearing Xiu Ji's words, he smiled lazily and looked out the door, "All under heaven belongs to the king, and all the people are his subjects. No matter who your master is, I can pay ten times the price."

There was a faint sound of thunder in the air, and the snowflakes were no longer scattered in the sky, but rolled together, gathering together, with a chilling sword intent. Xiu Ji's lips twitched, and he only had time to curse "bastard" in his heart, and in the wind and snow, a white light broke through the air.

The sword slashed down like lightning. He had swung the sword thousands of times in the waves, and he was confident in his speed and strength. But this time, the sword swung down, ice chips flew, and there was a trace of confusion in his heart. A bit of piercing coldness slowly spread from his bones. He trembled and lowered his eyes, and saw the small hole on the right chest of the black clothes. There was bitterness in his eyes after enlightenment. The sword's intention was in front of the sword. One move, only one move!

Xiu Ji gasped for air and turned to look at Huangfu Jue. Huangfu Jue was slowly getting up with the help of a couch. The jade crown that bound his hair was gone, and his black hair half covered his face. His narrow phoenix eyes were dark and unpredictable, and in his left hand he was holding a half-segmented sword tip that looked like ice and jade.

There was a faint cold snort in the air, and the wind and snow in the room disappeared instantly.

Xiu Ji fell on his back. Huangfu Jue looked out the door, touched the slightly concave point of Kuilong's soft armor, and sneered. He was a centimeter away from his heart. Even if he didn't want to kill him, he wanted to make him unable to move for half a month. However, he was proud of his status, so he retreated after missing the attack.

Huangfu Jue coughed softly, and dewdrops slowly formed on the lotus leaf, dripping onto the table.

That night, the star Rob.

A dark shadow nimbly climbed over the high wall of Weiyang Palace, pressed the acupuncture points of the palace maid on duty, and successfully slipped into the inner hall. However, when entering the room, he could not suppress his cough.

"Who?" Li Luo woke up with a start. Just as she opened her eyes, she was sent back to sleep by a finger attack.

Huangfu Jue lifted the bed curtain that was covered with smoky branches and flowers and quietly looked at the person in the bed.

Even in her dream, her brows were tightly knitted. Her hair was scattered on the pillow, and the hair on her forehead was wet with sweat. The silk quilt was curled up under her body, her face tilted to one side, and the round outline under her clothes could be vaguely seen.

Huangfu Jue stood there for a long while, then leaned over and gently pulled the quilt out from under her. His fingers inadvertently brushed the skin on her neck, which was warm and hot. His eyes darkened and he couldn't help but caress it a few times.

Yanzhi moaned softly, instinctively looking for a cool place. She waved her hands wildly, grabbed his hand, pulled it back under her cheek, and hummed comfortably.

Huangfu Jue laughed dumbly and simply lay down on the bed. The sweet and sticky aroma of peach blossoms filled his breath, and before his eyes was her delicate skin, which made his mind wander. He pressed his lips against her brows and whispered, "Little drunkard, you made me eat you, don't cry tomorrow."

I slid my fingers into her thick black hair and kneaded it slowly. I watched the space between her brows slowly relax. I felt an indescribable joy and peace in my heart. All the strange thoughts faded away, and I only cherished this moment of peace and tranquility.

Her face was facing him, her breathing was gradually slowing down, her sleeping face was pure and beautiful. His fingers gently rubbed her thick hair, and he easily found the slight bulge, and after carefully outlining it, it was exactly a half crescent moon.

He raised the corners of his lips slightly, and tenderness filled the corners of his eyes. Yanzhi, I finally found you.

Lord of the Snowland, I want to thank you very much. Only you can protect her willfulness so well and return it to me so completely.

Yanzhi's pair of black eyes stared blankly at Chengchen, who had hundreds of children and grandchildren with pomegranate patterns on his body.

It was already noon, and the palace servants who were serving the girls had been waiting for a long time. Linglong was whispering to them to change another basin of hot water.

The hangover wasn't very bad, but she didn't want to get up. There were still vague dreams in her mind, warm breath, and real touch. She was in a trance, afraid that if she opened her mouth, the dream would just be a dream, and she would never be able to find even a trace of warmth again.

Linglong lowered her eyebrows and stood aside, her heart was in a mess. The young lady did not explain why she fainted yesterday, and she could only vaguely guess. But the atmosphere in the palace was tense, and the number of guards was almost doubled. In addition to the important military officials, the doctors of the Imperial Hospital entered and left the Jiuzhou Qingyan Palace. She was nervous and almost wanted to announce that the young lady was not feeling well and had to stay in bed to rest.

There was a rustling sound coming from inside the tent, and Yanzhi half sat up. Linglong sighed inwardly and hurried forward to serve.

Yanzhi was in a daze the whole time, and it was not until after breakfast that she noticed that Linglong was worried. She fiddled with the nine-link jade in her hand and asked lazily, "What's wrong?"

Linglong bit her lower lip and spoke hesitantly, "Jiuzhou Qingyan Palace...something seems wrong. The imperial physician has gone in three times."

Yanzhi's face turned pale, and the Nine-Link Chain hit the table with a clang. She was stunned for a long while, then suddenly stood up and said, "Get ready, I'm going out."

My heartstrings were suddenly pulled very tightly, my throat felt dry and astringent, and there was a hint of inexplicable joy hidden in my hazy consciousness.

Master...

Along the way, she was sometimes sad, sometimes happy, sometimes resentful, sometimes angry. Her heart was heavy and unsteady. It was not until the sedan chair landed that she managed to calm down.

Holding Linglong's hand, he slowly got off the sedan. The sunlight was dazzling, and he couldn't help squinting. When he opened his eyes again, he saw Concubine Xian bowing, "Empress." Her voice was soft and weak, with a barely perceptible hoarseness. Unlike her usual elegance, she had a simple makeup today, with only a royal blue hairpin with jadeite beads on her head, a magnolia-green double-embroidered satin dress, and a plain face, looking a little haggard. Yanzhi waved her hand casually, picked up the white jade dragon-patterned steps, and walked up.

"Empress." Concubine Xian's voice was a little anxious, "The Emperor is meeting with the court officials, I'm afraid he can't see you." Seeing Yanzhi turned around and looked at her, her face flushed, and she whispered, "I thought that the Emperor was busy with the war in Western Xinjiang these days, so I made some ginseng soup, and it was Eunuch Fu who came to pick him up."

His dark-skinned eyes paused on her face for a while, then he pursed his lips and smiled, saying slowly, "'Xian Fei' is worthy of the name 'Xian', she is truly virtuous."

She looked down from above, smiling and talking, but she had the elegance and pride to look down on the world. Concubine Xian felt a chill in her heart, and felt that she could not escape from this icy gaze, and she took a half step back involuntarily. She had turned around, and her jade-colored skirt with broken branches and piled flowers passed by. In an instant, the jade steps were covered with flowers.

The virtuous concubine stood there in a daze, watching her walk to the top step by step, watching Fuquan come out to greet her respectfully, watching the moonlight disappear into the palace gate. Her eyes grew colder and colder, and her silver teeth clattered softly.

Why can some people stand inside the door so easily, while she has been planning her whole life and is always standing outside this threshold?

Fuquan led Yanzhi to the east side hall of Jiuzhou Qingyan Palace, where Huangfu Jue was indeed discussing court affairs. People in ochre, purple, crimson, and red, with cranes and unicorns, came out one after another. The first one was Yan Yanzi, the Marquis of Yan'an. When he saw Yanzhi, he was obviously startled, and there was a slight tremor in his voice, "I wish the Queen good health."

Yanzhi looked at him quietly, her figure still standing tall, but with white hair visible under the purple gold crown, and there was hidden pain in her eyes as she stared at him.

Yan Yanzi, a military god of his generation, a mighty jade pillar that could stop children from crying at night. But at this moment, he was just a soft-hearted father.

There was already a sting of moisture in her eyes, and she quickly turned her face away, "Father..." her voice was so low that it seemed like she was choking, "You have aged a lot, and you are so ugly..."

The important officials were stunned. Even if they had to climb out of a sea of fire and swords, they couldn't help but twitch their lips. Yan Yanzi's old face turned red, and he forced himself to keep a straight face. Before he could speak, the rouge had already gently brushed over him.

Shame on you, degenerate, trying not to laugh until you get hurt...

The author has something to say: Sorry, sorry, dear readers. I wasted a few days due to something else, but now I will return to normal.

☆, Beauty Pageant

Huangfu Jue was holding an ancient scroll, leaning against the bed. His face was slightly pale, which made his hair look like crows and his eyes look like jade. He looked less cold and more noble.

Seeing Yanzhi coming in, he put the book aside, stretched his limbs lazily, and smiled slowly, "You are a rare guest today! Could it be that my Shangyuan is too big and the Queen got lost?"

Yanzhi's eyebrows did not move. A palace maid with a bun on her head was kneeling at the head of the bed, holding a medicine soup, looking at her expectantly. She took the medicine soup and waved her hand.

The palace maids acted as if they had been pardoned, and they bowed and quietly left.

Yanzhi sat down on the edge of the bed very naturally. Huangfu Jue was startled, then his eyes moved slightly, with a smile on his face and his red lips half opened.

Qianmingzi, Codonopsis, Angelica dahurica, Red Peony Root... Yanzhi was slowly mixed in the medicine bowl. The bitter aroma of the medicine confused her consciousness. She felt sour and bitter in her heart. She was happy for a while and confused for a while. Although Huangfu Jue's face was pale, it was bright and smooth. The solar meridian was blocked and the cold air attacked the lungs. It was indeed injured by the Zhoutian Dharma of the Xueyu lineage. Master... you finally broke the precepts for Yanzhi.

When she was in a trance and put a spoonful of medicine into Huangfu Jue's mouth, he bit the silver spoon in his mouth, and slowly swept the remaining medicine with the tip of his tongue, with a seductive look. She realized that their posture was too intimate. Her face sank immediately, and she looked at the affectionate Huangfu Jue with a look of disgust, "Let go."

Huangfu Jue chuckled and raised his chin

lazily, "I thought you came to visit me after hearing the news. But after looking into your eyes, I knew it was too early for me to be happy. Yanzhi, I'm injured, are you happy?" His voice became lower and lower, and at the end, it sounded a little aggrieved and lost.

Of course, the master's sword greatly relieved the anger in the disciple's heart. Yanzhi remained calm and put the long-handled silver spoon to his lips again, "Your Majesty, you are too suspicious."

"Then, Yanzhi really has me in her heart." The voice was gorgeous, deliberately low, and gentle like the first petal quietly blooming on a branch.

Yanzhi felt a chill in her heart as she watched him swallow the medicine contentedly. Her expression changed faster than turning the pages of a book, and she sighed that he was so shameless and had no bottom line.

The bowl of medicine was quickly fed to Yanzhi, who had obtained what she wanted to verify. She stood up and was about to bow and take her leave.

The jade-colored skirt was pressed under him, "Your Majesty," Yanzhi said with a little anger.

Huangfu Jue smiled slightly, his brows and eyes were surprisingly gentle, "I have finished reading your travel notes, let Fuquan go with you to exchange for a few other books."

Yanzhi was furious. The book he took away last time was a unique copy from the previous dynasty, and it was the most beloved part of her dowry. If she hadn't been so afraid of him, she would have snatched it back long ago.

Huangfu Jue ignored her angry glare and pointed at the books on the square red sandalwood cabinet with landscape patterns, "What are you standing there for? Take it away."

Yanzhi took the book with a cold face, and Huangfu Jue said again, "Take the scroll beside it as well. All the interesting ladies in the capital are in it, see if there is one that suits your taste."

Yanzhi's body suddenly stiffened. She looked at the scroll tied with yellow silk ribbon with complicated eyes. She suppressed the urge to throw it away. She knelt slightly and said stiffly, "I will take my leave."

He grabbed the scroll and stood up and walked out without waiting for Huangfu Jue to speak.

Huangfu felt tired, his eyes slightly closed, and the corners of his lips slightly raised.

The incense in the Suanni Ruyi incense burner was filled with sandalwood, and the painted banana leaf plum vase was filled with iris orchids about to bloom. On the desk, coffee table, and acacia-patterned wooden floor, there were portraits of beauties everywhere, some looking up, some smiling sweetly.

Yanzhi sat on the rosewood chair with a sullen face, her eyes darting from one picture to another.

"Yanzhi," the mist in my mother's eyes had not yet faded, but her voice was calm and clear, "This is Zhishang's choice, you can't stop it. Since the emperor has given you the decision-making power, then choose a rear that can bring him the greatest benefits."

The rear, stable interests...Can the flesh-and-blood souls behind these vivid pictures of beauties be equated with cold materials and dirty power?

She could understand why her brother made such a choice, and why he couldn't accept that his freedom was based on her happiness, right? Two years, could he compete with Huangfu Jue in two years?

Thinking of those long and slanted phoenix eyes with flowing light, I sneered in my heart.

How can I allow others to sleep soundly under my bed?

When Linglong came in, she saw Yanzhi curled up in the deep of the chair, the longan on the floor was still rolling, and the vermilion skirt of the beauty on Cai Hou's paper was stained with dark stains.

She sighed and quickly cleared a space on the ground.

Yanzhi looked at her, and after a while she

said weakly, "Where is Li Luo?" She hadn't been seen for a long time, and the room was empty.

Thinking of what Li Luo said this morning, Linglong paused, put the scroll in her hand on the long table, and then said lightly, "Didn't you ask her to go out and find out the information of talented ladies in the capital?"

Yanzhi groaned softly. She had indeed forgotten. However, she glanced at the scroll and realized that there was no need to do so. The information Huangfu Jue had provided was already very detailed, even including the girl's private hobbies.

He was too lazy to move, and just stared at Linglong. His curled-up posture did not show his usual ethereal feeling, but instead he looked like an abandoned puppy.

After Linglong cleaned up the room, she could no longer maintain her cold expression. Standing in front of her, her eyes were filled with anger, "Miss, do you know how much you drank yesterday? Three jars of old Huadiao," she said slowly, word by word, "crying and laughing is not enough, you used a sword to force Lai Xi to find wine for you. Now, everyone in the harem knows that the master of Weiyang Palace can drink a lot."

Yanzhi shrank back into the chair again and stammered, "I was in a bad mood yesterday." She really didn't remember it, only vaguely remembering that she pulled out the sword inlaid with gold, jade and pearls from the wall, "I didn't say anything nonsense, did I?"

Linglong shook her head, squatted down, and said softly: "Miss, you must take good care of yourself."

Yanzhi put her head on her knees and rocked unconsciously. The initial sadness and despair gradually faded away, but she still had so many concerns that she couldn't let go. She said softly, "Linglong, it won't happen. I will get better."

After the morning court session, Yan Zhishang walked out of the hall with his hands behind his back. The sunlight rippled from the glazed golden ceiling. He squinted his eyes slightly, and then saw Li Luo standing next to the beast head on the corner of the corridor.

The small pavilion at the four corners is built against rocks on three sides, surrounded by water. Below it are crowded lotus leaves with occasional pink flower buds.

Yan Zhishang sniffed the tea and sighed, "Only three ounces of rime can be produced on Mount Heng every year. It seems that you are having a good time in the palace."

The slender fingers lifted the purple clay teapot, the mouth of the pot was slightly tilted, and the tea was clear and green. Yanzhi's eyebrows were calm, just like the misty Jiangnan, "The emperor is a very generous person."

Yan Zhishang was smiling the whole time, but his smile never reached his eyes. Even when he was so relaxed, his posture was still as straight as a sword drawn from its sheath. He looked at Yan Zhi and said softly, "What about the past? Have you forgotten everything?" Have you forgotten the snow on Tianshan Mountain, the gray wolf in the wilderness, and that... person? The smile on Yan Zhi's lips became fainter and fainter, gradually becoming transparent, and she looked straight into Yan Zhishang's eyes, "Brother, I did nothing wrong."

Yan Zhishang drank the tea in one gulp, the dark color in his eyes became heavier, "Yes, you did nothing wrong." But you don't know how much I wish you didn't do so well. The flame of heartache and resentment burned in my chest every night, almost burning my reason. How could my sister, who was not stained by dust, the most holy snow lotus on Tianshan Mountain, fall into the most filthy place in the world?

"Brother," Yanzhi said softly, "if you really think that I have sacrificed, then let me make my sacrifice more valuable. The Queen Mother will hold a birthday banquet next month, and there will be a hairpin flower competition. Please help me choose a sister-in-law that I like."

Yan Zhishang raised his eyebrows, his cold and hard lines added a bit of teasing, "Yanzhi, men and women are different." Seeing her troubled look, his mood suddenly became cheerful. His fingers stroked the celadon teacup with broken branches and flowers, looking at her black eyes thoughtfully, "Birthday party? There are so many surprises. Yanzhi, Huangfu Yu showed up."

"Where?" Yan Zhi's face was not surprised. It was a foregone conclusion, and their appearance was only a matter of time.

"The largest gambling house in Dingzhou." He didn't have to travel day and night to get back to Shengjing for the birthday party.

Although his tone was gentle, it was chilling. Yan Zhi looked at him quietly and smiled slowly, "Brother, no matter how confused Wan Zhao is, she is still your sister."

Her thick eyelashes drooped, covering her cold eyes. Yan Zhishang remained silent, sipping the tea in his hand. He only had one sister.

The tea fragrance is subtle and the summer lotus is speechless.

Yan Zhishang's glacial eyes suddenly surged with burning emotions, and he looked straight into Yan Zhi's eyes, "Two years, to protect your heart."

Yanzhi smiled bitterly in her heart. They knew each other too well. No matter how she tried to hide it, he would not believe it. However, Huangfu Jue's kingly charm was too low.

"Don't worry, I can take care of myself."

Watching Yan Zhishang leave, Yan Zhi's heart calmed down. She knew that there was an invisible barrier between them, and they could no longer speak freely as before. However, it didn't matter, he was still there, where she could see him.

Zhishang fought for her, and all she could do was to protect herself to the greatest extent possible.

As for Yan Wanluo, her hatred faded away. A woman who lost the protection of her family, put herself in the cusp of the storm, relying only on the favor of a man, her happiness was just a fleeting moment of beauty.

She spent the next few days in comfort. The assassination of Huangfu Jue was suppressed by someone with ulterior motives, the harem was peaceful, and Weiyang Palace faded from people's sight again. She was busy looking at flowers and playing with dogs every day, and went to pay respects to the empress dowager every other day.

But one day, she met Concubine Shu beside Mingyue Bridge.

She wore a gauze dress with pink clouds and double butterflies, a skirt with floral patterns and dew-stained lilies, her black hair was piled up in layers and folded into a bun, and a row of pearls the size of dewdrops were pressed on her temples. She was still as fresh as ever, but this beauty was no longer the crystal round dewdrops on the petals after the rain. Her eyebrows were already weathered, and her delicate face was covered with a shadow.

After the ceremony, she didn't want to hide the hostility in her eyes. Yan Zhiwei nodded and paused. At the moment of passing by, she suddenly spoke and said softly: "The Queen is Fengyi, a role model for the whole country. When she travels, she rides a phoenix chariot, and there are twelve palace maids and eunuchs. She wears a weft dress, decorated with twelve flowers, and two bobs. The female historian is by her side, and her daily words and deeds are all recorded in a book."

Yanzhi stopped, glanced across her face, and said calmly, "I am the queen, and also Yanzhi." First Yanzhi, then the queen.

Concubine Shu's eyes were filled with deep scorn. "Wang Yan is also from a noble family, and has been cared for by her father and brothers since she was young. Although the Wang family is not as famous as the Yan family in terms of military achievements, they are not unknown in the court. But since entering the palace, she has been walking on thin ice every day, and has never been casual for a single day."

Yanzhi smiled slightly, "If you have nothing to ask for, you can be like me."

She stood there casually, smiling calmly, the carved railings and painted walls, the broken walls and dilapidated buildings, were all floating smoke. Concubine Shu looked into her eyes and thought of Wen

Liangyuan's words, that people like the queen were raised by mountains and rivers. Sadness slowly welled up in her heart. She really didn't care. She really didn't care about what she had worked so hard to achieve. If it was Yan Wanzhao, she could still give it a try, but how could she really defeat such an enemy?

Seeing that she had nothing to say, Yanzhi smiled and turned away.

A sentence was delivered quietly with the wind, "This morning at the court, the Grand Secretary of Longyuan Pavilion and more than ten people from the Secretariat begged the Emperor to depose the Empress."

The person in front still walked very steadily, but his posture was beautiful in a different way, like clear water on flat ground and lotus flowers blooming with every step.

The author has something to say: My dear friends have been very cold recently. How about we have a snack with meat next time?

☆、Poison

Wen Liangyuan said that people like the queen were raised by mountains and rivers. Sadness slowly welled up in her heart. She really didn't care about what she had worked so hard to achieve. If it was Yan Wanzhao, she could still give it a try, but how could she really defeat such an enemy?

Seeing that she had nothing to say, Yanzhi smiled and turned away.

A sentence was delivered quietly with the wind, "This morning at the court, the Grand Secretary of Longyuan Pavilion and more than ten people from the Secretariat begged the Emperor to depose the Empress."

The person in front still walked very steadily, but his posture was beautiful in a different way, like clear water on flat ground and lotus flowers blooming with every step.

The slender fingers curled up and grasped the sky-blue bed curtain, and the lotus-colored jade arm exposed outside was covered with fine beads of sweat.

The quilt slid halfway under the bed, and the long black hair was tangled tightly. The slender waist was tightly restrained, and the fierce impact made the woman only half open her red lips and whimper. Her pair of blurred eyes were full of water, and even though her consciousness was blurred, she was still full of love.

The softness under her body began to tighten unconsciously, and her palms were filled with warm tremors. Huangfu Jue leaned over and pressed down, kneading the smooth peaks, and rubbing his lower body slowly, "You want it to be ready so soon? I won't allow it."

The flexible long legs wrapped around his waist, the woman half bit her red lips, twisting her body impatiently, the love that flowed from her lips and teeth was so tender and charming, "Jue'er, give it to me, Jue'er... um..." The sudden emptiness made her sob softly.

He easily flipped her body over, with her legs spread wide open. She only had time to let out a low cry before the violent attack choked her deep in her throat, shattering her sounds.

The curtains swayed like ripples on water, causing the candlelight to sway slightly. All that remained in the room were broken flesh and low gasps.

Huangfu Jue put on his clothes and got out of bed. The woman behind him was already lying on the bed like water, looking at his slender body with her beautiful eyes in fascination, "Jue'er, are you unhappy today?" He has always been a patient lover in bed, and rarely was he as passionate and wild as he was today.

Huangfu Jue held the white jade cup with a dragon pattern, his eyes flickering under the candlelight. He spoke slowly, his voice lazily after making love, "Tell Wang Shouren to keep his minions in check. It's not his turn to interfere in my family affairs."

The woman was silent for a while, then slowly sat up, the quilt slipped off, revealing her round shoulders and deep valleys. She pulled her black hair behind her back, her face was as beautiful as a painting, and her bright eyes were misty.

It was Wang Linbo.

"Jue'er, I haven't contacted my elder brother for a long time. However, you have spoiled the little girl from the Yan family too much." The voice was slightly hoarse, with just the right amount of sourness.

Huangfu Jue glanced at her with a slightly raised eyebrow, "Are you jealous?"

Wang Linbo stared at his handsome and evil face in fascination. He knew that the blood flowing in this perfect body was cold, but he was still incredibly attracted to him. As he approached, she pouted her red lips slightly, crossed her arms across his thin waist, and almost murmured to herself, "Jue'er is mine."

Huangfu Jue wrapped her hair around his fingers, slowly exerting force. Wang Linbo felt pain, and a trace of grievance appeared in his bright eyes. He raised the corners of his lips, looked into her eyes and said softly: "Remember what I said."

Wang Linbo fell on the bed and heard him tapping his fingers lightly from the outer room, then heard Fuquan's low voice, followed by the rustling sound of someone getting dressed. She almost held her breath and listened carefully until Amber came over to help her wash up.

She leaned lazily against Amber, letting her put on her underwear, "Amber, where are things going?"

There were purple marks all over her body. Amber replied in a muffled voice, "The things are ready."

Wang Linbo raised his head, looked at her carefully, and slapped her. "Pa", Amber's head tilted to the side, and five deep fingerprints appeared on her left cheek. Wang Linbo looked at her coldly, "Jealous? You are not worthy!"

Amber turned back stiffly and continued to dress her silently.

Wang Linbo's eyes suddenly filled with tears, and he touched her face with trembling fingers, "Amber, Amber, I'm not good... Don't be angry..."

Amber fastened the buttons of her tunic and held her hands, "Master, Amber is fine."

Wang Linbo looked at her, a big tear quickly slipped across the corner of his eye, like a helpless child, "Amber, he is angry, he is warning me. I can't be discovered by him, I can't..."

Amber held her tightly in her arms and whispered to comfort her, "The master arranged it himself, so there will be no mistakes."

Yanzhi stood beside the lake stone, looking at a newly planted osmanthus not far from the crabapple tree, with green leaves and dense flowers, and a gleam of light flashed in her eyes. She waved and Lai Xi came over. Yanzhi pointed at the osmanthus and asked, "When was it planted?"

"It was sent by Eunuch Hai from the Ministry of Internal Affairs yesterday. He said it was a rare plant that has been seldom seen for decades. It has double flowers and leaves, and its fragrance is the best for nourishing the qi and concentrating the mind. I picked the flowers and leaves, and the chief physician of the Imperial Hospital said the same thing."

Picking a small white flower, Yanzhi smelled the faint fragrance in the pistil, and the smile on her face deepened a little, "The fragrance is really good, find someone to serve it well." Lai Xiyiyue has his own rules for doing things, and Weiyang Palace is almost an iron plate. But if you see something interesting, don't let someone who doesn't have eyes keep it to death.

"Where's Li Luo?"

Linglong was happy to see Yanzhi's smile still on her lips, and joked, "She's crazy. She stays in the piano room practicing swordplay all day, and I can't control her."

Yanzhi was stunned, then smiled and waved her hands, "Go find her, I want her to pass a message to the eldest young master whom I admire most." She needed someone who could open up the information channels inside and outside the palace.

It is said that the wood-tea plant only grows deep in the Ten Thousand Mountains in Lingnan. It has two flowers and two leaves, one flower in the sun and one in the shade, and is a favorite of poisonous insects.

The drama in the deep palace was indeed

accomplished without bloodshed.

The person sent by Yan Zhishang arrived soon. She was an ordinary-looking girl. Yan Zhi asked a few questions and then had someone take her to the small kitchen.

As soon as she left, Li Luo couldn't help but said, "Miss, is there something wrong with that flower? I went to deal with it."

Yanzhi glanced at her calmly and said, "If you have too much energy, go to the yard to loosen the soil." This was her life-saving amulet, a plunder that her opponent had voluntarily given her. She stretched herself and lay on the beauty couch to take a nap.

There are several forces behind this flower, the most obvious one is Qipin's family, the flowers and plants in the Imperial Household Department are basically monopolized by her family. There must be a deeper hidden mastermind behind it, who went through a lot of trouble just for her.

The Suzhou embroidery silk was smooth and silky, the pillow had a faint scent of white orchid, and she couldn't hide the smile on her lips.

Huangfu Jue came during dinner.

He showed up more often, always drinking a cup of tea, eating a meal, sitting for a while and then leaving. Li Luo and Ling Long had become indifferent to him, and Yan Zhi basically ignored him.

Huangfu Jue came in and took a deep breath, "What a nice smell." He pulled a chair and sat down. There were only four dishes and a soup on the table, but they were exquisite and unique. A round plate with light pink crabapple flowers was filled with green or tender white dishes. In the middle was a large lotus leaf-shaped plate, and the soup inside had been boiled to a translucent, creamy consistency.

Huangfu Jue felt his appetite was whetted. He glanced at Yanzhi and said with a smile, "Did you change the cook?" There was a small kitchen in Weiyang Palace, and whenever he came without notifying them in advance, they would always cook for themselves.

Yanzhi scooped a spoonful of Mingzhu tofu and said lightly, "Your Majesty, do not talk while eating and do not talk while sleeping."

Huangfu Jue shook his head and sighed. Seeing that she only picked up the light chopsticks, he scooped a bowl of soup and placed it next to her. He also drank a sip and felt that the taste was delicious and endless. After tasting it carefully, it seemed that there were thousands of flavors spreading on the tip of the tongue. He didn't know what the ingredients were, and couldn't help but wonder: "What is it made of?"

Yanzhi didn't move her eyebrows, and put the spoon to her lips. Li Luo smiled and said, "Snake soup."

The young lady really asked her to loosen

the soil for the flower for a long time, and then dug out two big green snakes. The young lady flipped through an ancient cookbook and suddenly wanted to eat snake soup. She watched the golden clay stove stew for two hours.

Huangfu Jue was startled, then looked at Yanzhi with a smile in his eyes. He untied the jade pendant on his waist and asked Li Luo, "Did you make this? Reward!"

"Thank you, Your Majesty."

Huangfu Jue left the Weiyang Palace, the smile on his lips gradually faded, his eyebrows and eyes became a little cold, and he stood by the shimmering Taiye Lake for a while before he said lightly, "Go check where the snake came from."

"Yes." Fuquan bowed slightly.

The waves were swaying, the lotus fragrance was wafting, and looking at the emerald green in front of him, Huangfu Jue's eyes flashed with cold disgust. Such a noble and pure figure, but underneath was a pile of mud, so dirty and disgusting.

"Call Lian Liangyuan, I'm suddenly in the mood to... enjoy singing and dancing."

The author has something to say: Liu Liu's updates are very powerful, we should encourage her!

Flowers, collect, hug...

☆、Flirting

The silk pipes were thin and the singing was low. Huangfu Yu's feet were already light and floating, and he felt that the stars in the sky were spinning. The emperor's brother was too cruel. Five or six beauties with long sleeves and graceful hands were holding five-inch square golden cups. If he hadn't used the excuse of urinating, he would have died in the sea of wine and the forest of meat.

My heart was hot and I just wanted to follow the sound of water and take a good bath. Thinking that the Guanyuntai nearby was remote and sparsely populated, I stumbled and walked westward.

After finally reaching the water's edge and pulling off the golden hairband, she suddenly heard a song floating over the water. The song was very low, and was obviously spoken without thinking. Combined with the gurgling sound of the water, it had an ethereal and profound beauty.

Huangfu Yu was curious, so he held his breath and moved upstream. When he saw the white shadow, his eyes were fixed.

On the other side of the river, a blue stone was lying in the water, and a woman was leaning on it. She was dressed in white, with a fair face and black hair that fell straight behind her. Her snow-white lotus feet were kicking the water leisurely.

Huangfu Yu felt his heart pounding, and could only mutter foolishly, "Fairy, fairy..."

"Who's there?" Yanzhi was startled and stood up from the stone. Her snow-white clothes fluttered, covering her beautiful lotus feet.

Huangfu Yu felt that her angry eyes seemed to be filled with thousands of stars, and his mouth suddenly became dry. Seeing her glare at him, she lifted her skirt and walked away. He was very anxious, and he jumped into the air with a tiptoe.

Before Yanzhi could even scream, he held her tightly in his arms. The two staggered and fell to the ground.

Huangfu Yu used his body as a cushion and fell firmly on the bluestone, without feeling any pain. The beauty's black hair poured down on his face, full of the fragrance of a fresh bath. The softness of her chest pressed him tightly, and he could clearly feel the intense ups and downs. The cool aura of water and the exquisite curves reminded him instinctively that this was real.

He whimpered in his throat, opened his mouth and bit the slender neck, "Beauty, follow me."

Yanzhi's face turned pale, and she felt that he was full of the stench of wine and meat, which was disgusting. Her elbow crossed and hit the numb point on his waist. When his body was stiff, she broke free from his shackles. She only had time to take a step, but her ankle was pulled hard, and her body immediately lost balance and fell to the ground.

Huangfu Yu only felt the touch was warm and tingling, and the tingling sensation spread from the palm of his hand to the lower body. Immediately, there was a bang in his head and he pressed down hard.

Yanzhi listened to the heavy breathing behind her, and murderous intent slowly emerged in her eyes. She pressed the silver bracelet on her wrist lightly, and a touch of silver light appeared between her fingers.

Huangfu Yu could not wait to turn her over, and his lips fell on her like raindrops, murmuring: "Fairy... I... will be responsible... How about the position of concubine..."

Yanzhi pushed with one hand, and the silver needle stopped at the Huihai acupoint. There was a slight hesitation in her eyes. Suddenly, she groaned, and her pearly teeth had already bitten into her lower lip. His hand suddenly climbed up to the peak and kneaded it fiercely. Yanzhi's eyes flashed coldly, and the silver needle had already stabbed hard.

Huangfu Jue had just finished his morning court session and returned to Jiuzhou Qingyan Palace. Before he had time to change out of his court robes, Huangfu Yu rushed in.

Huangfu Jue frowned and looked him up and down: the golden ring on his head was crooked, his robe was wrinkled, and it was wet from the waist down. He took the sky-blue robe with sea dragon pattern from Rui Bai's hand, waved away the people in the room, and then asked calmly, "Where have you been fooling around?"

Huangfu Yu's eyes sparkled, and he took several deep breaths before he said quietly, "Brother, I met the Goddess Luo."

Huangfu Jue sneered and raised his eyebrows, "Did you see a ghost?"

"No, no, no... It's not a ghost! Brother, I'm done. I fell in love with her the first time I saw her... I want to marry her!"

Huangfu Jue changed into his robe and chose a belt with a gold-embroidered dragon pattern. He sat on the chair, took a sip of tea, and then asked casually, "Who do you like?"

"I don't know, I've never seen her before. She has long hair, big eyes, and smells good..." Huangfu Yu racked his brains to think of adjectives.

"Cough, cough, cough," Huangfu Jue almost choked to death on his tea. He looked at Huangfu Yu suspiciously, "You've been pure and aloof since you went out?" The harem is full of women like this.

"Oh, my brother!" Huangfu Yu slid down on the armchair in frustration. "She is very special. With her pair of jade feet exposed and playing in the water calmly, I felt that she could only be a fairy in the water. There was no scent of makeup on her body. I only realized yesterday that there really is a lotus flower emerging from clear water."

His words became softer and softer, and he was annoyed that he had offended the beauty last night. Huangfu Jue's expression gradually became serious, and there was a hint of gloom in his eyes as he looked at him, and he slowly said, "You can't ask me to drive everyone out and let you identify them one by one. If you have a pen and ink, draw it yourself."

Huangfu Yu held the pen and recalled the past. After a while, he followed the pen and a picture of a beauty was completed in an instant. He looked at it carefully and sighed regretfully, "It's just similar in appearance, but it should be enough to find someone."

In the painting, a beauty is walking on the water, her clothes fluttering in the wind. Her bright eyes are full of affection, as if she is smiling but not laughing.

Huangfu Jue covered her eyes with his hands, and spoke in an unusually gentle tone, "Yu'er, did you touch her?"

Huangfu Yu shook his head and said, "I have no memory of what happened afterwards. When I woke up this morning, my clothes were intact, so I guess I didn't finish it." He felt half regretful and half relieved. A woman like that deserved to be treated seriously.

Huangfu Jue smiled slowly, his eyes full of blood and gore, "Very good." Suddenly he raised his voice, "Prince Yu was disrespectful in front of the king, and he shall be punished with fifty strokes of the cane."

Huangfu Yu was shocked, "Brother, why are you doing this..." Before he could finish his words, his arms were strangled by the warriors in front of the palace who flashed in.

Huangfu Jue slowly rolled up the painting and said, "Go ahead. After the fight, I'll take you to see the person in the painting."

The scent of sandalwood wafts through the air.

The Buddha is sitting cross-legged, with his left hand placed horizontally on his knee in the mudra of concentration, and his right hand placed on his right knee, with his palm facing inward and his fingers pointing to the ground. His half-open eyes are gentle and compassionate, showing his love for all living beings.

The Queen Mother closed her eyes and meditated, chanting scriptures in a low voice.

Nianyu hurried in and called softly, "Mammy, Mammy."

Nanny Lai walked over and whispered something in Nianyu's ear. Nanny Lai's face changed. She knelt down beside the futon and said, "Master, something happened to the prince."

The Queen Mother slowly opened her eyes,

held the rosary in her hand, and bowed three times to the Buddha statue. Then she looked at Lai Ma with a reproachful look, "He is already an adult, he should be able to take responsibility for everything by himself, why are you so flustered?"

Nanny Lai smiled bitterly, "My Lord, the prince has caused quite a bit of trouble this time. The emperor was furious and gave him fifty lashes of the cane. After that, he was carried to the Weiyang Palace."

The Queen Mother's hand paused on the mother bead, "Did Yu'er offend the Queen?"

Nanny Lai's expression suddenly became strange. She hesitated for a moment and said, "I'm afraid I was drunk yesterday and recognized the wrong person."

The Queen Mother sneered a few times, "Evil son!" She closed her eyes and muttered Buddhist scriptures again.

Nanny Lai was anxious, "Master." The weather is so hot now, if someone is left under the sun, the sweat will get into the wound and he will suffer badly.

The Queen Mother sighed, "Desecrating the imperial palace is a capital crime. If he survives and comes back, it will be his good fortune."

Nanny Lai knew that the Empress Dowager hated these things the most, so she didn't dare to persuade her anymore and went to find out the news herself.

The inner hall of the Weiyang Palace was in a mess, as if it had been robbed. Huangfu

Jue was sitting on the only surviving chair. Yanzhi covered herself with the quilt and curled up deep in the bed.

Huangfu Jue sighed, "Are you still angry? Which hand did he use to touch you? I'll cut it off to make amends, okay?"

There was silence deep in the bed, not even the lightest tassel stirred.

Huangfu Jue snapped his fingers lightly and heard a shrill scream from the yard.

Yanzhi suddenly sat up and glared at Huangfu Jue. Unexpectedly, she was looking into a pair of bottomless black eyes. A tiny wound was cut on his forehead by the splattered porcelain, and a drop of blood slowly flowed to the corner of his eye. He turned his head to look over. Although his face was calm, his eyes were burning. He had never seen Huangfu Jue like this before. It was very strange.

The silent fire in his eyes was a little cold inside, a murderous intent. Yan Zhi was slightly startled, thinking that he was just pretending, but she didn't expect that he really had murderous intent. For the face of the emperor?

Family affection is indeed weak in the royal family, she thought vaguely, and the look she gave Huangfu Jue was a little strange, three parts puzzlement and seven parts contempt.

Seeing that he was angry, her anger subsided. Breaking so many things was very tiring. She got off the bed naturally, carefully walked around the broken porcelain pieces, poured herself a cup of tea, and said calmly, "Take the person away and don't pollute my land."

Huangfu Jue said nothing. When she passed by him, he stretched out his long arms, pulled her onto his knees, buried his head in the crook of her neck, and said sullenly, "I feel uncomfortable. Tell me, how should we punish him?"

Yanzhi's body was stiff, and she said coldly: "If the emperor is really unbalanced, Prince Yu's mansion has many concubines. Ah! What are you doing?"

Suddenly he bit her neck hard. Yanzhi covered her neck with her hands, and her eyebrows raised.

Huangfu Jue slowly pursed his lips, and stared at her with his long black eyes, "You are different, Yanzhi, you are different from them."

Yanzhi looked at him hatefully, lowered her eyelids for a long while, and said lightly: "The emperor's words are golden, that's different. I'm tired, the emperor and the twelfth prince, please go back."

Huangfu Jue held her and rocked her slowly. The dark emotions in his heart gradually settled down. He suddenly smiled and whispered in her ear, "Yanzhi, do you still feel uncomfortable when I hold you like this?"

Yanzhi was stunned, and a blush immediately spread from her ears to her cheeks. She felt ashamed and annoyed, and uttered two words through her teeth, "Shameless!"

Huangfu Jue chuckled and quickly kissed her earlobe. He let go of her hand before she completely turned hostile and straightened his face. "Twelfth brother did make a mistake, but fortunately it didn't cause a big disaster. I'll let him go to the Imperial Stables and feed the horses for a month, okay?"

Yanzhi snorted coldly, glared at him fiercely, flicked her sleeves, and walked straight to the side hall.

Huangfu Jue watched her figure disappear behind the flying figures screen, and felt his heart soften as never before. She was still here, standing beside him intact, as proud as ever. His tense emotions relaxed, and he couldn't help feeling a little tired. He always forgets that even if she is a flower, she is also a wintersweet covered with thorns. He can hold her hand, stand together at the top of power, and look at the beautiful mountains and rivers with a smile.

The author has something to say: Oh oh oh, Liu Liu is a backward element.

Dear ones, you are not alone in staying up late tonight.

☆、Sisters(Modified)

Yanzhi half leaned on the yellow pear wood

inlaid copper chair, with little Snowball nestled in her arms. She teased it lazily, using its tail to sweep its soft round nostrils. Snowball was impatient with her teasing and kept whining.

Linglong felt distressed and hurriedly picked up Snowball and said, "Miss, Snowball hasn't eaten yet. I'll go feed him."

With nothing to do, Yanzhi glanced at Li Luo who had a sullen face and asked, "Why is it so quiet today?"

Li Luo looked at her with a pout and said nothing.

"Are you blaming yourself, or were you scolded?" It was Li Luo who followed her last night. She suddenly wanted to drink, so Li Luo left her.

On ordinary days, there are not many people around the Weiyang Palace. People in the harem seem to avoid this area, and their vigilance is also lowered.

Li Luo's eyes turned red. "When I think of that bastard... if it weren't for the young lady's cleverness..."

Yanzhi looked at her and smiled, "The bastard you are talking about is the current Prince Yu, and... he is very likely the son-in-law of the Marquis of Yan'an."

Li Luo snorted in hatred, "He's just a playboy. The young lady lost her mind and abandoned her father and mother for him."

Yan Zhi was stunned. Yan Wanzhao always had a setback and was self-righteous. If she had not been in love with Huangfu Yu, how could she have done such a rebellious thing?

"Li Luo, let mother go to the palace this afternoon."

Yun Zishu did not come alone in the afternoon.

A young lady in palace attire, with her hair tied up high, her skirt covered with peach blossom mist and white silk skirt, slowly walked out from behind her, gracefully and elegantly, and knelt down, "Wan Zhao greets Her Majesty the Queen."

Her movements were slow and her pronunciation was mellow, revealing a deep-rooted superiority in her bones.

Yan Zhi smiled slowly, "Sister, long time no see." She looked at Yun Zishu again and said coquettishly, "Mother, when did sister come back? Why didn't you inform me in advance?"

Yun Zishu looked at her lovingly. The fact that Prince Yu was punished with fifty strokes of the cane had already spread all over the court. Everyone was saying that the queen punished her sisters because their reputations were damaged. Her daughter had suffered so much injustice, so she let her pretend to be confused and said lightly: "Wan Zhao returned home the day before yesterday, and today she should go to the palace to pay respects to the queen."

Yan Wanzhao smiled awkwardly, his eyes reddened, "Wanzhao is unfilial and brings shame to our family." After saying this, he looked at Yanzhi gratefully, "Fortunately, I still have my sister..."

Yanzhi looked at her, and suddenly smiled, and said slowly: "'If there is no him, there will be no me. I weep in the evening sun, and leave the family.' Although sister has lost her biological mother, mother has always regarded you as her own daughter, and father values you the most. Not to mention the emperor's grace, he has appointed you as the future queen. Sister's departure really chilled everyone's heart. Fortunately, sister is not too confused, and knows how to turn back after straying."

Yan Wanzhao listened quietly, tears welling in her eyes. She knelt down on both knees in front of Yun Zishu, buried her face in her skirt, and cried bitterly, "Mother, I am so foolish to have caused you and me so much trouble. Today, I have seen my sister, and I feel relieved. I will report to my father and go to Tiekan Temple to pray for my family under the green lamps and ancient Buddhas."

Yun Zishu glanced at Yan Zhi with a smile, then pulled Yan Wanzhao up and said, "What nonsense are you talking about."

Yanzhi looked at her coldly, sneering in her heart. As expected, she had learned a little about the sufferings of the people after going out, and knew that she had to lower her posture and kill people with a soft knife. She stroked Yingluo's hair and raised her eyebrows, "How can we go to Tiekan Temple? It is a well-known place of poverty. We are also royal relatives now, so if we want to go, we have to go to Dajue Temple."

Yan Wanzhao's crying, which had just subsided, rose again, and she used Yun Zishu's sleeve as a handkerchief. Yun Zishu said angrily, "You are already so famous, and you are still talking nonsense." He waved to Linglong, "Take the young lady to wash her face."

Linglong came over with a smile, Yan Wanzhao bowed with red eyes, and followed her down.

As soon as she left, Yanzhi's face turned stern.

Yun Zishu sighed, "Don't blame your father, he is the one who makes you happy."

Yanzhi snorted lazily. It was good for her to come, but some things could only be asked to the person concerned.

Yun Zishu stretched out his middle finger and smoothed the wrinkles between her brows, and said softly, "The emperor beat Prince Yu with a stick, but is it related to you?"

Yanzhi nodded, "He got drunk and behaved inappropriately, and provoked me."

Yun Zishu was stunned, and her heart suddenly felt empty. Seeing Yanzhi's sparse eyebrows and eyes, she opened her mouth, but all the words she wanted to say were stuck in her throat. She curled her fingers tightly and said slowly, word by word,

"Yanzhi, you have suffered so much, and mother will always get you back every bit of it."

Yan Zhi looked at her and suddenly laughed, "Can anyone bully Hong Niangzi's daughter? Prince Yu will probably be separated from 'sexual happiness' for three years." Yan Wanzhao had gone through so much trouble to marry him, but now she had to stay alone in an empty room. Besides, she really wanted to kill him last night, if she hadn't happened to come across his jade pendant and guessed his identity.

Yun Zishu forced a smile, Yanzhi pulled her hand, "Don't worry, mother. I asked you to come here to discuss something." Waving her hand, Li Luo handed over the scroll, "Look, I've noticed the youngest daughter of Mei Hanlin and the second daughter of Jiang Shilang. I think they're both good. Will brother like them?"

Yun Zishu held Yanzhi's hand, with relief and pity in his eyes, "Yanzhi has grown up, you have considered everything. Your brother's marriage is not suitable for the Wu family, nor for the Wen family. Qingliu is indeed the best choice. I have heard of the girls from these two families, and their personalities and character are both top-notch."

Yan Zhi threw the scroll aside and leaned sullenly on Yun Zishu's shoulder, "They are not worthy of my brother."

Yun Zishu smiled and shook his head, "Silly

child."

The mother and daughter leaned against each other for a while, and Yan Zhi raised her head, "Why did Daddy ask you to bring Yan Wanzhac?"

Yun Zishu was silent for a while, with displeasure in his eyes, "She knelt outside your father's study for a whole day and night holding her mother's spirit tablet. Yanzhi, her affairs are handled by her mother, you don't need to worry about it."

Yanzhi thought about it and suddenly smiled and said, "But Prince Yu has never come to propose marriage yet?"

Yun Zishu hummed lightly.

Yanzhi's eyes sparkled, "Dad is such a face-conscious person. Poor Wanluo, he really has to become a monk now."

Yun Zishu looked at her with a gentle gaze, "Since the emperor has made you the empress, the matter between Wanzhao and Prince Yu will not be pursued. But no one can guess what the emperor is thinking. Yanzhi, is he good to you?"

Yanzhi turned her face away and remained silent.

Yun Zishu sighed and said slowly: "I'm watching with cold eyes. I'm afraid the emperor has feelings for you. Yanzhi, no matter what, mother hopes you can be happy."

Yanzhi looked at the lush green tea trees in the courtyard. Happiness, in this deep palace? Her happiness can only be in the vast sea of clouds, the continuous snow-capped mountains, and can only happen between the eagle and the wolf.

How can there be love if there is no freedom?

Linglong quietly left the right side hall of the Weiyang Palace and closed the door. The light in the room became dim, and the Canaan incense gradually became stronger.

The light just stopped at the hem of her rouge skirt, rippling out the golden thread of hibiscus flowers and glass brocade. She was hidden in the shadows, with a clear light in her eyes, looking at her half-sister in front of her. She watched the hesitation in her eyes at the moment of closing the door quickly turn into determination, and she knelt down without hesitation.

"Sister, are you kneeling to me for the imperial power or for marriage?" The cold words still have the texture of pearls and jade even in this closed room.

Yan Wanzhao was silent for a while, her eyes slowly shifted from the relief of the dragon and phoenix on the wall, the night-shining pearl in the mouth of the phoenix head to Yanzhi, and then she spoke, "After mother died, what you have now is all my dreams. I dreamed that one day, your family would be able to kneel in front of me." She looked straight at Yanzhi, her back proudly straight, her eyes deep, "until I met him."

"He played rogue to me, tried his best to

make me laugh, flirted with me... and scolded me. At first I could still keep my composure, but later I could yell at him." A tear slowly slid down her perfect chin, the corner of her mouth slightly raised, and her eyes slowly softened. "That day, he secretly knocked me out of the small building. After I woke up, I cried and screamed like a shrew, punching and kicking him. He ignored my slap and kissed me on the corner of my lips. 'Yan Wanzhao, you are now the most beautiful woman in Shengjing.' There were five fierce scratches on his face, but he looked straight at me. I knew that I had completely lost. My previous life was the most beautiful mirror. Once it was broken, there was no going back."

Yan Zhi looked at her fiercely, her tone was gentle and charming, just like the sweetest glances between lovers. Such a revelation hurt her deeply, and she clenched her five fingers tightly to resist the pain in her heart, "You want to destroy the entire Yan family for your love?"

Yan Wanzhao stared at her steadily, with guilt in his eyes. "Whether you believe it or not, I never thought of disobeying the order. It was Brother Yu who kidnapped me from the Yan Mansion. It was during the escape that I learned his true identity."

Sarcasm slowly emerged in Yanzhi's eyes, "If he really cared about you, why would you come to me for help?"

"I want to marry into Prince Yu's mansion in a dignified manner. Yanzhi, only you can help me." A royal marriage cannot accommodate pure love. She needs the support of her parents' family and the recognition of the royal family.

Yanzhi looked at her and suddenly burst into laughter. As the laughter gradually subsided, tears oozed out of the corners of her eyes. After a long while, she slowly spoke, "Okay, I'll help you."

Huangfu Yu lay on the bed and hummed.

Huangfu Jue saw Han Lan's eyebrows twitching constantly, and his patience was running out. He took the cotton swab from his hand, lifted his clothes and sat down beside the bed, and said calmly, "Go and get the medicine."

Huangfu Yu turned his face away and immediately remained silent.

Huangfu Jue snorted coldly, "You flirted with my queen, and you still dare to show your disrespect to me?"

Huangfu Yu's voice came from the pillow, "Brother, is she really Yan Wanluo?"

"Um."

"No wonder you tried so hard to marry her. Poor me, I visited the Marquis of Yan'an's mansion so many times at night but never met her. Is it really not our destiny?" Huangfu Yu's voice was very low and frustrated.

After a while, Huangfu Jue's voice was heard, "Yu'er, I can give you anything you want, except Yanzhi."

He quickly applied the medicine and pulled it to his buttocks. "It's OK, it's just a superficial wound. After you recover, you can go to the Marquis of Yan'an's mansion to propose marriage."

Huangfu Yu struggled to move his body, turned around, and looked at him with resentment, "What about the work of the Imperial Stables?"

Huangfu Jue wiped his hands and said calmly, "I have to go."

With Huangfu Yu's return to the capital, the court and the country are calm but there are undercurrents. When the late emperor was dying, he wanted Huangfu Yu to inherit the throne, but Huangfu Yu refused. He has a good relationship with the emperor and is the legitimate son of the empress dowager, so he is very valuable among the kings. Although there are rumors that he has an affair with the eldest daughter of the Yan family, he has not yet been engaged, so it cannot be confirmed. The empress dowager's birthday is approaching, and the girls are all looking at the hairpin flower competition, competing secretly.

The two pillars of the capital, Yan Zhishang and Huangfu Yu, are the dream lovers of many girls.

Mrs. Yan also changed her low-key style and often appeared in the circle of noble ladies, bringing with her the person at the center of the storm – Yan Wanzhao.

Why didn't Wanzhao show up some time ago? I felt palpitations and went to a nunnery to recuperate for a while.

She was extremely beautiful, and her eyes were sincere. Even if someone asked her sourly, "Does your daughter like to go to the nunnery to recuperate?" (Yanzhi was not at home during this period, for the same reason as above)

She smiled and said, "Master is my old friend and has excellent medical skills. If you need help, just ask."

The Marquis's Mansion was powerful, and few families, except the truly wealthy, dared to reject them. Yan Wanzhao became active again in the social circles of the capital in a very high-profile manner.

The author has something to say: Well...Liu Liu is very hurt.

People work so hard, but the audience is still so bored.

anyone here?

☆、Birthday celebration

"Miss, it's almost time." Linglong reminded Yanzhi quietly.

Yanzhi put the book aside and asked, "Have mother and the others arrived?"

"Madam and the eldest daughter are here." Linglong was holding two skirts in her hands, one was a shark silk water pattern standing eight-treasure skirt, and the other was a Sichuan gauze phoenix pattern washing flower pleated skirt. "They were sent by the Sizhenfang yesterday. Which one should I wear?" Both were so exquisitely crafted that it was hard to choose.

Yanzhi glanced at it calmly and said, "Find something plain."

"Miss!" Linglong refused. All the ladies above the third rank were here today, so it couldn't be too simple. "You still have to accompany the emperor to arrange a marriage for the young master."

Stop the sorrow... Yanzhi felt a little irritated, closed her eyes, and pointed at something at random, "Come on."

Shuimu Mingse is the largest of the ten scenic spots in Shangyuan. It has the largest flower garden in the palace, with strange trees and rippling water. In the middle is a chrysanthemum-shaped fountain with a large lion head spraying water, forming seven water curtains, with pearls and jade splashing in a staggered manner. Hundreds of musicians from Changyin Pavilion are scattered around, and there is music everywhere, and every step is filled with stringed instruments.

There were already quite a few bright-eyed girls, gathered in groups of three or five, some standing by the water, some gathering in front of the flowers.

On the east side of the fountain, there were eighteen stone-carved screens with landscapes, birds and animals, and a rectangular table with huanghuali wood, mother-of-pearl and ivory stone, flowers and birds. The empress dowager and all the concubines in the harem sat inside.

The Queen Mother drank the wine Huangfu Jue offered her and said with a smile, "Your Majesty, you should go ahead and accompany the foreign ministers. If you leave here, it will be easier for the girls to relax."

Huangfu Jue smiled and stood up, "I wanted to see the birthday gifts they gave to my mother, but since my mother has sent them away, I will not stand in line." He looked at Yanzhi with his black eyes, "Queen, my share of the gift will be taken by you."

The Queen Mother smiled and poked his forehead, sighing, "How petty, even my mother is calculating."

Yanzhi glanced at him and met his gaze. She lowered her eyes and said calmly, "Husband and wife are one. What I am giving is naturally the emperor's."

The Queen Mother smiled and groaned, "Yanzhi, your mother loves you in vain. Your Majesty, please don't leave. I want to see what kind of generous gift you two will give me."

Yanzhi clapped her hands.

Li Luo came up holding a long narrow wooden box. Yan Zhi took it and placed it in front of the Queen Mother, saying in a gentle voice, "May you live like this day every year."

The Queen Mother smiled and said repeatedly:

"Okay, okay."

The rosewood box was wrapped in red silk, with a longevity pattern embroidered in gold thread. The empress dowager looked at the different shapes of the longevity characters and said with a smile, "This requires some effort." She untied the red silk and opened the wooden box herself.

Everyone's eyes changed. Inside the wooden box, there were layers upon layers of chrysanthemums. In the middle was a red lotus-shaped longevity guest, followed by light green, goose yellow, dark purple, and white. The most unusual one was the black imperial daughter flower in the right corner. When the lake breeze blew, the silk-like petals trembled a little, and a strange fragrance filled the air. This box was filled with flowers that would "kill all other flowers when they bloom."

These chrysanthemum varieties are certainly priceless, but the most rare thing is that the flowers that bloom in September all bloom in June.

The Queen Mother was overjoyed, "Oh, my son, how did you get this?"

Huangfu Jue smiled and glanced at Yanzhi, then picked up the bright red birthday gift and inserted it into the empress dowager's hair, "Your son, I borrow this flower to offer to the Buddha."

Seeing the Queen Mother happy, everyone tried to join in the fun. Only one voice came out indifferently, "No matter how beautiful the flowers are, they will wither in one day. They are not as good as gold and silver." The Queen Mother pinched a scarlet fruit with her fingers and put it against her lips, laughing. Everyone was silent for a moment. She seemed to be still unaware. She just smiled at the Queen Mother and said leisurely, "Sister, do you think it is or not?"

The Queen Mother's expression remained unchanged. She closed the wooden box, handed it to Chang Gui, and said slowly, "When people get old, they prefer these flowers and plants. They are dead things, but they have more conscience than people. If you treat them well, they will bloom in April and May, July and August."

Wang Linbo raised his eyebrow, and Concubine Shu beside him spoke first, "The Queen Mother can't just like flowers and plants. Yan'er's gift also took a lot of thought." She carefully held a delicate jade sculpture of Guanyin in front of the Queen Mother, her eyes full of expectation, "Yan'er has asked Master Yuankong of Dajue Temple to bless it."

The Queen Mother saw the halo of light flowing around the jade statue, her eyes were as bright as lacquer, and there was a hint of compassion. She put her hands together and chanted the Buddha's name softly, "Amitabha." There was a little more warmth in her eyes when she looked at Wang Yan, "Shu Fei is thoughtful."

Concubine Shu smiled shyly and glanced at Huangfu Jue. Seeing that he was also looking at her with a smile, her face couldn't help but blush and she returned to her seat.

Facing Wang Linbo's half-smiley eyes, she seemed to be startled, and her smile faded slightly. The delicate atmosphere at the banquet was instantly dispelled by the concubines' witty remarks.

When Concubine Xian stood up, Huangfu Jue had already nodded to the Empress Dowager, and he took Fuquan to the outer courtyard.

The surroundings immediately became deserted, and Yanzhi smiled coldly in her heart. After everyone had given their gifts and the sound of flutes and pipes could be heard on the dance and singing stages, she excused herself to change her clothes and walked out.

Li Luo was very careful today. In addition to herself, she also brought four young palace maids. The six masters and servants walked slowly along the stream behind the rockery.

In addition to the fragrance of flowers and mist, the air gradually became filled with the scent of lush green trees. Yanzhi looked at the apricot tree in front of her that two people could hug together and stopped. She looked at the green apricots on the branches, with a hint of melancholy in her eyes, "Li Luo, I want to eat apricots."

The flowers have faded and the green apricots have become small. When the swallows fly, green water surrounds the houses.

Under the tree in the drizzle, she looked at the steamed buns and beef jerky, her lips pouted, "I don't want to eat."

He glared at her fiercely, but still put his hand down, "What do you want to eat?"

What do you want to eat? He didn't want to eat anything, he just wanted to embarrass him. The girl who bought the umbrella secretly looked at him several times, she was unhappy.

Looking at the emerald green above my head, I suddenly remembered the apricot tree at home, which has the same sour and astringent taste. "I want to eat apricots."

He frowned slightly and looked at her in distress.

"I want to eat."

She looked at him so confidently. He was silent for only a moment and then disappeared in the rain and fog.

In May, the apricot blossoms were still on the branches, so where could she find apricots? She waited under the tree, secretly cursing him as an idiot and laughing at the same time.

The sun was about to set when he finally came back. She was already very angry, but when she saw the two wrinkled green apricots in his hand, her anger immediately turned into joy.

What happened next? Where did the man who ran all over the mountains to find a green apricot for her go? She felt hazy and couldn't help but put her hand on the cracked tree trunk.

I thought I could let it go, but memories are like vines that twist and crawl out from the cracks all the time, with branches connected to each other, rooted in the blood vessels, and when they are pulled out, it is excruciating pain.

There was a slight tremor on the tree trunk, and Li Luo stepped up to the treetop. She picked a few relatively large green apricots and floated down again. "Miss, this is for you."

"Pa pa pa," a high-five sound suddenly came from behind the stone, "What a beautiful body movement, girl." A man in black clothes appeared in front of them, his hair piled up like a pile of crows under the purple gold crown, and a lazy smile chewed on the corners of his mouth. When his eyes swept over Yanzhi, he was obviously startled and stopped.

Li Luo stood in front of Yan Zhi and looked at him warily, "Who are you?"

The man looked at her with interest, "You are quite skilled, little girl. Who is your master?"

□□Emperor Taizong won the world on horseback, and all the nobles practiced martial arts. It was normal for people from the Marquis of Yan'an's mansion, even maids, to know some martial arts. Yanzhi stopped Li Luo from making a move, "Li Luo, don't be rude, meet the Fourth Prince."

Huangfu Fang's smile deepened as he met Yanzhi's cold eyes, "People are deceiving me! The Empress is a kind-hearted woman, but they say she is a wooden fool." He flicked his sleeves, raised his hands to his forehead, and knelt down in an upright manner.

Yanzhi turned her body to one side and said calmly, "Your Majesty is a descendant of the royal family, why do you need such a big gift?"

Huangfu Fang stood up from the mud, his expression still carefree and unrestrained, "Don't be so optimistic, you should be punished."

There are few people with such genuine nature in the palace, and Yanzhi felt a flash of admiration in her heart.

Huangfu Fang was the fourth son of the late emperor. □□ respected black and valued purple, but he preferred red. He wore bright clothes and rode fast horses, sang loudly and got drunk. The late emperor loved and hated him when he was alive.

How could such a person be born into an imperial family!

"The flowers ahead are too flourishing, tending to be gaudy, which does not suit the prince's gentlemanly mind. Your Majesty should return to your seat." Yanzhi spoke calmly as she passed by him.

Success is the king and failure is the villain, and this has been the case since ancient times. When heroes have no way out and beauties have aged, it is inevitable to feel sad.

There was a long sigh behind him, followed by several clanging sounds, as if someone was knocking on the railings, "But the romantic love is always blown away by the rain and wind--" The tone was lazy and the ending was dragged out very long, but there was no charming meaning.

The author has something to say: I apologize, I apologize, Liu Liu used the excuse of paying New Year's greetings to be lazy.

Woohoo...are there any bricks...

☆、Kao

As soon as Yanzhi's figure disappeared, a palace maid appeared in front of Huangfu Fang, knelt down on her knees, and murmured a poem, "Recalling the lotus pond from afar, who is chanting about Duruo Island? I am afraid that I will not have dreams this beautiful night, but if I do, we will travel together."

Huangfu Fang leaned against the railing and replied lazily, "Get up."

The palace maid quickly handed a pink object to Huangfu Fang and said, "The shadows on the cloud platform are moving in the wind. I think it's an old friend coming." After saying that, she lowered her head and left.

Huangfu Fang twisted the silk handkerchief in his hand and smiled softly. It was indeed because the flowers were too abundant.

When Yanzhi returned to Shuimu Mingse, the hairpin flower ceremony had already arrived. Yan Wanzhao stood in front of a bush of peonies, her pleated skirt covered with golden petals, a white jade hairpin pressed against her temples, and a golden and jade flower in her hand. She looked around with a spirited look, and was a beauty of nature. Within three incense sticks, she had composed five poems in succession, defeating five other ladies who came to compete in flower-picking.

A total of twelve flowers are selected in the hairpin flower competition, with peony being the king of flowers and the competition being the most intense.

However, if she wanted to seize the title of the king of flowers in the past, it would not be so difficult. Yan Zhi watched the pink-dressed girl holding a top-ranking red flower walk up to Yan Wanzhao, and the two raised their hands in greeting and smiled slowly.

Yan Wanzhao's smile was still perfect, and her fingertips seemed to be casually wrapped around a strand of black hair. Only those who knew her well knew that this was a subconscious action when she was in a bad mood.

The Queen Mother was waving at her. After making sure that Yan Wanzhao saw her, she smiled from across the air, then walked up to the Queen Mother and slowly looked through the poems recorded by the female official.

"Yanzhi, I didn't expect that there are hidden dragons and crouching tigers in our boudoir. Take a look," the Queen Mother picked out a few pictures from the box, "how are they inferior to those top scholars in the previous dynasties?"

Yanzhi's eyes fell on one of the Xue Tao letters, with a hand holding a flower-pinned small calligraphy, the signature was Mei Xunyou.

"How can the deep valley bear the northern branches? Every year, the flowers bloom late. Do you know that it is the time when the ice and snow are piled up?"

Yanzhi chanted slowly, and every word was as pure as ice and snow, with a sense of loneliness and nobility. I couldn't help but be stunned. Such a woman is good, but her temperament is probably too aloof and difficult to get along with.

"Yanzhi, Wanzhao is worthy of her great reputation! 'The beauty of the country is drunk in the morning, and the fragrance of heaven is dyed on clothes at night'. It is both new and clever, but it does not lose the aura of a master. It is worthy of being the 'king of flowers'."

The Queen Mother took the paper roll that the female official had just presented to her with a smile, and looked at Yan Zhi, her eyes seemed to have deep meaning. Yan Zhi only felt a little irritated in her heart, and said lightly: "If the Queen Mother says it's good, then of course it's good."

The Queen Mother was startled, then relieved. She patted Yanzhi's hand and said softly, "Don't worry, Mother will make arrangements."

Her son was too disappointing. When something like this happened, the woman would always suffer. It was inevitable that Yan Zhi had some grudges in her heart. After dragging it on for so long, she should give the Yan family an explanation.

He immediately called over the female official, picked up the pen, and personally named the twelve flowers. He then ordered someone to make a copy and send it to the front yard together with the poem.

The eunuch in charge of ceremonies called the twelve flower mistresses forward in a long voice to receive the reward. The masters of each palace stood up, pinned the flowers on the flower mistresses' temples, and gave them rewards one after another.

The Queen Mother personally called Yan Wanzhao to her side, put the gold and jade seal in her hair, looked her up and down, held her hand and said with a smile: "This person is truly more beautiful than flowers."

Yan Wanzhao's cheeks were slightly red, her eyes were bright, and she said softly and coquettishly: "Empress Dowager - Mother -"

The Queen Mother had a kind look on her face, and her eyes already showed satisfaction with her daughter-in-law.

Yanzhi's mind was mostly on Mei Xunyou, who was following behind. She was dressed more simply than the others, with jewelry all white like white jade, pointed eyebrows, bright eyes, and a demeanor that was otherworldly. She felt cold in her heart. She was a beauty, but she was not suitable for Zhishang.

There were soft voices all around him, and bright-eyed girls everywhere, but his heart was uncertain. Could it be Jiang Qingluan?

Zhishang, your happiness is in my hands. Do you know that I am so scared and so cautious...

She was distracted and naturally didn't pay attention. As soon as Mei Xunyou raised his head, Concubine Xian and others changed their expressions.

Today's hairpin flower competition was organized by Princess Zhaoyang. Noticing that the empress dowager looked tired after she had awarded the twelve flowers, she arranged for her to rest indoors and sent Yan Wanzhao and two girls to chat with her. Turning back to Yanzhi, she smiled and said, "Empress, it's getting late. Shall we arrange for dinner?"

Zhaoyang was the eldest daughter of the Queen Mother. She was very brave and was the Queen Mother's favorite. Huangfu Jue also respected her very much. She looked at him from the side, her eyes slightly raised, and her expression was somewhat similar to Huangfu Jue. She asked questions, but the tone she used was not questioning.

Hearing the alienation in her words, Yan Zhi smiled slightly, "Imperial sister, it's up to you."

The Queen Mother's attitude has made it clear that Yan Wanzhao is the designated Consort of Prince Yu, while the daughter-in-law that Princess Zhaoyang prefers is Wang Yan's younger sister.

The Wang family and the Yan family have unknowingly become opponents of each other.

The banquet was not half over when Fuquan came calling quietly.

Huangfu Jue stood alone beside the waterfall, having changed into the same imperial robe he had just worn, a dark purple long robe with wide sleeves and a belt, with a smile on his face.

Seeing her walking slowly, the smile on his lips deepened a little, and he said softly: "Yanzhi, did I tell you that you look beautiful today?"

Yan Zhi lowered her eyebrows and said calmly, "Your Majesty is busy with all kinds of affairs, how could he pay attention to my dressing and makeup."

He had his back to the fountain, the tiny

drops of water in his hair gleaming golden, and he looked straight at her, but he smiled and said nothing.

The waterfall splashes like pearls and the petals of the albizzia tree fly all over the sky.

Yanzhi's irritability surged up for no reason, and her voice became a little colder, "What does the emperor want to call me for?"

Huangfu Jue smiled softly, "Have you chosen the person?"

"...Jiang Qingluan."

"I thought you would choose Mei Xunyou more."

Yanzhi was startled by his approach to her, "She is not suitable."

Huangfu Jue smiled at her and said, "Although from a man's perspective I prefer Mei Xunyou, but, as long as you like her."

"Your Majesty," Yanzhi raised her eyes, "will you arrange a marriage between Prince Yu and Wanzhao after the banquet?"

"Um."

"I have a request."

Huangfu Jue suddenly interrupted her, "Yanzhi, you are neither my subject nor my concubine." His voice was deliberately soft, his black eyes smiling, "No 'subject' will slap me."

His eyes were too hot, Yan Zhi barely noticed and turned away, "I... want to ask you to allow them to be together for the rest of their lives."

"A lifetime together," Huangfu Jue repeated slowly, "Why?"

Yan Zhi was silent for a while, "I am worried about Huangfu Yu."

Huangfu Jue approached her and stretched out his finger. Yanzhi subconsciously wanted to retreat. He had already picked a fallen flower from her hair. With joy in his black eyes, he said softly, "I thought you hated her."

Yanzhi said nothing. She vaguely knew why he was happy, but she didn't want to hide the growing disappointment in her heart. She hated him, but she added a time limit, three years.

Yan Wanzhao, you have been loved by someone for three years, but you are still sleeping in the same bed with different dreams. The man you love the most doesn't even touch you. Can your everlasting love withstand three years of indifference and suspicion?

The banquet ended suddenly.

The Queen Mother suddenly fainted, and Princess Zhaoyang hurriedly escorted her back to the Yanxi Palace. Huangfu Jue rushed over and asked Yanzhi to dismiss everyone.

Ning Yunshu gave a secret look as he left, his lips moving slightly.

careful!

She was very thoughtful and intelligent, and she immediately sensed that something was wrong with the end of the banquet. The Queen Mother fainted, but Princess Zhaoyang looked more angry than sad. There were many new faces with calm eyes among the palace maids at the banquet, and the uniforms of the imperial guards could be seen faintly outside the corridor.

Something unexpected happened in the palace. The author has something to say: Liu Liu needs to work hard. I read the article today and found that we are too slow to warm up. We need to make a breakthrough. Dear friends, give some motivation!

☆、Serial

In Minghua Palace, Concubine Xian sat beside the coral kang table, saying nothing. She is waiting.

Lian Pingting left the birthday banquet halfway through and has not returned since then. None of her people can leave, as the imperial guards are guarding outside Minghua Palace.

This chess piece was carefully selected by her and was just ready for use, but she didn't expect that someone else would take the lead.

She could only wait.

After Yanzhi returned to Weiyang Palace, she found the new kitchen helper, learned what she wanted to know, and then gave orders for dinner.

Everything was normal in Weiyang Palace. After the hour of Xu, the palace gates were closed.

Yanzhi was sitting next to a yellow pear wood carved dressing table. She had removed her makeup and was slowly combing her hair with an ivory comb.

Linglong spread out the peach-red silk quilt covered with lilies, put the dried chrysanthemum pillow core into the double carp-playing-lotus pillow, lit some benzoin, and whispered to Yanzhi, "Miss, go to sleep."

Yanzhi didn't say anything, just looked out the window and sighed softly.

How many people will remain sleepless tonight!

"Who are you?" Li Luo's low voice suddenly came from the hall, followed by a person's low defense voice, the sound of footsteps, and the sound of tables and chairs colliding.

When Yanzhi went out, Li Luo was stepping on a palace maid's chest and said angrily, "Miss, a stranger sneaked in."

The maid was wearing a light blue round-neck sunflower-shaped short shirt. Judging from her attire, she should be a maid serving tea. She raised her head, but her clear eyes were full of tears. Her black eyes looked straight at Yan Zhi, and she sobbed, "Empress, please save my prince!"

Li Luo exerted force on her feet and said in a hateful voice, "Who knows your prince? Sneaking into the queen's bedroom late at night clearly has ill intentions."

Her face was as pale as snow, her body trembling like a leaf in the wind, her forehead banging heavily on the acacia-patterned wooden floor, "Madam, I have a token of my love."

Yanzhi looked at the white jade tied with colorful silk threads in her hand. On the front was a pattern of flowing clouds and bats, and on the back was a seal character "放". When the late emperor was alive, he loved jade the most. When each prince was born, he would be given a piece of jade pendant with his name on it.

She held the jade in her palm, and the texture of the jade stung her skin.

She had never expected that her unintentional reminder during the day would become so true; nor had she expected that Huangfu Fang would treat her as a living driftwood because of her words.

She looked at Mu Lian'er who was kneeling in front of her and asked coldly, "Why should I save him?"

Mu Lian'er met her gaze and said word by word, "The prince said that he is not good at adding icing on the cake, but only at providing help in times of need. As long as he is alive, he is willing to fulfill one wish of the queen."

Yanzhi smiled slightly and said softly: "Is his life only worth one wish of mine?"

In Jiuzhou Qingyan Palace, two warriors in full armor appeared from behind the pillars, their swords half unsheathed, and they shouted in unison: "Stop!"

A white figure slowly climbed the stairs, the breeze blew past, and the faint scent of magnolia was faintly heard. She took off her veil, and her face was pure and beautiful under the moonlight, "It's me."

"Swish!" The sharp sword tip just brushed past her cheek, and a strand of black hair fluttered up and down.

Huangfu Jue held the hilt of the sword with his backhand, his eyes narrowed slightly, "Yanzhi? Why are you here?"

There was a strong smell of alcohol on him. Yanzhi almost held her breath immediately and quietly took half a step back, but was annoyed to find that she had not closed the distance at all.

Huangfu Jue supported himself on the wall, holding her in his arms, lowered his head, and said in a hoarse and low voice, "Why did you come to my bedroom so late at night?"

He was too close, and the tip of his straight nose almost touched her forehead. Yanzhi looked at her nose, and her nose looked at her heart, and she said lightly: "Your Majesty, I have a grievance to report."

There was a brief silence, his chin lifted by a finger, Huangfu Jue's slanted phoenix eyes could not see her reflection, full of dark whirlpools, making people sink deeply and almost drown. He slowly raised the corners of his lips, "Who has a grievance?"

Yanzhi looked straight at him, not retreating or shrinking, "Huangfu Fang was wronged."

Huangfu Jue's pupils shrank suddenly, and he slowly withdrew his hand, looking at her coldly, "Who told you, Yan Zhishang?"

Yanzhi shook her head, "Not Zhishang." He only told her that Lian Pingting was raped and murdered.

Huangfu Jue still stared at her closely and spoke softly, "Of course it wasn't Zhishang. He tried his best to protect you. So, was it Lao San's people who came to you?"

Yanzhi was silent. Even though she knew that he had been involved in political schemes all his life, she was still surprised that he found the answer so quickly.

Huangfu Jue snorted, pointed at the palace door, and said coldly: "Go back to sleep."

There was no light in the room, only the night-shining pearl in the corner reflected the faint moonlight. The moonlight poured down from the gilded window, shining directly on the couch. There was a woman lying on her back.

Yanzhi only took a glance, and then a pair of hands covered her eyes. The hands were slender, and there was a clear fragrance of the blue sky between the fingers. He sighed softly, "Yanzhi, be obedient. None of this is your business. Go back to Weiyang Palace and forget about it."

Yanzhi pulled his hand down, her tone light

but firm, "Huangfu Jue, I can't be the canary in your cage."

Huangfu Jue said nothing, but smiled softly for a long while, very lightly and coldly, "Well, even if I cover your eyes and ears, you will still see and hear what you should see." He turned her shoulders and looked straight into the depths of her eyes, "But, Yanzhi, are you sure you want to take this step?"

Yanzhi did not avoid his eyes, "Everyone has something she wants to protect."

Huangfu Jue stretched out his arms, pushed her away, walked to the table, and picked up the jade cup. After drinking a cup, he glanced over, his eyes and eyebrows were full of murderous intent, "Queen, please explain your grievances."

Yanzhi looked at the couch again. She was lying quietly, her face full of rosy color, as if she was just sleeping. Sadness, as thick as blood, quietly pressed on the tip of her eyebrows. She slowly spoke, "Lian Liangyuan's death has nothing to do with Prince Gong. At the beginning of the Si hour, I saw him outside Shuimu Mingse."

"Who is the witness?"

"I am the evidence."

"That is to say, my brother did not go to Guanyuntai to rape and then kill my concubine, but had a secret meeting with you, the Queen?"

Yan Zhi was startled, and her eyes quickly turned cold, "Huangfu Jue!"

Huangfu Jue raised his eyebrow and smiled softly, "You get angry so easily? Do you know how many people's plans will be messed up when you stand up like this, and how many hidden arrows will be stabbed behind your back?"

He stood up and took out a scroll from the secret compartment, his expression seemed to be nostalgic. When the scroll was opened, Yanzhi was startled. With the moonlight and pearl light, only the outline of the person in the painting could be seen, but the style and charm were very familiar.

Huangfu Jue saw Yanzhi staring at the bed in a daze, "Are they similar? In fact, they are only three-tenths similar. I don't like her, but I am greedy for the three-tenths of warmth she can bring me. Just because of this, she will end up like this." His voice became lower and lower, but it was icy cold, "Yanzhi, are you afraid?"

He stood there with a gloomy look, but Yanzhi felt an indescribable loneliness. She looked at the portrait and asked softly, "Who is she?"

"My mother." Only the virtuous concubine could remember what she looked like, and would go to great lengths to find Lian Pingting who looked a bit like her. In his heart, apart from the past, there was really nothing he could be nostalgic about.

"Why don't you find the real murderer and avenge her?"

He raised his lips, revealing his evil

charm. "Huangfu Fang's fiefdom is in the Sixteen Prefectures of Youyun, he commands 100,000 elite soldiers, and he has close ties with my fourth brother. No matter who set up the trap and who was the bait, I am willing to see this result."

Yanzhi looked at him with a cold face, and said word by word: "Huangfu Jue, you don't deserve to sit in your current position!"

He abandoned his woman and was suspicious of his brother. He was clearly a cold-blooded villain. She actually felt sympathy for such a person. How ridiculous!

Looking at her icy face, Huangfu Jue suddenly smiled and glanced at her with his phoenix eyes, "Just a few words of truth, and you can't listen? You are so active in pleading for Huangfu Fang, aren't you afraid that if he dies, Youzhou's troops will fall into the hands of Xiangyang Hou, which will be detrimental to Yan Zhishang's Northern Expedition." He waved to her and said lazily, "Come here, have a few drinks with me." In just a moment, he put away his fangs and sharp blades, looking playful and harmless.

Yanzhi was silent for a while, and finally said, "Okay, I'll drink with you."

The author has something to say: Liu Liu is working hard to update, so please don't lurk around, you should also bubble up once in a while.

Collections are welcome, flowers are welcome.

☆、Aftermath

Yanzhi was silent for a while, and finally said, "Okay, I'll drink with you."

It was indeed a good wine. As soon as it entered her throat, she felt a burning sensation that burned all the way to her limbs and bones. She picked up the vermilion wine jar, tilted her head back and took a big gulp. She almost moaned in pleasure. It was so comfortable. It had been a long time since she had felt her blood burning like this.

Under the moonlight, her black hair was like a waterfall, almost touching the golden glazed tiles. A drop of wine slowly slid down her slender neck and went straight into the deep valley. Huangfu Jue's eyes darkened and he raised the jar to his lips.

Set up a banquet and sit among the flowers, drink wine cups and get drunk under the moon.

Within an incense stick of time, Yanzhi's eyes were already blurred. She kicked off her soft shoes, bare her jade feet, and smiled foolishly at the moon, "Singing to the wine, how long is life." Holding the wine jar, she spread her arms and turned around on one foot.

"Be careful." Seeing her staggering and sliding down the eaves, Huangfu Jue slightly shifted his body and held her in his arms.

Yanzhi pouted her red lips slightly and pointed her slender jade finger directly at his nose, "I'm warning you, don't take advantage of me."

Huangfu Jue smiled softly, his dark eyes full of doting, "You have such a poor alcohol tolerance, and you dare to learn to drink like others?" Under her glare, he really let go. Yanzhi carried the wine jar and sat down with her back to him.

After a while, he felt a real touch on his back, and the fragrance of magnolia was blown to his nose by the wind. He remained calm and quietly softened his body.

"Huangfu Jue."

"Um?"

"It must be hard to be an emperor."

"fine."

"Will it be difficult for you if I let Huangfu Fang go?"

"A little bit, but it's not impossible."

A pair of beautiful arms were around his neck, and she leaned forward, looking at him seriously with her big eyes, "What do I have to do for you to let him go?"

Feeling the soft touch on her arm, her heart couldn't help but beat faster. He remained calm and asked calmly, "Why do you insist on saving him?" Before today, she probably hadn't seen the fourth brother. Yan Zhishang couldn't be the only reason.

Yanzhi paused, her voice somewhat frustrated, "He... looks like the second senior brother." Huangfu felt his body stiffen, then immediately relaxed, looking at the person who had buried his head in his shoulder, "Does your tooth hurt?"

Yanzhi raised her head, her lips tender and tempting, and looked at him hatefully, "I hate you." She missed her second brother, Tianshan, and her master.

Huangfu Jue's expression softened. He wiped the blood from her lips and said softly, "I will release Huangfu Fang. Will you agree to one condition of mine?"

Yanzhi narrowed her eyes and yawned slightly. "What are the conditions?"

Huangfu Jue held his breath and let her rub against his neck like a cat. He found a comfortable position and raised the corners of his lips slightly.

Before Yanzhi completely lost consciousness, she suddenly heard a murmur, "Promise me not to drink in front of other men."

Under the moonlight, her long eyelashes were like butterfly wings, and her sleeping face was innocent. His fingertips slid down from the tip of her eyebrows and gently touched her red lips. A sigh turned in his throat. Even at this moment, he did not dare to indulge his desire. This beautiful and cunning little beast finally had to take every step carefully, in exchange for her to rest assured at this moment.

Huangfu Fang, the fourth son of the previous emperor, governed the sixteen states of Youyun. He had 100,000 cavalrymen under his command and was always in confrontation with Tiele.

Lian Pingting, with a dance that moved the king, was promoted to Liangyuan as an exception. On the Queen Mother's birthday, she was found dead in Guanyuntai. In her hand was a fan pendant with the word "Let go" engraved on it.

Huangfu Fang was taken to the clan house. Qi Wang Huangfu Xi and Run Wang Huangfu Qing jointly signed with other old ministers to defend Huangfu Fang's innocence, and there were also Qingke as witnesses, so Huangfu Fang did not go to Guanyuntai.

When Huangfu Xi was making his death appeal, the clan office suddenly presented a pink silk scarf, saying that it was obtained from Prince Gong and should belong to Lian Liangyuan.

Time stood still on the spot.

Huangfu Jue smiled, his dark eyes swept over the ministers who were petrified on the spot, and left his seat in a huff.

Fuquan issued an edict: The emperor is depressed and ill, and will not attend court for the time being. The three courts will jointly try the case of Prince Gong, and Prince Qi will cooperate.

"Snap," the white jade hairpin in Wang Linbo's hand was broken, and he screamed and threw it at the kneeling eunuch.

Amber held her with one hand, winked at the people below with a cold face, and the little eunuch quickly stumbled out.

Wang Linbo's eyes were blurred, and he recovered after a long time in her arms, "That bitch... for that bitch..." Jealousy and madness had distorted her face, and her whole body was trembling, "He really likes it, really likes it!" She had known him for twelve years, and watched him struggle out of the rotten darkness, stepping on the bones step by step to where he is today. At the age of fifteen, he could hold a golden cup and drink the blood of the living, so what other reason could he give up the benefits he had?

Amber patted her back gently, and waited for her to calm down before speaking coldly, "The queen went to Jiuzhou Qingyan Palace last night."

Wang Linbo's body trembled, and he looked at her with slightly confused eyes, as if he was confused and puzzled, "It's her again, it's her again, why hasn't she died yet......"

The gilded red gold hook held up the curtain, leaving only a thin veil at the head of the bed, through which the graceful figure could be vaguely seen. A hand passed around the veil and touched the round shoulders.

The person on the bed snorted heavily and shook his shoulders. But he only smiled softly, and his hand had already circled around his chest like a fish. He avoided the bright red spot and slowly groped at the soft place.

Wang Linbo bit his lower lip and climbed up, his eyes full of spring, three parts of anger and three parts of resentment, "Huangfu Jue!"

After being teased by him, the thin nightgown was only hanging on her shoulders, and the beautiful scenery underneath was almost completely visible. Huangfu Jue smiled softly and sat down on the head of the bed. Regardless of her struggle, he pulled her over and put her on his lap. His hand slowly climbed along her calf, and his lips moved to her small ear, deliberately breathing into the ear hole, "Are you angry?"

His waist was firmly restrained by hers, and she could only endure his invasion from top to bottom. Wang Linbo moaned, and then he softened in his arms. He stretched out his hand to his arms and twisted it hard, gritted his teeth and said, "Enemy."

The slender legs were wrapped around his waist, and it felt like his waist was about to be broken. Wang Linbo looked at the man in front of him through the mist. Even in such a fierce sex, with the body entangled, his breathing was only slightly hurried, and there was still a carelessness in the depths of his eyes.

She struggled desperately to gather her strength and entangled her legs tightly, trying to hold him, to keep him inside her body forever.

Huangfu Jue leaned against the bedside, watching her delicate hands wandering around his waist and abdomen. He smiled lazily and whispered ambiguously, "Didn't I feed you enough just now?"

Wang Linbo stroked his chest, stabbed it with his five pointed fingers, and said faintly: "I really want to dig out your heart and see what it is made of."

Huangfu Jue had been smiling, but his smile slowly turned cold. "If you want it, I'll dig it out and give it to you."

Putting her face close to his warm skin, she sighed softly, "I'm not greedy. As long as I can occupy this little space, it's enough." She raised her index finger slightly in front of his eyes.

Huangfu Jue kissed her hand lightly, his dark eyes indifferent, "Don't do anything else, I will treat you well."

Wang Linbo's smile slowly froze, he straightened up and looked at him, "Jue'er, you should know how I treat you. Over the years, I have been trying my best to deal with you and the Wang family. Now, you are promoting the Yan family, where do you put the Wang family?"

The death of Lian Pingting alone not only reassured the Wang family, but also eliminated a major threat to him. Why should he blame her?

Huangfu Jue looked at her with sinister eyes, and slowly said, "Lin Bo, because it's you, I'll say it again: Don't do things behind my back, don't interfere in the court, such a woman is not lovable."

Wang Linbo's face turned pale, and he just stared at him blankly, keeping his lips shut without saying a word. It was not until he got dressed and went out that he threw himself on the bed and burst into tears.

At the hour of Xu, Fuquan conveyed the emperor's oral order, and Consort Shu of Gyeongbokgung Palace went to sleep with him. Concubine Shu took off her duck cloak and walked into the hall alone. Seeing Huangfu Jue concentrating on reading the memorials, she quietly rolled up her sleeves and stood aside to study.

Suddenly, Huangfu Jue snorted angrily and threw the memorial in his hand away, "Nonsense, all nonsense."

Concubine Shu hurriedly called out softly, "Your Majesty, be careful not to get too angry."

Huangfu Jue then looked at her, still furious, "Yan'er, these censors are really annoying! The death of a concubine has led to all sorts of trivial matters. Some people even listed the ten major crimes of Prince Yu, saying that he hoarded a large number of troops and formed a clique for personal gain. How ridiculous! I can't even trust my brothers, but they are all loyal to me."

This was the first time he expressed his emotions so directly in front of her. Wang

Yan felt a surge of joy in her heart and looked at Huangfu Jue with bright eyes, "Your Majesty should be happy. The censors dare to speak out and make suggestions, which shows that your Majesty is a wise ruler."

Huangfu Jue burst into laughter and put his big hand around her waist, "Yan'er is still the best person to share my worries. Yan'er, I have something to entrust to you."

Wang Yan looked at him with tenderness in her heart, "It is a blessing for me to share the worries of the emperor."

Huangfu Jue pinched her chin and smiled with satisfaction, "Yan'er, be good." He straightened his face and said, "Such a scandal happened in the palace, and I am very upset. But I believe that Prince Yu would not do such a thing. Yan'er, I will leave the matter of Lian Liangyuan to you. Everyone in the harem is at your disposal. You must cooperate with the clan office to find out the truth of the matter."

By saying this, he was clearly bypassing Concubine Xian and giving her the power to manage palace affairs. Wang Yan was excited, but she declined, saying, "Yan'er has only been in the palace for a short time, and there are other sisters..."

Huangfu Jue waved his hand, "Don't mention them, each of them has learned from it. Only Yan'er is truly devoted to me."

"Your Majesty." Wang Yan murmured softly, her eyes already red.

Huangfu Jue chuckled, "Silly child." He stretched out his arm, picked her up and walked towards the heavy curtains, "It's late, let's rest."

The author has something to say: Dear friends, Liu Liu is not used to saving half a chapter before publishing it.

If you are not in a hurry, you can watch it the next day. It is even better without a title.

☆、The truth

A rose bush fills the whole yard with fragrance.

On the Zitan chess table, the black and white pieces were already in a close fight.

On the other side of the chess table, Linglong was originally sitting, but now Huangfu Jue was sitting.

Yanzhi frowned and looked at the man opposite her, "Why doesn't the emperor go to court?"

Huangfu Jue picked up the white chess piece and stared at the chessboard, "The emperor is ill."

Yanzhi watched as the white pieces were gradually surrounding the black pieces, and she swept the chessboard in disarray, and asked Huangfu Jue directly, "When should I go to the clan house to record my statement?"

Huangfu Jue flicked his hand and a chess

piece shot steadily towards her forehead. "Have you heard that the queen went to the clan house to record her confession?"

Before Yanzhi could move, Li Luo beside her had already grabbed the chess piece and put it back on the chessboard with a cold face. Ever since Huangfu Jue visited Yanzhi at night and knocked her out with one finger, she had never been in a good mood every time she came.

Huangfu Jue raised his eyebrows and said lazily, "Don't worry, since I promised you, I will definitely do it."

Yanzhi hesitated for a moment, and quickly glanced at Huangfu Jue, "I was...drunk that day, and I forgot everything I said."

According to Linglong, she was carried back to Weiyang Palace by someone. She was entangled for two days, fearing that she had made some promise to sell her body.

"Forgot?" Huangfu Jue glanced over, his eyes narrowed, "You promised yourself that you would give birth to me." He stretched out a hand and waved it in front of Yanzhi, "So many sons."

Seeing Yanzhi staring at him blankly, her face turning pale and blue, he couldn't help but burst out laughing.

"Huangfu Jue!" Yanzhi was extremely angry. She blew the chess pieces into pieces and turned away.

Huangfu Jue smiled and leaned back on the red lacquered gold armchair, and a rose just happened to fall on his lips. He picked up the petal with his teeth, thinking of her angry eyes, which were unusually bright, just like this rose, blazing and dazzling.

He put the flower between his lips, chewed it bit by bit, and ate it into his stomach.

Huangfu Jue stayed in until after lunch.

Yanzhi's expression remained indifferent. She sat face to face with him and didn't even lift her eyelids to lift his.

Huangfu Jue waited until she finished eating, and he saw a trace of fatigue between his eyebrows and eyes, and then he spoke, "Yanzhi, I want to ask you for someone."

Yanzhi half closed her eyes. After losing all her martial arts, she had the habit of taking a nap. When the time came, she felt groggy and said, "No."

Huangfu Jue laughed, "Stingy guy." He hesitated for a moment, "Can I borrow it for a few days and then return it to you?"

Yanzhi closed her eyes completely and waved back, "Yiyue, accompany me to rest."

Yiyue walked up with a pale face and knelt upright in front of Huangfu Jue.

Huangfu Jue narrowed his eyes, and instead of getting angry he smiled, "Are you blind? You can't even tell who your master is?"

Yiyue trembled slightly, and without any reasoning, she just bowed her head to the ground. They were all picked by Huangfu Jue. Their family backgrounds were clean, and they had no connection with the forces in the palace. On the first day of the training, they were told that their only master was the master of Weiyang Palace. After being in the palace for a long time, she also knew some of Huangfu Jue's methods. Since she let Lian'er in, she knew that she could not escape today.

A pair of hands patted on the shoulders, and Yanzhi's cold voice sounded, with a little impatience, "Get up, no matter who you were before, I am your master now. Your Majesty, don't you agree?"

Huangfu Jue chuckled and helped Yiyue up with his own hands, "Stand up, if you kneel again your master will get angry with me."

Yi Yue's body shook slightly, but when she met his ruthless yet smiling black eyes, her face calmed down. "Thank you, Your Majesty." After paying her respects, she went to the bedroom, spread the quilt and burned some incense.

When Huangfu Jue looked up, he met Yanzhi's cold eyes and was slightly startled.

He had just used hidden power to injure the Yiyue meridian, and his technique was extremely skillful, and it would be difficult for ordinary people to detect it. His mind raced, his face remained expressionless, he approached with a smile, and said in a gentle voice: "Go to sleep later, be careful of indigestion."

Yanzhi glanced at him calmly, and with just one glance, he could see the coldness and disgust in her eyes. She pursed her lips tightly, walked around him, and wanted to go back to the inner room.

If she leaves, his three months of hard work will go down the drain. Huangfu Jue grabbed her, ignoring the stiffness of the person in his arms, and whispered in her ear: "Shh, don't move. I just injured Yiyue with my hidden power, you ask Li Luo to help her push the blood through the palace, at the Tanxia and Huizhong points. In the future, she will be grateful to you and will obey you in everything."

He spoke softly, noticing the body in his arms slowly softening, and the disgust in his eyes quietly receding.

Yanzhi pushed him away and snorted coldly, "Shameless and despicable means."

Huangfu Jue raised his eyebrows and smiled, pretending to be aggrieved, "Good intentions are not rewarded, and I am doing this for you wholeheartedly."

Yanzhi glanced at him sideways, thought for a moment, and said, "From now on, you don't have to worry about the people in my palace."

Huangfu Jue raised his hands, "Okay, okay, except for you, I don't care about anyone else."

Yanzhi spat at him and went back to her inner room.

As soon as Yanzhi entered the bedroom, Yiyue knelt in front of her, tears welling up in her eyes, but her voice was very calm, "Your Majesty, Lian'er is my biological sister. Back then, my family was poor, and Lian'er and I were sold to human traffickers by my father. Over the years, I have asked people to inquire about her, but there is no news about her. On the day of the Queen Mother's birthday banquet, we ran into each other by chance. Her features are still vaguely the same as when she was a child, and there are scars on her arms from burns when she was a child. She is really my sister, the little girl who pulled my sleeve and followed me." Her face was covered with tears, and she knelt heavily on the ground, "Your Majesty, Yiyue is ashamed of your trust. Your kindness, Yiyue will repay you in the next life."

Yanzhi smiled at her and said slowly, "I don't believe in ghosts and gods, and I don't believe in the afterlife. If you really want to repay me, do it in this life."

Yiyue opened his mouth, his eyes full of misery, but in the end he said nothing and kowtowed heavily.

Her forehead didn't touch the cold ground, Yanzhi's hand was the first to cushion it. The glass-like black eyes looked at her quietly, and his voice was still ethereal, with a hint of sympathy, "You have been with me for so long, you should know that I hate you kneeling at every turn. Do your job well and don't think too much. Since you are mine, I have the final say on whether you live or die."

Yiyue was stunned and looked at her blankly. Yanzhi pulled her hand back, undressed and went to bed. Through the soft curtains, she yawned and said softly, "Don't kneel anymore. Go down and find Li Luo."

Yiyue's body softened, and she sat on the ground in a daze. She understood Yanzhi's words, but she couldn't believe them. She was stunned for a while, and tears flowed down again. After a long while, she quietly retreated.

As soon as she left, Yanzhi opened her eyes. I felt a little irritated, and the more I lay there, the less sleepy I felt.

She was able to stay safe in the palace, and she knew in her heart that it was Huangfu Jue's protection. But knowing is one thing, and witnessing it with your own eyes is another.

A man like him is surrounded by beautiful women, so why is he so special to her that he can even be called indulgent?

The more I thought about it, the more confused I became. My heart was pounding. I kicked the golden silk quilt and jumped onto the cold floor barefoot. Only then did I feel a little relieved.

Huangfu Jue returned to Jiuzhou Qingyan Palace and called Han Lan. In front of him, he injured the palace maid next to him using the same method.

Han Lan examined the patient for a moment and shook his head. Huangfu Jue waved his hand and asked him to feel the pulse. He placed two fingers on the pulse for a moment, narrowed his eyes and said, "The coldness has entered the feet and Taichong. After half a month, the wind and cold will gradually appear." The pulse was unusually obscure and no one noticed it.

The palace maid was so frightened that she was trembling with fear and kowtowing on the ground.

Seeing Huangfu Jue looking at him with a half-smile, Han Lan shook his head and sighed, and the golden needle in his hand pierced the Shenting acupoint on her head like lightning. The palace maid shrank to the ground. A man in black flashed out like light smoke and dragged her behind the curtain of Nine Dragons Chasing the Sun.

Huangfu Jue said coldly, "Han Qing, where does your medical skills rank in the □□?"

Han Lan was startled, and his eyes immediately widened, "Your Majesty doubts my medical skills?"

Huangfu Jue tapped the tabletop with his slender fingers, thinking, "If I use the method just now, will it really not be discovered?"

Han Lan was relieved. He knew Huangfu Jue's cautious and suspicious character. "Your Majesty, don't worry. Your Yin Power has reached perfection. If you wait ten days, even I won't be able to tell your pulse."

Huangfu Jue thought of the tender body that had slowly softened in his arms just now, and thought of her eyes that had never shown any surprise from beginning to end, and he couldn't help but laugh softly. He fixed his eyes on Han Lan, and spoke in a low voice like a lover's whisper, "Won't anyone find out? I think you've been enjoying yourself for too long, and your bones are rusty."

Han Lan's knees became weak and he knelt on the ground involuntarily. He was still confused and could only say in a trembling voice: "Your Majesty...is stupid, Your Majesty...is stupid."

"From today on, all the maids and concubines under the age of 40 in your house will be expelled from the house. Go back and concentrate on refining medicine. If you keep sitting in the well and watching the world, I will cut you into pieces one by one." Idiot, killing people invisibly, almost made him lose all his previous efforts.

Han Lan rolled and crawled out of Jiuzhou Qingyan Palace, and Huangfu Jue was still angry. After a while, he suddenly smiled, "Xiu Ji, do you think I have found a treasure?"

The light suddenly dimmed, and Xiu Ji appeared out of thin air, with his sword leaning against the pillar. He spoke in a hoarse voice, "Bai Zizai is an expert in medicine, swordsmanship, and martial arts. Yan Zhi is his last disciple, so it's no surprise that he taught her everything he knew."

Everyone in the martial arts world knows that the Lord of the Snow Region has three disciples, each of whom inherits three unique skills from him. If he had not seen Yan Zhi with his own eyes in the Paradise Palace of Langya Mountain and slowly followed the clue of Ye Zi, he would not have been able to find out her identity in the Snow Region. Thinking of that amazing sword, his eyes turned cold and his fingers in his sleeves could not help but curl up tightly.

The rouge can only be his.

"Tell Ye Xiao that I will give her another seven days. If there are still poisonous insects in Weiyang Palace, she should come back and be a good bride to the king."

Xiu Ji smiled silently, "Your baby is a master of medicine, what are you afraid of?"

Clenching his fingers into a fist, he said slowly: "I can't give her any chance to turn the tables."

His little Yanzhi may not be cunning or shrewd enough, but that's just because she is too proud and disdainful. If he pushes her too far, the little fox will show her claws.

The author has something to say: Thank you all for supporting Liu Liu's articles!

Especially thanks to those who received and commented.

Without you, Liu Liu would have no spring for writing.

☆、First Night

His little Yanzhi may not be cunning or shrewd enough, but that's just because she is too proud and disdainful. If he pushes her too far, the little fox will show her claws.

Concubine Shu works very quickly.

In just two days, she had checked all the palace maids, eunuchs and guards on duty. She also got some very interesting things from Lian Liangyuan's personal maids Huamei and Ziluo.

On this day, he was waiting in Jiuzhou Qingyan Palace early in the morning.

After Huangfu Jue changed into his court dress, she smiled and took out something from her sleeves, presented it to Huangfu Jue, and said softly, "Your Majesty, I have fulfilled my mission. We have made some progress on Prince Gong's matter."

There were several pieces of letter paper, made of the finest Caihou paper, very smooth but with wear on the edges and corners.

Huangfu Jue took it and flipped through it, his face darkening, "So, Lian Pingting and Prince Gong have known each other for a long time?"

Concubine Shu nodded, "They met at the Lantern Festival, when the Lian family hadn't gotten into trouble yet. After that, they kept sending letters to each other for more than a year, and the news stopped after Lian Liangyuan entered the palace. I'm afraid these letters were preserved because of Lian Liangyuan's obsession."

She slowly leaned to Huangfu Jue's side and leaned her head on his shoulder. "Your Majesty, Lian Liangyuan shouldn't have private messages with men in the harem, but Zi Luo said that she just wanted to see Prince Gong for the last time, return the token of love, and make it over. Moreover, I also transferred Shuimu Mingse to the duty maids and eunuchs at Guanyuntai. They didn't see Prince Gong, so Prince Gong should not have kept the appointment." As she spoke, she looked at Huangfu Jue's face through her long eyelashes. Seeing that his face softened slightly, she sighed softly, "Just because of this selfish thought, she ended up with such a miserable end. It's also retribution for her."

Huangfu Jue snorted coldly, "She deserves to die. If she hadn't dismissed the servants and wanted to meet with Prince Gong privately, how could she have given someone the opportunity to take advantage of her."

His expression finally eased a little, and he put his arm around Concubine Shu's soft waist, "Yan'er did a good job, the rest is up to the three officials. What reward do you want?"

Concubine Shu shook her head, her eyes full of smiles, "I have the Emperor by my side,

I am luckier than any other woman in the world, I have no more extravagant thoughts."

Huangfu Jue stared at her for a long while, then suddenly smiled, "Having Yan'er is also my blessing. However, I must give her a reward. Let me think about it. How about promoting her to Imperial Concubine?"

Even when she arrived at her own palace, Concubine Shu's heart was still in the clouds. When she saw Concubine Wang, she was not surprised. She bowed and called out with a smile, "Aunt."

Wang Linbo's misty eyes swept across her slightly fluffy hair. Her cheeks were still red, but his eyelids quickly dropped. He took a sip of tea and said calmly, "Is it done?"

"Well," Concubine Shu smiled slightly, twisting the silk thread on the edge of her skirt with her hands, her eyes a little dazed, "Aunt is right, the emperor seems to be very satisfied with this result."

She hated Lian Pingting so much that she wanted to eat her alive. She wanted to publicize her scandal, but her aunt stopped her. Her aunt was right, the dead would never be her enemy. Today, she pretended to sympathize with him, and the emperor was very happy.

Imperial Concubine... Imperial Concubine, just one step away...

Wang Linbo chuckled, held up his chin with his bare hands, and said with moving eyes,

"Yan'er, you have to know that there are some things that cannot be seen by the eyes, especially - a man's heart."

Concubine Shu came back to her senses and said with a little displeasure, "Aunt, I will definitely be able to capture the emperor's heart."

Although she was slightly angry, there was still a girl's innocent look between her eyebrows. Seventeen years old, still as young as a flower. Wang Linbo felt a slight bitterness in his mouth, sour and hard to swallow. When she was her age, she was just as confident. But now, what did she grasp?

Huangfu Jue is a devil living under the sun. Even if he has the heart, he is just a stone that cannot be warmed up.

Concubine Shu was so absorbed in the tenderness of Huangfu Jue that she didn't notice Wang Linbo's strange and compassionate look. Even if she had noticed, she wouldn't have understood.

A woman immersed in love is always blind and stupid.

That night, the apricot blossoms cast shadows and the lights were still on.

Wang Linbo stared blankly at the window until the Udumbara flowers bloomed quietly and the night dew wet her veil.

He didn't come after all.

Tears flowed from the corners of her closed eyes, like beads that had broken off the string, silently splashing onto the white jade windowsill.

"Master, take a rest." Amber said softly, with deep worry and pity in her eyes.

Why didn't she come? She had spent so much effort to set up this situation. But all was ruined by his words. She also secretly followed his wishes and asked Concubine Shu to get sufficient evidence to help Prince Yu escape.

When he saw Concubine Shu, he should have guessed what she had done behind his back. She was already showing weakness, using a very low profile.

Why doesn't he come tonight?

A very low laugh escaped from her red lips. "Jue'er, are you going to abandon me? You would rather spend your energy on Wang Yan than look at me again. Is it because she is young or because she is obedient?"

After nightfall, Huangfu Jue dressed lightly and left Jiuzhou Qingyan Palace.

Going south from Jiuzhou Qingyan Palace and bypassing Qujiang Pond, there is a fork road, which leads to the harem in the southeast and the three pavilions in Shangyuan in the southwest, namely Yifu Pavilion, Luomei Pavilion and Xinghua Shuying. The first two pavilions in Shangyuan are for people to enjoy, but Xinghua Shuying is where Concubine Wang lives. Because Concubine Wang loves apricot flowers the most, when the late emperor passed away, she was so heartbroken that she insisted on moving to Xinghua Shuying to keep company with the apricot flowers all over the sky and remember the late emperor.

Huangfu Jue was walking towards the southwest, but he paused and looked towards the southeast.

After a short delay, a group of people carrying lanterns came in a hurry. When they came closer, they seemed to have never expected that the emperor was here in disguise, and they knelt down hurriedly to pay their respects.

Fuquan saw that the leader was Lai Xi, and before Huangfu Jue could speak, he asked the reason. It turned out that the queen was not feeling well, and wanted to go to the Imperial Hospital to summon the imperial physician.

After Fuquan finished asking the question, he took a step back and glanced at Huangfu Jue from the corner of his eye. Huangfu Jue remained calm, and he had already walked up the southeast stone egg road. He said calmly, "Fuquan, go and call Han Lan."

Yanzhi was ill, and Dr. Han immediately determined that it was the cold that attacked her internally and caused her to have a high fever. The people in the outer room knelt down in a sea of people, and only Li Luo looked up and glared at Huangfu Jue.

Huangfu Jue narrowed his eyes, but before he could react, Yanzhi's mumbling drew his attention away.

After only half a day, her lips were

already cracked. I had to get close to her to hear her vague murmurs, "Snowy... Snowy... Master... Snowy..."

Her dry lips twitched slightly, and her brows were tightly furrowed. At this moment, she was no longer as cold as usual, but with the determination and fragility of a child.

Snowland, Snowland, only in dreams can you indulge yourself, just say these two words. Huangfu Jue didn't know that there was deep pity and a hint of frustration in his eyes, and his slender fingertips just touched her cheek, but then retracted.

When he turned around, his face was already cold. He glanced at everyone and looked directly into Li Luo's eyes. "It's the hottest day of the year, how could the Queen catch a cold?"

Li Luo ignored Linglong's pulling and looked at him angrily. After he left, the young lady became restless and walked around barefoot on the ground. She drank another bowl of honey and snow frog soup with ice. Before the hour of Xu, she started to have a fever. If it weren't for him, how could a person like the young lady end up being bedridden every two or three days.

She thought so, her tone was naturally stiff, and she just stiffened her neck and said, "I don't know."

Yi Yue, who was standing beside him, kowtowed hastily, "Your Majesty, please forgive me. It was this servant who served the Majesty, and Li Luo really didn't know. The Majesty took a nap and stepped on the ground barefoot, so she must have been exposed to the cold."

Yanzhi had a weak body and was very careful about her diet and sleeping. Other palace ladies had changed into wooden clogs long ago, but she still wore thick silk shoes.

Huangfu Jue raised his eyelids, his gaze turned cold, and he said indifferently: "As a personal servant, you can't take good care of your master. Go to the quiet room and reflect on yourself."

The quiet room, two meters square, with four white walls, is a way for palace maids to punish themselves when their masters do not want to use the board. If they are not given food or water, they often suffer mental breakdowns before they starve to death. They are not panicking about this, but about the fact that serving as a personal servant means three people. If they all leave, who else can Yanzhi trust?

Before Linglong could speak, Huangfu Jue waved his hand, and several eunuchs who served in front of the emperor came to them. Linglong pressed Li Luo's hand, shook her head slightly, glanced at Yanzhi, and walked out first. Although Li Luo looked angry, she still followed him out.

The room soon became quiet, with only the sound of sand slowly flowing from the golden leak.

Huangfu Jue played with Yanzhi's hand, as if he had thought of something, and smiled slightly, "You are the most protective of your shortcomings. You will be angry again after waking up." His lips pressed on her hot lips, slowly moisturizing the cracks, "Wake up, I'll wait for you."

Yanzhi had a very long dream.

I vaguely remember that when she was a child, she was soaking in a hot spring in the mountains. Suddenly, snow came from all directions, and the hot spring was quickly submerged. She was buried in the snow, and her internal organs were freezing cold. She opened her mouth to call for help but couldn't. Suddenly, the scene changed again. She was walking tremblingly in a cave in the center of the earth, with churning magma below. She didn't dare to open her eyes, but just held on to her master's sleeve tightly. Suddenly, she stepped into the air, her body fell sharply, and the flames jumped violently. She screamed.

"ah--"

She suddenly opened her eyes and looked into a pair of anxious and compassionate eyes. Her eyes gradually became moist, and she murmured, "Master..."

Huangfu Jue was startled, and slowly sat up from his bent position. He patted her hand that was rushing towards him, and narrowed his eyes, "Yanzhi, what did you call me?"

Her breathing was still rapid, and her scattered eyes slowly gathered together, becoming disappointed and cold little by little. She closed her eyes, with an undisguised look of loss, "It was a dream, Your Majesty."

She was sweating all over, her limbs were sore and weak, and she barely raised her eyes to look around. Only the jade-green purple bamboo lamp illuminated the dim light in the room, and there was no one around. She asked, "Where's Linglong?"

Huangfu Jue's face was hidden in the shadow of the curtain, and his expression could not be seen clearly. He only heard a faint voice, "He's not here."

I felt like banging my head against the wall because of my headache, and I pounded my head with my hands out of frustration, "Where are Li Luo, Yi Yue, and Lai Xi?"

The slender fingers, with the scent of ambergris, touched the temples on both sides with moderate force, "Not even one."

Even the dullest brain had a hint of alertness at this moment. She grabbed his hand and tried to get up.

The light was dimmed by the shadow, and Huangfu Jue had moved behind her.

She felt weak all over and had to lean on him. Her throat was swollen and dry. She coughed softly a few times, and a glass of water was handed to her lips.

After taking a few sips of water, her throat felt better. From her angle, she could only see the corners of his lips tightly pursed. "Where are my people?"

The water cup was placed heavily on the table, "Heavenly Prison."

With his eyes half closed, he waved his hand randomly, and said impatiently, "Your Majesty."

Her hair was wet and tangled in wisps, and her face was as pale as paper, but his heart softened as never before. "If it happens again, I will put them all in jail."

He put his hand over her eyes, feeling her eyelashes gently scratching his palm, and his tone softened, "Go to sleep, you can see them in the morning."

This night is his.

The author has something to say: I'm not trying to be lazy, the baby is sick.

I should be able to update daily this week.

Liu Liu needs to work harder!

☆、Stalemate

Her hair was wet and tangled in wisps, and her face was as pale as paper, but his heart softened as never before. "If it happens again, I will put them all in jail."

He put his hand over her eyes, feeling her eyelashes gently scratching his palm, and his tone softened, "Go to sleep, you can see them in the morning."

This night is his.

Yanzhi was ultimately no match for Huangfu Jue. The benzoin burning in the stove, coupled with the medicinal effect, made her fall asleep again quickly.

Occasionally, when I am half asleep and half awake, I can always smell the fresh scent of ambergris.

When Yanzhi opened her eyes again, Li Luo and Ling Long were waiting by the bed, and Huangfu Jue was nowhere to be seen. Her fever had subsided, but she was still lazy and listless. She washed and took medicine as usual, and did not say a word about last night. Li Luo opened her mouth several times, but when she saw her expression, she closed it again in dismay.

News from the harem always spread quickly. At half past the hour of Si, Lai Xi came in to reply. Concubine Shu had joined forces with the Imperial Clan Court to investigate the case of Lian Liangyuan.

It turns out that Lian Pingting had admired Prince Gong before entering the palace. When she heard that Prince Yu had entered the palace, she asked the palace maid to send a message through Luopa, and asked to meet Guan Yuntai. Prince Gong understood the righteousness of the matter and did not go. While Lian Pingting and Guan Yuntai were waiting, they were seen by a guard from the imperial army. The guard saw that Lian Pingting was beautiful and there was no one around, so he had evil intentions and raped and killed her.

The emperor was furious and immediately issued an edict: the guard was to be executed by slow slicing and his entire clan was to be implicated; Prince Gong was released without charge; Lian Pingting was of bad character, so she was stripped of her title of Liangyuan and demoted to a commoner and buried.

Yanzhi was leaning against the head of the bed, slowly stirring a bowl of cardamom soup with a small hollow long-handled silver spoon. She said nothing when she heard the words, but a sad look appeared between her brows. She handed the bowl to Linglong, shook her head and said she didn't want to drink it anymore.

Linglong looked at her face and said with a smile, "Miss, you have done what you promised Prince Gong, you should be happy."

Yanzhi lowered her eyes and remained silent. The peaceful sleeping face under the moonlight appeared before my eyes again.

Lian Pingting is just one of the millions of pitiful women in the palace. She pretended to be gentle and kind when she came to Weiyang Palace, but she was tired of it; she became a victim of the interests of all parties, but she felt pitiful and lamentable. Grace is only temporary, but pain is lifelong. The beauty like water, turned into dust in the blink of an eye. The man she regarded as the sky could not even give her justice.

Raped and then killed by a guard? In the deep palace, there are guards everywhere. If there is no deliberate planning and layout, ordinary guards can't even see the concubines' hair. It's ridiculous that all the civil and military officials in the court have become deaf and blind in front of their own interests.

When Huangfu Jue arrived at noon, Yanzhi was frowning at the medicine bowl. He curled his lips, exempted everyone from the formalities, sat directly on the bed, and stretched out his hand to Li Luo.

Li Luo was startled, but the hand holding the medicine did not move.

Huangfu Jue glanced at her with a dark, unfathomable look in his eyes. Li Luo's mind faltered, and she reluctantly handed over the bowl.

Huangfu Jue scooped up a spoon, blew on it, and said lightly: "Go down."

Li Luo pursed her lips and looked at Yan Zhi. Her dark eyes were looking at her thoughtfully.

Feeling wronged for no reason, Li Luo turned around and left the house. As soon as she entered the main hall, she saw Linglong looking at her seriously.

Linglong took Li Luo to the side room and closed the door. Her expression gradually turned cold and stern. "Li Luo, do you know what you are doing?"

Li Luo bit her lower lip, looking stubborn. Linglong stared at her without blinking, "This is not the Jianghu, nor the Marquis' Mansion, and you are not an ignorant child. You know better than me why you entered the palace! Who are you looking at? That's the emperor! Your own life doesn't matter, don't implicate the young lady and the Marquis' Mansion." At the end of her words, she was already speaking harshly. Li Luo's abnormal behavior was not the first or second time. The young lady didn't say anything, but she couldn't tolerate it anymore.

Li Luo opened her mouth and her eyes turned red. She quickly wiped her eyes with her hand and said angrily, "So what if he is the emperor? I just look down on him. If it weren't for him, how could the young lady become like this today?"

"Li Luo!" Linglong scolded, "Is this your duty as a servant? The young lady knows what's going on. No matter what happens between her and the emperor in the end, you have no right to interfere!"

Seeing her angry, Li Luo still said with all her might: "You have been following the Madam, but I have been accompanying the young lady for half a year. The young lady is so happy and carefree." And that person, that person is so proud and persevering...

Linglong looked at her deeply and said slowly, "The past is not important to me. I only care about what the young lady likes and needs now. If you can't adjust your mentality, I will report to the young lady and let you return to the Marquis' Mansion."

After he finished speaking, he stopped

looking at her, took a set of tea sets with blue and white porcelain flowers, and went out.

Li Luo stood there silently, her face turning red and white, tears falling down her face.

Yanzhi drank the medicine cooperatively, holding a secret pickled plum in her mouth, leaning on the ivory orchid pillow, quietly looking at Huangfu Jue.

Huangfu Jue's eyes flickered, his eyebrows and eyes were smiling, "Why are you looking at me like that?"

Yanzhi lowered her eyes and said coldly: "I want to see if you have a heart."

Huangfu Jue smiled softly, grabbed her hand, placed it on his chest, and asked softly, "Do you feel my heart beating?"

Through the thin silk robe, it was easy to feel the strong heartbeat in the palm of my hand, and Yanzhi's face quickly turned red. She struggled a few times, but couldn't get away. She simply made her five fingers into claws and stabbed hard.

The nails, which had been maintained for several months, were very long and sharp. Huangfu Jue exclaimed, and with a smile, he held her hand, intertwining his fingers and palms, "Little wild cat, your nails are going to break, and you won't be able to play the piano."

Yanzhi squinted at him, her breathing slightly rapid.

Huangfu Jue put her scattered black hair

behind her and straightened his face. "Don't think about anything anymore. Lie down and go to sleep."

Yanzhi raised her head and looked straight into his eyes, "Why don't you let her go with a clear conscience?"

Huangfu Jue looked at her, his smile faded, his brows and eyes were cold, and he said slowly: "No woman in the harem is clean, no matter how you wash, it is impossible to be white. Yanzhi, I promised you this time. Next time, no matter whose business it is, don't interfere again."

Seeing her pale face, her eyes were like the water in a cold pond, deep and clear, looking at him coldly. Huangfu Jue stood up and said in a light tone, "I will come to see you when I have time. When you feel better, I will take you out for a walk. You don't have to stay in the house all day and have wild thoughts."

On this day, there were angry shouts from time to time in Jiuzhou Qingyan Palace. Zhou Yifu, the Minister of Works, reported the flood in Jiangsu and Zhejiang and requested to open the dike to release the floodwater. Huangfu Jue threw the memorial in his face. From the three provinces to the six ministries, all the officials who were discussing the matter lowered their heads in disgrace. Yan Yanzi originally wanted to present the list of people to be drawn up by the military for the Northern Expedition, but seeing that the emperor's mind was unpredictable, he could not help but glance at Fuquan.

Fuquan was an old and experienced man, and he knew the emperor's thoughts accurately. Normally, he would give some hints, but today he looked straight ahead, only at the small piece of land under his feet. Yan Yanzi was puzzled, so he slowed down his request. He didn't know that Fuquan was slightly annoyed with him because of his daughter.

Fuquan was Huangfu Jue's man, and his master's mood was his heaven. Today, it was thundering and raining, so he naturally had a gloomy face and was in a bad mood.

At dusk, Concubine Xian came to Jiuzhou Qingyan Palace. She had lost a lot of weight, but her expression was calm and peaceful. She was wearing a plain pleated skirt with scattered flowers, and a silver magpie flower on her hair. She knelt in front of Huangfu Jue and kowtowed.

Huangfu Jue looked at her with a half-smile on his face, "Why are you kneeling for no reason?"

Concubine Xian looked at him, her heart growing colder. She had been with him for so many years, and her biggest thing every day was to figure out his thoughts. Now that they were face to face, so close, she finally understood one thing — she could not enter his heart, no matter how hard she tried.

He is a natural king on the grassland, who

only likes plundering and killing. He will not eat prey that is offered to him.

She looked at him calmly, "Your Majesty, I failed to judge people and brought shame to the royal family. I come here to apologize."

Huangfu Jue's slanted phoenix eyes were very dark and charming, still the dark color that she couldn't see through, staring at her steadily. For a moment, she almost held her breath, thinking that he had seen through her. But he soon lowered his eyes and said casually, "You have worked hard these years, it would be good to take a break."

The virtuous concubine trembled, and finally kowtowed silently, and only stood up after a long time.

After she left, Huangfu Jue's expression became very strange, as if he was disdainful, disgusted, or deeply bored. He just leaned on the couch with a dull look, holding a Buddhist scripture copied by Mani himself, and didn't turn a page for a long time.

Fuquan checked the time and coughed softly, "Your Majesty, how about going to Weiyang Palace to take a look? I heard that Lai Xi asked for two more jars of wine from the imperial kitchen."

Huangfu Jue snapped the book shut and snorted coldly, "Nosy!"

Fuquan smiled, bent down, and slapped himself lightly, "I am a talkative person.

I am old, and I can't keep my mouth shut. When I followed Concubine Xiao, I didn't say a word all day long. It was a common thing. Your Majesty remembers Concubine Wan, she was also a strong-willed woman. She had a husband at home, but was abducted by the late emperor. She didn't say a word all day long, either holding a knife or banging her head against the wall. The late emperor didn't get angry, he just put her on the bed when he came. After a few months of fussing, we had a child, and gradually she learned to talk and laugh again."

Huangfu Jue looked at him and couldn't help laughing. He scolded, "Old thing, do I need you to teach me how to be a woman?" He paused and said softly, "Yanzhi is different from them."

Too soft will break, too hard will break, her temperament is so clear. How to climb down this rose without breaking the thorns is the source of his troubles. Before he has completely obtained her, he will never allow anything to taint her purity.

"Go to Weiyang Palace and give her subordinates a warning. They have been spoiled by her and are no longer in good shape. Ask Xiao Dezi to summon Xiangpin over. Send someone to Minghua Palace to keep an eye on them."

Fuquan nodded in agreement and opened his mouth to speak before leaving.

Huangfu Jue's eyes turned cold, and he said slowly: "Fuquan, remember your identity."

Fuquan turned around silently, a flash of disappointment in his eyes.

Huangfu Jue had not been to the gate of Weiyang Palace for two days. Yanzhi's illness came and went quickly, and she recovered in less than two days.

On this day, there was an unexpected visitor.

Yanzhi had just met Sixi from the small kitchen and given him some instructions when Linglong came to report that Huangfu Yu wanted to see her.

Yanzhi was silent for a while, then smiled coldly, "Bring the man to the flower hall."

When the maid came up to refill the tea for the third time, Huangfu Yu saw a bright-eyed little girl coming out from behind a folding screen with figures inlaid in pastel colors. She was also wearing a light pink stand-up collared maid's outfit, but the cuffs had wide railings with white gold lines. She must be a well-known maid in Weiyang Palace. She bowed with a smile, her big almond eyes full of apology, "Don't blame me, Your Majesty. There are few people coming to the palace, and the little girl is so narrow-minded that she didn't recognize you and left you out in the hot sun. Your Majesty just woke up from her nap, Your Majesty, please follow me."

The flower hall was very bright, and the whole room was filled with golden sunlight. Huangfu Jue was already sweating profusely, and he drank a lot of herbal tea to quench his thirst. However, he had already made preparations to apologize, so he was not annoyed, but nodded and smiled and followed her.

After passing through the flower hall, turning around the corridor eaves, and going around the Mingtang, he found that these young palace maids actually led him slowly into the inner room. My heart couldn't help but jump with excitement, nervous and expectant. She, she, is she going to see me in the bedroom? Could it be that she also fell in love with me that night?

The author has something to say: Rolling around and asking for a harvest...

☆、Jifeng

Huangfu Yu walked around without touching the ground, his mind wandering. The little palace maid led him through a long corridor, opened a small door on the side, turned back and smiled at him, "Your Highness, the Queen is over there under the wisteria flowers."

Huangfu Yu was startled. The sunlight outside the door almost hurt his eyes. This was clearly the back garden of Weiyang Palace. He walked down the stairs in a daze and couldn't help but look back.

The maid had a clear sneer on her face, and when she saw him looking at her, she lowered her head. He suddenly realized that she had gone through so much trouble because she was angry.

After seeing the people under the flower stand, all the slight unhappiness in my heart turned into a pounding heart.

The fairy that night was sitting beside the stone table, wearing red clothes and black hair, with bright eyes and white teeth, and she was extremely beautiful. He rushed to the front and bowed to the ground, "Huangfu Yu greets the emperor's sister-in-law."

Her delicate hands brushed her hair, and her scarlet silk sleeves slid down, revealing her plump arms. She glanced at him and said softly, "Your Highness Prince Yu, why did you come to my Weiyang Palace?" Her eyes were too bright to contain the overwhelming force. Huangfu Yu's breathing stagnated, and he pinched his thigh desperately, then he opened his legs and sat across from the stone table.

"Sister-in-law, Huangfu Yu came here this time to apologize to you and to accept a request from someone." He looked at his nose and took out a jade pendant from his arms, "My third brother left Beijing yesterday and asked me to give you this jade pendant."

Yanzhi smiled lightly, her cool fingertips brushing his palm inadvertently, "Private exchange is strictly prohibited in the palace. Your Highness is indeed a brother with deep affection."

My heart felt numb and the stone bench under my butt seemed to have grown thorns. I resisted the urge to slide off the chair, bit my tongue, and uttered two words, "Where..."

He stole a glance at Yanzhi, and there was a tiny light falling on her hairline, her face was a light golden color, and from such a close look, her skin was flawless. He looked at her and felt a little infatuated.

"Sister-in-law," he stuttered, "my third brother asked me to ask you a question: You have never met him before, so how come you recognized him at first sight?" You still have to ask such a question. He is so ugly, who wouldn't come out?

The hand pouring the tea paused for a moment, and a smile suddenly appeared.

She had seen him three years ago. Youyun was not far from the Snow Region, and he was a famous dissolute prince. Ye Zi took her and hid in the largest brothel in Jizhou for two days before she saw his true face.

What happened next? She thought vaguely, yes, then Ye Zi was kicked by her master and locked up in Xuanbing Cave. She cried and vowed never to talk to her master again. So much time has passed, it seems like a lifetime ago.

The green tea poured steadily into the cup, and the air was filled with the refreshing tea fragrance. She smiled at Huangfu Yu and said, "My Lord, I received your question. Is there anything else?"

It was so beautiful, as if spring had returned to the earth and all the flowers were in full bloom. His heart trembled, his legs softened, and he knelt on the ground with a plop, his cheeks flushed, "Sister-in-law, I did something disrespectful to you that night. I apologize to you. I was drunk and mistook you for Wan Luo. Sister-in-law, please forgive me for this misunderstanding."

He spoke with his eyes closed, and eventually the words became more and more fluent, with a look of genuine regret on his face.

Suddenly, there was a faint sigh in my ear, and the gentle fragrance of magnolia filled my nose. A very ethereal and ethereal voice said, "Is it really similar?"

Huangfu Yu looked at Rulan's outstretched hand, not daring to breathe, extremely tangled, tears streaming down his face. "Brother, mother, who will save me? The fairy has become so sentimental, I'm about to make a mistake."

He covered his face with his hands and burst into tears, "Sister-in-law Huanghuang, my brother Huanghuang and I have a bond as strong as rock. If you... don't forgive me... I will have no face... to live... ahhhh..."

Yanzhi sat back on the stone chair. The weather was very hot, and she still had the soft fox fur under her. She looked at him coldly for a long while, "Get up."

Huangfu Yu rubbed his eyes and saw that the fairy had a stern and icy look. "Your Majesty is the emperor's right-hand man. Yanzhi dare not keep you here. I offer this tea to your Majesty. Let's not talk about the past."

Huangfu Yu blinked, looked at the cup of green tea in front of him, and thought to himself that women are really fickle.

When Huangfu Yu walked out of the backyard, looking back every few steps, Yanzhi looked at the Longquan Ice-patterned Cup he had just used for a long time, and a smile slowly appeared at the corner of her lips.

He is indeed a very interesting person.

He is a smooth talker with a slick appearance and a slick tongue, but he has the desire but not the courage to do it. Is such a person really sincere?

Huangfu Yu ran all the way back to his Mirror Lake Water Moon. Woohoo, Huangfu Fang, that bitch, one Ferghana horse is not enough. At least a hundred horses are needed to soothe his sensitive and fragile heart. Send a letter immediately, 800 miles away.

That night, Jinghu Shuiyue wailed constantly. It was said that Prince Yu had a stomach upset and had been holding the toilet for the whole night.

The white-bearded imperial physician was gloomy, which was a symptom of deficiency fire. Why did His Royal Highness Prince Yu keep saying that he must have taken laxatives? How did he know? His Royal Highness Prince Yu drank a bellyful of lemongrass and walked a few steps quickly. The drug effect spread throughout his body. Add a cup of bitter platycodon, ice and fire collided, and naturally he had severe abdominal pain and diarrhea for three days. When His Royal Highness Prince Yu was lying on the bed, it was not unreasonable to say that beautiful women were horny.

When Huangfu Yu kicked the door open, the two people entangled on the desk hurriedly separated. The woman screamed, and ran behind the bed with her clothes in her arms, her white legs bare.

Huangfu Jue was naturally upset when his good time was interrupted. He straightened his clothes with a gloomy face and scolded, "You are becoming more and more unruly!"

Huangfu Yu frowned and was about to speak when his face suddenly turned pale and he rushed out, holding his stomach. When he came back with a depressed look, Huangfu Jue had already drank his tea leisurely.

"Are you still having diarrhea?"

Huangfu Yu lay on the table and hummed twice.

The woman hiding behind the bed had tidied her clothes, came out with a red face, bowed, and left quickly.

Huangfu Yu looked at the slender waist that was twisting very quickly, and thought of the two slender legs just now, "You look unfamiliar, which palace are you from?"

Huangfu Jue smiled and said casually, "Do you like it? I'll give it to you."

Huangfu Yu made a bitter face, "I am cultivating myself now." He looked up at Huangfu Jue with a strange look in his eyes, "Brother, you hunt geese all day long, will you get your eyes pecked by a goose one day?"

Huangfu Jue just smiled and said nothing. After a while, he said in a gentle voice, "Did you get humiliated by Yanzhi?"

Huangfu Yu cried out, "For you, I sold my body and my beauty. If I continue like this, I will die. I gave up my most precious face to please her. You can't just leave me alone."

Huangfu Jue snorted, "You have to clean up the mess you made yourself." Seeing his miserable appearance with cold sweat dripping down his face, his tone softened a bit, "If it was really her who did it, it would only be a flesh wound, nothing will happen."

Huangfu Yu looked at him, thinking of the day before yesterday when he was practicing for Prince Gong. When he entrusted him with the jade pendant, he smiled meaningfully, "Fourteenth, your tenth brother is finished." His eyes darkened, and he asked hesitantly, "Brother, did you really marry Yanzhi just to contain Xueyu?"

Huangfu Jue's eyes were stern, and the

relaxed atmosphere between the two brothers disappeared. He slowly stood up and stood in front of the window, "Yu'er, don't worry, I will help the old man fulfill his last wish."

Outside the window, there are lush flowers and trees, while inside the window, the figure is aloof and proud, yet faintly desolate. Huangfu Yu sighed and said softly, "You know I don't care at all. I'm just afraid that you can't recognize your own heart. If a proud woman like her finds out one day that you set a trap for her, I'm afraid it will be difficult for her to have both."

Huangfu Jue turned around, his eyes were extremely cold, like lightning in the dark night, "She will never know, never. As long as you continue to play your love-sick role well, and marry Yan Wanzhao back to your Prince Yu's Mansion safely."

Being glared at by him, Huangfu Yu shrank his head and pouted his lips in grievance. He just made a mistake that all men would make. He has been beaten and knelt down. What else do you want him to do?

Huangfu Jue exhaled slowly, his hands trembling slightly in his robe sleeves, and slowly clenched into fists.

To the northwest, after passing Youyun, Shiloduoduo Lake and the Death Desert, there is a mountain that towers into the clouds and is covered with snow all year round. It is Tianshan Mountain - a mysterious forbidden area in the martial arts world and the gate to the Snowland School.

The Snow Region existed before the founding of the country. The disciples of the Snow Region roamed the world, some were the heads of aristocratic families, and some were local heroes. They had long been a transcendent force in the world. If it weren't for the strict order of the Snow Region that the disciples were not allowed to get involved with the royal family, it would not be difficult to change the dynasty.

How can I allow others to sleep soundly beside my bed? □□The emperors of all dynasties have been secretly planning to destroy this super power in one fell swoop. By the time of Huangfu Jue, the royal family had accumulated power for a hundred years. However, the master of the Snow Region of this generation is a master of profound skills, and his three disciples are also geniuses. The royal family is afraid of making a move and can only restrain it secretly.

Before leaving, Huangfu Yu looked back at Huangfu Jue again, "Brother, the woman just now was from the palace of Concubine Xian, right?" Seeing the sneer on Huangfu Jue's lips, he confirmed his guess. He couldn't help but curl his lips secretly. This man is simply a woman's nightmare. When he is ruthless, he can make you wish you were not born in this world.

"Royal brother, I know you don't want to hear it, but if I don't say it, no one else will dare to say it. After all, Wen Liangyuan is pregnant with your child, and you should also have a child." As he spoke, he already had one foot outside the threshold, waiting for Huangfu Jue to get angry and run away at any time.

Strange thing, the normally strong scales didn't move at all today. He was startled, turned around and looked, and met a pair of dark eyes. Huangfu Jue was smiling, with a very strange smile on his lips and eyes, "Yu'er, I promised Yan Zhi that you and Yan Wanzhao will be together for the rest of your lives. After a hundred years, I will pass the throne to your son, okay?"

"No!" A miserable howl was heard from Jiuzhou Qingyan Palace, startling several gulls and herons.

Yan Zhishang went to war. The day after Huangfu Fang returned to his fiefdom, he led the 30,000 vanguards of the Northern Expedition Army to the northern border. Before leaving, he only sent two words to Yan Zhi.

wait for me.

These two heavy words were gently hidden in the softest corner of her heart. No matter what happens in the end, no matter whether it is a cliff or a steep cliff, somewhere in this world, there is always someone silently guarding you, with the same mind and blood.

I burn a censer of incense and play some music, hoping you take care.

Lian Pingting's case disrupted the Queen Mother's birthday banquet, Yan Zhishang's marriage was granted, and Concubine Xian gave up the power to rule the six palaces and contemplated her mistakes behind closed doors. The only one who benefited was Concubine Shu. Huangfu Jue told the harem that Concubine Shu was kind and fair, and could be a role model for the harem. She was promoted to Imperial Concubine and given the title "Min". From then on, Concubine Shu was favored and stood out.

The Wang family has reversed its previous decline, and its followers are now active in the court.

When the first fallen leaf fluttered down the branch, Yan Zhishang won a great victory at the Heishui River. Twenty thousand cavalrymen wiped out the fifty thousand elite soldiers of Tiele. The court and the public were jubilant, and the marriage between Yan Wanzhao and Prince Yu was also put on the agenda.

The author has something to say: Thank you for your support, Happy Valentine's Day!! 1 There will be a climax soon, don't be anxious.

☆、Confidant

Lian Pingting's case disrupted the Queen

Mother's birthday banquet, Yan Zhishang's marriage was granted, and Concubine Xian gave up the power to rule the six palaces and contemplated her mistakes behind closed doors. The only one who benefited was Concubine Shu. Huangfu Jue told the harem that Concubine Shu was kind and fair, and could be a role model for the harem. She was promoted to Imperial Concubine and given the title "Min". From then on, Concubine Shu was favored and stood out.

The Wang family has reversed its previous decline, and its followers are now active in the court.

When the first fallen leaf fluttered down the branch, Yan Zhishang won a great victory at the Heishui River. Twenty thousand cavalrymen wiped out the fifty thousand elite soldiers of Tiele. The court and the public were jubilant, and the marriage between Yan Wanzhao and Prince Yu was also put on the agenda.

Weiyang Palace has always been very peaceful. Yiyue was grateful to Yanzhi and took care of her food, clothing, housing and transportation. She was actually more attentive than Li Luo.

Huangfu Jue was very busy. The war in the northern border was intense. He spent most of his time in Jiuzhou Qingyan Palace handling government affairs. When he occasionally returned to Weiyang Palace, he only saw Yanzhi's back.

Ever since the case of Prince Gong, she had

always treated him indifferently.

Yanzhi tended to the flowers and plants in the yard every day. The place where the camellia was originally planted had been replaced with a plum tree with green calyx. As early as July, the Ministry of Internal Affairs sent a large number of rare flowers and plants to replace the flowers and plants in the yard. She stopped them twice. When the green fruits of the camellia gradually turned red, Huangfu Jue suddenly came one day and said that Tu Luo had sent a good horse and wanted to give her a foal. She liked it very much and lingered in the Imperial Stables for a long time. When she came back, the camellia had been dug up. She was heartbroken, but she couldn't get angry at Huangfu Jue's pretending to be ignorant.

However, apart from attracting two green snakes at the beginning, the tea plant did not attract any poisonous creatures. She began to suspect that she had made a mistake and that it might indeed be a mutant sweet olive.

She naturally didn't know that on that day, the Shadow Guards in the palace were having a grand party.

The bald bull held the jar of wine and drank it, crying bitterly, and said to the cool woman in black: "Sister, it's been two months, two months without a drop of wine!" The cool girl snorted coldly and kicked him down. What was the wine? She almost married the shemale king.

When Yanzhi began to feel lonely in the harem, she made her first friend in the harem, Wen Ruyu from Cui Linglong Pavilion.

It was a coincidence that Xueqiu suddenly ran away one day, and when the people in Weiyang Palace were anxious, Wen Ruyu sent her back. Her belly was already obvious, but she didn't care about these cats and dogs. After a conversation, Yanzhi found that she was knowledgeable and generous, and she liked her a little. She had been in the palace for a long time, and there was no one around her who was like-minded. It was rare to meet someone who was involved in medicine, divination, and astrology. After a few visits, the two of them started to get along.

But there is one more thing that makes her treat him sincerely.

Once, Wen Ruyu brought chestnut cakes and saw Yanzhi looked tired, so she asked. Yanzhi was having her period during those days, and she was irritable and couldn't sleep well at night. After hearing this, Wen Ruyu brought her Dasheng Yiyinqin the next day and said she had a new song and wanted Yanzhi to appreciate it. Yanzhi was originally a music-deaf person, so she readily agreed.

This song was plain and harmonious, like a bright moon rising from the sea and wind blowing through pine waves. Yanzhi only felt relaxed and happy. Unconsciously, she felt tired and slowly closed her eyes.

When she woke up again, the sun had already set and the sky was full of red clouds. Wen Ruyu closed his hand, and with a lingering voice, he smiled and said to her, "Madam, did you sleep well this night?" She immediately put her hand into her sleeve, but she could still see blood stains on her green jade fingers.

Although she acted as if nothing had happened, she was deeply moved. She was pregnant and was about to become the mother of Huangfu Jue's first child. Yet he was still so kind to her, which was truly a sign of his deep affection.

Although Huangfu Jue took good care of her, she found it difficult to let down her guard. Wen Ruyu made her feel the first unadulterated warmth since she came to the palace.

Huangfu Jue got out of the two-day and two-night military meeting and came to Weiyang Palace. As soon as he entered the inner room, he saw Yanzhi hurriedly hiding something behind her. He pretended not to know and sat aside. Yanzhi breathed a sigh of relief and quietly reached under the quilt again. Suddenly, he heard his low and smiling voice, "Yanzhi, what good things are you hiding?" In a flash, he had reached out from under the quilt.

"Tsk tsk," he turned over a piece of soft red silk in his hand, with a light yellow tie and two embroidered green water plants.

It was obviously a small bellyband. He smacked his lips and said, "It's so small!" He glanced at the towering chest, "Can you wear it?"

Yanzhi felt embarrassed, snorted, and reached out to grab it.

"Ah!" Her hand touched the embroidery needle. Before she could withdraw her hand, Huangfu Jue had already grabbed it, "Why are you so impatient?" As he said that, he put her finger in his mouth and sucked it gently.

"You..." Yanzhi was anxious and was about to scold him, but when she saw his eyelashes drooping and his expression focused and gentle, her heart suddenly became confused and she swallowed the rest of the words.

Huangfu Jue suddenly raised his head and met her stunned eyes. He was stunned for a moment, then his eyebrows curved, and he held her hand in his palm, saying lazily, "Are you touched? You finally found my good side, right?"

Yanzhi glanced at him and picked up the bellyband he had just thrown on the couch.

Huangfu Jue followed her with his eyes. Suddenly he leaned close to her and whispered, "Yanzhi, are you ready to fulfill your promise?" Seeing her puzzled look, he slowly curled and stretched out his five fingers.

Yanzhi's face flushed, and she thought of how drunk she was that night. She pushed him and said, "It's too hot." She finally said reluctantly, "That's for baby Ruyu."

She was busy sorting out the impetuous emotions that he had aroused, and did not notice the cold light that flashed across his eyes.

He spoke slowly, "Ruyu, Wen Ruyu? When did you become so close to her?" He had withdrawn the secret guards since the poison was no longer in the Weiyang Palace. In the past few days, the war in the northern border was raging, and he was actually negligent. With Yanzhi's temperament, it would not take a day or two to win her favor. Someone was deliberately trying to get close to his baby, but he didn't get any news about it.

Looking at their folded hands, Yan Zhi felt annoyed, pulled her hands out, and said coldly: "Ruyu is fine, she is about to give birth, you should spend more time with her."

Huangfu Jue frowned, "Is there a woman as fickle as you?" Seeing her sullen and silent, his mood suddenly improved, and he squinted at her, "Yanzhi, after Prince Yu's wedding, I will take you out for a walk."

Women's thoughts are often very strange, and they are best at saying one thing and thinking another. Perhaps, when she doesn't understand, her concern will show up as awkwardness.

Go out, Yanzhi was stunned for a long time. Since she stepped into this nine-story palace, she never thought that one day she would be able to go out.

Seeing her staring at him blankly, with all kinds of emotions in her eyes, Huangfu Jue sighed softly, suddenly leaned forward and kissed her on the lips, "Yanzhi, you really can make me heartbroken."

"Bang!" Fuquan's head turned sharply to the side. Without even wiping the blood from his lips, he knelt straight on the ground.

Huangfu Jue stared at him coldly, with silent fire in his eyes, and uttered every word from his lips, "Fuquan, you are so brave!" Only he could suppress the news, help Wen Ruyu clear the obstacles, and let her slowly approach Yanzhi.

Fuquan looked at him, tears mixed with blood flowing down his cheeks. He choked and said, "Your Majesty, I can't bear it. That's your first child. That's your blood. You can be a good father!"

"I don't need a child!" Huangfu Jue interrupted him harshly, his black hair fluttering in the wind, his eyes flashing red, "Fuquan, you have crossed my bottom line."

Fuquan kowtowed heavily, his face calm, "After I leave, Your Majesty, please take care of yourself."

He staggered to his feet and walked out. Huangfu Jue's charming voice slowly rang out, "You have been with me for many years, and you are the closest person to me. Go back to your hometown to retire."

Fuquan paused, and his upright body suddenly hunched over, "Thank you, my emperor, for your grace."

The meandering stream gurgled, orioles sang on the acacia trees, and a cream-colored figure walked out of the mist, walking slowly and with a noble demeanor.

"Sister," Concubine Xian slowly turned out from behind Iris and said with a smile, "Sister, where are you going?"

The figure turned around and it was Wen Ruyu. She held her waist and bowed with difficulty, "Sister, I'm just about to go for a walk."

"Really?" Concubine Xian said slowly, "Sister has been out too often these days. Be careful not to harm the child."

Wen Ruyu's eyes sparkled, and she said gratefully, "Sister is so good to Ruyu."

Xian Fei smiled, and looked at her belly with a gentle gaze, "Sister will naturally treat you well. No one else can treat you well except you." She came over and helped Wen Ruyu's arm, "It's foggy, go back to the house. General Manager Fu has returned to his hometown. The palace is in chaos now. Don't go out these few days."

Wen Ruyu was startled when she heard this and suddenly looked up at her. The virtuous concubine smiled gently, but there were tiny sparks in her eyes, burning and compelling.

The powerful eunuch Fu returned home, and all the suspicions in the palace soon subsided. Haigui succeeded as the chief steward of the imperial court and continued to take good care of the Weiyang Palace. Yanzhi did not have any doubts.

Yanzhi has been very busy these days. The wedding date of Prince Yu and Yan Wanzhao is set for the eighth day of this month. The empress dowager is old, and she is busy running around the Yanxi Palace every day.

Finally, one day she had some free time, and she watched Linglong and Yiyue pick out things to prepare for the gift. Yiyue took out a rectangular box from the rosewood cabinet with dragon and phoenix patterns, and before Linglong could even wink, Yanzhi had already taken it.

The body of the zither is still red, and the five strings are still broken. My fingers gently stroke the gong and shang scales, and the sound of the zither lingers. If the zither had a heart, it would cry.

The rare and famous piano was lost in the world. It should have been a betrothal gift from the proudest man, but it was found by the elder brother and became a witness to this absurd marriage.

It turned out that she and he were not destined to be together.

Not daring to think about it anymore, her heart ached, and she hurriedly put it away, along with her most obscure thoughts.

"Wen Ronghua hasn't been here for a long time, right?" Linglong happened to speak.

Yiyue added, "I heard that Cui Linglong

Pavilion is very humid, which is not good for children. Concubine Xian has already brought Ronghua to Liuyunpu to wait for the birth of the baby."

Yanzhi was startled and her brows slowly furrowed.

Yiyue saw it all, and whispered to Yanzhi while removing her makeup at noon, "Master, Wen Ronghua is one of the most charismatic people in the palace, but her child may not be as she wished."

Yiyue's hands were very deft, her ten fingers flew and she quickly removed the hairpins. In the blurry bronze mirror, she looked calm and composed, as if she was talking about the weather.

Facing her eyes in the mirror, Yan Zhi said slowly: "If you know anything, just tell me."

She let her hair down in a bun and tied it up loosely behind her, half of her black hair cascading down over her crescent-shaped white gown. It was just the simplest dress, but it made her look extraordinary. Even though they were facing each other every day, Yiyue's eyes were filled with amazement. Looking at the watery face in front of her, she said softly, "Your Majesty, you are different from these women in the harem. You have a broad vision and a broad heart. You don't know what they can do to win favor. Wen Ronghua's family is in decline, but she is pregnant with the emperor's first child. If it was a son, it would be the emperor's eldest son. Without the protection of Concubine Xian, she would never have lived safely until now. Your Majesty, have you ever thought that Liang Yuan is not qualified to raise a prince?"

A vague thought flashed through her mind, but she immediately suppressed it. She just remained silent, as calm as still water.

Seeing the obvious rejection in her eyes, Yiyue still spoke slowly, "My queen, if you really don't want to be close to the emperor, then you should take this child into your arms."

Yanzhi raised her hand to stop her from talking, and said in a deep voice: "Yiyue, I know you are doing this for my own good, but don't say such things again." She stood up, with a bit of loneliness in her eyes, "I am also a child, and I know that children are the apple of their mother's eye. If you take away a mother's child, you are digging out her heart."

Yiyue was silent for a while, "Even if it's not you, it will be someone else."

Yanzhi's eyes were filled with determination, and she said slowly, "Since she knows me, I will fight for her. If it fails, I will let her bring the child to Weiyang Palace."

Yiyue stopped talking, looking at her quietly with strange eyes.

Yanzhi was stunned, thought for a moment, and laughed at herself. She closed her eyes and leaned against the soft blanket. After a while, Yiyue heard her say lightly: "Life is like a dream. If you always plan like this, how can you be truly happy for a day. I just want to know that she plays the piano for me, relieves my loneliness, and is my friend. This is enough."

After hearing this, Yiyue smiled quietly, put down the tent, and quietly retreated.

The next day, Yanzhi asked Li Luo to deliver some snacks and fruits to Liuyunpu. After Li Luo came back, she said that she had seen Wen Ronghua and that he was in good spirits. She also brought a message saying that the queen was busy with the wedding, so she did not disturb her during the move. She would come to visit again when everything was quiet. Yanzhi felt relieved.

Soon it was the eighth day of the ninth lunar month. Yanzhi, wearing a golden silk phoenix-embroidered dress and a phoenix crown with pearls on her head, went to Prince Yu's mansion with Huangfu Jue to officiate the wedding.

It was a grand wedding. The wedding procession from the Yan'an Marquis's Mansion stretched for ten miles all the way to Zhide Road, with red ribbons and colorful decorations and the sound of gongs and drums.

The Minister of Rites personally presided over the ceremony and praised loudly: First bow - to heaven and earth, second bow - to parents.

Yanzhi looked at the two newlyweds kneeling down and felt that they were performing a silent farce. Although they were very close to each other, it seemed as if there were mountains and oceans between them and she could not blend in at all.

It's really hard to accept.

After the ceremony, she left the hall on the pretext of getting dressed.

Many female relatives came that day, and Prince Yu's mansion had specially set up a quiet room for them to rest and change clothes. The room Yanzhi stayed in was obviously carefully prepared. There were yellow pear wood furniture, and the treasure box only placed blue and white porcelain from the Ru kiln. There was a pot of excellent red crane taro on the carved flower table. There was even a short-legged chaise longue in the room, facing a laurel tree in front of the window, and it was covered with a snow-white fox fur cushion.

As soon as Li Luo came in, she smiled, "The steward of this palace is quite a sensible person. This room looks like the young lady has cleaned it herself."

Yanzhi snuggled into the fox fur coat, still feeling irritated. She looked at Li Luo and said lazily, "Go ask when they can go back."

Before Li Luo could respond, she heard a deep, lazy male voice laughing, "You just came out, and you're already thinking about going back?"

Huangfu Jue stood with his hands behind his back, and came out from behind a huanghuali screen carved with green stone and a dragon pattern. He raised his eyes and looked at Yanzhi mischievously.

Linglong and the others all paid their respects and then left respectfully.

Huangfu Jue walked up to Yanzhi, flicked her forehead with his finger, and smiled lovingly, "Lazy cat!" He stretched out his hand to her, "You stay in the palace all day long. It's hard to get out, but you don't want to go out for a walk. Yu'er has invited the most famous circus troupe in Jiangnan. Let's go and have a look."

Yanzhi shook her head.

The most famous opera troupe in Jiangnan was the Li Family Troupe in Huizhou. She had watched it when she was ten years old. When she was ten years old, her internal strength had just been completed and the cold poison in her body could be controlled. Her master took her to almost all the fun places in China.

Huangfu Jue saw that she looked depressed, so he stopped smiling, reached out his hand to hold her, sat down next to her, and looked at her face carefully. "What's wrong? Who are you mad at?"

As soon as he approached, Yanzhi wanted to jump down barefoot, but Huangfu Jue grabbed her waist and couldn't move. Huangfu Jue glanced at her and stretched out his tone, "You are mentally unbalanced, naked jealousy."

Yanzhi just snorted but didn't say anything. He could always grasp her emotions easily and it was useless to hide them.

Her elder sister was wearing a bright red wedding dress, worshipping heaven and earth with her beloved, she must have been very happy and sweet. She would never have such a feeling in her life, so what if she was jealous?

Huangfu Jue looked at her with a gloomy face, and suddenly asked: "Am I really inferior to him?"

Yanzhi was startled, then her face turned pale when she understood what he meant. He had never mentioned it since she revealed her true feelings. Although he teased her from time to time, he never really got angry at her cold words. With his deep personality, he said such words, which made her feel embarrassed and surprised.

He squinted at her, his demonic aura increased greatly. She simply closed her eyes and said lightly: "Things that you don't have are naturally the best."

The room suddenly became very quiet. Although Yanzhi closed her eyes, her body was tense and the hairs on the back of her neck stood up.

She could feel Huangfu Jue's warm breath on her soft neck, and she couldn't help but lean back quietly.

"It's such a small place, where can you hide?" His voice whispered in her ear, as light as the wind, but with a chill of ice. His hand pressed hard, and Yanzhi fell on him involuntarily, "Yanzhi, why don't you know how to pity the person in front of you?"

The author has something to say: Dear friends, if you are more enthusiastic, I will let Jue Ye...

Hey, you decide whether to eat porridge or meat.

☆、Northern Tour

The incense burner with four-petal cirrus patterns was filled with the scent of lilies, and Huangfu Jue's footsteps were silent. Through the soft curtains, he could clearly see that the body lying on the bed with its back facing forward suddenly stiffened.

Yanzhi, are you afraid of me?

Huangfu Jue opened the curtain with one hand, and held it up with a gilded purple gold hook. He stood by the bed and looked at her for a long time. Her body was curled up like a fetus in the mother's womb. From behind, she felt that her thin shoulders were even more adorable.

He sighed softly, "Yanzhi, are you blaming me or yourself in your heart?"

Yanzhi desperately grasped the corner of the quilt to suppress her trembling. From the moment she heard his voice, she felt panic in her heart. She was actually afraid of him. If he had forced her, she would have fought hard afterwards. But she couldn't accept that she couldn't control her body, those shameful moans, and trembling feelings. She couldn't close her eyes all night. When she closed her eyes, she saw those obscene scenes in front of her.

She was a doctor and knew clearly that she had not taken anything containing aphrodisiac ingredients. Because she knew this, she felt even more painful.

"Go away, go away..." As soon as he spoke, he found that his voice was very dry and no longer as ethereal as usual.

Huangfu Jue frowned and hugged her with the blanket. She screamed, punched and kicked, and struggled desperately. Huangfu Jue didn't say anything, simply stifled her struggle, and hugged her tightly, letting her punches rain down like raindrops.

Yanzhi was tired from beating him, so she rested her head on his chest and cried bitterly.

Huangfu Jue lowered his eyes, his expression difficult to discern. He gently patted her back with one hand, and used his other hand to slowly comb her hair with his fingers.

After two days and two nights of suffering and another round of crying, Yanzhi gradually lost her strength. As she fell into a daze, she felt a warm sensation on her back. Huangfu Jue slowly passed the Qi to her with his right hand, calming the disordered breath in her body. With his left hand, he took out a handkerchief and gently wiped the tears from her face.

On the night of their wedding, he had wiped her face in the same way, but his mood was completely different. Yanzhi was filled with resentment and turned her face away.

Huangfu Jue smiled softly, leaned her halfway on the bed, leaned over to take the bowl, tasted a spoonful himself first, then scooped a spoonful and handed it to Yanzhi's lips, "Eat, only when you are full will you have the strength to beat and scold."

Yanzhi just closed her eyes, her chest rising and falling slightly. In just two days, she had become as haggard as a lotus leaf withered after frost.

Huangfu Jue was silent for a while, then he gently but firmly lifted her chin with two fingers and pressed his lips against hers.

Yanzhi opened her eyes in shock and anger, and a mouthful of sweet porridge had already passed through her lips and tongue. Huangfu Jue's eyebrows curved, and his lips just stuck to hers, neither advancing nor retreating.

After Yanzhi swallowed a mouthful of porridge, he stood up and asked with a smile: "Do you want to eat it yourself or do you want me to... feed you?"

Yanzhi looked at him with hatred, and when the silver spoon was passed to her lips, she finally opened her mouth. Neither of them spoke, and the bowl of porridge was soon finished.

After finishing the last bite, Yanzhi closed her eyes, and her body slid down, but was held by Huangfu Jue. He kicked off his boots and leaned against the head of the bed with her. He took her hand, his fingertips were cold and slender, and kissed it on his lips. He looked at her sideways and said slowly, "I promised you that I would wait until you were willing. I didn't do it. It's my fault." He put her cold and stiff fingers in his palm and rubbed them, "Yanzhi, since you disdain the world's etiquette, you should know that everyone has desires, and you don't need to be afraid."

She closed her eyes, an abnormal blush appeared on her cheeks, and her breathing was slightly rapid.

Huangfu Jue looked at her with a gentle expression, and his slow voice was like the spring breeze blowing over the branches of young girls in March, natural and peaceful, "When men and women admire each other, they all have the urge to touch each other. If you like her, you will want to own her. Yanzhi, I like you."

Her long eyelashes covered her eyes, trembling slightly like the wings of a butterfly. In the candlelight, she was as beautiful as glass, but also as fragile as glass. Even if you didn't get close to her, you could tell how stiff her body was.

Her body already had his memories.

He picked up a strand of her hair and played with it between his fingers. Huangfu Jue's eyes darkened and his slow voice had a magical magnetism, "You moaned and cried under me, your eyes were charming, and you were happy too..."

"Stop talking, get out!" Yan Zhiwu interrupted him with a scream, tears rolling down her cheeks, and pointed at the door, "Get out—"

Huangfu Jue's dark eyes stared at her, dark and complex, as if filled with thousands of emotions. Suddenly he smiled gently, "Yanzhi, I am your husband. We have worshipped heaven and earth and entered the bridal chamber. Even if we really did it that day, it would be the most natural thing."

Yanzhi was startled, panting for a few times, and suddenly tore open her shirt with both hands, revealing most of her tender chest. She looked at him coldly, with a strange fire in her eyes, "Your Majesty, you are the emperor, do you want it? I'll give it to you!"

Huangfu Jue frowned and really leaned forward. Yanzhi subconsciously wanted to dodge, but stopped abruptly. She closed her eyes and pulled her clothes open a little more with both hands.

She felt a wet touch on her chest, and then a pair of hands pulled her clothes up. He did it slowly but firmly, and even tied the silk ribbon around her waist.

Wrapping her tightly and holding her in his arms, Huangfu Jue smiled bitterly and sighed, "Yanzhi, I really miss you, but I want your heart more. That day, it was not your fault. You were too young to understand that the relationship between men and women is a very happy thing. You can think of it this way. I shamelessly took advantage of your desire. I swear, if you don't take the initiative to pounce on me in the future, I will never touch you even if I suffer internal injuries."

The person in her arms stopped trembling. Her voice was hoarse, nasal, and full of weariness, but surprisingly clear-headed. "Swear on your kingdom!"

"Okay, the sixth-generation monarch Huangfu Jue swears here: I will never take the initiative to invade Yanzhi. If I break my oath, the Tiele cavalry will trample through my sixteen states."

Yanzhi calmed down, and suddenly she felt complicated. No matter what, this oath was too heavy.

Huangfu Jue glanced at her secretly. What he wanted was nothing more than a turn of events like this. He smiled and patted her head, "I have made the vow, you should be relieved. In five days, I will be inspecting the sixteen cities in the north. Do you want to come with me?"

Yanzhi suddenly opened her eyes, not hiding

the surprise and surprise in her eyes.

In the north, there is a clear sky, vast grasslands, herds of cattle and sheep, and there is also Zhishang. A little further north is the continuous... Tianshan Mountains.

"Eat well, sleep well, and make up for what you have lost in the past two days. Then I will decide..." Seeing her eyes slowly rising and her murderous look revealed, Huangfu Jue hurriedly comforted her, "Okay, okay, I must take you with me. How come you can't even take a joke?"

He leaned back and murmured, "It's late, and I have to attend court early tomorrow. I'm going to sleep."

He really closed his eyes like that.

As soon as he closed his eyes, the enchanting temptation, the noble aloofness, the unpredictable temperament that made people love and hate him all disappeared. His face was calm and peaceful, his hands folded in front of his chest, and there seemed to be a glow flowing around him.

Yanzhi bent her knees and sat up, her hand reaching out halfway and then stopped in the air.

His breathing was even, long, steady and peaceful, and he had actually fallen asleep. She sat there for a while, her expression changing several times, and finally she regained her composure. She placed the colorful Shu brocade quilt between the two of them and lay on her side.

After an unknown amount of time, Huangfu Jue's lips slowly curled up.

The emperor was preparing to tour the north, and the six ministries were in a commotion. The Ministry of War and the Ministry of Rites were busy as hell. However, a group of upright people in the Censorate strongly advised that the emperor should stay in the palace when the army was deployed in the northern border.

Almost no one paid attention to what these old men with tall hats and wide sleeves and white beards were shouting at the top of their lungs in the court. Anyone with a little bit of common sense knew that the emperor was not as indecisive as the previous emperor and his wishes never changed.

From the imperial court to the localities, everything was spinning frantically around the emperor's northern tour.

Huangfu Yu ended his leisurely vacation. During Huangfu Jue's northern tour, he was the regent. Huangfu Jue left him two people, the Secretary of the Central Secretariat Pei Yan and the Nine City Military Commander Cen Xi.

Wang Shouren and Yan Yanzi both wanted to accompany the emperor.

Countless people at the center of power in the capital city looked thoughtful.

That night, the sky is dotted with stars.

Amber looked at the woman in black in front of her with a cold face. She took off the hood of her cloak, revealing a pair of sparkling eyes.

"Do you know how dangerous this is? The Emperor could be here any minute tonight."

The woman in black looked at her calmly, with a hint of pity in her eyes, "No, dear sister. The emperor went to the concubine's place, and he will stay in the Purple Palace tonight."

Amber looked at her viciously with a sinister expression.

The woman smiled slightly and said slowly, "I thought you should be happy." She moved to the side and easily took her fist. She sighed, "Sister, you have regressed again. It seems that the activities of the false phoenix and the fake phoenix are also very exhausting."

Amber's eyes were red, and her body rushed straight towards her. In an instant, their fists, fingertips, and knees collided dozens of times like lightning. In close combat, the moves changed so quickly that there was no sound at all.

"Stop!" A lazy voice sounded coldly, and the two of them separated quickly. Wang Linbo walked into the hall, looking at the woman in black with his smoky eyes, not hiding his annoyance, "Mu Mei, what's the matter, brother?"

The woman in black clasped her fists and smiled softly, "Dowager Concubine, the Prime Minister asked me to tell you that you must find a way to get Concubine Shu to accompany him on his northern tour. The Emperor stayed at the Weiyang Palace last night, Dowager Concubine, please put the overall situation first, and the Wang family must seize the master to be the crown prince."

Wang Linbo smiled coldly, "Overall situation, whose overall situation?" Although it was already night, she was still dressed up. There was a light golden powder on the corners of her eyes, and at this moment, her eyebrows and eyes were cold, and she was actually a bit bewitchingly beautiful.

Mu Mei stopped smiling and said word by word: "The Prime Minister's overall situation is the Concubine's overall situation. If it weren't for the Wang family, how could the Concubine, at her age, hold two emperors in her lap?"

Wang Linbo's body trembled, and he stared at Mu Mei. After a while, he said, "You are just a dog of my brother. You dare not bark without the master's order. What you said just now, is it my brother's intention?"

Mu Mei lowered her eyes, "I have offended the Concubine Dowager, and I will go back to apologize. But the Prime Minister is not going to abandon the Concubine Dowager for Miss Yan'er. The Wang family needs a crown prince, Concubine Dowager, you will never give birth to the next heir to the throne."

"Okay, okay," Wang Linbo smiled instead of getting angry, with golden phoenixes flying on his temples and pearls waving in his ears. "Go back and tell him that I will risk my life to let his precious daughter accompany me, so let him wait to hold his grandson."

Mu Mei hesitated for a moment, "The eldest son of the royal family can only come from the Wang family, Wen Liangyuan..."

Wang Linbo had stopped laughing long ago. He looked at her without blinking with his bright eyes, and said softly, "Why are you not talking? Go ahead and say it."

Her eyes were like the most poisonous rattlesnake, cold and strange, curled up in the corner, ready to jump up at any time and bite you like lightning. Mu Mei's words were forced into her mouth by her gaze.

Even though she knew she didn't know martial arts, she still involuntarily lowered her calves slightly and took a defensive posture.

She finally understood why the Prime Minister had such a complicated look on his face before leaving.

Lin Bo... Alas, Mu Mei, if she is willing to take action, then so be it. If not... then it depends on God's arrangement.

One thought makes you a Buddha, one thought makes you a devil.

She and Huangfu Jue were originally taboos, and they were mandala that could only bloom in the dark. It was no surprise that she became paranoid and twisted.

She might give up herself for the Wang

family, but she would never give up Huangfu Jue for the Wang family.

After Mu Mei left, Wang Linbo sat down in front of the dressing table as if nothing had happened. "Amber, my eyebrows are a little blurry. Please help me draw them up."

Holding the inkstone, she re-drew her eyebrows long and thin. Seeing her looking left and right with satisfaction, Amber couldn't help but said, "Master, you can't interfere in Concubine Shu's affairs."

Wang Linbo looked at her with a smile and said, "Silly child, do you really think I'm a fool? They all wanted to help Wang Yan to the position, so I followed their lead and gave her a push." Whether there was a cliff or a smooth road ahead, that depended on her luck.

The woman staring at the mirror, smiling but with ruthless eyes, does anyone still remember that she was also a simple and lovely girl in her twenties?

Amber said, "What if she really has a child?"

As her red lips parted, she exhaled a sweet breath, "Then, this is the day of my death." The one who killed her must be her brother who always talked about morality. But, how could there be a child? How could a man like him let Wang Yan give birth to his child?

Brother, you have really lost this game.

September 16th is a good day for breaking

ground and traveling. Huangfu Jue decided to go on a tour to the north on this day.

In the Weiyang Palace, Linglong and a group of young palace maids checked the things they were going to take, bottles, jars, clothes, and jewelry, and packed six large red copper-covered silver-rimmed boxes.

Yanzhi looked lazy these days, and just loved to curl up on the short-legged chaise longue and read. Yiyue was afraid that she would hurt her eyes if she read for too long, so she liked to tease her and talk to her.

Once, when they were alone in the study, Yiyue said to her solemnly, "Madam, Linglong and Yiyue have grown up, what are your plans?"

Yanzhi put down the book, surprised at first, then silent, "Did you figure it out?"

Yiyue nodded. Yanzhi smiled, "It's okay. I've asked my brother to pick out a few good families for her. After the northern tour, I'll let her leave the palace."

Yiyue smiled with relief and said nothing more. In the deep palace, it was not uncommon for someone close to you to be stabbed in the back. After returning from Prince Yu's mansion, Li Luo's behavior was too abnormal.

She didn't like to serve Yanzhi, and every day she either went out or stayed in the yard. She was no longer the talkative and cheerful person she used to be, and there was always a gloomy look between her brows. What was most worrying was her overly strange expression towards Huangfu Jue.

Yiyue had been in the palace for a long time and had seen many palace maids using their masters to gain power. She just thought that Li Luo had developed feelings for Huangfu Jue. Little did she know that her guess was completely different from the truth.

During her nap, Yanzhi was still vaguely thinking about how to talk to Li Luo. She could vaguely understand what was on her mind, but she had always resisted talking to her. That memory could only quietly emerge in the most peaceful moments, and it belonged only to her.

He is her leaf, she is his rouge. They are always innocent and their world is always theirs. There is no suspicion and no betrayal.

But before she could find the right opportunity, something happened in the evening that made her lose interest, and she never had another chance again.

Yanzhi had already removed her makeup and was picking lantern flowers with a small pair of silver scissors. Yiyue came in hurriedly, "Madam, Wen Liangyuan is here."

Yanzhi was startled and quickly straightened her clothes to go out.

It was indeed Wen Ruyu, but she was dressed as a palace maid, with her hair in a bun, a sunflower-shaped blouse with a stand-up collar, and a stone-blue plain cloak tied on the outside. The cloak was wide and covered her abdomen. From the back, she really looked like an ordinary palace maid.

Her face was filled with deep weariness. Seeing Yanzhi coming out, she still bowed gracefully, "Ruyu is so rude. You asked to see me so late at night and disturbed your peace."

"What happened?" Yanzhi was startled, and hurried forward to support her hand, and put her middle and index fingers on her wrist. After checking her pulse, she felt relieved and asked.

Wen Ruyu just looked at her with trepidation in her eyes, and asked softly, "Madam, are you going to accompany the Emperor on his northern tour?"

Yanzhi nodded. The light in Wen Ruyu's eyes dimmed and disappeared. She smiled softly and looked down, "If the queen leaves, she won't be able to see Ruyu's baby being born."

Yanzhi felt that her smile was extremely bleak, and she was secretly guessing. She said softly, "There are still a few days left, and the imperial decree has not yet been issued. I wanted to go see you tomorrow, but you rushed here at night, why don't you care about the child?"

Wen Ruyu's eyes turned red, and she hesitated to speak. She just said, "I was stupid too. I heard that the queen was leaving, so I was worried and came here in a hurry."

Yanzhi looked at her thoughtfully, "Ruyu, we have known each other for a long time. If you have any questions, just tell me directly."

Wen Ruyu's face turned pale and she held her hand tightly, "My Lady, please don't leave, okay?"

Yanzhi said in a deep voice: "Ruyu, you are afraid. What are you afraid of?" What could have happened that made her hide from others and come here so late at night?

Wen Ruyu shook her head. "It has been like this for the past few days. Nanny said I was suffering from prenatal anxiety. But my queen, I am really afraid that I will suffer alone with this child. You are not here, the emperor is not here, and I am alone..."

Yan Zhi said gently, "Don't be afraid. The Queen Mother is still in the palace. You are on good terms with Concubine Xian, so she will definitely protect you. As for the child, when I come back, I will talk to the Emperor and ask him to let you take care of him yourself, okay?"

Wen Ruyu's eyes were full of shock, her lips trembled a few times, tears rolled down her cheeks, and she choked and said, "Your Majesty..." Yanzhi tried to comfort her with a few kind words, but her brows did not relax.

After sitting for a while, she insisted on leaving despite Yanzhi's pleas to stay.

Yanzhi had no choice but to ask someone to carry her on a sedan chair and let Laixi go to see her off.

When Wen Ruyu reached the door, she suddenly turned around and smiled, "My queen, please give the baby a name."

Yanzhi was startled. This seemed to be Huangfu Jue's responsibility. Seeing her earnest eyes, he couldn't bear to refuse, "Okay, let me think about it."

Wen Ruyu smiled again and said slowly: "I can trust your knowledge. When the children are older, I will ask you to teach them lessons, okay?"

Yanzhi only felt bitterness in her heart, and a chill gradually rose. Although she smiled and looked gentle, what she said was clearly the words of entrusting an orphan to someone else.

The author has something to say: This is the second update. Staying up late is really hard, but I feel happy when I see the messages from you.

Let Liu Liu be happy until she dies.

☆、Prepare

She smiled and spoke with a gentle look, but her words were arranged in great detail. Yanzhi felt a chill and almost suspected that she was entrusting her son to someone else.

With a "huo" sound, Yanzhi suddenly sat up from the bed, her eyes confused, and she screamed in surprise: "Ruyu, Ruyu!"

Yiyue was on night duty today, so she quickly put on her clothes and sat up, calling softly, "My queen, my queen, wake up!"

Yanzhi's eyes gradually came into focus, and she looked at Yiyue's face. She hurriedly grabbed her hand and called out in a hoarse voice, "Yiyue, where's Ruyu?"

Yiyue knew she was having a nightmare, so she smiled softly and said, "Don't be afraid, Madam. Wen Ronghua has returned to Liuyunpu safely. Have you forgotten? Lai Xi personally sent him back. You must be dreaming. You must know that dreams are the opposite of reality."

Her voice was neither hurried nor slow, and was pleasant to the ear, like the faint scent of Canaan, which had the power to soothe people's hearts.

Yanzhi let out a long breath and touched her cheek, which felt cold and damp.

She pulled the quilt tighter, feeling cold all over. There were only two lights in the corner of the room, and the bookcases, tables and chairs were all dim, like ghosts.

"Yiyue, please turn up the light."

Yiyue responded, took a cloisonné lamp and placed it on the plum blossom round table in front of the bed, and added a handful of lily incense to the incense burner.

The small candle flame struggled and jumped up, illuminating a space, and Yanzhi felt her heart come alive.

Seeing her dazed look, Li Yue moved a red wooden stool and placed it beside the bed. "My lady, if you can't sleep, I will talk to you."

Yanzhi stared at the candle flame absentmindedly, "I just dreamed of Ruyu. She was covered in blood, holding a small baby in her arms, crying, 'Madam, save me, Madam, save me!'"

Yiyue said softly, "Your Majesty, you are just too worried. Worrying makes you confused. You had such a dream because you were thinking about Wen Ronghua. Liang Yuan's current status is so important that no one would dare to harm her."

Yanzhi's eyes were filled with melancholy. "Ruyu's expression is very strange. I feel uneasy. I always feel like something is going to happen."

Yiyue lowered her eyes and smiled softly, "Ronghua knows that the queen treats her very well and knows that the queen will leave the palace for a while, so it is natural for her to be reluctant to let her go. She is pregnant with the emperor's eldest son, and everyone is watching her. It is inevitable that she is worried and emotionally disturbed."

Yanzhi thought silently. Ruyu must have some hidden reasons in her heart. If it wasn't something urgent, she wouldn't be so flustered.

However, she had her own plans for the Northern Tour and had to go.

He kept thinking about it, but couldn't make a decision. He sat quietly for half an hour before he finally suppressed his uneasiness. He asked Yiyue to turn off the lights, and then he lay down again.

I have already decided in my heart that I will go to the Empress Dowager's palace tomorrow and ask her to take good care of me.

The candlelight flickered, and Yiyue's face looked slightly gloomy.

Wen Ruyu got off the sedan chair at the door and waited for Lai Xi to leave before going through the side door. Before she could ask Xiao Dezi who was waiting for her, she heard a series of short muffled groans, as if someone was covering his mouth and unable to shout. Her expression changed and she hurried back to her courtyard.

Hongshao was still wearing the lotus-colored double-breasted shirt that she usually wore. She lay motionless on the spring stool, with blood stains all over her body from waist to thighs.

Concubine Xian looked at her, first happy and then surprised, "Sister, why are you dressed like this? I was afraid you were thirsty, so I sent you some papaya juice, but I only saw this damn girl wearing your clothes to deceive me. Sister, what's going on?"

Wen Ruyu supported her waist and slowly squatted down to feel Hong Shao's breath, tears flashing in her eyes. She heaved a sigh of relief when she saw that she was just fainting temporarily.

Although Concubine Xian smiled, her eyes were as sharp as needles. She just smiled faintly, "Sister, you must have misunderstood. I don't like this shirt anymore, so I gave it to Hong Shao. As for my sister's outfit, I just want to go out for a walk and take a breath."

Concubine Xian stopped smiling and said, "Sister, the Emperor is so kind that he allowed you to move here to rest and take care of your baby. If you act willfully, neither you nor I will be in any good. Sister is a smart person, and you should remember that all this is the Emperor's will. If you insist on doing something foolish, no one can help you."

Wen Ruyu's face turned pale, but he remained silent.

Xianfei walked up to her and reached out to touch her belly. Wen Ruyu dodged and her hand stopped in mid-air.

She stared at Wen Ruyu intently and said slowly, "Sister, we are the only ones in the harem who have no one to rely on. You only have me, and I am the only one who sincerely hopes that the child will be born. Since you have given up on the emperor, you should understand that Yan Wanluo is even more unreliable! The Yan family and the Wang family are birds of a feather!"

Wen Ruyu's smile gradually faded, and she looked at Concubine Xian with a dim gaze,

"Sister, although Ruyu is stupid, she can tell who is sincere and who has ulterior motives. Sister, don't worry, Ruyu will never do stupid things again."

Xian Fei was startled and looked at her coldly for a long while. Suddenly she smiled and softened her voice, "It's good that you understand. It's late at night, so I won't disturb you. I will take Hong Shao away with me."

Wen Ruyu's face turned pale as he watched the young eunuch dragging the unconscious Hong Shao out, biting his lower lip deeply with his silver teeth.

Concubine Xian smiled and glanced at the kneeling palace maids and eunuchs in the room, and said softly, "Everyone, stand up. If you dare to instigate the master again, you will end up like Hong Shao."

Everyone in the room was silent. She then smiled, took Liu Shang's hand, took light steps, and left.

Wen Ruyu's face was as white as paper, and her teeth were chattering. The spring stool in the room had not been removed yet, and there was blood on it. She put her hand on it with trembling hands.

The slender jade fingers, with the bright red bloodstains, are like plum blossoms in the snow, desolate and gorgeous.

She slowly placed her hands on her belly, tears flowing silently. "Child, you must remember that this is the first human blood you have ever known."

She will no longer sing for you, talk to you, or make beautiful clothes for you.

Mother, I want you to remember this forever.

Haigui bowed quietly beside him, but Huangfu Jue hesitated for a moment when handing over the memorial.

At this moment, he suddenly remembered Yanzhi's tearful eyes.

Her eyes were filled with tears, rolling in her eye sockets like dewdrops, but her expression was still stubborn, and she would stare at him fiercely with her eyes wide open.

He smiled unconsciously, withdrew his hand, and added a few words to the secret letter.

The camera moves, and the enemy is trapped. Leave the mother!

Haigui put away the secret letter and bowed, "Your Majesty, it's midnight now. Shall we sleep together?"

Huangfu Jue was still smiling, his dark eyes curved, "Let's go to Weiyang Palace."

After passing Qujiang Lake, Huangfu Jue slowed down his pace. Lotus lanterns floated in the water, twisting and turning, forming a huge Chinese character "儿".

Stopping Lai Xi from following him, he swam upstream following the light.

The new moon is cold and the starry eyes are weary. A woman in palace dress stands on a lake rock, placing a lotus lantern in the river.

Her hands were as white as snow, her eyes were as clear as water. She looked in the direction of Huangfu Jue, seemingly intentionally or unintentionally. She smiled, her tone was delicate and lazy, with a hint of weariness, as if she was indescribably happy, "Jue'er, you are finally here."

Being overwhelmed by the red waves, they lingered until death.

She just clung to him, moaning softly, crying softly, her body was weak and boneless, and she just kept trying to please him.

Tears flowed from the corners of her eyes, soaking the butterfly and flower pillow. Her unpainted face already had fine lines on it.

Jue'er, am I old? Am I still your eyeball?

The violent impact made her voice shattered, leaving only a pair of eyes smiling sadly and beautifully.

Jue'er, I'm going to Qingping's place. Please love me well, for the last time.

On September 14, the imperial edict was issued to the six palaces: The Queen, the Imperial Concubine, and the Concubine Qi will accompany the emperor on his northern tour. The harem will be temporarily managed by the Concubine Xian, and no one should make arbitrary decisions. If Wen Liangyuan gives birth to a prince, she will be promoted to the rank of Concubine. The Queen Mother is old, and each palace should guard its own gates and not cause any trouble.

In Guanju Palace, Concubine Xiang was like a madman, smashing everything she could. She slapped the maid beside her with a thin, ice-silver belt. This was the pendant she always carried with her, and it was covered with pearls and jade. The edges of the gems slapped her face until it was covered with blood, but the maid just closed her eyes and cried, not daring to block it with her hands.

She sat in the mess, pulling her hair and crying loudly.

Since she learned that the emperor would take his concubines with him on his northern tour, she was overjoyed for three days and even took out her fox fur snow robe from the bottom of her box. She thought she could win the emperor's favor with this, but she didn't expect that she would become the biggest joke in the harem.

The second concubine and the third concubine, Concubine Shu was promoted to Imperial Concubine, and was favored by the emperor. Concubine Xian regained power in the harem. If Wen Liangyuan could give birth to a son, she would rise to the top. Even Concubine Qi, who had a cold personality, was allowed to serve the emperor. But she could only guard the Weiyang Palace alone.

The beauty is still here, but the emperor's favor has already ended. She is unwilling to accept this, very unwilling!

At 7:00 p.m. on the 19th, Huangfu Jue

ascended the altar to offer sacrifices to heaven. At 9:00 p.m., a large motorcade left Xuanwu Gate, crossed Zhuque Street, and exited the Tonghua Gate of the Outer Palace, leaving Shengjing.

Huangfu Jue's carriage was in the middle, with a black wood carriage with animal heads squatting on the four corners and nine golden dragons playing with pearls. The carriage was as big as a small house and was pulled by eight horses. Behind it was Yanzhi's phoenix-dragon chariot with six horses. The carriages of the imperial concubine and Qipin were all pulled by four horses and were carved with red sandalwood. Such a large team only went out of the city for more than ten miles in a day.

At noon, the convoy stopped and a guard came to report that lunch would be had in the suburbs.

When Yanzhi got off the car, she was distracted.

The sky is clear and the wind is gentle, my shoes step on the soft and warm ground, and I breathe in the air with the scent of earth, making me feel like I am in another world.

Linglong and her friends chose a place sheltered from the wind, spread a large felt cloth, and placed the food they had prepared early in the morning on it.

Royal Concubine Red, Han Palace Chess, Mantuo-style sandwiches, and even a carved fruit platter. Yanzhi smiled, which was very elegant.

Wang Yan seemed to glance at this place, but did not approach. Her people chose a place on their own. Concubine Qi did not get off the car. The three women were each doing their own thing.

The imperial guards in bright silver armor surrounded them from a distance. Yanzhi searched for a long time but did not see the person she wanted to see.

She hadn't seen her father for several months since she had taken a close look outside Huangfu Jue's study. He was clearly in the team, but it was so difficult to take a look at him. She felt a little disappointed.

It was the same young guard with a tiger head embroidered on his chest, with a pair of bright eyes under his helmet. He knelt on one knee from a distance and said, "Empress, it's time to get on the carriage. The team will set off soon and arrive in Fufeng County before dark."

Fufeng County is the Jiangnan of the northern frontier and the richest county in the Huaibei area.

The author has something to say: I am in a very difficult situation and have hit a bottleneck.

I have prepared a cute gg, where is the best place to put it?

☆、Drug

It was the same young guard with a tiger head embroidered on his chest, with a pair of bright eyes under his helmet. He knelt on one knee from a distance and said, "Empress, it's time to get on the carriage. The team will set off soon and arrive in Fufeng County before dark."

Fufeng County is the Jiangnan of the northern frontier and the richest county in the Huaibei area.

When they arrived at Fufeng County, the cold moon was silent in the west sky. The entry ceremony was very low-key, and only the county governor Li Chengqian led a group of officials to welcome them ten miles out of the city. When Yanzhi and the others arrived at the city gate, they changed to a sedan chair and went straight to the palace.

Yanzhi was very tired. Although she was just walking in the carriage, her hands and feet were still sore and numb. The head in charge of the palace was very knowledgeable. He didn't say anything nonsense and arranged a bath first.

She lay down in a large wooden barrel. The water was very warm. Linglong dropped a few drops of rose oil into it, and a faint fragrance emanated.

Li Luo's hands vigorously massaged the acupuncture points on the shoulders and back, and Yanzhi let out a comfortable sound.

Even if she were set free and allowed to

ride a horse and whip it, she would not be able to enjoy the world. She had been at ease for too long, and laziness had seeped deep into her bones.

When Yanzhi, dressed in a fresh and clean manner, sat down beside the huanghuali throne-style mirror table, the housekeeper came to greet her through the curtain and asked about the arrangements for dinner.

"Linglong, just say I'm tired and bring the food in."

Linglong responded and went downstairs to give orders.

Yiyue used a large lotus green towel to carefully wipe Yanzhi's hair. Seeing her black hair smooth and round with water drops dripping down, she couldn't help but praise: "The queen's hair is in great shape."

Yanzhi smiled faintly, "No matter how good it is, it's just three thousand strands of troubles. Only when they are gone can we be free."

Seeing her sad face, Yiyue smiled and changed the subject, "Your Majesty, although this palace is small, everything is well-equipped. I just looked at the bedroom, and the clothes and quilts are all your favorite comfortable and soft things. This lady in charge is not a simple person."

Yanzhi's heart moved, and after thinking about it, a sneer appeared on her face. How could a palace in a small county have things comparable to those used by the emperor? I don't think it was because of the cleverness of the mind, but because someone came down early to prepare.

Their next journey was to leave Imjin Pass, cross the Yellow River, go to Xiping County, pass Bayan Mountain, and finally reach Youyun. This journey was more than 5,000 miles. If he could arrange everything like this, how much manpower and material resources would it take.

Throughout history, those who were arrogant and extravagant have all ended up ruining their country.

The meal was delivered quickly, along with a young eunuch. Yanzhi recognized him as Haigui's apprentice, who also served in front of the emperor.

She was still young, so her voice was only clear. "The Emperor is entertaining the local officials of Fufeng in the front yard. The deer meat on the table is the most heart-warming, so he took some and gave it to the Empress, and told her to rest early after a long day's journey."

Yi Yue hurriedly took it, and stuffed a small gold ingot into his hand with a smile, "Thank you for your hard work, eunuch." The young eunuch took it with a smile on his face, bowed and left.

Yanzhi saw that the small Tiansu was brightly colored and she was actually hungry. She tasted it and found it was delicious. She smiled and said to the three of them, "Don't be busy. Sit down and eat. This is not the palace, so there are no such strict rules."

Linglong and Yiyue sat down first. Yiyue saw this and sat on half of the bench. Li Luo laughed first, "Sister, if you do this, Miss will feel uncomfortable."

Yiyue took the silver chopsticks and tried all the dishes. Then she took the small celadon plate with broken branches and put some of the dishes that Yanzhi liked. Then she picked up the bowl and chopsticks in front of her and said with a smile, "Although the rules are not as strict as those in the palace, you still have to be careful of ears. Sister, you have to be careful too. You should call me Empress instead."

Li Luo was startled, and her smile slowly faded. Linglong smiled and said, "Sister is really careful. After all, there are no outsiders in our palace. But if you still call me like that outside, it will definitely cause trouble for the queen."

Li Luo stole a glance at Yan Zhi and saw that she was just eating with a faint smile and a calm expression. She felt bitter in her heart. She didn't change the title at the beginning to comfort the young lady. Now, she is more and more content to be a "mother".

Could it be that she really had forgotten that person?

Seeing Yanzhi's chopsticks reaching for the

bowl of Xiaotiansu again, she hurriedly said, "Madam, didn't you dislike eating venison before? When we were in Fuzhou..."
"Li Luo!" Yan Zhi frowned slightly, "The past is the past. Where in this world can we find an unchanging human heart?"
Her tone had never been so harsh. Li Luo opened her mouth, and seeing the impatience in her eyes, her eyes suddenly turned red.
"I'm full." She lowered her head and rushed out.
Yanzhi remained silent, while Linglong stamped her feet in anger, "This damned little evil star is really possessed by a ghost. Madam, it's all because of you who spoiled her."
Yanzhi held them both with her hands and said calmly, "Ignore her. She won't be making trouble for many days."
The next day, Yanzhi was supposed to receive a high-ranking imperial lady, but she declined the invitation due to illness. When the backyard was quiet, Linglong found two pieces of clothing from the bottom of the box. Yanzhi happily put them on and applied some makeup on her face. In the blink of an eye, a handsome young man appeared before her eyes.
Linglong burst out laughing, "My little... Madam, if I hadn't seen it with my own eyes, I really wouldn't have recognized it."
Of course, this is also my most important skill.
"Your Majesty, I sent Li Luo to buy rouge,

Yi Yue went to help you with the rewards, and the Emperor went outside the city. Your Majesty, shall we leave now?"

Yanzhi lifted her chin with a folding fan and said, "Beauty, follow the young master." Her voice was already neutral and clear. The word "Beauty" curved on the tip of her tongue and came out lightly, full of frivolity.

Linglong not only blushed, but she hadn't seen her smile like this for a long time. Although she was nervous, she was still very happy.

Yanzhi took Linglong to the backyard secretly. Since Huangfu Jue had left, the imperial guards beside him must have followed him, so she was sure she could avoid the guards in the backyard.

As expected, there were few guards along the way. Yanzhi used a stone to divert the attention of the guards and made a few meows to easily divert them away. When they arrived at the corner gate of the backyard, it was locked with a rusty lotus cross lock on it.

Yanzhi secretly breathed a sigh of relief. Large houses usually had this kind of door. Although it was abandoned after being used as a palace, it was not blocked off.

She took out a piece of wire and flicked it a few times. With a click, the lock opened. The two of them clapped their hands excitedly.

The woman in black covered her eyes,

screamed, and kicked the bald man beside her who kept making secret gestures. He was mobilizing their secret guards in the hope of allowing someone to escape more safely and secretly.

"She is really Bai Zizai's last disciple? Really! Ahhhh, my idol is shattered, shattered!"

The master and servant walked around the street at ease. Because of the emperor's arrival, there were soldiers at almost every alley. But the street was still bustling, and the shops were all newly renovated, with shiny red paint and bright tiles.

The two of them only picked up exquisite and novel little things to buy along the way, such as small clay figurines with silver foil, root-carved Buddhas... After a while, their hands were full.

In a porcelain shop, Yanzhi said she wanted to go to the toilet, handed her things to Linglong, and followed the shop assistant.

Linglong continued looking at the porcelain and waited for her.

There were two porters resting in front of the store. One of them was stretching his legs to bask in the sun, and when someone kicked him, he just laughed. Suddenly his expression changed, and he cursed: "xxx, I got fooled."

Linglong was still looking at the porcelain leisurely, asking the waiter about the price from time to time.

The two porters walked briskly and ran towards the toilet in a hurry.

The toilet was empty.

Night Owl sniffed the faint scent of lilies in the air, his face livid, his eyes glowing faintly, "He's changed his clothes, but he hasn't gone far. Tiezhu, gather some people."

The long ancient alleys have stone walls covered with moss, there are sundries in front of every house, and the air is filled with the smell of decay, dampness and mold.

A young man was walking hurriedly. He was wearing an ordinary green shirt and a small hat, was short, had a dark face, but his eyes were as bright as stars.

"Bang bang," he stood in front of a vermilion door and pulled the pull ring hard.

After a long while, a hoarse voice finally shouted like a broken gong, "There are no corpses left."

The young man raised his lips and said in a clear and compelling voice, "You old man, come and open the door. If you don't come, I will really kill someone."

The sound of footsteps and cursing could be heard in the yard.

The door was only slightly opened, revealing a head of messy white hair. His small, soybean-sized eyes blinked hard, and he was about to close the door.

"Old Deer Head, if you dare to close the door, I will immediately go to the street and shout three times: The master craftsman Ou Yezi is here!"

"You stupid girl! Your master has mountains of gold and silver, but you come to raid my lair. Bai Zizai is a fake, a rotten person... Ouch, you stupid girl!" The door was pushed straight open and hit his mouth with spit flying.

Yanzhi looked at her with a smile, a little mischievous pride in her eyes, and suddenly sighed, "Grandpa Lu, after so many years, why is your mouth still so smelly?"

Her expression changed dramatically from joy to sigh. The old deer head was stunned for a moment, muttered a few words, and turned away.

He crouched in the greasy kitchen, groping for a long time without knowing where he had hit. The iron pot in the middle suddenly moved, revealing a big hole in the middle. He slipped in, followed by Yanzhi.

Three advances and three retreats, nine consecutive and nine verticals.

When they were in the dark room, the old deer head suddenly changed into a different person. His body suddenly grew in size, and cold light flashed between his eyes.

"Girl, since you took that brat to trick my Wu Gou away last time, no one has come for five years." His sharp eyes shot straight at Yan Zhi, "Girl, why didn't that brat come?"

Yanzhi smiled and turned her gaze to the fir wood weapon rack. "Grandpa Lu, do you have a long sword suitable for killing enemies on the battlefield? Also," she took out a blueprint from her arms, "I have thought of a few small things, please see if they are suitable."

Huangfu Jue's smiling face suddenly became solemn and his eyes narrowed suddenly.

The officials of Fufeng County who were sitting next to him felt that the power of heaven was unpredictable, and they were trembling with fear.

Haigui bent over. In the September weather, a drop of sweat slid down from his temple, tremblingly falling from his chin to the redwood floor.

"Bang!" Everyone seemed to have heard this soft sound, and they all rolled down from their chairs and kowtowed to the ground.

"Guard the city gate and don't move for an hour. Tell Ye Xiao that I will give her an hour." Huangfu Jue's lips moved and he suddenly glanced at him.

There was a sticky murderous aura with a bloody smell, and between the pupils, all one could see were mountains of corpses and white bones.

Haigui shrank back and took small steps back.

Huangfu Jue smiled again, and glanced under the throne with his dark eyes, "Why are you kneeling down? Get up quickly."

The old deer-head's eyes sparkled, and he sneered, "The old witch was right when she said that there is no good man in the world.

Girl, don't be sad, grandpa will kill him."
Yanzhi sniffed and glanced at him, "You are not a good person either. You come here and trick people into crying. Stop playing the sentimental card and find something for me quickly. I'm in a hurry."
The old deer-headed monster snorted, and with a sullen face, he dragged out an iron box from under the cabinet. "The sword is called seamless, made of black iron, five and a half feet long, and weighs eighty-one pounds. It is most suitable for fighting on the battlefield, or for two armies to confront each other. But girl, I can't give my grandpa's things to you, but not to a stinky man."
Yanzhi smiled happily, but ignored his last words. The old monsters of the master's generation didn't buy into anyone's accounts, but they all loved her very much and always responded to her requests.
"How about the picture? Is there any way to make it?"
"Your two things are just the current 'Gypsophila' and 'Zhuge Crossbow' with different designs. You can't embarrass your Grandpa Lu. But girl, if you want to promote it in the army, with the level of smelting in the court, it won't work even if they give you another hundred years."
The old deer head was proud and disappointed. "Gypsophila" and "Zhuge Crossbow" are already the pinnacle of close-range hidden weapons. The girl can

improve them with just a few strokes, and their power is many times greater. She only studied with them for two months back then. It would be great if they could pass on their skills.

Bai Zizai, that sinister guy, is really lucky.

Yanzhi thought for a while and said, "Grandpa, my situation is special now and I can't stay in Fufeng County for long. After you make these two things, throw them into the yard of the county garrison." She stood up and handed him a letter and a small Hetian jade seal.

She bit her lower lip, tears rolling in her eyes, and said softly: "Grandpa, I'm leaving."

The old deer head looked at her gloomily, "Girl, what injustice have you suffered?"

The autumn wind was howling, Huangfu Jue's wide sleeves were billowing up, his black hair was flying, his phoenix eyes were filled with boundless vastness, and his joy and anger were unpredictable.

Behind him, sixteen riders were arranged in a fan shape. There was a dead silence in the air.

The incense burner in Qilin's mouth has burned halfway.

Yanzhi smiled at him, but couldn't hold back her tears. "I'm just afraid that you're old, and next time I come, I'm afraid I'll have to look for you in a mass grave."

The old deer head's expression relaxed, and a gleam of light flashed in his eyes. He waved his sleeves to cover up and said, "Go, go."

He was already old and experienced, and he could see that the once quirky little girl's brow was now tinged with sadness. But the girl was grown up, so naturally she would have her own worries, and asking her would not reveal the truth.

The red light of sandalwood flashed and then disappeared silently.

Huangfu Jue raised his hand.

"Your Majesty, the target has appeared." A rider came running like a whirlwind, his bald head shining in the sun.

Yanzhi and Linglong walked out of the porcelain shop talking and laughing.

Yanzhi's eyes glanced around her imperceptibly and she continued to talk about the cloisonné Eighteen Immortals figure vase she had just bought.

Linglong said, "Sir, this road is bustling, there are so many new people."

Yanzhi smiled and said, "Maybe people here like to go out at this time."

Suddenly, a girl selling flowers stopped them. In her basket were fresh butterfly flowers. She glanced at Yanzhi and said, "Girl, buy some flowers."

Although Linglong liked it, she shook her head when she looked at the things in her hands.

The flower girl bit her lower lip. Her deep

eyeliner and brown eyes gave her a unique beauty. She leaned towards Yanzhi and said, "Sir, don't you love this flower?"

As we got closer, the scent on her body became stronger. It wasn't a floral scent, but it made people want to inhale it again and again.

Yanzhi held her breath calmly, picked a bud from the basket, and inserted it into the flower girl's temples, "Long'er, pay."

Linglong didn't understand what was going on, so she paid obediently. The flower girl seemed both shy and happy, her eyes chasing Yanzhi.

Yanzhi took two steps, then suddenly turned around and smiled, "My family has a house and a garden, and I have six wives and concubines, and countless maids. Girl, are you willing to come with me?"

"Young Master, Young Master..." The flower girl blushed and ran away with a stomp of her feet.

"Hahahaha…" Yanzhi laughed out loud.

The flower girl threw the flower basket into the stinking ditch, took off the butterfly flower on her head, and looked at me with anger. "Six wives and concubines, countless maids. Could she really see through my disguise? How is it possible? How is it possible?"

The fortune teller next to him poked the flag that had been predicted accurately on the ground and said with a bitter face, "Boss, you should think about how to be punished when you go back."

The flower girl suddenly smiled slyly, her eyes bold and passionate, "I can't get a piece of meat in my mouth, but I suddenly throw myself into my arms and take off my clothes. He must have exposed his wolf body immediately. How can he have the energy to mess with me?"

The boss's words were so obscene and evil that the fortune teller suddenly had a bad feeling. "Boss, is there going to be a problem?"

She waved her hand and said, "Don't worry, this is the top-grade aphrodisiac from Paradise Palace. It is colorless, invisible, soundless and odorless. The emperor fell for it back then. The quality is absolutely guaranteed."

The author has something to say: I am really in a hurry. I have read everyone's messages and will reply when I have time.

Ah, isn't it true that women only love bad men?

Please raise your hands if you support Jue Ye.

☆、Love

Yanzhi and Linglong swaggered back to the inn through the main gate.

Before the guards could stop him, Haigui was already walking over, "...Sir, please come in, the emperor is waiting for you."

Green ants and new wine, red clay stove.

The room was as warm as spring. Huangfu Jue was only wearing a heavy purple robe with gold patterns and was drinking by himself.

Seeing her come in, he curled his lips and said lazily, "Are you back? What did you buy?"

He was so indifferent that Yanzhi couldn't help but be stunned.

Somehow, she knew clearly that he was angry. She felt a little uneasy. She put all the bottles and jars she bought earlier in the outer room. She only had a fat clay doll wrapped in tin foil in her hand. After thinking for a while, she put it in front of him and said, "Here you go."

Huangfu Jue looked at its silly face and thought it was very cute, so he couldn't help but paused with his hand holding the glass.

Yanzhi sat opposite him, poured herself a cup, raised her hands, and drank it in one breath, "I just wanted to have fun, don't blame others."

She drank too fast, and her face turned red. Her hair was tied up with a jade crown, and her eyebrows were flying into her temples, which made her look quite handsome. Huangfu Jue watched, and the restlessness that had been clamoring for the whole morning slowly subsided. He sighed and took the cup in front of her, "Eat something to fill your stomach first."

Yanzhi glanced at him stealthily and asked,

"Are you not angry anymore?"

Huangfu Jue glanced at her and said slowly, "After all, he is heartless. It's useless to be angry to death."

Yanzhi blushed as he continued, "Don't sneak out next time."

Yanzhi hummed softly, and suddenly felt an indescribable feeling in her heart.

She dined by herself while Huangfu Jue drank slowly, and there was a very warm and harmonious tacit understanding between the two of them.

This was the first time the two of them had spent time together naturally since Prince Yu's wedding.

Halfway through eating the Yanzhi rice, she suddenly felt hot. She glanced at the charcoal stove, thought for a moment, went back to her room, changed into a thick satin outer robe, and put on a shirt with a four-happiness pattern, paired with moon-white pants, and tied her black hair up high, feeling very refreshed.

When she came out, Huangfu Jue couldn't help but look at her again, "Why is your face so red? Are you sick?"

His hand reached out to Yanzhi, and Yanzhi had no desire to hide. His hand was beautiful, slender and handsome, and it felt very cool when it was placed on her forehead. Yanzhi sighed comfortably.

When his hand moved away, Yanzhi actually felt a little reluctant to leave.

Seeing her watery eyes following him,

Huangfu Jue's heart moved. He slowly drank the wine in the glass and said, "Finish the meal."

Yanzhi responded randomly, picking up the rice in the bowl with chopsticks. She felt a little irritated, but just thirsty, so she picked up the wine glass and took a small sip. The cool liquid flowed down her throat, and she squinted her eyes comfortably.

Huangfu Jue watched calmly, and when she came to take the wine jug again, he blocked it with his hand and said lightly: "Don't drink, you're going to get drunk."

Yanzhi frowned, half leaned over, and reached out to grab it, "How can you be drunk? It's only two glasses."

She had a musk-like scent that was getting stronger and stronger. Huangfu Jue unconsciously let go of her hand.

Yanzhi felt a fire in her heart, warm and comfortable. She supported her chin with her left hand, held the wine glass with her right hand, squinted at Huangfu Jue, "Actually, Daddy is right, you are really good-locking, you are the best-looking man I have ever seen. No wonder you have so many women in your harem, each of them is willing to die for you."

Huangfu Jue raised his eyebrow, "You are getting better and better at speaking."

Yanzhi loosened her collar with her hands, frowned and said, "How strange, why is it getting hotter and hotter?" She shook the wine pot, "Could it be a century-old wine?" She stood up and reached out to take off her coat. Huangfu Jue's eyes darkened, "Be careful not to catch a cold."

Before she finished speaking, Yanzhi had already taken off her outer coat, revealing a tight-fitting jacket made of Songhua silk. She came to Huangfu Jue and almost lay on him. "To be honest, you're not such a bad person. Come, let's have a drink."

Huangfu Jue helped her up, only to feel his touch burning hot, and his eyes slightly turned away, "Yanzhi, stop making trouble."

Yanzhi's long eyelashes flickered, and she stretched out her hands to hold his face over, with their noses almost touching. "Why are you so serious today? Usually... don't you like to touch me?"

Huangfu Jue said in a hoarse voice, "Baby, you are playing with fire."

Yanzhi tilted her head, looking a little puzzled. "Playing with fire?" She sat on his lap naturally, and slid her hand into his collar. She felt the coolness and comfort of the touch. "Why?"

Huangfu Jue's throat slid up and down, and her face was already pressed against him, rubbing against him, and she was sighing in comfort.

He was stunned for only a moment, and Yanzhi had already torn his outer robe into tatters. The room was warm, and he was wearing thin clothes to begin with, and now he was only left with his underwear.

He gritted his teeth and said, "Yanzhi, what did you eat?"

What did you eat? This was Yanzhi's last conscious words.

She didn't eat anything, but just smelled the secret incense of the Paradise Palace, touched the stamens of the butterfly orchid, and drank some wine, and then she was poisoned and lost her mind.

It's very hot, the blood is boiling hot.

She seemed to be running in an endless sea of fire, with flames spewing out of her mouth.

Huangfu Jue soaked her in the bucket, and watched her slide down, her hands and feet thrashing. After a moment's hesitation, he lifted her up again. Her eyes were already confused, and her silver teeth bit her red lips fiercely.

Huangfu Jue looked at her strangely and put his finger to her lips. She immediately opened her mouth and bit it, as if she was crying or biting. Huangfu Jue slowly stroked her hair hesitantly.

He rarely hesitated like this, especially since his lower body was badly swollen.

As the sweet and fishy blood entered her throat, Yanzhi's eyes became slightly clearer. He looked into her eyes, "Yanzhi, who am I?"

Yanzhi shook her head irritably and tried to hold his head down, but he avoided her and asked, "Who am I?"

"...Huangfu Jue..." That little bit of

liquid could no longer satisfy her needs. She just thought he could give her more.

Huangfu Jue held her hand with his backhand, "Very good, you still know who I am. Yanzhi, you have been drugged, and your body cannot be immersed in cold water. I can help you, but you can't blame me afterwards."

Finally I touched his lips, happily taking in more coolness. I dazedly saw a piece of paper, dazedly pressed my handprints on it.

No, still no. She cried softly, what should she do to put out the fire in her heart? Subconsciously, she thought it was him, he made her suffer so much pain. Her pink legs and jade arms all wrapped around her, scratching and biting.

A soft sigh was heard in the dimness.

Her body was then carried away, she let out a sharp cry, and was wrapped in a brocade quilt.

Huangfu Jue whispered to comfort her, "Baby, don't worry." His hands had already torn the bed curtains into pieces and tied her up tightly. A hand slithered in like a snake.

Squeeze, pump/insert, fireworks explode.

Yanzhi only felt that her body was rushing down with the hundred-foot waterfall. The rushing water and the noisy sound of water made her heart feel like it was being pulled by an extremely thin steel wire, and her heart was blocked in her throat.

The turbulent water splashed down the bottom of the pool, and the broken jade splashed and the pearls were dotted. Large handfuls of water mist rose up, like a bunch of white flowers blooming.

Blooming, stretching, falling, a day of flower rain.

She finally managed to scream. It was extremely thin and long, lingering and winding among the flowing clouds and waterfalls.

Brief fainting.

It feels like the peace of the mother's womb.

There are warm water waves rippling gently. Strange disharmony, familiar touch, just want to fall asleep deeply in this tranquility.

Who sighed softly beside her ear, like the breeze lingering on the mountaintop? Who called out softly and anxiously, determined to wake her up from her dream of the moon and flowers?

She insisted on falling into a deep sleep until the familiar flames spread again.

Several lives and deaths, several dreams and awakenings.

When I opened my eyes again, the sun was already setting, casting a thousand-colored shadows on the window screens, giving off a strong sense of spring.

Before Linglong could be surprised, she was stared at by her pair of black eyes.

Stubborn, obstinate, and with a desperate ferocity.

She pulled off the quilt from under her

body and took off her middle clothes in the blink of an eye.

There were bruises all over the ivory-like skin.

Yanzhi stared at the deep and light red, her face pale. A messy picture flashed through her mind quickly.

She climbed down to his lips.

She ripped his clothes at random.

It was wrapped up like a silkworm pupa, groaning and crying…

She bit her lower lip deeply with her silver teeth, forcing back the tears in her eyes. Even though she was ignorant, she knew what the swelling and pain between her legs meant. Since he had to use such a dirty and despicable method! It was ridiculous that she was so naive that she actually believed his oath.

His body seemed to be immersed in a cold pond, but his face was burning hot. His body was tormented by ice and fire, and his heart was filled with resentment, sadness, hatred, disappointment, embarrassment, and other mixed emotions. He wished he could pierce his heart with a sword and break him into thousands of pieces.

Linglong called out anxiously, "Miss, it's not what you think. The emperor, the emperor didn't...he didn't really consummate the marriage with you." Her face turned red, and she hurriedly handed a piece of paper to Yanzhi, "The emperor said that if you wake up and are angry with him, he will give you this paper."

The messy handwriting is vigorous and unrestrained.

I am poisoned by love and suffer from the torment of love. If you help me, I will definitely be grateful and will not be ashamed or angry, resentful or resentful.

Although the two words "Yanzhi" in the signature are crooked, they still have the style of Izumo, and it is undoubtedly her handwriting.

The paper rustled between her fingers. Yanzhi suddenly looked at Linglong. Her cold eyes sparked with sparks. She spoke every word from her lips, "Help? How can he help me get rid of the lustful poison if he hasn't taken my body?"

Linglong's face was so red that blood seemed to be dripping out. She leaned close to Yanzhi's ear and whispered a few words.

Yanzhi's face turned pale and blue, "Where's Huangfu Jue?"

"The Emperor took three showers last night and caught a cold. He is now going to rest."

The author has something to say: I stayed up too late last week and my cervical vertebrae hurt, so Liu Liu broke her promise.

Bow and apologize.

I can't type today because I read the article again. I want to revise it. Find some bugs and cut some branches.

I'd like to recommend a piece of writing

to you all, Ji Yue Jiao Jiao's &ltDon't Escape, Stubborn Princess&gt, it's a very sad and lovable article.

☆、Hike

Yanzhi had a fire in her heart, rolling and rolling, but she couldn't get angry. Her sore limbs reminded her of the absurdity of last night. She stayed in bed all day and ignored everyone.

She thought herself smart in vain, but ended up falling into the hands of a despicable man.

She was totally unaware of the attack, so the flower girl must be the most suspicious. Such a skillful technique, such a top-notch meth, must be someone extraordinary. Either a medical saint or a poison master.

Huangfu Jue!

There wouldn't be such a master around her for no reason. That woman must be related to him.

I was annoyed that he took advantage of everything and pretended to be a gentleman. I believed that the cold shower was also a trick he played to inflict pain on himself.

There were footsteps outside the house, very light and steady. Yanzhi immediately closed her eyes.

There was a low conversation. His voice was slightly hoarse, and he asked her about her daily diet, and then he coughed softly.

He moved to the bedside and stayed there

for a long time.

Yanzhi only felt sweat in her palms and tried to make her breathing even.

She could clearly feel a pair of eyes falling directly on her through the thick curtains. She felt that even the brocade quilt and clothes were exposed. Her body seemed to be crawling with small insects, making her feel itchy and tingling. She wanted to scratch them immediately.

There was a voice in my heart saying loudly, open your eyes, Yanzhi, he bullied you, question him harshly, don't be a coward.

His limbs seemed to have consciousness of his own. No matter how the voice urged him, he just lay there stiffly and could not move.

The footsteps finally sounded again, and there seemed to be a chuckle mixed in with the muffled cough.

Yanzhi immediately became alert. The hateful voice seemed to be at the door, with a thick nasal tone, soft and dragging, "Wake her up later, and have more dinner. The army will leave the city tomorrow, and we will have to sleep outdoors for the next few days."

Although the voice was low, it was not suppressed as before, and she could hear it clearly.

Yiyue lifted the bed curtain and saw a pair of bright and clear eyes, which clearly contained a hint of anger. Knowing that she must have been awake just now, he smiled secretly in his heart, but did not show it on his face. He said softly: "My queen, since you are awake, you must have heard what the emperor said. You will leave the city tomorrow, so you must be in good spirits. According to me, the emperor cannot be blamed this time. Last night, we were waiting outside the house. You used both soft and hard methods, but the emperor still tied you up like a silkworm pupa. He really acted like a saint."

Seeing Yanzhi's cheeks flushed, her eyes were filled with anger and shame. She stopped talking, but said to herself as she brought the clothes: "I never thought that the emperor would be so kind to people."

Yanzhi sneered slightly after hearing this.

He has three thousand rivers, but he will never drink from them. Is such a person worthy of talking about love?

The winding mountain road, the large patches of rhododendrons seemed to be burning the entire mountain, and the convoy was winding like a snake.

As the carriage bumped along, I felt lazy all over. Through the gap in the curtains, I saw a pair of geese flapping their wings in the sea of clouds, and I couldn't help but sigh.

Amidst such ups and downs, Yiyue continued to sew, while Linglong smiled at her from time to time, and seemed to be in a very good mood.

In the evening, the sunset glow spread

layer by layer, and the distant mountains and nearby waters all relaxed in this hazy golden light.

The convoy stopped.

The young guard with bright eyes came over shyly. Yanzhi already knew that he was the captain of the Imperial Guards Shenwu Battalion, named Qin Jian. He seemed to be responsible for her safety. In the past few days, she could see him when she stopped the car to settle down.

He was holding a beautiful little mare in his hand. It was snow-white and had big, gentle eyes like ripe purple grapes in summer.

Yanzhi was overjoyed.

"Grape!"

The filly snorted at her affectionately.

Seeing her running towards him, Qin Jian lowered his head in panic, his face slightly flushed, "Empress, the convoy will be stationed here. In front of us is Luoxia Mountain, the scenery is very beautiful..."

Before he could finish his words, he smelled a faint scent of magnolia. A white hand quickly snatched the reins from his hands, and a white shadow fluttered onto the horse's back.

"Thank you." Her once clear and ethereal voice now had a lively and lively tone. She sat upright on the horse and smiled at him.

"drive--"

"Empress, Empress, come back first!" Yi Yue shouted angrily, but she could not catch up with him. The man and the horse were already ten feet away.

Yanzhi just raised her hand, and her slender fingers drew a beautiful arc in the air.

Yi Yue was so angry that she stamped her feet. She hadn't even changed her clothes yet, but she ran out in her long sleeves and gorgeous skirt. It must be cold on the mountain, so she could only glare at Qin Jian with hatred.

He had quietly mounted his horse and was chasing down the mountain road.

It seemed like he hadn't seen her for a long time. Grape was very excited and ran as fast as she could. Yanzhi lowered her body and held the intricate Suzhou embroidered woolen skirt in front of her. The wind was strong, but the blood in her bones was heating up little by little.

Gradually, red leaves appeared on the roadside. Palm-sized red leaves rolled in the air and hit her face, stinging her painfully. She did not dodge, but just galloped through the sky full of red leaves. The mountain was very quiet, and it seemed that there was only one man and one horse spiraling up the mountain road.

The depression that had been weighing on her heart for days was left behind, and all she could see were the red leaves all over the sky and the vast sky.

Luoxia Mountain is not steep, and can accommodate four horses. The whole mountain is covered with maple trees, clusters of deep red and light red, as delicate as red flowers, bright and eye-catching. Occasionally, the mountain is covered with bluestone walls and green vines.

She and the horse were like a white cloud emerging from a mountain, floating freely in the quiet autumn.

When Huangfu Jue raised his eyes, he was stunned.

The phoenix hairpin and pearl flower had been thrown away somewhere, her black hair fluttered in the wind, and her skirt was lifted in front of her, revealing only her milky white silk pants. She leaned forward, almost sticking to the horse's back, and rushed straight towards him.

A pair of eyes, however, are surprisingly bright. They are as sparkling as the surface of a lake that has just been broken, and as cool as a new mirror that has just been opened. They contain the spiritual energy of mountains and rivers, and carry infinite charm.

The sound of horse hooves seems to be stepping on my heart.

Unconsciously, a smile appeared on his lips. Huangfu Jue shook the reins, and the jade dragon under him took a few steps and stopped across the road.

Seeing him, Yanzhi was just slightly stunned. Grape must have been brought out by Qin Jian under his instruction. She already knew he would be here. She pulled the reins and Grape slowed down. Three feet away, it stopped.

The haze that had just dissipated came back quietly when he saw him. He frowned, glanced at him, and snorted softly, "The ghost is still there."

In her seventeen years, she had never met such a man, who was both good and evil, hot and cold, and seemed careless, but he was very thorough in many matters. She hated him so much that her teeth itched, but she couldn't find a place to bite.

Huangfu Jue saw her standing there awkwardly, swinging the small horsewhip with her slender hands, frowning slightly, with a natural and silly smile in her eyes.

Yulong took a few steps to her side, and before he could speak, he put his fist to his lips, coughed a few times, and then sighed: "If you don't look at her, you'd think she's a wild girl who ran away from a family."

Yanzhi just glanced at him.

When she was riding the horse, she felt the blood rushing up. When she stopped, she felt the mountain wind invade her body and shivered. "A-choo—"

Her waist suddenly tightened, and she was carried by Huangfu Jue to his horse. The cloak with a fox fur collar covered her head.

"Don't move!" Huangfu Jue frowned, and put his cloak around him to cover her carefully. When he was so close, he realized that his touch was cold.

The warm masculine scent, mixed with a hint of ambergris, made Yanzhi anxious. "Huangfu Jue--" he struggled hard, but could only buy himself a few inches of space. His arm was like an iron hoop, unable to advance or retreat.

Huangfu Jue lowered his eyes and let her make a fuss. When the cold air on her body dissipated a little, he spoke lightly, "I can let you go. If you get sick, I will take the life of your maid in Weiyang Palace. Every day you are not well, there will be one less person."

Yan Zhi was extremely angry and glared at him fiercely. She met his gaze directly, and there was a rare serious look in his eyes. Her lips were pursed, and the color of her lips was dull and pale.

It seems that his cold has not yet healed.

Her heart was in a mess, his slender fingers were clasped around her waist, his hands were extremely beautiful, clear and powerful. She couldn't help but think of the madness of that night.

She was not completely oblivious to that extreme pain and pleasure.

The person in his arms suddenly became quiet. Huangfu Jue was slightly surprised. Seeing her cheeks turn light red, his heart moved and his slanted phoenix eyes were shining.

"Huangfu Jue," Yanzhi suddenly asked, "Did you send secret guards to follow me?"

Huangfu Jue's eyes flickered and he smiled slightly, "Good idea. If you are always so disobedient, setting up secret guards will be a precaution."

Yanzhi snorted softly, and after a while she said calmly, "The flower girl I met on the road yesterday was very suspicious. She might be the one who drugged me."

Huangfu Jue patted her head and said, "Don't worry, I'm here."

Yulong walked back slowly.

The sky is full of red leaves.

The man's eyes were slanting, his temperament was noble, and his expression was doting; the woman's eyes were slightly angry, and besides being cold, she had a natural aura and charm. The two rode side by side, seemingly intimate, but the woman's back was straight.

Li Luo looked at the two people from afar, her eyes as deep as water.

Yulong passed by her without raising his eyes. Yanzhi turned around as if she wanted to say something, but was blocked by Dede's horse hoof.

A red leaf fell, reflecting the sparkling pearl on her neck and the snow-white fox fur in her hand. Her hands were shaking, and Qin Jian wanted to pull up the reins to catch up, but he looked back at her worriedly.

Li Luo looked at him coldly, kicked the horse hard in the belly, and the horse rushed out like an arrow.

The author has something to say: My mother-in-law is sick, the children are too noisy, and I am exhausted.
Sometimes I really want to give up, but I am still obsessed.
Even if this book is not separated from my flesh and blood, it is the result of my heart and soul and I cannot bear to part with it.
And to my dear readers, this is all my motivation.
Liu Liu will never give up!

☆、Night Banquet

When we reached the foot of the mountain, we could see bonfires, people coming and going, and the strong smell of meat wafting over in the wind.
The place where we will camp tonight is an open plain in front of Luoxia Mountain. Outside is the bronze chariot, and the black arrows have a cold metallic texture. The cavalry and infantry form a huge semicircle, surrounding the dragon chariot.
The soldiers were in armor and did not kneel before the king. Wherever they walked, red tassels fluttered on their lowered helmets.
Huangfu Jue avoided the crowd and sent her back to her tent. When he let her off the horse, he leaned over and plucked a dry leaf from her hair. His dark eyes were full of teasing, "Wild girl, go back and wash up

quickly, the dinner is about to start." His tone was intimate and natural, and his doting was obvious.

Yanzhi quickly raised her eyes to look at him with a strange expression, and it was unclear whether she was angry or happy, and she didn't say a word.

Linglong and the others had been waiting outside for a long time and escorted her into the tent.

After drinking a bowl of ginger honey water, her complexion became rosy. Linglong put aside her worries and said angrily, "My queen, it's not the same outside as at home. You ran out without caring about anything. What if you catch a cold? If it weren't for the emperor, you would really want to kill me!"

As they were talking, Yiyue brought in the jewelry box. Seeing Yanzhi's lazy expression and drooping eyelids, she exchanged glances with Linglong and said with a smile, "Madam, I just saw Qin Jian and his men carrying a huge elk. They said that the Marquis had shot it and it will be the main meal tonight."

Yanzhi hummed softly.

Daddy can kill a tiger alive, so he can hunt anything. I should be able to see him at the dinner party. It will be too late if I don't talk about it now.

Seeing that Yanzhi had perked up, Yiyue secretly winked at Linglong, and they both worked together. In just one stick of incense, they had finished applying Yanzhi. She wore a simple horse-like bun, with three silver hairpins inlaid with jadeite, grass bugs and gemstones on each side, and a crabapple flower was drawn on her forehead with silver powder. She wore a brocade dress with colorful satin and hundreds of flowers, and a silver-white belt with gold-rimmed and oriental pearls. She was graceful and elegant, like a bright moon shining brightly.

After the makeup was done, the two were very satisfied. Yiyue sighed, "Your Majesty is worthy of being called the most beautiful woman in the country."

Linglong smiled without saying a word, her expression full of pride.

Yanzhi said calmly: "No matter how beautiful it is, it is only skin deep and will return to dust sooner or later." She glanced at the two of them and said, "You two are a little weird." Especially Linglong, who often looked at her and smiled these days.

Yiyue touched her face and pretended to be nervous, "What's weird? Eyebrow color or foundation?"

Her mischief reminded Yanzhi of Linglong, "Where's Li Luo? I just saw her."

Linglong snorted heavily, "We asked her to deliver the clothes, but she ran away in a hurry. Who knows where she is now?" She had a gloomy face all day long, and was alienated from everyone. She sat in the carriage with the servants. Because she was good at riding, she was allowed to chase after her. Unexpectedly, the clothes were not delivered, and she disappeared. It was really getting more and more outrageous.

Yanzhi was silent and thoughtful after hearing this, with a hint of loneliness in her eyes.

Li Luo, actually had such an obsession. Just now on the mountain, she clearly saw her eyes, hurt, stubborn, and unbelievable. She was nakedly accusing her of betrayal.

She stood up and said calmly, "Let's go."

Open air barbecue.

Huangfu Jue occupied the main seat, leaving Concubine Qi to serve wine. Yanzhi and Wang Yan sat on the left and right, respectively, sitting with their father.

The emperor's holy will is that regardless of whether they are the monarch or the subject, they should only talk about family relationships.

The bonfire was blazing, and the faces of the people were all red. All the people present were his loyal subjects, drinking from golden cups and eating meat with great pleasure. The feast was filled with joy.

Yan Yanzi looked indifferent, but he had drunk the wine from the glass. His eyes were surprisingly bright, and when he looked at Yan Zhi, one could see the tenderness in them.

Yanzhi sat beside him and asked for a charcoal barbecue herself, leaving Yiyue's carefully dressed-up to Liushui.

Next to her father, she still seems to be that naughty and clever little girl.

Yan Yanzi looked at the extra black skewers of meat on the plate, a hint of smile in her eyes, and bit them slowly in her hands.

Yanzhi looked at him nervously, "Daddy, can I eat it?"

Yan Yanzi touched her head and nodded with a smile.

There were twinkling stars in Yanzhi's eyes, and she smiled slowly after a while.

Opposite the two of them was the Chief Censor Kong Zeqing, the Grand Secretary of the Palace, and the President of the Royal White Deer Academy. Although they were in the wild, he was still dressed in a tall hat and a wide belt. He did not touch the food and wine in front of him. He clenched his fists, trembled with his lips, and stared at Yan Yanzi straight, as if he was eager to stand up.

Wang Shouren put his hands in his sleeves and smiled, "The Queen and I are indeed a father and daughter with deep affection."

Kong Zeqing panted heavily, "It's inappropriate, inappropriate!"

Wang Shouren smiled at him and said, "Sir, please speak carefully in front of His Majesty."

Kong Zeqing's face suddenly turned red. Just as he was about to speak, Yan Yanzi raised his head and glanced at him unintentionally, his eyes gleaming with a sharp edge. He had been killing for many years, and his murderous aura had almost become real. Kong Zeqing felt like ice and snow, his mind was lost, and he forced himself to say something. For a long time, his face was pale, and he kept saying, "Man...man..."

Wang Shouren laughed out loud and raised the golden cup, "My Lord, I offer you a toast. Zhishang guarded the northern border and won nine battles in a row. My Lord, you have taught your son well!"

You are good at educating your sons, but what about educating your daughters?

Her Yanzhi face remained expressionless, her wide sleeves with phoenix pattern were loosely rolled up, revealing her fair white undershirt, and she was concentrating on flipping the row of skewers of meat in front of her.

Yan Yanzi smiled slightly and drank the wine in the glass, with infinite satisfaction in his eyes, "Your Majesty is right, Yan's greatest pride in life is these two children."

Kong Zeqing stood up tremblingly, and said with great sorrow: "My Lord, this is wrong. The Queen Mother has entered the East Palace. She is the mother of a country and the master of all concubines. You and she are the monarch and the minister. How can you still regard it as an ordinary father-daughter relationship!"

He was a veteran of three dynasties, and

had served three generations of emperors and empresses. Which one of them was not virtuous, kind, and graceful? Who had ever seen such a willful and unruly empress?

It is not the blessing of the country, it is not the blessing of the country!

Yanzhi burst into laughter, her eyes were as clear as glass, and she spoke slowly, "Are you teaching me a lesson? The emperor has already said that tonight we will only talk about human relations. You don't even follow the emperor's will, so how can you openly criticize the ministers?"

She was smiling and talking happily, with a childish look on her face, but her words were extremely cold and showed no mercy at all.

Kong Zeqing was shocked and angry. He stumbled to his knees in front of Huangfu Jue's desk and said in a hoarse voice: "Your Majesty, this old minister..."

Huangfu Jue had been looking at Yanzhi with a smile, and finally spoke up, saying slowly, "The elder is drunk, go down and have a rest."

Kong Zeqing's eyes widened, and he was in great pain. He had never drunk a drop of alcohol, so how could he be drunk? Gu Yong came up and wanted to make a direct remonstrance. However, he could only call out "Your Majesty" before being dragged away by Haigui and his men.

Huangfu Jue's black eyes seemed to be smiling, his gaze slowly passed over everyone's faces, and he said lazily, "The autumn dew is cold, why not drink a few more cups."

His tone was slow, but everyone felt a chill in their hearts, and they raised their glasses quickly. Qingliu sighed in his heart, saying that Kong Ge was talented and famous, and his career was prosperous, but now it was probably over.

The dragon has a reverse scale that cannot be touched.

In the past, Lin Yujian, the Grand Secretary of Longtu Pavilion, and twelve people from the Zhongshumenxia jointly submitted a memorial, stating that the empress did not cultivate virtues as a woman and was incapable of managing the harem, and they earnestly requested that she be deposed.

The emperor only said one thing: What does my family affairs have to do with you?

Within half a month, these twelve people committed crimes one after another and disappeared from the court. Although the Yan family was powerful, they could not cover up everything without the emperor's approval.

Unexpectedly, the flood of the Yan family drowned all the veterans of three dynasties. Many people were looking at her, most of them were cautious and tentative, only Zhengzhong's gaze was the most unscrupulous. Yanzhi just focused on the skewers in front of her, occasionally chatting with Yan

Yanzi.

The maids presented the golden roasted deer legs, and Jinlan's figure danced past. Yan Yanzi leaned over to help her cut the meat, and heard her say very softly, "Daddy, on October 13, I'm going to Wutuo Mountain."

The silver-engraved knife easily cut the meat into even small pieces. Yan Yanzi looked at her deeply and said in a gentle voice, "Eat it."

The delicious venison tasted like chewing wax in her mouth, so she frowned and swallowed it slowly. When she looked up inadvertently, she met Huangfu Jue's slightly raised eyes, which were full of interest. He beckoned her, wanting her to come over.

She frowned, unwilling to give up the rare comfort around her, and wanted to ignore it, but Huangfu Jue's voice sounded immediately, "Queen, I also want to try your cooking skills."

She was only a few steps away from Huangfu Jue, but there was a gaze following her like a shadow. She didn't need to look back to know that it must be filled with naked jealousy and resentment.

The man in front of her had bright eyes and a smile on his face, but he pushed her to the forefront step by step.

The author has something to say: Thank you all for your support, woooo, Liu Liu can only bow deeply and keep writing to try to repay your maintenance.

A stable update should be possible next.

☆、Bath

Someone had already placed a rose chair next to the throne. Yanzhi simply walked to the throne and placed the black gold tray in front of Huangfu Jue.

Huangfu Jue looked at the blackened skewers of meat, making a smacking sound with his mouth, but his hand reached out from under the black lacquered wooden table and grabbed a corner of her skirt.

Unable to turn around, Yanzhi glared at him angrily, but Huangfu Jue pretended not to see him. He held an iron rod and looked it up and down, as if hesitating whether he should eat it.

The stalemate lasted too long, and I just felt that the laughter of the crowd had subsided a little.

Yanzhi suddenly smiled, as bright as the first moon breaking through the clouds. She leaned her hands on the table and said, "Your Majesty, don't you want to try it?" She slightly suspended her left foot and kicked upwards fiercely.

A strange look flashed across Huangfu Jue's eyes, and the corners of his lips curled up slightly. Looking at Yanzhi's eyes, he felt an indescribable weirdness, and his heart was in chaos. It was dangerous!

One kick missed.

The slender ankles were tightly held.

A rosy blush appeared on her cheeks, and her pearl-like eyes were filled with shame and anger as she stared at him.

Let go!

No—let go! He stared at her lips and said silently with a smile.

The low laughter suddenly became louder, and even the hearty laughter of a military officer could be clearly heard.

A drop of sweat slowly seeped out from the tip of her straight nose. If eyes could kill, there would be thousands of transparent holes on his body.

A smile gently seeped into her eyes, and as soon as he loosened his hold, the small lotus feet broke free like a swimming fish.

Before she could feel relieved, his face suddenly leaned closer and his expression was serious, "Shh, don't move." His thumb gently rubbed the corner of her eye, wiping away a little black mark.

"Dirty little cat." He murmured.

Being so close and slightly tipsy, she could clearly see deep into his eyes, where her figure was.

The eyes were like black jade, with soft ripples, and there seemed to be a very small whirlpool, so deep that it seemed to drown people.

"Bang!" The colored glass shattered to the ground. The imperial concubine said in a gentle and proud voice, "It's okay, my hand slipped for a moment."

Yanzhi's heart trembled, and she

immediately took a few steps back.

Huangfu Jue watched the tenderness in her eyes disappear in an instant, and returned to his seat without any reluctance, the smile on his lips slowly dissipating. He turned his head slightly and met Wang Yan's passionate and painful gaze. He smiled casually, "Yan'er, how can you be so careless!"

A clever maid beside him offered him wine as red as agate. He smiled and picked up the glass, motioning to Wang Shouren. He never looked at her again.

Yanzhi didn't live to see the end of the banquet.

Yan Yanzi almost drank the wine, but he kept an eye on her. When he heard her sneeze, he apologized to Huangfu Jue and insisted that she go back to rest.

That night, I really had a stuffy throat and nasal congestion.

Yanzhi was so angry that Huangfu Jue sent three imperial doctors but none of them could cure her. When the fourth doctor came to Huangfu Jue with his head covered, the emperor sighed and said, "Let her be."

When everything was in harmony, the eighth-generation monarch of □□ secretly broke into the house to pick flowers.

Yanzhi glared at the man who casually took off his shoes and got on her couch, and gritted her teeth and said, "Huangfu Jue, what are you doing?"

Huangfu Jue tucked her quilt tightly and

put his hand on her forehead. "I came to see you. My silly girl got angry and scolded four imperial doctors away. I had to come and see you. Well, why are you angry?"

In the dark night, his deep voice was like flowing water, with a peaceful rhythm and tenderness.

Why are you so angry?

The imperial doctors were all trembling with fear, saying that she was weak and timid and should just rest. They sighed and were extremely anxious because it was just a gust of wind.

Naturally she would be angry.

She remained silent, her lips pursed stubbornly, but he could easily see through her disguised strength and said slowly, "As for the imperial physician, you should think of a way out for everything. You should treat one point of illness as five points, and don't take their words to heart." He pinched her cheek gently, "I will always make you fat, accompany me for fifty years, and go to see the scenery of various countries."

Scorn slowly surfaced in Yanzhi's eyes. Fifty years, what a hell!

"I'm sleepy, please do as you please." He buried his head in the quilt and closed his eyes.

The darkness is thick and confusing, but consciousness becomes clearer.

I felt a warm touch on my head. After I

moved away, I heard him sigh with a smile, "What should I do? You're still a little coward."

For a long time, the room was silent.

There was a long lasting fragrance in the car.

The lavender tuberose was sealed in a crystal bottle with a slender neck, and the fragrance diffused from the mouth of the bottle.

This was found by her pillow this morning. When she opened her eyes, she looked into the numerous flower stamens, rolling with tiny, crystal clear night dewdrops.

She had clearly thrown it out of the window, but I don't know who picked it up and kept it with such great care.

The journey was very tight that day, and the lunch was hastily eaten in the car. Yanzhi was in a daze and felt drowsy in the car. Occasionally opening her eyes, she saw the long, oblique purple petals reflecting a hazy luster in the refraction of the crystal.

There is a magical beauty in her dignity, something he would like.

In the evening, they left Imjin Pass.

The wind suddenly became stronger, and sand and stones flew onto the hood of the car. There was always a particularly bumpy section of the road. Yiyue and Linglong could do nothing, so they just chatted. They were afraid that she would sleep too much and have a hard time at night, so they always talked about her.

Yiyue was originally from the south and had never left Shengjing since she entered the palace. She almost held her breath while listening to the sound of the wind outside the car. "Miss, this wind is too terrible. It seems like there is a child crying."

Yanzhi closed her eyes and said in a tired voice, "This is nothing. The real strong winds in the north can blow away herds of cattle and sheep, and even tents."

Yiyue's eyes widened. "Really? We won't run into each other, will we?"

Linglong smiled and pulled her over, "Don't be afraid, sister will protect you." Yiyue spat lightly and scolded, "Whose sister are you?" The two of them laughed together.

Linglong was tickled by Yiyue until her whole body went limp, panting and calling out "gocd sister" repeatedly. Yiyue let her go and asked Yanzhi quietly, "Miss, is the wind really that strong?"

Yanzhi's lips curved up and she smiled and nodded. Yiyue closed her eyes and chanted Amitabha.

Of course there is wind that can blow away people and animals, but it is in the desolate Gobi Desert north of the Tianshan Mountains. There are also the most simple and hospitable Volkhan people, and the hot Shaodaozi wine.

In such a closed carriage, the whimpering of the wind can still be clearly heard. Such bad weather is not suitable for traveling, but the bugle to stop the advance has not sounded. Yanzhi was puzzled and couldn't help but open her eyes, "Yiyue, go ask where they are going to camp."

Yiyue nodded and went to the front of the carriage to ask the driver. The wind was too loud and she could only hear the people outside shouting their answers. Yiyue turned around and frowned, "Your Majesty, they don't know either. They said they had asked for instructions, but there has been no instructions from above."

Yanzhi hummed and guessed in her heart which camping site they might choose.

When the emperor goes on tour, defense is the most important thing. Water, swamps, and mountains are not acceptable. And in this kind of weather, Dad is also in a dilemma.

The wind was getting stronger and stronger, and they waited in silence. When the carriage finally stopped and Qin Jian announced that the tents were ready and asked the queen to move, Yanzhi clearly heard Yiyue and the others let out a long sigh.

After a day of riding in the carriage, it was hard to stay alert. Yanzhi ate a few mouthfuls of food and went to bed.

Haigui suddenly asked for a meeting outside the tent. When he came in, he bowed and said that the emperor had found a rare item in front and asked the queen to move aside.

Yanzhi let her hair down, her long black

hair all fell to her chest. She supported her chin with her hand and yawned slightly. "Reply to your master, just tell him I'm asleep and we'll see tomorrow."

Haigui smiled and said, "Your Majesty, the army will have to leave tomorrow. I have prepared the phoenix chariot, which will be here soon." He was a smart man and good at flattery, so he was so humble this time that he could not help but nodded.

The wind died down, but the chill was strong. Wrapped in a rouge, I could feel the phoenix chariot going up and down, as if it was going up a mountain road.

Not long after they had traveled, the sedan chair touched the ground and someone whispered, "Your Highness, we've arrived."

Yanzhi waited for a while, but no one came forward to serve her. It was quiet all around, with only the rustling of the jungle and the chirping of mountain birds.

Yanzhi was suspicious, but she smelled a very familiar fragrance. She just snorted in her heart and closed her eyes without saying anything.

Sure enough, someone laughed quietly, and a hand reached into the tent. The dragon-patterned obsidian ring on the little finger took Yanzhi's hand and said, "Madam, please get off the sedan."

The corners of her lips unconsciously raised, and she said angrily, "You are playing tricks." As soon as she stepped out of the sedan chair, her eyes were covered by the wide sleeves.

Huangfu Jue whispered in her ear: "Don't peek, your husband is going to perform magic. One, two, three, to the left; four, five, six, to the right..."

Yanzhi followed him in a daze, and unknowingly became curious. When he suddenly left, she couldn't help but hold her breath.

There was a pool filled with mist, and outside it were piles of jade stones. Within a few steps, there were lush grass and colorful fallen petals.

There is actually a hot spring here!

Because of it, the small area is as warm as spring. Although it is almost winter, there are still flowers blooming.

She was still in a daze, and Huangfu Jue had already stolen a kiss on her lips, his black eyes smiling deeply, "Madam, do you like this gift from your husband?"

Changshan is covered with white wax like an elephant, Tianchi is separated by mist like a poet. The clouds on the building lift the curtain to reveal the sun, and the hot spring water washes the fat.

The author has something to say: Ahem, the beauty is about to come out of the bath, ladies and gentlemen, the curtain is still drawn, do you want to open it?

Ding ding ding, the rich ones support the show with money, the people support the show with people, the ones with flowers smash the flowers, the ones with bricks hit the bricks...

☆、Hearing the Flute

There is actually a hot spring here!
Because of it, the small area is as warm as spring. Although it is almost winter, there are still flowers blooming.
She was still in a daze, and Huangfu Jue had already stolen a kiss on her lips, his black eyes smiling deeply, "Madam, do you like this gift from your husband?"
Changshan is covered with white wax like an elephant, Tianchi is separated by mist like a poet. The clouds on the building lift the curtain to reveal the sun, and the hot spring water washes the fat.
The hot spring was bubbling and bubbling, with a faint sulfur smell that was too familiar. Yanzhi couldn't help but take two steps forward.
Deerskin boots stepped on the soft grass, and the fragrance of wild flowers hit the hem of the skirt. There was a thin mist in the mountains, and the water in front of me was sparkling. I scooped water in my hands, and it was warm and smooth.
In such a mountainous area, there is an open-air hot spring formed by the gushing earth energy.
Yanzhi's eyes sparkled, and she turned around and smiled, "Your Majesty, please call Linglong over."
With the help of this hot spring, she can

regulate her body and not be afraid of the future journey.

Huangfu Jue shook his head, picked up a stone by the spring and sat down, looking at her with interest without blinking, making it clear that he didn't want to leave.

Yanzhi was stunned, then she felt ashamed and angry, and glared at him fiercely. After struggling for a while, she couldn't resist the desire deep in her heart, and slowly pulled open the silk belt around her waist.

Huangfu Jue raised his eyes, obviously surprised, and then smiled endlessly.

Yanzhi held the belt in her hand, walked up to him, and said with a hint of arrogance in her voice, "Close your eyes."

The long ribbons fluttered in the wind, as soft as algae in the water.

Huangfu Jue really closed his eyes.

The silk brocade belt went around her eyes, covering her charming eyes. Her fingertips were tied into a complicated knot.

Huangfu Jue tilted his head quietly with a smile on his face.

The moonlight broke through the clouds and shone on his face, making his cheeks look almost transparent, ethereal and soft.

Yanzhi stared at him for a moment with a complicated expression.

She couldn't guess his mind, couldn't understand his intentional or unintentional feelings, and couldn't understand her own bitter and confusing mood.

How could it be such a coincidence that there was a hot spring in the camp. Since he didn't say anything, she pretended to know nothing. The army marched against the wind and camped at the foot of the mountain, which had nothing to do with her.

The sky is as black as ink, and the stars' eyes are tired.

Her figure is extremely graceful in the hazy water vapor, her white hands spin lightly, her frosty feet play in the water, just like a lotus blooming in the water.

A man lies on his back on the bluestone beside the spring, with his head resting on his head. He has a clear and elegant demeanor and a carefree mood.

These mountains and these waters are full of vitality and elegance because of these two people.

The moon is idle, the flowers are falling, and the years are quiet and good.

The sound of water was sparse, Yanzhi was humming softly, and the smile on Huangfu Jue's face never faded.

The valley was silent when suddenly a flute sounded. The sound was vague and hard to detect at first, but gradually became clear. The white moon shines, the bright moon casts a shadow, and the song "Autumn Lake Moon Night" is played. The music has a twist and turn, and the fingering is good, but it lacks a sense of tranquility and remoteness, and has a sense of emptiness and desolation.

Huangfu Jue sat up and looked directly at Yanzhi. Although his eyes were bound, he could still hear the sound and tell where she was. He asked calmly, "What's wrong?"

The rouge quickly broke through the water. The water dripped from the ends of her hair, and her fingers tried hard to tie the belt of her underwear, but she couldn't do it. There was only one voice in her heart shouting frantically: How could it be him, how could it be him! How could he be here, how could he...

Huangfu Jue was silent for a moment, and still smiled when he spoke, "You finished washing so quickly? I thought..." He slowly approached, and the air was filled with a scent similar to the fragrance of flowers, which became stronger and stronger. "I will sleep outdoors in the deserted mountains tonight."

Yanzhi clutched her clothes tightly, her consciousness suddenly scattered. His words seemed so close yet so far away, she could hear every word clearly, but she couldn't make out the meaning. She looked at him, at a loss.

Huangfu Jue raised his chin slightly and called out tentatively, "Rosy?" His fingers had already reached for the silk ribbon above his eyes.

Yanzhi held his hand tightly, and said after a while, "We're done washing, let's go back, I want to go back."

Her voice trembled uncontrollably, and her fingertips were cold. He paused for a moment, then exerted force with his fingers and palms, causing the pieces of silk to fly everywhere.

The pain and despair in her eyes had not yet faded, and she looked straight into his slanted phoenix eyes. Her face was sad and dejected.

Huangfu Jue's eyes turned cold, and he quickly embraced her in his arms, holding her tightly and holding her across his knees. He grabbed her slender bare ankles and roughly put on shoes and socks. He narrowed his eyes and looked at her fiercely, "What are you crazy about?"

Yanzhi closed her eyes, the sound of the flute was still clear and distant.

At this moment, she just wanted to run away. She would rather go crazy than suffer this awake. She leaned her head on Huangfu Jue's shoulder and said in a low voice, "My head hurts. It hurts so much."

Huangfu Jue was silent for a while, then said slowly: "You deserve the pain for running out like this without caring about anything." He stopped talking, held her and sat down, tied the fox fur coat around her, and wiped her hair carefully with a towel.

Yanzhi was upset and knew that she had revealed her identity too much. He acted as if nothing had happened, but she must have been suspicious. After thinking for a while, she forced herself to speak, "Isn't the mountain closed? Where does the flute sound come from?"

Huangfu Jue used his fingers as a comb, sliding them slowly down her hair. A faint white vapor rose where his fingers passed.

When her hair was half dry, she broke off a peach branch, and with her fingers as sharp as knives, she cut it into a long hairpin and tied her hair up loosely.

He looked focused, as if he hadn't heard what she said.

He tucked the last strand of hair behind her ear, and slowly stroked her cheek with his fingertips before he sighed with satisfaction.

The flute sound was lingering, rising and falling at the high point, mournful and mournful, like the blood-crying of a cuckoo or the wailing of a monkey.

Huangfu Jue looked past her to the vast mountains, and said with a smile, "'Thinking of the years in the mountains and seas, the solitary light shines on oneself, and the heart and liver are as cold as ice and snow'. This person is playing alone in the mountains, and I am afraid he is also a heartbroken person. If you want to see him, I will try to invite him to show up."

Yanzhi was startled, staring at him with wide eyes, and said in panic, "No, I don't want to... I don't know who he is... um..."

Huangfu Jue had already grabbed her chin fiercely, and his lips pressed down with a rage that could destroy the world. Yanzhi was already stunned, and only when the tip of her tongue was sucked over did she know how to resist.

Huangfu Jue tightly held her waist, forcing her to get close to him, and ravaged her with his lips and tongue. Yanzhi finally regained her sanity in the midst of the storm. Huangfu Jue was really angry. Apart from her weak struggle, she was only filled with fear and anxiety.

An unknown amount of time had passed before Huangfu Jue, breathing softly against her forehead, his eyes dark and cold, wind blades raging, said slowly: "I hate people lying to me the most. Yanzhi, you never need to lie to me." He put her on the stone and stood up.

Yan Zhi was startled. Seeing his fingers clasped together, she knew he was going to call someone. However, she could not let him see Ye Zi no matter what. She jumped up and grabbed his hand, and said hurriedly: "Huangfu Jue, I just feel that the song is familiar, not for the person who plays the flute. Even if it is someone I know, it is a thing of the past."

He looked up at her with a strange expression, half-smiled, and said slowly: "Really? Is it over?"

Yanzhi's face was miserable, and her voice was urgent and fast, "Yes, yes, I told you a long time ago, have you forgotten?"

He was extremely upset. Why was he here? It

was still a thousand miles to Tianshan. October 13 was coming soon. Why wasn't he in Tianshan?

She was so stubborn, almost looking at him with hatred. Her lips were reddened by his kiss, and tears were faintly visible in the depths of her eyes. Huangfu Jue looked at her, his eyes gradually softened, and he held her hand tightly with his backhand, "As long as you say it, I will believe it." He raised his hand to straighten the wooden hairpin in her hair, and smiled slightly, "Let's go back."

As he spoke, he tucked his right hand behind his back, formed a circle with his thumb and index finger, and shook it three times quickly.

Yanzhi was almost stunned as he pulled her for a few steps. He let her go so easily, which made her even more uneasy.

I didn't realize it when I was climbing up, but although the mountain is not high, it is extremely difficult to walk on. There are protruding rocks on the narrow road, and I have to be careful at every step.

All the palace servants who were carrying the sedan chair disappeared. Huangfu Jue squatted down, turned around and smiled at her, "Come on, I'll carry you."

He was so excited, it was obvious that he had planned it all along. Yanzhi was stunned for a moment, and said nothing, silently leaning behind him. She didn't have the strength to walk down the mountain, and didn't want to talk anymore. Perhaps deep down, she also began to rely on the warmth he gave her.

She was so well-behaved and obedient, holding his shoulders with both hands, her body was fragrant and soft, Huangfu Jue's eyes darkened, and the corners of his lips slowly curled up. He carried her lightly and went down the mountain step by step steadily. He smiled and said, "You girl, you look so thin, but I didn't expect you to be so heavy."

No one behind him said anything, only the long hair fluttered to his nose, itching him so much that he couldn't help but sneeze. Yanzhi burst out laughing.

Huangfu Jue pretended to be angry and said, "How dare you do such mischief!" He tickled her thighs with his fingers. Yanzhi giggled and kicked her legs against him.

Huangfu Jue was suddenly excited and let out a clear whistle. He then flew over the rocks like green smoke.

Yanzhi didn't dare to move anymore. She hugged his neck tightly with both hands, but she made a hoarse sound.

Huangfu Jue laughed out of anger. This little girl actually treated him as a mount. As the camp approached, Huangfu Jue slowed down and called out softly, "Yanzhi?"

"Um?"

Huangfu Jue listened to her delicate and lazy nasal voice, and the corners of his lips curled up slightly, "In the whole world, there is only you."

"What?" His voice was so low that it was almost a whisper.

Huangfu Jue pointed a finger at her forehead and said, "I mean, you are so lucky to be able to ride a real dragon as a mount."

Yanzhi snorted complacently.

Seeing the figure, Huangfu Jue put her down. Yanzhi smiled and bowed. Huangfu Jue looked at her deeply and said, "It's not as sad as you imagined, right?" Yanzhi's smile gradually disappeared, and she was stunned. He suddenly pointed at her heart and stared at her, "I'll wait for you to empty it."

The author has something to say: I dare not make any more promises and can only bury my head in writing. Seeing everyone urging me to write more, I feel really ashamed.

You're too slow to warm up, I can't stand it myself, Master and Brother, please bubble up quickly.

☆、Emperor's Wrath

He stood there, slender and graceful, his eyes slanting, looking at her gently and firmly, his eyes deep, as if countless stars were twinkling. His index finger lightly pointed at her chest.

Yanzhi, empty your heart.

Yanzhi stared at him in a daze. He was indeed a very handsome man. In terms of appearance alone, his master and senior brothers were slightly inferior to him. His actions were all graceful. If she said that she had never been moved by him, she would be deceiving herself. However, ——

He could never give her what she wanted.

Taking a deep breath, she smiled softly and bowed again, "Yanzhi's heart is too small. Even if it is empty, it can't hold an emperor. It's late at night. I have to go back. Linglong must be waiting anxiously. Your Majesty, please take a rest."

He took two steps back and turned around resolutely.

Huangfu Jue watched her leave, his eyes dark and dark. After a while, he slowly raised the corners of his lips, mocking and cold.

"Master," the man in black appeared out of nowhere and knelt before him.

"How?" Her eyes slowly moved over his shoulder, and her words were spoken softly and charmingly.

"It is the Zhoutian Great Freedom Sword of the Snow Mountain lineage. It should be the young master of the Ye family in the South China Sea. There is also a woman beside him. It seems that she passed by unintentionally. She was not kept."

The hand that was stroking the ring paused, as if muttering to himself, "...woman?" His dark eyes suddenly showed interest, "What are the casualties?"

"Three dead and two injured. Night Owl lost one arm and stabbed the woman with a sword."

"Where is the injury?"

The man in black was silent, "...It seems to be wounded in the right chest."

Her phoenix eyes narrowed slightly, her expression was very happy, she glanced at the man in black, and uttered two words from her red lips, "Idiot!" Her slender jade-like fingers touched her forehead, and she sighed, "Ye Xiao is still the one who pleases me the most. Leave this matter to her, and come back to me after it is done."

"yes."

Huangfu Jue raised the corners of his lips, and his fingers wandered around his neck. The sword light chilled the sixteen states, and here, the coldness of the sword seemed to still remain.

"Dong", the black hair fluttered, brushed past the cheek, and went three inches into the wall.

His eyes were crazy, staring at him intently, "My name is Ye Zi."

The mouth opened and closed silently, and Ye——Zi——suddenly burst into silent laughter, with a look of mockery on his face.

For the next three days, the sky was clear and the weather was fresh, but Huangfu Jue ordered the army to stay where they were and only took his men to hunt outside the city.

Yan Yanzi made several remonstrations, but he just laughed it off.

On the evening of the third day, senior military generals including Yan Yanzi were summoned.

Huangfu Jue stood beside the marching map with his hands behind his back and said slowly, "I have decided to change the route to the northwest, cross the Yellow River from Xingling and go straight to Youyun."

Yan Yanzi's expression changed drastically after hearing this, and he stamped his feet and said, "Your Majesty, this is absolutely not possible. Changninggu has already made preparations to receive you, and the route must not be changed without permission."

Huangfu Jue just smiled and said nothing, glancing at Wang Yulan.

The Wang family has been a family of aristocrats for centuries and has always disdained the military. Wang Yulan is considered the first person to do so in decades.

Wang Yulan bowed and stepped out, smiling, "Since the emperor is worried about the war in the northwest, I think this is feasible. Xingling is under the jurisdiction of the Northwest Army and has always been a military stronghold. Send a pigeon to tell Nie Qingyuan to prepare to receive the emperor. The trip should be safe."

Yan Yanzi snorted coldly and glared at Wang Yulan, "A son of a wealthy family should not sit idle. The emperor's northern tour was originally to supervise the war, how could he go deep into the front line? If something goes wrong, Wang Yulan, can you bear the responsibility?"

His tone was stern, and Wang Yulan laughed dryly, "My Lord, General Yan has driven the Tiele out of Yumen for more than a hundred miles, and there is no more war in the northwest. Youyun also has Prince Yu in charge. My Lord, why worry about nothing?"

Yan Yanzi raised his eyebrows and was about to speak, but Huangfu Jue coughed lightly, "You don't have to argue." He pointed his finger at the march map and stopped at the northwest of Youyun. "I will never cross the border of Youyun. I will stay for a maximum of seven days and then return according to the original route."

Qin Duan stepped out. He was the descendant of the famous general Qin Qiong, and he inherited the title of nobility and served as the commander of the imperial guards in the capital. At this time, he looked worried, "Your Majesty, Xingling is a natural barrier, and there is only a floating bridge on the river. How can the ladies get across?"

Huangfu Jue raised his phoenix eyes and glanced at everyone, with an expression that was hard to tell whether he was happy or angry. He said slowly, "That is your business."

Yan Yanzi returned to the tent, where counselor Dongfang Qi was waiting. Seeing Yan Yanzi looked unhappy, he asked, "My Lord, is there something wrong?"

Yan Yanzi waved her hand, "Let's not talk about it for now. Is there any news about Juntian?"

Dongfang Qi nodded, his face solemn, "It was indeed Young Master Ye Zi, and he was accompanied by the granddaughter of Hainan Yang's family. The little girl was hit by a sword, and the two fled westward. Lord, Juntian and the others were just following the secret guards from a distance, and judging from the situation, it seems... the secret guards did not kill him."

Yan Yanzi listened quietly, his eyelids half closed, and after a while he snorted coldly, "Our emperor is the best at matters between men and women. Young boys and girls, sharing life and death, healing naked, it is natural that they are most likely to develop feelings. He did this just to make Yan Zhi give up."

Dongfang Qi was worried, "My Lord, could it be that the Emperor... has already known about the relationship between the young lady and Xue Yu?"

Yan Yanzi said coldly: "I have long suspected that the secret guards around the emperor are the people in the underworld who were found on the Internet when he disappeared. Even if they don't know Ye Zi herself, they will know the swordsmanship of Xueyu. There is no eternal secret in this world. The day I met Yun Shu, I was prepared for this day. I took all precautions, but my Yanzhi, Yanzhi..."

Dongfang Qi sighed, "The young lady's entry into the palace is really a coincidence. If the emperor did it on purpose, then his mind is too terrible. This move really hit the weak spot of the Marquis Xueyu. However, the emperor seems to be sincere about the young lady. The soldiers were killed and injured in the previous few days of marching against the wind, and it was just to go to Xiufeng to see the hot spring, which is good for the young lady's health."

Yan Yanzi closed her eyes in silence, cracks appeared in her steel-like eyes, and she slowly said, "Whether it's true or false, I just want my Yanzhi to be happy. If it's a dead end, even if it means death, I have to protect my daughter."

"Send a message to Yanzhi, the fish is out of the net, tell her not to worry. Ziqi, come here, the emperor suddenly changed the marching route, I'm afraid he has other intentions."

"Bang!" The gilded finger-file knife in Yanzhi's hand fell to the ground. She paused for a moment, then quickly bent down to pick it up, her expression unchanged.

"Cross the river from Xingfeng and go straight into Youyun?"

Linglong nodded, "Yes, they said we should reach Youyun first, and then return along the previous route."

Yanzhi sat quietly and smiled for a long while. She looked very healthy. Three days of conditioning had restored her skin to a smooth and smooth state. In the sunlight, it was faintly transparent. Her smile was very clear and shallow, like the first bud on a branch in early spring, which was blown away by the cold wind before it bloomed.

The freshly manicured nails dug deeply into the palm of my hand, unable to suppress the sudden panic and surprise that arose in my heart.

How would she feel if she really set foot on that land?

"Linglong, does daddy have anything else to say?" she asked softly.

"Everything is fine, don't worry Miss."

Everything is fine, everything is fine. She repeated in her heart over and over again, that's all.

It is better not to meet than to not meet. It is better to forget each other, forget each other in the world, forget each other in the years.

On September 29th, they arrived at Xingfeng. While passing through the six counties, Yanzhi kept claiming to be ill and rarely went out. All activities that needed to demonstrate the majesty and dignity of the royal family were attended by Huangfu Jue and Wang Yan.

Huangfu Jue seemed very busy and rarely showed up. But no matter where he went, Yanzhi would always have a pot of seasonal flowers in his car in the morning.

The further west you go, the lower the

temperature.

One day, Yiyue came in wearing a brocade cape and blowing on her hands, and said with a smile: "It's too cold, Miss, look."

In her hands she held a pot of small daisies, with linear petals lying on dark green leaves. They were still full of vitality despite the frost and wind.

Yanzhi put down the book, touched the tender center of the flower with her fingers, and smiled.

Linglong said happily: "It's so cold, but there are still flowers blooming."

Yanzhi smiled and sighed, "It was born and raised in nature, but it must be moved to a place with fireworks. Yiyue, why did the car stop?"

Before we got close to the river, we could already hear the roar of the rushing water. We should be heading straight for the ferry, but for some reason, the car was gradually slowing down.

Yiyue placed the flower on the compartment, turned around and giggled, "I asked Li Luo to go ask Captain Qin, but she has been gone for quite some time and hasn't come back yet."

Thinking of Qin Jian who was so shy that he couldn't speak when he saw her, Yan Zhi couldn't help but smile knowingly. Li Luo seemed to get along very well with him. They could often be seen talking to each other these days. It was good this way. Li Luo's mind had shifted, and the secret worries should fade away.

After being in a daze for a while, the felt was lifted and Li Luo came in. Her face was pale and her eyes seemed a little dazed. She sat down without saying a word.

Yanzhi frowned slightly and asked calmly, "What happened?"

Li Luo's eyes slowly turned and looked at her. Her lips moved and after a long while she spoke, "···Murder, Miss. So many people died···"

Yanzhi sat up straight.

Li Luo went to look for Qin Jian. She waited for a long time by his tent but he didn't come back. Instead, she saw soldiers in uniform walking past in a line. She was curious and followed them. People around her recognized her as the Queen's personal maid. Those who dared to stop her were glared at by her and rushed through under the name of Yanzhi.

She came to the river amidst a large group of soldiers. When Qin Jian heard the news and hurried over, it was too late.

Li Luo saw clearly that many people were tied with heavy stones, their screams drowned out the roar of the river, and they were pushed into the turbid and swirling river one by one by the expressionless soldiers around them.

The lives of the people turned into ripples on the river surface.

She was horrified, her screams were muffled by a hand, and Qin Jian half dragged and half carried her to a remote place. With a gloomy face, he told her that Nie Qingyuan had failed to build the bridge, delaying the emperor's trip, and the emperor was furious, so he threw all the people from Xingfeng into the Yellow River to build the foundation for the bridge.

Li Luo cried bitterly. She grabbed the hem of her rouge dress, and her tears soaked the fish-shaped satin on her knees. She was still so young, as tender as the yellow of a willow tree in March. She had never seen such a cruel scene.

The car suddenly became very quiet.

The smile on Yanzhi's lips gradually turned pale and powerless, and she touched Li Luo's hair unconsciously, "...Okay...don't cry, when the emperor gets angry, there will be corpses scattered all over the place...who told you to watch this kind of excitement..."

"Miss," Li Luo suddenly raised her head, her eyes full of fear and hatred, "Lord Nie is a good man. Qin Jian said that he was framed by Wang Yulan. Miss, the emperor... the emperor..."

Yanzhi's heart suddenly sank, and for a moment, she actually wanted Li Luo to shut up. Yiyue quickly took her in his arms and took over the conversation, with pity and resentment, "Drink some calming tea to calm your nerves. You are from the Marquis's Mansion, but you are so brave. I heard that there are people in the capital who follow the execution. Lord Qin was punished, so he must have violated the law. Even if it is unjust, it is not our business to interfere. Don't be afraid, sister will sleep with you tonight."

Her face was slightly pale, but her words were soft and gentle, slowly soothing Li Luo's emotions.

Yanzhi felt chest tightness and asked Linglong to open the car window.

The distant mountains were all light blue, the horizon was faintly black, and a cold wind blew in through the cracks, bringing with it a damp, fishy smell of sandalwood.

If they were experienced herdsmen, they would have already moved their cattle and sheep to the leeward hills early, because the weather was about to change.

The author has something to say: Please collect it.

Woohoo my poor...

☆、In distress

Yan Yanzi personally supervised the construction, and the floating bridge was completed after one day and one night. Time was so tight that they only had time to widen and thicken the original iron ropes, which could only accommodate two horses passing side by side, but the imperial phoenix chariot could not pass through.

Huangfu Jue simply left the flag carriage at Xingfeng, leaving only the most ordinary blue cloth oil-covered carriage. It seemed that he wanted to go on a tour incognito.

All the palace ladies got off the carriages and walked across the bridge.

The sky was so low that one could feel the dark clouds with one's hand. The wind swirled up, and the brocade and feather cloak fluttered.

The river roared wildly, as if thousands of people were crying and howling.

Yanzhi walked step by step, looking vaguely at the tip of her toes. The person in front of her suddenly paused, and a hand stretched out from the sleeve of the double-sided embroidery with gold edges.

Yanzhi stared at the hand in a trance, as if she saw pairs of hands, some rough and some tender, scratching and twisting, trying their best to reach into the air.

She recognized Nie Qingyuan, he was her father's old subordinate. He had a full beard and liked to ride the strongest horses and drink the best wine. Such a rough man, but he had a pair of skillful hands. There was still a beauty kite made by him in the storeroom of the Marquis' Mansion.

It was this pair of hands, slender, beautiful, and clean like the spring water flowing from the snow-capped mountains, that killed hundreds of lives in an instant. There was a hint of disgust in her eyes, and she stopped subconsciously.

Huangfu Jue turned his head slightly,

looked at her with inquiring eyes, and grabbed her hand.

"Your Majesty," Yan Zhi said softly, "Does this sound like many people crying?"

Huangfu Jue's eyes were filled with cold sneer, and he tightened his grip, "Are you quarreling with me just because of this? Are you going to kill Nie Qingyuan for me?"

Yanzhi looked at him, clearly catching the ruthless coldness in his eyes. She sighed, "Huangfu Jue, even if the country is a chessboard and all things are pieces, they are still living creatures with flesh and blood. Even if you call yourself a chess player, it is inevitable that one day you will not be deeply trapped in the chess game."

Huangfu Jue seemed to be stunned for a moment, then he smiled and said, "Yes, this vast country is my chessboard. Whether I sacrifice a pawn or a rook depends on my mood. If you are afraid that I will kill innocent people, you should always be by my side to remind me."

There was a little pride in his eyes, like a child who found candy that an adult had hidden. Such a fickle man could have a hundred emotions in the blink of an eye.

Such a man is like the exotic flower Mandragora from the Western Regions, once you get addicted, you will become addicted, leading you step by step into the hell of depravity.

Yan Zhi snorted coldly, "The emperor is

just like a street scoundrel."

She did not walk side by side with him, but took a step back. Her wide sleeves flowed down, covering their clasped hands, but could not hide the jealous gazes of others.

When the tip of my toes touched the hard ground at the bridge head, I heard Huangfu Jue's charming voice, "Yanzhi, even if I betray the whole world, I will never betray you."

Fog.

The overwhelming fog enveloped all the valleys, big and small, in an instant.

Huangfu Jue looked at the valley quietly, with dark eyes surging.

Yan Yanzi hurriedly approached, his face solemn, "Your Majesty, the fog is too heavy. There is no sign of support. We can't wait any longer, we must camp. And I am worried... if the fog doesn't clear, there might be frost."

Huangfu Jue exhaled a breath of white air, his voice still calm, "Yes, the weather is getting colder and colder. Call the Queen to my place and prepare to set up camp."

Yanzhi sat in the car, listening to the urgent reports outside one after another, her heart tightening.

They were now in the Dadou Valley. If it was a sunny day, the terrain would not be considered dangerous, but at the moment the line of sight was only a few meters. If it got darker, the situation would be difficult to estimate.

"Your Majesty," the deep and deep voice said, it was my father.

"Tell me--" The man opposite was still calm and composed, his fingers flying as he brewed Kung Fu tea.

"The spies reported that there is a canyon ahead that is only wide enough for bicycles. Five miles later, there will be an open area that can be used as a camping site."

Huangfu Jue smiled with his phoenix eyes, pushed the tea in front of her, leaned forward to wipe the crumbs of Fuling cake from her lips, and said lazily, "Go forward."

"Yes." Yan Yanzi responded in a deep voice, and then said, "Your Majesty, the imperial concubine is a little depressed and she wants to see your Majesty."

Huangfu Jue raised his lips and said, "I am in charge of military affairs, so I don't have time. Let the Prime Minister go. I believe she won't feel depressed staying with her father."

Yan Yanzi did not leave, and continued: "Your Majesty, it is too dangerous to ride a bicycle. It would be better to let the imperial guards join the carriage team and provide protection in sections."

Huangfu Jue looked at her with sparkling eyes, and slowly traced her lips with his middle finger. Seeing Yanzhi glaring at him fiercely, he couldn't help but chuckle and said casually: "We are not as good as you in this matter, just make your own decision."

Yan Yanzi said: "Even so, please ask the Queen to get off the carriage, and I will dare to ask to get on the Emperor's sedan chair."

Yanzhi was stunned. His father's words clearly meant that this trip was risky and he had to accompany him to protect him.

Huangfu Jue's smile gradually faded, and he said calmly: "Wherever I am, the Queen will be there. Marquis Yan does not need to worry, just command from the front."

"I obey your command." After seeming to hesitate for a moment, the footsteps slowly faded away.

Yanzhi was suspicious and was about to speak when Huangfu Jue suddenly leaned forward and said with a smile, "Yanzhi, what did the Marquis say just now? Is he more worried about you or me?" He complained half-truthfully, "He's obviously afraid that I can't protect you and wants to take you away from me."

Yanzhi felt cold in her heart. The situation had actually gotten so bad. She had lived in the snowy mountains for many years, so she naturally knew how terrible the climate in the mountains could be. She stood up suddenly and said, "I have to go back."

Linglong and Yiyue were in the car behind. If anything happened, they would definitely rush to find her. In the rush and chaos, the 70% hope of survival would be reduced to 30%.

Huangfu Jue held her hand tightly and said, "I have already told your maids. If you go back, I am afraid they will have to trouble you to take care of you. Sit down, it's okay, look at what I have prepared for you."

He took out a large bundle from the carriage's deck, untied it, and saw that it was full of snow-white fluffy fox fur and a black furry black bear fur coat. Huangfu Jue brought it to Yanzhi, who was naturally very clean, and turned her face away in disgust.

Huangfu Jue laughed and sighed, "Silly girl, this is a good thing that can save your life."

He closed his eyes and leaned back, "Hurry up and change it."

Yanzhi had already felt the cold, and even though she was holding the heater in her hands, the chill still spread from the soles of her feet.

He took out a set of fox fur clothes, which were very delicately made, with almost no trace of stitches. The cuffs and lapels were embroidered with ancient butterfly patterns. Yanzhi liked it very much, but she also knew that she could not stand the cold. She stole a glance at Huangfu Jue, turned her back, untied the feather satin cloak, and put it on.

As soon as she sat down, Huangfu Jue opened his eyes and saw that she was only wearing a fox coat. He shook his head and sighed, "You prefer flashy things." He naturally took her hand.

Yanzhi struggled a few times and found a constant stream of heat coming from his palm. Although she stopped struggling, her expression remained cold and indifferent.

Listening carefully to the sounds outside, there were only the clattering of horse hooves and short horn calls. The whole team seemed to have suddenly fallen silent, and the sky and the earth seemed eerily empty.

Yanzhi said softly, "How bad will the situation be?"

Huangfu Jue kept looking at her with a smile, his eyes soft and focused, "If it's just fog, at most someone will fall off the cliff, and the damage will not exceed a hundred. If there are other situations, it's hard to say."

In other cases, Yanzhi looked at her purple fingertips. Does the sharp drop in temperature count? In just a moment, she felt that the car was filled with cold wind, leaving only a little warmth in her palms.

The man in front of him was still smiling, and the lives of thousands of people could not make his smile fade. He could not suppress the hatred that rose in his heart. If it weren't for his stubbornness, how could he fall into the current situation!

If the emperor and half of the ministers of a dynasty were buried here, half of the dynasty would have collapsed.

Huangfu Jue put the black bear fur coat on her, opened his arms to hold her, and whispered: "Don't look at me like that, it breaks your heart. In your heart, am I guilty of the most heinous crime?"

As soon as I was in his arms, the chill was banished by warmth, and he had a faint scent of pine resin. While my mind was still hesitating, my body had already found a comfortable position on its own.

Yanzhi leaned her head on his shoulder, feeling as if she was leaning against a warm stove, and she did not forget to snort coldly.

Huangfu Jue smiled and patted her head, "If you feel sleepy, take a nap."

Being able to sleep is a blessing. Tonight, I am afraid that many people will never wake up again after falling asleep.

There is always a warm current surrounding my body, feeling lazy and my consciousness gradually becomes blurred.

A long, shrill sound.

Yanzhi suddenly opened her eyes, surrounded by the faint light of the Night Pearl. A soft voice sounded above her head, "Awake?"

Yanzhi woke up almost instantly, her eyes sparkling with shame and anger. He wrapped his arms and legs around her, holding her in his arms, the two of them almost intimate.

The anger came quickly, and she didn't know why. She almost broke away from his embrace viciously. Huangfu Jue was startled, then laughed, and stretched out his tone, "Little liar——" The tone was tender and meaningful.

As soon as Yanzhi came into contact with the air, he shivered.

The temperature has dropped so low.

The car was like a huge block of ice, without a trace of warmth.

There was no sound outside, no snorting of horses, no rumbling of wheels, and the long scream just now seemed to be just an illusion in her dream.

The carriage was no longer moving forward.

Yanzhi's heart grew colder and colder. Her shame, anger and anxiety froze in an instant. Her dark eyes turned to Huangfu Jue quietly, "Where are we now?"

Huangfu Jue stretched his limbs on the couch, looking lazy, "I don't know either. I only know that if you don't wake up, we will be buried alive. Come here, escape with your husband."

I hooked my fingers towards her very soothingly, as if to say, "The flowers on the roadside are in bloom, let's go enjoy them together."

The author has something to say: There will be two updates in the evening.

Please accept me because Liu Liu works so hard.

One day it goes up and one day it goes down, is there such a sad thing? Woohoo...

☆, Trapped

The temperature has dropped so low.
The car was like a huge block of ice, without a trace of warmth.
There was no sound outside, no snorting of horses, no rumbling of wheels, and the long scream just now seemed to be just an illusion in her dream.
The carriage was no longer moving forward.
Yanzhi's heart grew colder and colder. Her shame, anger and anxiety froze in an instant. Her dark eyes turned to Huangfu Jue quietly, "Where are we now?"
Huangfu Jue stretched his limbs on the couch, looking lazy, "I don't know either. I only know that if you don't wake up, we will be buried alive. Come here, escape with your husband."
I hooked my fingers towards her very soothingly, as if to say, "The flowers on the roadside are in bloom, let's go enjoy them together."
When the rouge came out, I realized how bad the situation was.
The car door was split open by Huangfu Jue's palm wind, and snow flakes flew all over the sky. Snowflakes fell all over the sky, and everything was white. When she stepped on it, it was knee-deep snow. In such a snowy place, she could hardly move.
Huangfu Jue smiled lightly, easily pulled her out of the snow and carried her on his back.

Even with her on his back, Huangfu Jue still left no trace on the snow. Dozens of figures appeared silently around him, all dressed in eunuch clothing, and the leader was Haigui.

Haigui bowed and said, "Your Majesty, please let me come."

Huangfu Jue glanced at him coldly, "How dare you? Lead the way."

Haigui remained calm and walked away with his head down.

Yanzhi suddenly said, "Let him carry me." He had been using his inner strength to help her ward off the cold, and he must be tired.

Huangfu Jue snorted coldly, "Even if he is a waste, he is still a man. You don't even have to think about it."

Yanzhi was stunned, almost laughing and crying. If she hadn't heard it with her own ears, she would hardly believe that Huangfu Jue would say such childish words.

The heavy snow covered all traces. They were as fast as bullets, rushing out of the valley like a meteor. All they could see along the way were horses neighing and wailing with their legs stuck in the snow, but no sign of people.

Yanzhi's eager search.

They were in the middle of the team, and it was impossible that no one in the front was left alive. Although she knew that Daddy was unlikely to be in trouble, she still hoped to see him. Moreover, Yiyue and

Linglong, two weak women, were worried in such weather.

She couldn't see anything. There were dense snowflakes everywhere. She opened her eyes with tears. Finally, Huangfu Jue seemed to have noticed something. He stopped, tied her cloak tightly, and even covered her face with fur. He smiled and coaxed her, "Hold on, we'll be there soon."

His breath was still, his hands were steady and dry, but his eyes had lost some of their sharpness. Yan Zhi was silent, lying quietly on his back. Hearing his soft and drawn voice, "Be good..."

She naturally didn't know that not far ahead, rows of soldiers fell down, and the dense snow had not even had time to completely cover their armor.

There were more and more dead bodies, all of them lying face down on the snow, without any of them hugging or entangled with each other.

Huangfu Jue's eyes gradually felt as cold as needles, and his toes stepped on the open space next to him.

The sky is vast, the snow is endless, and their figures seem to merge with the world, as dissipated as light smoke and drifting like light smoke.

"Roar, roar, roar—" It seemed to be the roar of a group of beasts, and there was a faint resonance between heaven and earth, "Boom, boom, boom—"

Yanzhi only heard Haigui's cold and shrill

voice, "Protect the emperor! Protect the emperor! It's an avalanche!"

Before she could react, Huangfu Jue had already pulled her into his arms, pressing her head tightly against his chest. He still smiled gently and said, "Don't be afraid, I'm with you."

Her heart strangely calmed down, and a vague thought flashed through her mind. If it is true, it is not bad.

Next, my ears were filled with whistling sounds, like thousands of horses being silenced, thunder falling from the sky, like ghosts crying, and like wolves howling. His body kept spinning and bumping against each other, sometimes fast, sometimes slow, but the one thing that remained unchanged was the eternal warmth in his chest.

Time seems to be very long.

She twisted her fat arms and legs in the hot spring, "I don't want to take a bath, I don't want to take a bath. I want to go out and play with my senior brother."

The master smiled good-naturedly and sprinkled handfuls of flower petals into the hot spring. "Yanzhi is a beautiful girl, she won't play with a stinky boy. The master picked the most beautiful flowers in the world for Yanzhi. After Yanzhi soaks in it, she will become fragrant and delicious."

She looked at her master with tears in her eyes, "What's the point of being so naive? I can't even play with my fellow brothers."

The master smiled very gently, "When Yanzhi grows up to be a beautiful girl, the best man in the world will come to marry Yanzhi."

Her eyes widened, "The best, like Master?"

The master touched his face, nodded, and said seriously: "Of course, your brothers are far inferior to him."

The chubby girl became slender in the dazzling white light. There was a beautiful person, as graceful as Qingyang.

In the winding corridor, she was wearing a bright red dress that made her skin look dizzy. She pushed open a door excitedly, "Senior Brother——"

"Hush!" A woman sat up lazily, and placed her index finger on her lips, seeming a little shy and timid, "He just fell asleep."

The brocade quilt with peony branches slid down, leaving a few bright red kiss marks on the jade-white shoulders.

"Yanzhi, Yanzhi!" Who was calling so persistently in her ear? She tried desperately to cover her ears. Don't call me, don't call me! Liar, liar, all big liars!

"Liar!" Huangfu Jue was stunned when he heard her utter these two words coldly as soon as she opened her eyes. He grabbed her neck for a long time and asked with gritted teeth: "Who do you say is a liar?"

Yanzhi stared at him steadily, then smiled slowly and asked softly, "Am I beautiful?"

Huangfu Jue was startled, and he touched her forehead with his hand, and asked in surprise: "Did you hit your head, or are you talking nonsense because of a fever?"

Yanzhi looked at him without blinking, "It's this face you like, right?"

Huangfu Jue gently curled the corners of his lips, bent his middle finger, and flicked her forehead fiercely. After hearing her cry of pain, he said, "Since I like you, I naturally love your face. You are such a heartless little thing, you want to tear down the bridge before you even cross the river."

Yanzhi stared at him blankly for a long while, her long eyelashes slightly closed, and when she opened her eyes again, they were clear and bright, and she smiled gently, "You're still alive...Are you hurt?"

One glance was enough to see their situation.

It was a small cave, with a pearl between his fingers emitting a faint light, which should have been pinned in her hair. The two of them huddled together, and the heavy clothes were stripped off by Huangfu Jue, surrounding the two of them. The light from the pearl was too weak, and she couldn't see Huangfu Jue's face, but she knew very well that except for a slight dizziness on her head, the rest of her body was unharmed. She calmly stroked Huangfu Jue's arm and looked up at his face.

Huangfu Jue smiled grimly, slid his arm down, held her waist, and looked at her at eye level, "Do you know you're worried about me?"

Through the thin clothes and intimate contact, she could clearly feel the warmth radiating from his body. Her heart trembled, and her fingers could only grasp him vaguely.

"Yanzhi," he whispered softly, "I am glad that we are all still alive."

His eyes were so close to hers, filled with joy, so deep, so much that it almost overflowed and flowed into her heart.

A faint sigh disappeared between the touching lips and tongues.

His kiss came down softly and gently, as if protecting a newborn baby, so cautiously, so solemnly and lovingly. Just gently rubbing on the lips, it seemed to have expressed all the lovesickness in his life.

Yanzhi slowly closed her eyes, and a tear slid down from the corner of her eye.

A corner of my heart collapsed, and inexplicable emotions quietly grew in the ruins.

After the kiss, Huangfu Jue still pecked her lips a few times, holding her hand tightly, his body as hard as iron, and whispered softly: "What a little devil who is killing me."

Yanzhi looked at him, her clear eyes suddenly became misty, and her hand slowly reached out from behind his back.

Blood, a palm of sticky blood!

Huangfu Jue smiled gently, quickly wiped the corner of her eyes with his fingers, and licked the tip of his finger with the tip of his tongue, "I have always wondered what your tears would taste like if you cried for me. It turns out that they are so bitter."

Did she cry? She wiped her tears with her hand and found them. Yanzhi was shocked. It turned out that he could affect her emotions in this way.

The wound was deep, flesh and blood were rolling, and the bones were visible. He randomly sprinkled some hemostatic medicine on it, and the bleeding stopped. The back was covered with bruises and contusions.

Yanzhi's hand slid gently over her, and her mind automatically emerged with the scene of him hugging her tightly, using his body as a cushion, and being crushed by the snow. Despite this injury, he still used his true energy to keep her warm. Even though he had a good foundation, if it weren't for the spiritual medicine that barely kept him going, he would probably have died.

The expression in her eyes changed several times, she hesitated and struggled. In the end, she just sprinkled the medicine he handed over on the wound, tore off her underwear and wrapped it up carefully.

After everything was sorted out, Huangfu Jue still held her in his arms. His expression was normal, but his face was slightly pale. The corners of his lips curled up slightly, and he whispered, "Be good and let me hold you for a while."

He leaned his head against the snow wall behind him, closed his eyes, and his breathing gradually became long and calm.

Yanzhi curled up against his chest, listening to his slightly rapid heartbeat gradually calming down, with a blank look in her eyes.

She knew everything, but she could do nothing. She had at least three more appropriate methods than his current method of forcibly gathering strength through secret techniques, but she could only wait silently, waiting for him to recover his strength and lead her out of the predicament. Or, she would never be able to get out.

The author has something to say: Liu Liu is very conflicted.

Extreme depression, fear, anxiety...

This month has been such a waste...

☆、Heartbeat

The expression in her eyes changed several times, she hesitated and struggled. In the end, she just sprinkled the medicine he handed over on the wound, tore off her underwear and wrapped it up carefully.

After everything was sorted out, Huangfu Jue still held her in his arms. His expression was normal, but his face was slightly pale. The corners of his lips curled up slightly, and he whispered, "Be good and let me hold you for a while."

He leaned his head against the snow wall behind him, closed his eyes, and his breathing gradually became long and calm.

Yanzhi curled up against his chest, listening to his slightly rapid heartbeat gradually calming down, with a blank look in her eyes.

She knew everything, but she could do nothing. She had at least three more appropriate methods than his current method of forcibly gathering strength through secret techniques, but she could only wait silently, waiting for him to recover his strength and lead her out of the predicament. Or, she would never be able to get out.

Half an incense stick of time later, Huangfu Jue had opened his eyes. He put all the warm clothes around Yanzhi and began to feel around the walls. After knocking and hitting, he used his long sword to find the gap and slowly drew a circle. He exerted force on his palm, and the round ice block was slowly pushed open by him to create a gap, and the cold wind poured in.

If there was wind, they could get out of the cave. Although she was shivering with cold, Yanzhi's eyes gradually brightened up. Huangfu Jue stopped his hand when there was just a gap between them. He turned around and smiled at Yan Zhi, "Wait for me obediently."

Yanzhi nodded gently and said, "Be careful."

Huangfu Jue waved his hand and dodged out.

It was very cold. Even though Huangfu Jue had put more ice on her from the outside, she still couldn't stop the shivering all over her body. She curled up as much as she could, burying her face in the bear's short and thick mane, and immediately began to miss Huangfu Jue's warmth.

I have already gotten used to it, used to his care and his pampering. I don't know when I started to become so familiar with his smell.

He is really a very patient man.

When she was in Weiyang Palace, she did what she wanted most of the time, and he was happy. She slept while he read, and she played chess while he watched. Even if she looked cold at him, he would always act as if nothing had happened. He said he wanted her, but he didn't force her. There were so many concubines in the harem, but nothing had to happen to her. Her food, clothing, and daily expenses were all exquisite, and rewards never stopped.

She never thanked him.

If it weren't for him, she would have been the happiest and freest person in the world. If other women with the surname Yan could have obtained his kindness, they would have been able to do so as well. Besides, there was always a hazy and lingering shadow in her heart.

But I never thought that I would be so heartbroken.

Master, Master, I couldn't help but call out in my heart, tears falling.

October 13th is coming soon. Do you miss Yanzhi? Yanzhi was buried alive in the snow. Did you know that? Yanzhi is very upset now. Tell me what I should do...

When Huangfu Jue came back, Yanzhi had already put on her clothes and was groping around in the cave. Her movements were very strange, her joints were incredibly soft, and she could stretch her muscles to the maximum extent. She did it very slowly, and Huangfu Jue watched silently for a while. She only did one movement, leaning back and pulling her hands back. She was wearing a lot of clothes inside, and the black bear leather coat was round and bulging on her body. When she moved, it was a bit funny and funny.

Yanzhi paused and panted slightly, "Can we go out?"

Huangfu Jue smiled without answering, and naturally took her hand, "Your hands are still so cold." He pulled her tightly towards him.

Yanzhi was silent for a while, and then she asked softly, "Is there no way?" If she was washed down by the snow flow, she might fall into the crack of the mountain wall.

Rubbing his chin slowly on the top of her head, Huangfu Jue smiled softly and said,

"There is no place in the world where there is no road. It's too dark now. Let's go out when it's light. Are you hungry?" He took off a sachet from his waist and handed it to her.

There was a faint scent of ambergris, and there was no spice in it, but some dried fruit candied fruit. Yanzhi picked up an apricot, and a smile appeared on the corner of his lips. This should be the plate on the carriage just now, and he actually grabbed a handful in a hurry.

Put it in your mouth and chew it slowly. It tastes 70% sweet and 30% astringent.

Yanzhi stepped away from his embrace and said with a smile, "Let's take a break. The movements I just made were taught to me by a nun when I was a child. She said they can help you stay healthy. I moved a little bit just now, and it can help you stay warm."

Huangfu Jue lowered his eyes, his expression indifferent, and uttered two words softly from his red lips, "Come here."

Yanzhi was startled, her smile slowly faded, and she sighed, "You are too tired, you must rest. I can do it myself."

Huangfu Jue snorted coldly, and squinted his eyes, "You can? You can still tremble and turn purple? If I rest, I will have to hold a cold corpse in my arms tomorrow morning."

Yan Zhi smiled and said softly, "I promise you, if I can't make it, I will call you."

Huangfu Jue glanced at her with a half-smile, sat directly on his cloak, and threw off his coat, "Come and help me change the medicine."

As expected, blood slowly seeped out of the bandage. He must have used gravity again. Yanzhi had no choice but to bandage him again. When tying the knot, Huangfu Jue suddenly asked, "Yanzhi, do you know medicine?"

She paused for a moment, "Well... I learned some from my master." She put his clothes on and rolled up the bandages he had taken off. "Okay, start regulating your breathing."

She had just taken two steps when she was hit by a strong force from behind and fell back into Huangfu Jue's arms.

"Huangfu Jue!" Yanzhi tried to stop him in a panic. He strangled her with one hand, and with the other hand he stripped her down to her underwear in an instant, and held her in his arms contentedly.

Yanzhi was so angry that she gritted her teeth. What a hooligan, what a scoundrel, how could he take off a woman's clothes so smoothly?

The place where their skin touched immediately became warm, but Yanzhi's heart sank. His pulse was vigorous and strong, and he was solid on the outside but weak on the inside. Wasting his own energy like a moth flying into a flame would undoubtedly lead to his own destruction.

Noticing her unusual silence, Huangfu Jue chuckled and stroked her hair with his fingers, "Silly girl, what are you thinking about?"

Yanzhi looked into his eyes and said softly, "Why are you so nice to me?"

Huangfu Jue looked at her quietly, as if he was looking for something. After a long while, he half-closed his eyelids and said lightly: "When you can understand your own heart, ask me again." He wiped the corners of her eyes with his fingers, slightly surprised, "Why are you crying again? Could it be... Are you afraid that I will die?" He lifted her chin, looked at her with flowing eyes, and said in a low voice as if to coax her, "What are you thinking about, Yanzhi..."

Yanzhi looked at him, her eyes, which were always clear, were now as hazy as smoke and water. "I'm afraid. I'm afraid of your heart. I'm afraid that I can't give you what you want."

Huangfu Jue's lips curled up slightly, his curve was cold, and there was a bit of boredom in his eyes, "In your eyes, am I someone who would risk his life for a woman? Hmm?"

She just felt her heart twisted into a ball, and she couldn't say a word. Of course he shouldn't be, but... She wished she had never studied medicine, and wished she was ignorant.

Huangfu Jue waited for a while, then smiled

softly, "Of course I won't, and I will never do that. So you don't have to feel guilty. Just be good, and we can go out tomorrow."

He closed his eyes, his brows slightly furrowed, and under his pearly eyes, there was a hint of gloom and indifference.

Yan Zhi was in a daze for a while, then suddenly smiled. It didn't matter if it was true or false. The only person she could lose was this person. She was not the little daughter of the Yan family, nor was she the master's little apprentice. She could only be Yan Zhi.

I don't know when I fell asleep, but my hand was always on his chest.

Huangfu Jue opened his eyes quietly, his hand already touching Yanzhi's sleeping spot.

There was another person in the cave, wearing black clothes and with black hair, it was Xiu Ji. Looking at the two people leaning against each other, Xiu Ji, who had always been expressionless, couldn't help but raise his eyebrows, "Did you succeed?"

Huangfu Jue's slanted phoenix eyes were dark and unpredictable, and he looked at him coldly. He put on his clothes and rouge, casually put on a long gown, and walked out. "why you?"

"The secret guard saw the signal and I was there, so I went."

Huangfu Jue raised his eyes and asked, "What's the situation outside?"

"Without a leader, there will naturally be chaos. Yan Yanzi has taken control of the situation. Xueyu seems to have heard the news, and Bai Zizai's sword maid has come down the mountain." After taking a closer look at him, Xiu Ji showed surprise on his face, "How did you get hurt like this? Do you want my help?"

Huangfu Jue shook his head slowly, "If you interfere, all my efforts will be wasted." He rubbed his brows, "They came so fast... Let the secret guards stay away from them."

When Yanzhi woke up, Huangfu Jue was no longer by her side. The snow wall at the entrance of the cave was tilted, and a large patch of sunlight was reflected in, making her feel warm.

When he left the cave, his steps were a little hesitant. He heard the sound of his clothes tearing through the air, and his body was hidden behind the snow wall.

There was only a piece of open space outside the cave, and beyond that was endless emptiness. Huangfu Jue leaned on his sword, knelt on one knee on the snow, covered his mouth with one hand, and coughed softly. In an instant, blood oozed out from between his fingers. He looked at it, his face indifferent, and wiped it with snow to eliminate the traces on the ground.

When Huangfu Jue stood up, he saw Yan Zhi. She looked at him silently, her face almost the same color as snow, her eyes dark and calm. He had never seen such a look in her eyes, filled with so many emotions, heartache, pain, pity, despair, all intertwined together. Such beauty, like glass, refracting colorful light.

She was finally moved.

The author has something to say: There will be another update in the evening.

Liu Liu worked hard and updated twice a day. Dear friends, please accept me quickly!

☆、Life and Death

There was only a piece of open space outside the cave, and beyond that was endless emptiness. Huangfu Jue leaned on his sword, knelt on one knee on the snow, covered his mouth with one hand, and coughed softly. In an instant, blood oozed out from between his fingers. He looked at it, his face indifferent, and wiped it with snow to eliminate the traces on the ground.

When Huangfu Jue stood up, he saw Yan Zhi. She looked at him silently, her face almost the same color as snow, her eyes dark and calm. He had never seen such a look in her eyes, filled with so many emotions, heartache, pain, pity, despair, all intertwined together. Such beauty, like glass, refracting colorful light.

She was finally moved.

Huangfu Jue was surprised, but he immediately regained his composure. There was a hint of fatigue between his eyebrows, but his expression was normal. He walked over naturally, put his arm on her cheek, and said softly, "Are you awake? The light is too strong, be careful of your eyes."

Yanzhi forced a smile, let him hold her hand, and walked out of the cave.

They were indeed washed into a crevice under the cliff by the snow flow. The inside was sunken, and it was impossible to find them from above.

Huangfu Jue said slowly: "It's only thirty feet above. If there is a foothold, it will be easy to go up."

Yanzhi remained silent. The mountain wall was covered with snow, smooth as a mirror. It was not easy to find a foothold. His true energy was already in disarray. If he lost his strength, he would be crushed to pieces.

Huangfu Jue patted her head and said, "Come in. You will only cause trouble if you stay aside. I have already dug two footholds. It will only take a moment to get up."

Yan Zhi grabbed his hand with her backhand, and said in a panic, "Wait a little longer, there must be people looking for us outside. Daddy will find us."

Huangfu Jue smiled, "Silly girl, you can't wait for me." He leaned over and kissed her gently on the cheek, "Be good."

It was a very light and clean kiss, but Yanzhi felt her heart instantly in turmoil.

Yanzhi brought out his mink coat and leaned against the cave entrance. Huangfu Jue took two pills, took a breath, and then flew up again.

I don't know how long it took, I could only see snowflakes falling from the sky from time to time, like clusters of silver flowers blooming in the air. Occasionally, the wind brought them to her face, like crystal drops of water.

After waiting for too long, she became conscious and scenes from the past flashed before her eyes. She sometimes laughed and sometimes frowned.

Master, Daddy, Mother, Senior Brother... and Ye Zi, she could finally pronounce the name calmly, without the pain that penetrated deep into her bones, but only melancholy and bitterness.

If we cannot meet again in this life, I hope you will not be sad. After all, there is still someone accompanying me in this eternal burial place.

Huangfu Jue had never been so embarrassed.

The golden crown was gone, and the thick black hair was covered with snow. His face was covered with blood and mud, and his clothes were torn to pieces. He staggered a few steps before steadying himself, but he smiled happily, "It's done."

Yanzhi stared at him blankly, and seeing the pale color on his lips, she could not feel any joy. After hesitating for a while, she finally put her hand on his arm, but it trembled instantly. Huangfu Jue embraced her and said lightly, "You are standing in the wind, and your hands are already so cold." He put her hand in his arms and sat down together.

His face was pale, and his features looked even colder. He seemed extremely tired, and did not speak again after he sat down.

Yanzhi's hands slowly wrapped around his waist and hugged him tightly. His body suddenly stiffened, then slowly relaxed, leaning most of his weight towards her.

His eyelids were tightly closed, but the corners of his lips were deeply raised.

A distance of thirty feet.

A person who has mastered the art of lightness only needs to lift it up lightly.

Huangfu Jue had already found the third foothold with her on his back. He calculated it very accurately, and every time he ran out of energy, a small pit would appear.

Yanzhi counted silently in his heart, five feet, ten feet, fifteen feet... His heart rate was very fast, and the true energy was rolling in his body, but he could still find the landing point very accurately.

Twenty-five feet.

The top of the cliff is right in front of us.

She could see a figure on the top of the cliff, waving and shouting excitedly, but her heart sank to the bottom in an instant.

Huangfu Jue's figure paused in the air, and he spat out a mouthful of blood.

Taiyin is damaged, and Qi and blood flow backwards.

Yanzhi's hand tightened, and her thumb pinched hard into the left side of his neck, "Ah!"

The two men fell down rapidly, "clang--" Huangfu Jue exerted his strength, and the sword in his hand cut through the snow wall, causing snowflakes to fly in vain.

"Miss, catch it." Suddenly, a two-foot-long soft rope appeared in the air and chased after them. Huangfu Jue grabbed it.

It was very quiet, and only the pounding of the heartbeat could be heard. After a while, Huangfu Jue's low laugh was heard, "Hehehe... I haven't experienced this feeling for a long time, Yanzhi, are you afraid?"

"I'm afraid..."

"Silly girl, at least I'm here with you. If you really fall like this, it's actually not bad."

"Miss!" The person who leaned out from the top of the cliff was Li Luo, her voice already hoarse, "Miss, come up quickly!"

Huangfu Jue sighed, "Silly girl, I have no strength left. You climb up first."

Yanzhi let go of his neck, held the rope, and moved slowly. When she passed him, he leaned over and kissed her on the cheek, saying softly, "Don't be afraid. If you fall, I will definitely catch you."

Yanzhi had no distractions, she grabbed the rope and climbed up step by step. Girls don't have much strength, Li Luo is now lying on the ground, she must hurry up, and then pull Huangfu Jue up with Li Luo.

His meridians are now disrupted and half of his body must be unable to move.

Finally reaching Li Luo's hand, Li Luo cried with joy, "Miss..." Yan Zhi didn't bother to say more, she turned over and directly grasped the soft rope, "Li Luo, let's work together! Li Luo?" Seeing her stunned expression, Yan Zhi couldn't help but scolded her. Li Luo lowered her head and responded.

The soft rope moved upwards little by little, with a lazy smile on his lips.

"Miss?" Li Luo's voice sounded a little strange. "Do you really like him?"

Her whole mind was focused on what was going on below, and she only groaned softly. Li Luo suddenly became excited, "I don't believe it... How can he compare to Master Ye Zi... He has countless women... He is a murderer... Miss, you promised Master Ye Zi that you would marry him..."

Li Luo's hand had already loosened. She didn't have time to think about it and just pulled back.

"Miss, you can't let Master Ye Zi down!" Li Luo's voice calmed down, her hands and feet were cold, and she screamed: "No——"

Huangfu Jue's hand had already climbed to the top of the cliff, and the soft rope was hissing towards his throat like a venomous snake. He raised his head, his phoenix eyes were cold and ruthless for a moment, and his whole body was deadly and cold. After seeing the white figure rushing towards him, his expression slowed down.

Let go, lunge forward, and clasp your fingers and palms together.

Yanzhi tightly grasped Huangfu Jue's hand, but her body took a step into the air. Behind her was Li Luo's heart-wrenching cry, "Miss——" At this moment, her mind became particularly clear, her arms hugged a protruding stone, and her fingers immediately bit it hard.

"Crack!" There was a very crisp sound. Maybe her arm was dislocated or her nail was broken. She couldn't think of anything else.

Hold on tight and never let go.

Huangfu Jue held his sword against the stone wall, looking at her with a gentle smile in his black eyes, and spoke in a low voice like a sigh, "What should I do, girl? I suddenly want to kiss you."

She bit her lower lip tightly with her teeth, and the acrid taste rushed to her throat and eyes. Below her was surging clouds and a cliff, and her strength was as gentle as a reed. He still smiled like that, and his smile was like the spring breeze blowing through the willow branches in March.

Well, if I let go like this, time can stay at this moment forever.

Huangfu Jue looked at her and stopped smiling, "You're crying again. You never cried before." His eyes were dark and deep, slowly revealing his deep and strong emotions. He called out softly, "Crazy girl, stupid girl, silly girl..."

The stubborn eyes suddenly showed doubt, and the black crystal-like eyes stared at him steadily.

His eyes were deep, but the corners of his lips were slightly raised. His soft voice was already dry and hoarse, "You dead girl, if you dare to let go, I won't let you go even if I become a ghost!"

Yanzhi's body trembled suddenly, tears fell like beads from a broken string, and she murmured softly, "Alu, Alu..."

Huangfu Jue smiled slowly, with emotions surging in his eyes, and he slowly repeated, "You little bitch, if you dare to let me go, I won't let you go even if I become a ghost!"

As soon as he finished speaking, his hand slipped out of Yanzhi's palm like a fish and pushed her palm like lightning.

Yan Zhixin was still in a daze, but she was involuntarily pushed high into the air by his force, "No, no - Alu, Huangfu Jue!" She was terrified and stretched her hands forward in vain.

His fingers slowly stretched out, like a Udumbara. Blood continued to flow from the corners of his mouth, but his slanted eyes were still smiling.

Farther and farther away, Yanzhi despairingly discovered that her struggles were in vain, and there was only cold air left in her clenched fingers.

His smiling brows were gradually twisted in tears. His thin face and narrow slanted eyes always had a vicious and cold expression. "Aolu, Aolu!" His voice was full of tears and his heart was broken.

It turns out it was you, it turns out you never forgot!

Two people rushed down from the top of the cliff like lightning, one of them caught Yanzhi, and the other swooped down like an eagle, and after a few turns, he caught Huangfu Jue.

Watching the man carrying Huangfu Jue and using the force from the sword pit to climb up, Yanzhi felt her body go limp and spat out a mouthful of blood, "Daddy..." She had fallen into endless darkness.

The author has something to say: After giving it some thought, this is all that can be put into this chapter.

Let me write about the childhood stories of Jue Ye and Yan Zhi.

It is said that it was a time when two children were innocent.

☆、Extra: The miserable green boy

"Miss, Miss!" The maids in long dresses decorated with emerald flowers ran around hurriedly, "Is it over there?" "What about the Buddhist hall? Have you checked the kitchen? Miss said that the Buddha's hand cake is delicious." "Miss, Miss..." People gradually walked away.

A figure rustled out from behind the rose bushes. She had a double-ringed bun and a pink top. Her big eyes rolled around before she brushed off the dirt and stood up. She kicked the branch under her feet in anger, pouting, "I hate you. Why are you attending a martial arts conference? You only leave me here. Master and my brothers are all bastards!"

Baiyun Temple on Cuiwei Mountain.

This is a sacred place with ancient trees and vines, lush grass, fog and clouds, and peach trees at the ferry.

Back mountain.

The spring gurgled down from the rocks, and the fish in the water played happily. A pair of snow-white feet kicked the water, and she held a handful of fine grass in her hand, occasionally throwing it into the water. Although she was small, her hands were very skillful. Every time she moved her hands, a fish would float up with its white belly turned up, and soon it would wag its tail and swim away.

When she was having fun, she giggled and muttered, "Stupid fish, stupid fish, ah, where are you hiding..."

Suddenly, her pretty little nose wrinkled, "Where's that fishy smell? It's so stinky?" Her nose was very sensitive and she could detect any strange smell. Second Brother loved to tease her and said that her nose was more sensitive than Huang Huang's.

The gurgling water was suddenly mixed with traces of blood, and soon the stream was filled with white fish bellies.

She quickly took out her little feet and swam upstream excitedly to find the culprit who had ruined her fun.

Not long after walking, we found a man upstream, half of his body stuck in the stream, motionless.

She was born in a wealthy family, and could tell at a glance that this man was either rich or noble. Although his clothes were dirty and torn, they were the cloud-patterned brocade that her father loved to wear. She mustered up the courage to kick him twice, but when he didn't react, she pulled him up by his feet.

The eldest lady was so tired that she was panting heavily. She stepped on his butt a few times with her pointed little feet and said angrily, "You are as heavy as a pig."

After circling around him twice, the little girl was very hesitant.

His injuries were very serious. There were three knife wounds and seven sword wounds on his body. The wounds were already black and purple, and his body was only slightly moving. Even if he was not dead, he was not far from death. But the master often said that except for him, seven out of eight men in the world were stupid and eight were bad. He was struggling and reluctant to give up such a good opportunity to practice his medical skills.

She was shocked when she saw his face. His entire cheeks were covered with a light green. Even so, it could be seen that he had thick eyelashes and a straight nose. He was clearly a slender and delicate beautiful boy.

Such a beautiful thing...can't just die like this.

After much difficulty, they found a cave and moved him in. Then they excitedly sneaked back to the alchemy room and brought back a large pile of medicine.

I carefully applied ointment all over his body, and it took a lot of thought to detoxify him.

Is it the Heartbroken Red or the Love Knot, the End of the World Grass or the Red Dust Tears? How about trying them one by one?

After taking the medicine, she stared with her eyes wide open. One stick of incense, two sticks of incense... it was too long, and her eyelids closed unconsciously.

When I woke up again, my life was already in someone else's hands.

Someone was holding my throat tightly in his hand, and a pale green face was close at hand, with slender eyes red, "Who are you..."

She burst into tears, her face covered with tears and snot. She kicked and hit him with her hands and feet, "Ahhh... bad guy... bad guy..." Master was right, all men in the world are not good.

He glared at her fiercely and tightened his

grip tightly.

Her hands and feet gradually became weak and she clapped them softly on him. Her eyes had begun to roll up like a dead fish.

Wuuwuwu, Master, help me, Yanzhi will be obedient from now on, it hurts so much, it hurts so much, Master, help me...

He suddenly twitched, blood oozing from his facial features, his eyes widened in unwillingness, and his body fell straight backwards.

The little guy cried desperately, "Ahhh... cough cough cough..." His round body rolled and crawled out.

After returning, the maid was overjoyed, but the master had not come back yet. She lost her temper, drove everyone away, and hid in the house crying. For two consecutive days, she was awakened by nightmares at night and dared not leave the house during the day.

On the third day, he calmed down a little. Wiping the bruises on his neck, he slipped out again with Huang Huang, feeling angry.

The cave was filled with the smell of blood and decay. His face was covered in blood and he was already barely breathing. She knew that the antidote she had used must be wrong and the drugs conflicted with each other. She felt relieved but also a little guilty. She kicked him hard a few times. When she heard his low and vague moans, she felt compassion again.

He flexed his fingers for a long time and

made up his mind, "Let's try again. If it still doesn't work, just accept your fate."

This time she learned her lesson. After taking the medicine, she hid far away from the cave. After a while, painful howls were heard in the cave. Yanzhi hugged Huanghuang's thick neck and was ready to run away. Huanghuang was their mountain dog in Tianshan. He barked at the cave entrance with disdain and licked the palm of his little master with his tongue.

His pain only lasted a short time, and after rolling a few times, he became motionless.

After feeling frustrated, she regained her fighting spirit, threw the cakes she had brought with her into the hole, and went back to ponder.

On the second day, the Nine-Transformation Snow Soul Heart was extracted from the hundred-year-old snow lotus of Tianshan Mountain.

On the third day, Tiansha Ancient Temple had Xiaohuandan, the holy medicine for healing.

...

It has to be said that the girl was really lucky. Although her medical skills were not very good, she had a wealthy master, and the emergency medicines he left for her apprentice were enough to equal the collection of an entire sect.

Although the medicines he took were not completely effective for his condition, they were all miraculous medicines for healing and nourishing the body. So many medicines, some strong and some mild, collided with each other in his body. Although they made him suffer from excruciating pain and made him live a life worse than death, they managed to keep him alive.

On the sixth day, he finally opened his eyes. There was darkness and emptiness in his eyes. He looked at her quietly, "Who are you?" His voice was hoarse and rough, like coarse sand grinding on his body.

The little girl who was peeking out of the cave jumped up as if frightened and ran away without looking back.

When he came back, he had a high fever all over his body, and his face was no longer green, but looked like a cooked shrimp. He curled up into a ball, mumbling, "...Mother...fire...Mother...Mother..."

She squatted beside him with a worried look on her face, but he grabbed one of her hands and held it tightly, "...Mother..."

The devil is your mother! After kicking her several times, he did not let go, but hid her hand deep in his arms, "Mother..." As she listened, her eyes became red. Although he was pitiful, he must have a very good mother. Her mother sent her to Tianshan when she was very young, and usually cared about other people's daughters.

She is a poor child, and he...seems to be too.

A high fever can really damage your brain.
She struggled to carry him back into the stream. As soon as he opened his eyes, he jumped out of the stream and used his fingers like blades to coldly cut off several strands of her hair.

She burst into tears, what a liar, he just called me his mother and now he wants to hurt people.

After crying for a long time, she didn't feel the expected pain. She quietly opened her eyes and saw him staring at her blankly. Water drops fell along his hair, his eyes were black and moist, and he seemed... even more handsome than the master.

One big and one small, one ignorant, the other at a loss, they began to look into each other's eyes affectionately for the first time.

From then on, she often ran to the back mountain.

After his fever subsided, he was awake longer and longer every day. He could find useful things from the things she brought.

Every time she saw him, she was very happy and would always chatter for a long time. Most of the time he just listened quietly. When he didn't talk, she called him "Alu" because his face was green when she saved him. She giggled and gestured to him, but he didn't get angry.

He seemed very hungry and would eat whatever food she brought him. At first, he would throw up after eating but would immediately continue eating.

She would burst into tears when she saw him. His clothes were of such good quality, but he was actually a hungry child.

She started to make a fuss about eating meat, so the cook prepared a table full of meat dishes. She managed to hide two chicken legs and took the opportunity to run to the back hill during her afternoon nap.

For some reason, a big hole suddenly appeared on the soft ground, and she fell heavily into it, hitting her forehead on the hard stone.

She fainted. When she woke up, she burst into tears, calling out A-Lu's name until her voice became hoarse. She was bleeding so much, she was scared and cold, and gradually she could no longer speak.

She kept the chicken leg in her arms, and she hoped that it would be hot when she saw Aolu.

It was Ah Lu who saved her, although his expression was strange, a mixture of coldness and disgust. But when he jumped in and hugged her, she was so happy that she could only shed tears and took out the chicken leg from her arms tremblingly.

A'lu's injury finally healed, and when she came to look for him she often couldn't find him.

She didn't always get out smoothly. After she hadn't seen him for three days, she got up early and waited for him at the cave entrance. When he came out of the cave, there was obvious surprise in his eyes, and he walked out without saying a word.

She chased after him, calling his name. He walked very fast and disappeared from her sight once he went around the foot of the mountain. She became anxious and ran as fast as she could, lifting up the hem of her skirt.

That day she was wearing a very beautiful long plum blossom gauze skirt. She walked too fast and stepped on the silk ribbon, falling down in embarrassment.

She grimaced in pain and tears streamed down her face.

As she was crying, Ah Lu's figure appeared, standing in front of her with her arms crossed, looking at her impatiently. She burst into laughter and limped after him.

He didn't wait for her, but slowed down.

Ah Lu kept walking up the mountain, and at some point, she had a wooden bow and arrow in her hand. But they walked around the mountain that day and found nothing.

She went from being very happy at the beginning to being depressed and finally just lying on the stone and refused to move.

Ah Lu said stiffly, "Wait," and then disappeared.

When he came back, he was holding a snow-white rabbit in his hand. She cheered and hugged it, looking at him pitifully, "It's so cute, can you please not eat it?"

Ah Lu glanced at her coldly.

As she walked down the mountain, she talked to the little rabbit and pulled its long ears while giggling. But the little rabbit suddenly bit her hard, kicked its hind legs, and ran away at lightning speed.

She screamed and ran after him with red eyes. The moss was smooth and covered with vines, and she slipped down the mountain stream.

"Ah—ah—"

She screamed with her eyes closed, her body miraculously hanging in the air. She opened one eye, and the strange rock under her head shook slightly. At this moment, the force pulling on her feet suddenly weakened, and she was teetering in the air. She screamed, "Alu, if you dare to let go, I will not let you go even if I become a ghost!"

In the end, it was A-Lu who carried her down the mountain because her leg was broken.

Ah Lu's back was very thin and creaky, but she fell asleep contentedly.

She was very happy at that time because A-Lu was no longer as cold as before. She had a very beautiful dream, dreaming of flying a kite with A-Lu.

That was the last time she saw A-Lu.

The master finally came back, and she just greeted him and ran out excitedly. Because she had half a roasted rabbit in her arms, she wanted to give it to Ah Lu.

The master's expression at that time was

very shocked.

That day she searched all over the mountain but couldn't find Ah-Lu. So she waited at the cave entrance, thinking Ah-Lu would come back.

She waited until the sun set and the sky was full of stars. The master came, held her in his arms and sighed, "Yanzhi, if he misses you, he will definitely come back to see you."

In the end, she never waited for A-lu, and later her master took her back to Tianshan.

For a very long time, she would always think of Ah Lu. He was her only friend. She had a master and a senior brother, but no friends.

The author has something to say: Yanzhichunchun's first love, uh, may be a little young... isn't she very cute and very loli?

Friends who are new to the article, please collect it.

Next, let's sing sweet...

☆, lingering

It turns out it was you, it turns out you never forgot!

Two people rushed down from the top of the cliff like lightning, one of them caught Yanzhi, and the other swooped down like an eagle, and after a few turns, he caught Huangfu Jue.

Watching the man carrying Huangfu Jue and

using the force from the sword pit to climb up, Yanzhi felt her body go limp and spat out a mouthful of blood, "Daddy..." She had fallen into endless darkness.

In the dimness, I seemed to hear many voices. Someone was shaking beside the bed, crying softly, and sighs lingering in my ears. I searched anxiously, but could not find the voice I wanted to hear the most.

When she opened her eyes, she saw Yan Yanzi's relieved face. He stroked her hair with his big hand and said, "Good girl, it's good that you're awake." He seemed to have not slept for a long time. His eyes were bloodshot and there was a stubble on his chin.

Yan Zhi moaned softly, the past came flooding back, her heart was in a mess. She stared at Yan Yanzi blankly, her eyes suddenly moistened, "Daddy..."

Looking at his daughter's misty eyes, Yan Yanzi just twisted the corner of the quilt for her lovingly and said in a deep voice: "The emperor is fine. With father here, you don't have to worry about anything. Just have a good rest." Seeing his daughter's eyes, which had always been clear, covered with a little sadness and filled with grief, the father felt sad.

He was fine…hazy and eyes closed again.

A bright light was getting bigger and bigger in front of her eyes, and the soft rope came in front of her eyes like a snake. Yanzhi suddenly woke up!

Holding Yan Yanzi's hand tightly, she spoke with difficulty, "Daddy, Li Luo..."

Yan Yanzi raised her hand to interrupt her, "Li Luo is in the torture chamber now. She told me everything. Don't be sad. She will definitely not be able to survive."

Li Luo, she is too foolish! Yan Zhi let go of her hand dejectedly, treason! He is not A Lu, he is Huangfu Jue, the emperor of a dynasty... He closed his eyes, and a tear flowed from the corner of his eyes.

His Majesty was in danger and narrowly escaped death.

The people in the headquarters were already in chaos. The civil servants headed by Wang Shouren pointed at Yan Yanzi's nose and cursed him, calling him a wicked villain with wolfish ambitions. Yan Yanzi wanted to save people in a hurry, so he sent people to imprison them.

Huangfu Jue was still asleep when thirteen officials of the third rank and above knelt outside the courtyard. The military officers were in full armor and glared at them angrily.

When Yan Zhixing came, she only glanced at them lightly, and walked straight to Wang Shouren, her eyelids drooped, her expression cold, "What do you mean, Wang Cheng?"

Wang Shouren knelt on the ground and said, "Empress, we are here to see the Emperor."

"The emperor hasn't woken up yet."

"I will wait!"

Yanzhi raised her eyelids, her brows brimming with anger, "The reason why the emperor was attacked is unknown, and the Western Tour is complicated. Wang Chenggui is the head of all officials, why is he so negligent in his duties?"

Wang Shouren raised his eyebrows, looked at her with a gleam in his eyes, then put his hands in his sleeves, lowered his eyes again, and said coldly: "It is better for the Queen to avoid suspicion in this matter."

Yanzhi smiled, her eyes as cold as water slowly moved around him, "The Prime Minister is a smart man, why bother yourself with trivial matters and mislead others and yourself." She entered the hall with fluttering sleeves.

Pei Lingmin, the Minister of the Secretariat, looked at her from behind, his eyes thoughtful, and murmured, "It seems our queen has changed her temper, ouch..." He suddenly covered his stomach and cried, "Prime Minister... I need to go to the toilet... How disgraceful, how disgraceful..."

Wang Shouren closed his eyes, his sleeves shaking violently. Pei Lingmin, you old man, you are not afraid of Yan Yanzi, but you are frightened to death by a few words from a yellow-haired girl. The day Yan Yanzi is dethroned, it will be the day you wrap up your body.

Wang Yan was standing by the bed, her eyes

red from crying.

Yanzhi stopped her greeting, walked around the bed, and said calmly: "Go down."

Wang Yan's eyes widened instantly, her face full of disbelief.

Yanzhi looked at her again, as if thinking that she didn't hear clearly, and said again naturally, "Go down, you are not needed here." Since she was here, everyone else was redundant.

Wang Yan glared at her fiercely, full of resentment and anger, and finally left angrily.

Yanzhi sat down beside the bed and gently stroked Huangfu Jue's face with her fingers. Such eyebrows, such eyes... When she dreamed of A Lu later, she could no longer see his face clearly. She never thought that he would come to her in this way.

Suddenly, she felt an itchy feeling in her palm, and she quickly withdrew her hand. After waiting for a long time, he still didn't open his eyes. Her throat suddenly felt dry, and she poked his forehead with her finger, gritting her teeth and said, "Big liar!"

Huangfu Jue suddenly raised the corners of his lips, quickly hooked his hands around her head, and said lazily: "If you don't lie to me, how can you know that someone is so bad."

Yanzhi lay on him in a daze and bit her lip, "...Are you really Ah Lu?"

His dark eyes looked at her tenderly, his

fingers stroked her temples, felt for the small crescent moon, and said softly, "Silly girl."

Yanzhi sniffed and felt her eyes turn red again. She pouted, "... liar, why didn't you tell me? You made me..." You made me think you were being nice to me for some other reason. She said bitterly, "You wanted to strangle me to death back then. You left without even saying goodbye. How could you bear to jump off a cliff and die alone?"

Huangfu Jue kept laughing, and suddenly raised his head to block her mouth. He barged into her mouth rudely, and domineeringly sucked away all the air. He didn't let her go until she was panting and her eyes were drunk. His eyes were as dreamy as a dream, "Silly girl, it's good to see you again!"

Yanzhi's eyes were blurred with tears, but there was a big smile on the corner of her lips. Yes, they are all still alive.

Huangfu Jue gently kissed the corner of her eyes, "Crybaby..." His hand touched her arm, "...Are you hurt?"

Yanzhi shook her head and said that it was just a dislocated arm and some minor abrasions, nothing serious.

With just this action, beads of sweat appeared on Huangfu Jue's forehead. He felt a little exhausted, but he still lingered on her.

Yanzhi glared at him and told him to lie on

his side. Her hands and feet were weak, so she lay on him for a long time. After thinking for a while, she smiled secretly, put her hair down and went to serve him the meal.

The meal was prepared, and she chose lily and red date porridge and two light side dishes.

Huangfu Jue didn't get up, but just looked at her and smiled.

She had no choice but to move a plum blossom stool, sit at the head of the bed, and feed him one spoonful at a time.

Huangfu Jue swallowed a mouthful of porridge and suddenly laughed, looking at her with his phoenix eyes, "Yanzhi, if you keep looking at me like this, I'm afraid I'll get hungrier and hungrier."

Understanding his implication, Yanzhi blushed, but she did not look away. Huangfu Jue and A Lu, blending together like this, she only felt strange and new, and could not help but want to take another look.

Huangfu Jue looked at her, smiled bitterly and sighed.

The bowl of rice was soon finished, and Yanzhi refused to serve more. She scooped half a bowl of lotus root, corn and pork ribs soup and slowly fed him.

Huangfu Jue took only one sip and frowned, "Salty."

Yanzhi looked at him suspiciously. The imperial chefs accompanying the army were all dead. This was made by the private chef of the Yingzhou prefect. The food served to the emperor must have been prepared with great care. How could it be salty?

She tasted it herself. The soup was delicious, smooth and not greasy. "How is it salty? You..." Huangfu Jue leaned over, staring at her lips, and said, "Really not salty? I want to taste it..." His lips covered hers and he sucked. Yanzhi felt the tip of her lips being held in his mouth, so soft that it was about to melt. Unconsciously, her arms had already wrapped around his neck, trying to respond to him.

Huangfu Jue made a sound, his lips became hotter and hotter, guiding her hands to move down to her body, murmuring, "Baby, I'm going crazy... Just give in to me..."

When her hand touched the iron-hard object, her face turned red and her heart beat fast. She pinched it hard and struggled to get up. Huangfu Juejun's face twisted, he gritted his teeth and said, "You are such a cruel little thing!" Suddenly his eyes flickered, and he said in a low voice, "Sooner or later I will punish you severely."

Yanzhi had already stood far away, her face as red as the peach blossoms in bloom in March, and she was looking at him with a giggle.

She hadn't smiled like this for a long time, her eyebrows and eyes curved, and joy seemed to overflow from her dark pupils. Huangfu Jue narrowed his eyes and hooked his finger at her.

Yanzhi shook her head, her smile becoming a little more mischievous, "I just remembered that there are still twelve people kneeling in the yard. You must be busy, I dare not delay you."

She must have done it on purpose to wait until now. She turned around with a smile, as light as a cloud. "Rosy." Huangfu Jue suddenly said.

"Huh?" She turned around.

Huangfu Jue looked at her quietly and said softly, "Come over in the evening. I'll wait for you to eat."

"Yeah." She nodded imperceptibly, and her heart suddenly filled with joy.

In your eyes, am I someone who would risk my life for a woman? Of course not, never.

He smiled slowly, "You silly girl, if you dare to let go, I will not let you go even if I become a ghost."

He is A'lu, whom she has been thinking about all the time, Huangfu Jue who never tells the truth, and also the little thief who quietly stole her heart.

She was willing to accompany him like this, eating and chatting in a plain way, just like the most familiar family member.

When she came at night, the house was silent. Haigui and his men were standing by the eaves of the corridor. When he saw her coming, he was happy and whispered, "Your Majesty, the emperor was very angry this afternoon. He refused to take medicine and refused to eat." After that, he personally put the tray with banana leaf pattern in the hand of the palace maid into her hand.

Yanzhi looked at him with a smile and said softly, "What if I don't come?"

Haigui's stiff face became even stiffer.

He was the most capable person around the emperor, and must be the best at guessing his master's mind. But she didn't like him spying on her all the time, her feelings were just a matter between the two of them. She was not a concubine who was fawning and competing for favor, and he was not her emperor.

Huangfu Jue would not refuse to take medicine because she was angry, nor would she be complacent because of a eunuch's intentional flattery.

She didn't like Haigui, partly because of his gloomy and thoughtful personality.

Huangfu Jue got off the bed and sat at the table to read the memorials. Yanzhi looked at him quietly for a long while. His face was much paler and there was a bit of fatigue in his eyes.

She had never seen him so tired. Even when he was seriously injured, there was always a wild beast in his eyes.

Huangfu Jue put down the memorial in his hand, smiled and opened his arms to her. She walked over obediently and let him hold her on his lap.

Huangfu Jue leaned his head on her shoulder and smiled softly, "My Yanzhi is still the most fragrant and the cutest. Those old men are really annoying."

Yanzhi's hand went around the back of his neck and kneaded it slowly, her tone carrying a hint of anger, "Didn't Han Lan say that you are seriously injured and need to rest."

Huangfu Jue tilted his head and kissed her hand, "Are you heartbroken?"

Yanzhi's hands relaxed, she hugged his neck tightly, and whispered in his ear: "You are mine, and I will naturally cherish my things."

Huangfu Jue fell silent, holding her face with both hands, his dark eyes slowly scanning hers, "Yanzhi, Yanzhi...do you mean what I think you mean?"

Yanzhi's face flushed and her eyes were drunken, but she did not back down. She nodded slightly under his extremely serious gaze.

She was suddenly held in his arms and could feel his body trembling slightly.

Huangfu Jue laughed softly, "Little thing, you're making me suffer so much."

Holding her tightly like this, it was as if he had melted her into his bones and blood. Kisses fell densely, on the corners of her eyes, on the tips of her eyebrows, on the tip of her nose...

Huangfu Jue's hand suddenly stopped, he took a few deep breaths, took his hand out from under her clothes, and slowly fastened her collar.

Yanzhi's eyes had long since turned into a

pool of spring water; she looked at him tenderly, letting him do whatever he wanted. Her black hair was half scattered on his knees, and there was a hint of spring in the corners of her eyes and eyebrows, which made her look charming. Huangfu Jue smiled bitterly, raised his head and took a few sips of herbal tea, and coughed softly.

Yanzhi reached out and snatched his teacup, and scooped out a bowl of clear soup from the casserole. He had both internal and external injuries, and drinking soup was the best way to nourish his vitality.

Lying on his lap, she looked puzzled, "Why don't you continue?" He seemed to have always wanted it, and abstinence was not conducive to the regulation of Qi. Before coming, she had made sufficient mental preparations.

Although lovemaking consumes physical energy, it can help release the depression, and proper release is good for his body. Moreover, after understanding her own heart, she does not reject his closeness.

Huangfu Jue closed his eyes, and at this moment, he suddenly missed her previous cold and aloof appearance.

Coughing a few times really diverted her attention, and she frowned and went to bring him medicine. Staring at her legs, her eyes were a little gloomy. He hurt the heart meridian and triple burner meridian, and his left hands and feet felt weak. Yanzhi sat for a long time, and there was a sense of numbness.

He kneaded the acupuncture points on her legs with his hands and watched her blow the medicine carefully, her brows gradually softened.

The lotus has already blossomed, and is about to sway with all its charm, right within his reach. She is his, and no one can take her away.

The author has something to say: It's not easy for Mr. Jue either, so let him be proud for a few days.

Brothers, wait a little longer. Spring has already arrived, so how far can summer be? Let the harvest be more intense.

☆、Catching an adulterer

Huangfu Jue closed his eyes, and at this moment, he suddenly missed her previous cold and aloof appearance.

Coughing a few times really diverted her attention, and she frowned and went to bring him medicine. Staring at her legs, her eyes were a little gloomy. He hurt the heart meridian and triple burner meridian, and his left hands and feet felt weak. Yanzhi sat for a long time, and there was a sense of numbness.

He kneaded the acupuncture points on her legs with his hands and watched her blow the medicine carefully, her brows gradually softened.

The lotus has already blossomed, and is about to sway with all its charm, right within his reach. She is his, and no one can take her away.

At night, the two lay side by side in bed.

"Alu, I am your savior."

"Um."

"You have to be very good to me and not have other women."

Huangfu Jue raised the corners of his lips in the darkness, and groped her fingers, intertwining them, "Hmm."

"Alu, why didn't you say goodbye to me and made me cry for so long?"

The smile froze on the corner of his lips, and thinking of the man who looked down upon him coldly, he spoke slowly, "I must be strong to protect my little princess."

Yanzhi hummed softly, "Alu, will you lie to me in the future?"

"If I lie to you again, I will be bullied by you for the rest of my life."

Yanzhi fell silent.

Only at night could she call him A-Lu so unscrupulously, and only when he was A-Lu would he make a promise that belonged only to her.

She shook his hand, "Alu, when did you recognize me?"

"At first sight." Those eyes, bright as cat's eyes, turned slightly, and were full of spirit. They were both smiling and charming, and they admired each other's gracefulness. He smiled slightly in the darkness.

With just that one glance, he knew that he had kept her in his heart for many years.

"At first sight?" Yanzhi frowned, thinking back to the day of her wedding, when she had applied layers of rouge. If she hadn't been mentally prepared, she might not have recognized herself. "You're lying!"

Huangfu Jue just smiled without saying anything. He tilted his head and his warm breath brushed against her ear. "Why can't you sleep?"

It was already midnight, well past her usual bedtime, but there was no trace of weariness in her voice.

She twirled a strand of his black hair around her fingers, and felt the words twirling around her tongue like that, "…A-Lu, do you have anything to ask me?"

Li Luo…Li Luo, such a vivid and beautiful life, she didn't want to die because of her after all.

Huangfu Jue's voice was slightly nasal and rose slightly, "What do you want me to ask?"

"Li Luo…what are you going to do with her…she is actually…just a child who knows nothing."

Li Luo had been in the torture chamber the entire time and had not been interrogated by anyone. He seemed to want to suppress the matter.

Huangfu Jue sighed, untangled her hair, and said calmly, "She is yours, you can handle it yourself, but you can't keep her by your side. A servant who is too stupid will bring trouble to the master."

Yanzhi breathed a sigh of relief. She had a vague premonition in her heart, but she was still surprised to hear him say it. She half-raised herself and looked at him with sparkling eyes, "Alu... I didn't know you were so kind."

Huangfu Jue twitched his lips, half-smiled, and slapped her down with his palm, "Go to sleep obediently."

When Yan Zhi returned home in the early morning, she invited Yan Yanzi over and told him what Huangfu Jue meant.

Yan Yanzi sighed, "Child, you are still too soft-hearted." Then he smiled again, "If the emperor does not pursue the matter, she is unimportant." The sunlight shone through the window screens covered with a thousand colorful shadows onto his face, and his relatively cold eyes also showed a bit of warmth.

"Your health is not good. Even if the emperor protects you, you will definitely be infected with the cold. The other day, my men found a snow frog fruit that was almost ripe. I have asked Linglong to make soup for you."

Yanzhi looked at him, then quickly lowered her head, her long eyelashes hiding the emotions in her eyes.

Snow frog fruit does not appear for a hundred years, and once it matures, it will separate from its mother body and dissolve into the soil. People who collect herbs often have to wait for one or two years, and pick them immediately after they mature and put them in a jade box to preserve their medicinal effects. How can ordinary warriors have the ability to identify and pick herbs?

In some things, we are just deceiving ourselves.

Yan Yanzi patted her head, her eyes full of understanding, "Child, people always have to look forward."

Yanzhi nodded, "I understand, Daddy, what did the emperor say about the avalanche?"

Yan Yanzi smiled and said, "It has been a long time since Wang Shouren wanted to overthrow our Yan family. He is still far from getting what he wants. However, I plan to resign the title of general this time."

Yanzhi was startled, "But the emperor has doubts about you?"

Yan Yanzi shook her head. "The lack of centralized military power has always been a hidden danger in the emperor's mind. Your brother has won many victories in a row and is destined to stand out in the military. My title of general is just an empty title. Dad has let your mother down a lot in this life. When you three siblings are settled, I will resign and take your mother to travel around the world."

After Yan Yanzi left, Yan Zhi lay on the chaise longue, deep in thought. Linglong really brought the snow frog soup, and after serving her to drink it, she hesitated to speak, "Miss, Li Luo she..."

As soon as the medicine entered my mouth, my internal organs immediately felt warm. I held the last mouthful in my mouth, not wanting to swallow it.

When Linglong's eyes had become misty, she spoke weakly, "Pack her things. The people coming from Northern Xinjiang to pick her up are under my brother's command. Let her go find my brother. If there is a chance, ask Qin Jian. If he is willing, then you can go with us." This was the last thing she could do for her.

Linglong knelt down while choking with sobs, "I will wait for Li Luo to thank the queen."

They were the closest people to Yanzhi, and Yanzhi told them about this after she woke up. Huangfu Jue kept his word, and they were all well protected. Because they fell behind, they escaped the most violent range of the avalanche. Yiyue's legs were frozen and she was unable to move. Linglong blamed herself for a long time because of Li Luo's matter.

Now that I have received the confirmation, I am surprised and happy.

The next day, Yan Yanzi really pleaded guilty in front of the emperor and tried to leave. Huangfu Jue refused, so Yan Yanzi knelt for two hours behind Wang Shouren. Huangfu Jue reluctantly agreed, but only removed his title of general, still commanding the imperial guards. He also comforted Yan Yanzi with kind words, and the relationship between the emperor and his subjects became very harmonious.

Wang Shouren was humiliated by Huangfu Jue's teacup smashing, and he accused him of forming a clique for personal gain. In a rage, Wang Shouren closed himself in and claimed to be sick. The imperial concubine cried in front of the emperor with a sad expression, but failed to persuade the emperor to change his mind.

The troops on the northern tour suffered heavy losses at Xingling.

More than ten thousand of the fifty thousand imperial guards were killed, several elders in the court died of fright and freezing, many concubines were reduced to being among the guards, and some were even worse, being buried under the snow, with no trace left of their bodies.

The troops from the northern border who came to welcome the emperor were led to another place by the maze, and someone deliberately shouted loudly to cause an avalanche. It was obvious that there must be spies in the army who wanted to take the opportunity to rebel. Huangfu Jue stopped in Yingzhou and instructed Yan Yanzi to reorganize the army. He also issued five golden orders in a row to summon Huangfu Fang to come and protect the emperor.

Yan Yanzi was demoted, Wang Shouren claimed

to be ill, and the civil and military officials on the northern tour were unprecedentedly united because of the attack on the emperor, and they were ready to fight as they stared at Huangfu Fang who was about to arrive.

When Yanzhi visited Huangfu Jue for three consecutive days, she met Wang Yan, who looked depressed. She waited outside Huangfu Jue's room and was very humble when she saw Yanzhi. Sometimes she would prepare soup and ask Yanzhi to bring it in with pleading.

After one or two times, Yanzhi's heart became more gloomy. When she met Huangfu Jue, she refused to stay any longer. She only chose the most reasonable meal for him and then returned to her own courtyard. Huangfu Jue knew her knot in her heart and could only patiently deal with her slowly.

On this day, Yanzhi had made plans early to go to the market. After the hour of Si, she went to Huangfu Jue's yard.

As soon as I entered the hall, I heard the sound of a woman crying softly.

Yanzhi glanced coldly, stopped Haigui's report, and quietly went to the bedroom.

In the room, Han Lan was packing up silver needles. Huangfu Jue was lying on the bed with the brocade quilt only draped around his waist, leaving his entire back exposed.

Wang Yan knelt at the head of the bed, pulled Huangfu Jue's hand and placed it on her face, sobbing. She wiped her tears for a while, and then used her other hand to pull the quilt up. The hand moved very slowly, and the thin fingers almost slid slowly. In the end, the palm was pressed against it and gently kneaded.

The room was connected to the floor heating, and there was a charcoal basin on the floor, but Yanzhi felt the heat in her palm slowly dissipating. She watched like this, watching Wang Yan almost half pressed against him, but Huangfu Jue still didn't move.

Han Lan suddenly raised his head, and when he saw her, there seemed to be a strange smile in his eyes, and he slowly said, "Hello, Queen."

Her heart suddenly calmed down, her eyes swept across him gently, and she said lightly: "Han Qing, there is no need to be so polite."

Her eyes fell quietly on Huangfu Jue, watching him put on his clothes, sit up hurriedly, and throw Wang Yan to the ground in embarrassment. She laughed softly.

He personally helped Wang Yan up, looked at her red and swollen eyes, and the scarlet bra under her thin Yunfei Baihua Feidie brocade dress. His slender hand gently brushed her bare chest and said slowly, "Your Highness is so cold-resistant. I really envy you."

After saying that, he stopped looking at her and smiled at Huangfu Jue, "Since Your Majesty has a beautiful woman by his side,

I'm going to ask for leave and go out for a walk."

After Huangfu Jue was surprised, his black eyes smiled and he reached out to pull her, "I'll go with you."

Yanzhi took a step back and was right behind Wang Yan. "The emperor is busy, Yanzhi will take his leave."

His steps became faster and faster, and he felt a breath stuck in his chest with nowhere to vent. As soon as he left the yard, a man came from the opposite side and almost bumped into him. He heard him say, "This old minister greets the Queen."

Yanzhi snorted coldly and walked away.

This person was the Secretary of the Central Secretariat Pei Lingmin. He smiled and said, "Your Majesty, please wait. I have something to say."

He walked a few steps to Yanzhi, and seeing her angry eyes, he didn't care at all, and said with a smile: "Your Majesty's phoenix body is important, and you also need to be happy. I have heard that your Majesty loves flowers. The other day I got a pot of Yulouyin. I wonder if I can have the honor of inviting your Majesty to come and see it?"

Yanzhi frowned. She didn't know many officials in the court, but she recognized him as one of the people who knelt down to make a petition a few days ago. She said coldly, "If you have anything to say, just say it."

Pei Lingmin was not surprised at her words. He paused for a moment and said, "Your Majesty, let me make it short. The attack on the emperor had nothing to do with Prince Gong. The people in the court wanted to divert the blame. I have received great kindness from Prince Gong, so I have no choice but to ask for help from Your Majesty today."

Yanzhi stared at him quietly and spoke slowly, "You have found the wrong person. I have no relationship with Prince Gong, and I have no knowledge of the affairs of the court. If there is nothing else, please do as you please."

"Your Majesty," Pei Lingmin's eyes were burning, "if Prince Gong is in danger, the real murderer will never be brought to justice, Youyun will fall into the hands of others, and your brother might be in danger. The prince is about to hand over the personal jade pendant to your Majesty, and he must trust you very much. I don't ask for anything else, I just hope that your Majesty can persuade the emperor when necessary and think of the relationship between brothers."

Yanzhi stopped him with her hand, "I don't like people threatening me, nor do I think I have that much influence on the emperor. The old man is old, and it is inevitable that he will be confused. Yanzhi will forget what happened today, and please forget it too."

After saying this, he turned away. Pei Lingmin stretched out his voice and said behind him: "I respectfully send off Her Majesty the Queen..."

The author has something to say: Second update.

Liu Liu is becoming more and more diligent.

I am very happy to see your messages. Thank you!

☆、Light up the lights

Yanzhi stopped him with her hand, "I don't like people threatening me, nor do I think I have that much influence on the emperor. The old man is old, and it is inevitable that he will be confused. Yanzhi will forget what happened today, and please forget it too."

After saying this, he turned away. Pei Lingmin stretched out his voice and said behind him: "I respectfully send off the Queen..."

Yanzhi took Linglong out directly. The guards seemed to have received the news and no one stopped her. Several people dressed in casual clothes followed her into the crowd, while the other two people, wearing green clothes and small hats, stood behind her with their hands clasped.

Yanzhi was depressed. When she arrived at the shop, she didn't even look at it. She just ordered something and someone paid for it. The shop owner was overjoyed and wanted to flatter her, but was stopped coldly. After walking most of the most famous Qingyi Lane in Yingzhou City, she felt a little relieved. She took Linglong with her and went to look for the unique shops.

Finally, they came to a lantern shop, the owner was a middle-aged scholar. The lanterns were very delicate and lovely, and there were impromptu scenes on the lanterns. Yanzhi couldn't put them down. She chose a set of palace lanterns of plum, orchid, bamboo and chrysanthemum and a beauty lantern, and asked Linglong to pay happily.

She was a smart person, and she amused the owner with just a few words. Seeing that she was interested in lantern making, he explained it in detail and gave her some rare lantern structure drawings. When the two of them left the store, they were holding bamboo strips, rice paper and other things in their hands.

Yanzhi smiled and said to Linglong: "I'll make one for you when I get home. It will be better looking than this."

Linglong nodded, looking quite pleased with herself, "Everything Miss does is the best."

The two of them walked around for a while, and the sun was setting in the blink of an eye. The person following them did not seem to be urging them at all, but was only paying attention to the people and things around them.

Yanzhi was no longer interested, so she

bought a bunch of snacks and brought them back to Yiyue, then turned back.

Huangfu Jue was waiting in her room. Holding a book in his hand, he leaned on the chaise longue where she usually lay, looking at her with a smile.

Yanzhi pretended not to see it, washed her hands, and let Linglong help her remove her makeup.

Huangfu Jue waved his hand and let Linglong go down. He walked behind her, looked into the mirror with his eyes tilted, and laughed softly, "You are so angry that you are very stubborn. Could it be that you are still jealous for ten years?"

Yanzhi threw the long hairpin onto the table without even raising her eyelids.

Huangfu Jue was not annoyed. He took the topaz comb and slowly combed her hair. "She came to see me because of Concubine Qi. This morning, Concubine Qi hanged herself. If you don't like this kind of thing, she has to come forward."

Yanzhi was startled and turned around to look at him, "Is Concubine Qi dead? Why?" That woman with indifferent eyebrows and eyes, who had always lived a peaceful life, how could she seek death for no reason?

Huangfu Jue lowered his eyes and said lightly: "She has an affair with the guard." On the night of the avalanche, he only cared about Yanzhi. Concubine Qi had no one to rely on, and it was the guards in the palace who saved her. The two of them were intimate with each other, and they couldn't control themselves.

Yanzhi's heart tightened, and she grabbed Huangfu Jue's sleeve, "Did you force her to do that?"

Huangfu Jue's eyes flashed with sarcasm, "She is not that bold."

Yanzhi looked at him hatefully, shook her hands, stood up and lay on her side on the bed.

Huangfu Jue followed her and held her in his arms, "Even if you are angry, you should calm down after spending three thousand taels of silver on me." He then laughed softly, "You are so petty, you are not like an adult at all."

Yanzhi pinched his arm fiercely and said bitterly, "Are you very proud of yourself?"

Huangfu Jue actually nodded and said slowly, "I'm very happy that you're angry like this." He hugged her tightly and rocked her slowly in his arms, "I'm the only one who's always worried about gains and losses, thinking about this and that. You should also try this feeling."

His body temperature had been low since he was injured. She kept her hand on him for a long time, but it didn't warm him up. His words came slowly, but they flowed into her heart simply.

There was no reason for her to be so angry. It was just that she could not tolerate things that she had ignored before. Thinking about it in her mind was one thing, and seeing it with her own eyes was another. Hearing him pour out his heart made her heart confused. She lowered her head and fiddled with his fingers, silent.

He held her like this, his face pressed against the top of her head, his breathing gradually becoming calmer.

Since Yanzhi got the drawings from the middle-aged scholar, she spent most of the day in the house learning how to make lanterns.

In just two days, she made two thousand-petal lotus lanterns, one for Yan Yanzi and one for Huangfu Jue's yard.

Since the last time, she had a vague resistance to going to Huangfu Jue's yard. Huangfu Jue summoned her, but she refused to go three out of five times. Huangfu Jue had no choice but to come and bother her when he was free.

She was actually fascinated by it. After becoming familiar with the lanterns, she began to study it herself. She painted eight fine-brush beauties on rice paper and found extremely thin bamboo strips and iron wires, and refused to let anyone else do the work for her.

When Huangfu Jue came, he often saw her naked and dressed in plain clothes, kneeling on the ground, thinking hard. He wondered, "Is she really crazy?" Later, Yanzhi closed the door tightly and refused to see anyone.

On October 12, Huangfu Jue's patience had

run out, and she walked out leisurely. There were two dark circles under her eyes, but her expression was extremely happy.

"Your Majesty, are you free tomorrow night?"

With a look of nostalgia in his eyes, he said casually: "This world doesn't need another bastard like me..."

As soon as he finished speaking, his body shook slightly and he looked at Yanzhi vigilantly. He only had time to stretch out his hand before he fell straight down.

The blade deftly rested on the index finger, Yanzhi smiled at Huangfu Jue and whispered: "...I am finally free."

The author has something to say: Posting silently...

☆、115 Chapter 115

Pang Tong had a gloomy face, holding a person in his arms, and rushed through the alley, "Get out of the way!"

The egret chicken in the fat lady's hand was knocked away, the fortune teller with a goatee fell over, and the child who was eating candied haws opened his eyes wide in fear.

There was chaos and cursing all along the way, but the person in his arms kept laughing.

A gentle, silver bell-like laugh. When Pang Tong brought the bowl of noodles to her with a "bang", she was still laughing.

Her eyes narrowed into long crescents, and she looked very proud and clever. She smiled all the way, and her jade-white face was stained with a faint blush. Pang Tong took a glance at her and swallowed the word "crazy woman" whole.

He sat down next to her, stole a few glances at her, and said in an annoyed voice, "Eat quickly. After you finish eating, we'll go to where you want to go."

Yanzhi smiled and supported her chin with her hand, "Pang Tong, I just did something that no one has ever done before, and I am very happy."

A smile that is too strong is like flowers blooming on branches, revealing a sense of desolation and desolation for no reason.

Pang Tong ate his soup in big gulps and snorted in between, "Hypocrisy."

Yanzhi just smiled and said nothing. After taking a few bites of noodles, she asked with a smile, "Pang Tong, how do you know my identity?"

Pang Tong squinted his eyes and said, "Little Princess of the Snow Region, is she very noble?"

He really knew it.

"Even if you are not noble, it is not something that a mere disciple of the Paradise Palace can know. Who are you working for?"

Her only connection with Paradise Palace was at Tongtian Peak five years ago. He knew her, could it be that... he was the masked man?

The body shapes are indeed somewhat similar, but the voices can be changed.

"Don't move." She shouted. A pair of hands climbed up his face.

Facing her serious gaze, Pang Tong closed his mouth in dismay. Her palms were cold and delicate, and when she rubbed them on his face, he felt tingling. When her palms were placed across his face, there was a soft and gentle fragrance.

Her eyes gradually changed from clear to confused.

Pang Tong held his breath unconsciously, and a trace of embarrassment crept up behind his ears.

Yanzhi frowned and said softly: "...It's not you." Although the eyes revealed after covering her face with her hands had a similar evil look, they were frivolous.

Those eyes were extremely bright, arrogant and bold.

.... The corners of the eyes should be tilted upwards, the pupils should be a light amber color, and the eyelashes should be long and graceful, but they only make people feel elegant......

She was suddenly stunned, and bitterness slowly spread from the bottom of her heart.

She couldn't let go, she only remembered him.

Is he awake? Is he looking for her frantically? She has already written down the things to pay attention to after the

injury. Can Han Lan take good care of him?
Pang Tong looked at her carefully, snorted, quickly pushed the table, and said in a strange voice: "You are so fickle that you are devoted to others so quickly!"
Yanzhi stood up, with a little sadness in her eyes. After thinking for a moment, she said, "Pang Tong, was there a man wearing a mask in the Paradise Palace five years ago? ... He should have been very outstanding."
Pang Tong's eyes flickered, and he said disdainfully: "Male favorites? If not a thousand, there should be at least eight hundred."
Yanzhi looked straight at him, "Where did you go after the Ji Le Palace was wiped out?"
"People always strive for higher positions, and whoever has money is the boss. What you want to ask can be answered in four words: 'No comment'. In our business, we also have credibility."
Yanzhi frowned slightly and said calmly, "The Tanzhong acupoint is aching slightly, and the Qi is stagnant when practicing the Baihui acupoint. The Qi Nu Gong is only suitable for pure Yin physiques. Once a man practices to the ninth level, he will go crazy at best, or his meridians will be broken and he will die from reverse bleeding."
Pang Tong raised his eyebrows lazily, "I will send you to your destination. The mountains are high and the waters are long.

We will never meet again, whether we are destined to meet or not. When you come to my grave in the future, just remember my life-saving grace and add some paper money."

Yanzhi remained silent.

He did save her twice.

Pang Tong smiled, "It takes some talent to be a villain. If you don't want to wait for someone to take you back to the palace, you'd better set off early, Your Majesty."

Tongjitang is a century-old brand with branches all over the country. The black gilt-edged plaque can be seen from across the street.

Yan Zhi asked Pang Tong to stop. He raised his eyebrows and asked, "Why don't you go back to the Marquis' Mansion?"

Yanzhi shook her head, looked at the plaque in front of her with complicated eyes, and said softly: "I have my own arrangements, you go ahead."

Her eyes were deep, filled with longing for home and hesitation, but her steps were light and firm.

Someone suddenly grabbed his arm, and Pang Tong's voice was filled with inexplicable irritation, "You can't go."

Yanzhi was not annoyed, she smiled and said, "I'll be fine."

Tongjitang is Xueyu's property. If the master still stays in the capital, the head manager of Tongjitang will definitely know his whereabouts.

Pang Tong frowned, put his arm around her waist, and without letting her speak, he took her to the bookstore next door. While flipping through old books, he whispered to her quickly, "Something happened at Tongji Hall three days ago, and the people there are no longer reliable. You'd better go find Yan Zhishang now."

Yanzhi's heart suddenly panicked. Three days ago, when Huangfu Jue had the accident. She weighed the pros and cons quickly. She couldn't stay outside for long. It would be difficult to escape after Huangfu woke up. She couldn't look for Zhishang. The Marquis' Mansion was the power center of the imperial city, and every move was monitored.

Also, she had an inexplicable obsession in her heart: she must see the master first!

She took off the jade pendant tied with colorful silk at her waist and said, "Go to the west of the city and find a jade shop with the same seal. Take it with you and someone will come to see you. I'll wait for you at Qingshui Shop."

Pang Tong glanced at her slightly protruding belly with disgust.

Yanzhi's face was a little pale, and her voice was as calm as before, "I can take care of myself. The city will be under martial law at any time, so you should be careful."

Pang Tong disappeared in the crowd. Yanzhi gathered his cloak tightly around him, held his waist, and blended into the crowd with some difficulty.

It was already bright outside and there were many people walking on the street.

She tried to concentrate. There didn't seem to be any major incidents in the palace. Although there were many soldiers patrolling the streets, they didn't look nervous. It seemed that the Queen Mother didn't take any action. Perhaps Huangfu Jue's unexpected awakening disrupted their deployment.

He... didn't know what he was feeling now. His family was betraying him, and she had also deceived him. He must be in great pain.

A clear voice suddenly sounded beside me, "Big sister, are you looking for someone?"

She was startled and found a little girl in red pants and a red jacket standing next to her, about seven or eight years old, looking at her with concern with her big round eyes. There was also a young man with an impatient look on his face next to her.

It turned out that she had been standing there for a long time.

Her eyes were twinkling, and she looked like a little girl. Yanzhi felt tender in her heart, and gave the paper flowers she bought to the little girl, and patted her head, "Thank you, sister is fine. There are many people on the street, go find your parents quickly."

The little girl skipped and jumped holding the boy's hand.

A young boy's voice could be vaguely heard, "...stranger...you are...stupid..."
In a trance...
A long time ago, there was also a little girl who chased after a skinny boy, calling out all over the mountains and plains, "Alu...Alu..."
Pang Tong brought people quickly.
Yan Zhi was startled and slowly stood up, "Big Brother..."
The man dressed in snow-white clothes, handsome and extraordinary, who turned around and came out after Pang Tong, was indeed Duan Kaiyang.

☆、116 Chapter 116

Duan Kaiyang was making tea, and the fellow disciples were speechless for a moment as they looked across the steamy Boshan stove.
Duan Kaiyang pushed the teacup in front of Yanzhi, smiled, and slowly said, "Why are you so willful and want to leave the palace at will?"
His voice was as gentle as before, but it was also a little distant.
Yanzhi lowered her eyes, her mind drifting like tea leaves, she only called out softly, "...Senior Brother..."
The light in Duan Kaiyang's eyes dimmed a little, and he smiled nonchalantly, "What do you want to know? Why should I do it?"
Yanzhi's hands clenched quietly in her sleeves.

She did feel a little resentful towards her senior brother. If something really happened to him, she thought, she would rather die in his place.

"...I saved him, brother, I want to see the master."

Duan Kaiyang looked at her with an unpredictable look in his eyes. After a long while, he slowly spoke, "So, your identity has been exposed?"

"Well," the voice was a little louder and had some emotion, "Is this what Senior Brother wanted?"

How could she explain her extraordinary medical skills to Huangfu Jue? The Snow Region had nothing to do with the dynasty, and she had also implicated her father and Zhishang. Her move had exhausted herself and the entire Yan family.

She could no longer stay by Huangfu Jue's side, nor could she be the Queen of the Celestial Empire. After all, she could no longer drag down her master.

"What do I want?" Duan Kaiyang stared at her with a strange look on his face. He repeated it again, as if suddenly realizing, "No, that's not what I want. I want him to die."

"Brother!" Yan Zhi scolded in a low voice. Looking at him, she was angry and anxious, her body trembling slightly, and she tried hard to soften her tone, "What's wrong with you?"

In her memory, the eldest brother had never

been like this. He was always smiling like spring breeze, gentle and doting. She was suspicious and frightened, and when she stood up, her body couldn't help but sway.

Duan Kaiyang leaned over from the opposite side, grabbed her arm, his face slightly stern, and used two fingers to feel her pulse.

She grabbed his sleeve with her backhand and met his gaze, "Big Brother, what happened?"

Duan Kaiyang lowered his eyes, a gentle internal force came from his heart sutra, and his tone contained a hint of blame, "How can a person with a double body be so impetuous? Have you thrown away all the skills you used to cultivate your energy?"

His tone made Yan Zhi calm down a little, but she still did not give up asking, "Big Brother..."

Duan Kaiyang used a little force to make her sit on the chair. He let go of her hand, with a half-smile on his face, "Yanzhi, you are still like this. You only see the people you want to see. Before, it was Ye Zi, now, it is Huangfu Jue. What about the others? Aren't they important?"

His tone was indifferent, but his expression was somewhat bleak, and he was tired and frustrated. "If one day, the thing you hold in your palm and put in your heart that you don't want others to see is trampled underfoot and becomes tattered, anyone would want to kill them."

Yanzhi stared at him in a daze, her expression gradually becoming serious, "Brother... This is my own choice, I don't blame anyone. Big Brother and Master will always be the people Yanzhi respects the most. I won't regret it, and Brother doesn't have to be sad."

Duan Kaiyang raised his eyes quickly, his eyes were sharp and dark, and he looked at her with a smile, "Okay, never regret it." He quickly added, "I hope he will never make you regret it."

Yanzhi frowned, feeling flustered for a moment. The implication in the eldest brother's words...she really had never thought about it. Suddenly, she couldn't think of anything in her heart, like a mess, tangled and entangled. Such a mess also made her feel empty, as if something was suddenly lost.

Tears suddenly welled up in my eyes. These men... only make me feel guilty. How hateful.

Through tearful eyes, she heard Duan Kaiyang sigh and smile bitterly, "Silly girl... do you really take it seriously?" He reached out to wipe her tears, his heart slightly panicked, and he turned his face away.

Duan Kaiyang paused and took his hand back as if nothing had happened.

Taking a sip of tea, he said calmly, "If it weren't for you, Huangfu Jue should have been taught a lesson. He took over the Ye family in Hainan and the southern waterways. He stretched his hands too far."

Yan Zhi was shocked. The Ye family should belong to Ye Zi. She didn't know that Huangfu Jue had conquered the Ye family. However, a wealthy merchant like the Hainan Ye family must rely on a certain authority. There would be no essential difference between relying on the Snow Region or relying on the royal family.

He sighed in his heart and said awkwardly, "Brother, you are all the people I value most. I cannot accept any of you being hurt. Snow Region has a strict order... not to involve the royal family. I... have already left him, so stop it."

Huangfu Fang is controlled by his second brother, and this time the attack on Beijing must be driven by Xueyu. Because he loves her, does he have to force the man she loves into a desperate situation?

Perhaps she had no right to argue about right or wrong, but their behavior still hurt her.

If he really died, she would not be able to forgive anyone.

Duan Kaiyang's mouth curled up with a hint of ridicule, "You want to see me to plead for him?"

Yanzhi looked him straight in the eye without flinching and said softly, "Yes, if you insist on killing him, then kill me first. If he dies because of me, I will never live alone."

"Crack", with a slight popping sound, Duan Kaiyang's teacup cracked inch by inch, and when he spread his palm, silver flakes flew away. His face remained calm, and he smiled and said word by word: "Good, it's worth it that Master and Senior Brother love you."

Yanzhi felt a pain in her heart and her eyes turned red, but her expression remained stubborn.

After a long while, Duan Kaiyang slowly spoke, "Master has left the capital to find the Three-legged Golden Crow for you. If you don't follow me back to the Snow Region, you won't be able to see him. Do you want to stay, or go with me?"

Tears rolled down and fell on the back of his hand. He felt lost and annoyed at the same time, and he didn't feel relaxed at all when he forced his senior brother to make a promise.

Shaking his head, "I can't leave, Senior Brother, thank you..."

She agreed to keep the child.

With a small sob, she walked around Duan Kaiyang and wrapped her arms around him, "Brother, I'm sorry... take good care of Master... take good care of Ye Zi..."

After a long time, a pair of hands hugged her back, hugged her tightly, and then let go.

"If you want this, I won't force it."

Duan Kaiyang and Pang Tong seemed to be familiar with each other. Before leaving, he said to Yan Zhi, "I will leave Beijing today. You and Pang Tong will go to the Shen family's villa in the north of the city. I will contact Zhishang. You must not go out casually and rest assured to take care of your pregnancy."

Yanzhi thought for a moment and said, "Pang Tong's internal energy is not in the right way. I want to ask Master to let him become Xueshan's disciple."

"I'll make the arrangements once this matter is settled."

He had already stepped out of the door, dressed in white, and finally turned back, "Don't you ask me why I killed you in public?"

Paiyun Palm and Broken Heart Needle are his famous skills.

Yanzhi lowered her eyes, "...Senior Brother doesn't want to hide it from me."

There was a light brown ivory-inlaid Guangyun Twelve Mansions screen in the room, and the hazy smoky color was reflected around her, implying a slight anger.

Duan Kaiyang smiled and strode out of the house.

The king has the intention, but the goddess has no dream.

He just didn't want to accept it and wanted to know if he was still her most trusted senior brother.

If it is love, it will make people crazy.

The author has something to say: La La La... Daily update

☆、117 Chapter 117

Shen's villa.

The two-story house has its own gate and courtyard, with luxuriant flowers and trees and deep shadows of tung trees.

Apart from her and Pang Tong, there was only a deaf-mute couple guarding the gate of the huge courtyard.

Pang Tong seemed to be living a very happy life, drinking and singing every day, playing the flute and enjoying himself. He was not seen going out, nor did he come to disturb Yanzhi.

Yanzhi, however, became more and more irritable day by day.

She hadn't received any news for three days. That evening, Pang Tong fished out a silver carp from the backyard pond and cooked fish soup with great interest.

Yanzhi smelled the fishy smell and felt very irritated. She left the table with a cold face.

If it was still the first time they met in the garden, she would never believe that he could cook. Although there was a mute couple, he still took care of most of the three meals. He made fish soup probably because she had a poor appetite.

I felt bad for losing my temper for no reason before going to bed. After thinking for a while, I went to the next door and knocked on Pang Tong's door.

With a push, the door opened. No one was in

the room.

Yanzhi walked slowly around the room and returned to her own room.

The bamboo shadows danced, and the moonlight came in, illuminating the deserted room.

He would leave sooner or later. It's just that when people are helpless, they will rely more on familiar things. He didn't say anything, so she pretended not to know.

I lay on my side on the bed, hugged my body, and watched the fetus in my belly move a little. I waited quietly for it to calm down.

This was the only warmth she could get in the long night.

When she fell asleep, she had decided not to wait any longer.

As soon as she walked out of the room, she was stunned.

Pang Tong was leaning against the blue stone under the wisteria, twirling a jade flute in his hand. He was wearing purple clothes and had black hair, looking refreshed.

Seeing her in a daze, he glanced at her and spoke lazily, "...Good morning."

The sun's shadow had reached the wisteria trellis. Yanzhi remained silent, ignoring his ridicule, but still felt a little happy in her heart.

Since he is back, he must have gone to get information last night.

On the table were crystal buns and tofu

pudding from Xia Ji, a famous breakfast shop where people lined up half the street to buy buns.

She ate two steamed buns and drank half a bowl of tofu pudding. Although she didn't feel like vomiting, Yanzhi still put down her chopsticks.

After staring at Pang Tong and finishing his meal, Yan Zhi said softly, "Where did you go last night?"

Pang Tong narrowed his eyes and held up two fingers. "Good news, bad news, which one do you want to hear?"

Yanzhi looked at him quietly, "Of course I have to listen to everything."

"The good one, the one in Jiuzhou Qingyan Palace, is not dead and attended the morning court today. The bad one, the Yan Mansion was raided."

"Impossible!" Yan Zhi suddenly opened her eyes wide, her face frosty, staring at Pang Tong, "Impossible. He has always trusted Daddy, and Zhi Shang has the Black Family Army at his disposal. Even if he knew my identity, he would never attack the Yan Family!"

Pang Tong raised his beautiful eyes and spoke slowly, "So, he wants to lure you out."

Yanzhi took a few breaths, pressed the Shenting acupoint hard, and tried her best to calm down the surging blood. Calm down, calm down!

She had a secret premonition in her heart

that if nothing had happened, Zhishang would have contacted her long ago.

Before I knew it, my teeth had bitten through my lower lip and I tasted blood in my mouth.

Huangfu Jue, Huangfu Jue!

Without saying a word, she stood up and walked into the house.

Pang Tong frowned and stood up to stop her. Yan Zhi said expressionlessly, "I won't act impulsively. It won't help if I go out."

Pang Tong's face was unusually serious. "Things are not as simple as they seem. The inner nine cities have implemented a curfew. All officials are hiding in their homes at night. Not only the Yan family is under lockdown, but also the Xiao family. I will go and find out tomorrow."

He slowed down his tone a little, "You should have confidence in it." His eyes swept over her slightly bulging belly, "It is the first official prince of the Celestial Empire."

Her eyelids drooped, hiding the light that flashed in her eyes. That man had always been unscrupulous and shameless, and it was hard to expect him to have any affection for his family.

However, her face was pale and indifferent, and her lips were as light as a withered crabapple tree. She couldn't help but want to say something that clearly showed that she didn't agree with him.

Yanzhi forced a smile.

Do you trust him? If you can really open your heart and trust him without reservation, why would you leave in a hurry when he is still not sober?

No matter how hard you try to mend the cracks, there will always be traces left. She can save him with all her heart, but she can no longer love him blindly.

The next night Pang Tong went out as he was told, and Yan Zhi stood by the window, waiting quietly.

Pang Tong came back very late.

When Yanzhi came in, he was biting the bandage with his teeth. Seeing her suddenly come in, he raised his eyebrows in surprise, then smiled and said, "It's just right, the miracle doctor is here."

His wound was very deep, slanting from the shoulder blade to the neck, and the flesh around the wound was torn, exposing the white bones. He should have dodged to the side, otherwise, the arrow would have pierced his throat.

Yanzhi looked at his wound in silence. The wound was too deep and had to be sutured.

"How did you get hurt?"

"I went around to the backyard of your house and ran into a mad dog. I shot it with an arrow. Tear up - fuck, your ancestors..." Pang Tong's handsome face twitched, and his entire back suddenly stretched like a bow. A piece of the table was dug out and he almost fainted.

A pot of the purest Shaodaozi was poured

all over his back, and as his muscles twitched subconsciously, the needle had already been inserted.

The best sewing needle, the long cowhide thread, the smooth and flowing sewing movements.

Sweat beads rolled out one by one, and Ma Shan was absorbed by the cotton cloth. The female doctor even had a faint smile on her face, "You are so talkative, you deserve to be beaten." When the needle was pulled out, a long piece of meat was brought out, and a long inhalation was heard immediately, "By the way, next time you meet a dog that can shoot a shocking arrow, roll away as fast as you can."

Pang Tong was almost out of breath, and snorted, "Your dog?"

Yanzhi finished the thread neatly, "My father's loyal warrior."

As long as Juntian is still alive, Daddy will definitely be fine.

Using the herbs at hand, she made a paste and applied it to the wound, then re-bandaged it. Yanzhi slowly squatted down, looked directly into Pang Tong's eyes, and said softly, "...Thank you."

She had never had a close relationship with this man, but he had been saving her since the second time they met.

Pang Tong snorted, turned his eyes away, and said angrily, "Who cares? I'm starving. Are you going to starve your lifesaver to death?"

Yanzhi's silent smile.
Finally, there is the second good news

☆、118 Chapter 118

The food she cooks won't taste good.
The noodles were made of water, some of which had turned into a paste. She tasted them and found them tasteless. She hesitated in the kitchen for a while, but finally decided not to bother the old couple and brought them out.
Pang Tong looked at her with disdain.
Her expression remained unchanged as she said calmly, "During the recovery period, you should eat lighter meals."
He snorted, and didn't say anything else, finishing the bowl of noodles.
Yanzhi breathed a sigh of relief.
After the meal, the medicinal effect of rosemary began to take effect, and Pang Tong gradually began to lose energy.
Feeling that he was glaring at her angrily, Yanzhi pulled the quilt over him and said softly, "You need to rest."
She was indeed in a hurry, but she could still wait for a short while.
Pang Tong woke up in just two hours. He was in good health, and his wound was only slightly red and swollen, but he did not have a fever.
Last night, he went to the home of Guan Chaobing, the Minister of the Ministry of Revenue. Guan Chaobing's favorite concubine

was his old lover.

Xiao Jiaohong hadn't seen him for a long time. She was pleasantly surprised and clingy to him. When she heard his passionate words, he let her know a lot of information.

"...... The consumptive Xiao family member personally led people to seal up the Yan Mansion... Good man... please move... Hmm... enemy... searched out a lot of gold and silver... dozens of sealed carriages... haven't come for a long time... missed them so much... bad brother... the Xiao family is so proud... the imperial edict then reached their house... the dead old man said he killed a lot of people... he went to court yesterday... and hasn't come back yet... good brother... don't worry... "

After leaving Xiao Jiaohong, he went to the Changning Marquis' Mansion. The seal on the gate had just been torn off, but there was no one inside. Not only was Yan Zhishang missing, but his lovely wife, concubines, maids and servants all seemed to have evaporated from the face of the earth.

He was suspicious, but still went to visit the Marquis of Yan'an's Mansion.

The man must have shown mercy when he shot the arrow, otherwise he might not have come back alive.

I told Yanzhi the important points, and she listened attentively. The sunlight shone on her cheek, and her skin was as transparent as ice and snow, and she was flawless and beautiful.

He turned his eyes away without leaving a trace.

Yan Zhi's mind was moving quickly. The incident in Yan Mansion should be the work of the Queen Mother. She still took action, but failed when Huangfu Jue suddenly woke up, and the Xiao family collapsed. Zhishang should not be in the capital, his armored army is in Shuofang, Henan. With the army in hand, even Huangfu Jue had to worry.

I just don't know where my mother and sister-in-law are.

She broke the medicine bowl, looked at Pang Tong and spoke slowly, "Juntian is a first-rate assassin, especially good at tracking and stealth. He will definitely find this place. Pang Tong, what are your plans for the future?"

Pang Tong narrowed his eyes and glanced at her. When he was harmless, he looked like a lazy cat. "After getting rid of this trouble of yours, the sea will be wide for fish to leap and the sky will be high for birds to fly."

Yan Zhi smiled sweetly, her cold face was like the blue sea and silver waves, with a cold light suddenly breaking and flowing slowly. She thought for a while, "Even if you don't say it, I can guess that the person behind you is plotting something big. Since you have betrayed him, your future will not be easy. The phoenix will not rest unless it is on the phoenix tree. Talents like you are welcomed by us in the Snow Region."

Pang Tong simply closed his eyes and said lazily: "I just like to be a pheasant in the mountains and villages, leading my flock of chickens to live a carefree life."

Yanzhi's eyes flashed with worry. Although she had only been with Pang Tong for a short time, she knew that he was sensitive and delicate under his unruly side, and he was very careful about his reputation. It was useless to persuade him again.

She sighed and told him the formula she had memorized. "This is a method I got from an ancient book. You should practice it for two weeks when the sun and the moon alternate. But you can no longer practice the Qi Nu Gong." She handed him a jade box and said, "There are three Fire Ganoderma Jade in it. If you are really in danger, maybe they can save you."

Pang Tong took the paper, glanced at it, and put it in his arms, but he did not take the jade box. He sneered: "I don't want this Laozi elixir, you can keep it for yourself."

She was in poor health and had to seek medical treatment and take medicine in the palace every day. The medicine she could carry with her must be life-saving medicine. Putting the rouge in front of him, she said with a smile, "Medicine is the easiest thing for a doctor to make. If you don't want it, wouldn't it be difficult for me to think about other things?"

Without waiting for him to refuse, she stood up, looked at him deeply with eyes full of smiles, and said in a serious tone, "I will never forget your noble character. Now that we are apart, take care of each other."

Pang Tong didn't say anything, but raised his finger and shook it.

Juntian will never appear in a place where there is light.

Yanzhi looked at the figure that almost merged with Fengweitong, and was not surprised. She smiled slowly, "Juntian, long time no see."

The man in black had an ordinary appearance, his eyes were silent and persevering, "Hello, young lady."

The news that Juntian brought was similar to what Yanzhi had guessed.

The Queen Mother placed Huangfu Yu under house arrest. Xiao Yu, following the Queen Mother's order, investigated the Marquis of Yan'an's mansion and placed Yan Yanzi under house arrest in the clan residence. He was the only one under house arrest, as Ning Yunshu had already left home. Yan Zhishang had already left the city that night, and Jiang Qingluan was sent back to her parents' home by him.

The hidden power of the Xiao family is deep-rooted and thriving, and they are in distant contact with Huangfu Fang. Even if

Huangfu wakes up, the outcome is still a 50-50 situation. The Queen Mother failed because she raised a son who was alienated from her.

She placed Huangfu Yu under house arrest, preparing to force him to ascend the throne after the plan was accomplished.

"Miss, let him go," Juntian's voice was as flat as his face. "The Queen Mother summoned all the officials and said that the Emperor had forged an imperial edict to usurp the throne and wanted to depose the Emperor. Prince Yu suddenly appeared, guarding the gate of Jiuzhou Qingyan Palace, holding a sword across his neck, and threatened to commit suicide if anyone dared to take a step forward. When the situation became chaotic, the Emperor appeared."

What happened next was very simple. Si Cenxi protected the emperor, and Huangfu Fang came to the court alone. Naturally, the empress dowager was defeated.

After listening to this, Yanzhi was speechless for a long while.

Yan Wanzhao did not lose his original intention after all, and finally saved the Yan family with his actions.

After a long while, he spoke softly, "Where are my father and mother now?"

Juntian's voice was rarely hesitant. "The Marquis is still in the clan residence. The emperor has issued three orders but he has not come out. Madam, he left the residence seven days ago. It seems that he had an argument with the Marquis."

Yanzhi was startled. In her memory, her parents rarely had red faces. She felt sad. Her father was in prison, her mother was missing and died in Henan. They had hardly been together before, but it was not like now that they were separated as a family and felt panic.

"What did Daddy say?" He came so late, he must have asked Daddy first.

Jun Tian said: "The Marquis said that if the young lady is still well, she should go to Fufeng County. The emperor has left the palace."

Huangfu Jue was half awake and half unconscious.

When he was awake, his face was grim and his words were short, often just one word, "Chase!" When he was unconscious, his breathing was rapid and his face was ferocious. He also killed several of the palace maids who served him closely while he was unconscious.

He had been chasing Dexin for two days and two nights since he left the palace. The traces ahead were still vague. The distance between them remained at thirty miles, never getting farther or closer.

The continued high fever had burned out all his patience. The sky was filled with burning red. No less than ten groups of officials had died for their remonstrances, and he had executed three of them in a row.

Si Cenxi knelt on the ground, blood gushing out from his forehead where the teacup had hit him, but he still kept his back straight, "Your Majesty, the dragon's body is more important. I am willing to issue a military order. If you don't capture this man, you will chop off my head."

Huangfu Jue was panting heavily, his eyes were raised, bloodshot, and he said, "Get lost—"

He goes after her, but what does he use to chase her?

He would never see her again, either alive or dead. She was on the top of a snowy mountain, far away from the mountains and rivers. He could not hear her voice or touch her warmth.

No one can, he will never allow it!

She disappeared from his sight like this! Even if he had to go to hell, he would bring her back.

Si Cenxi wanted to remonstrate again, but Huangfu Jue's phoenix eyes were already filled with murderous intent.

"Your Majesty!" Haigui crawled in, speaking in a high-pitched voice, "The Empress, the Empress is in Fufeng County, Qingyao sent a message—"

The hot wind blew past him, his collar was grabbed by someone, and he met a pair of strange and murderous eyes.

Huangfu Jue asked very slowly, "She is in Fufeng County?"

Haigui nodded with difficulty.

The phoenix stared at him for a long while, and finally closed it unwillingly. Before pressing her body against him, she uttered two words clearly, "Return."

Yanzhi never thought that the senior brother would deliberately mislead Huangfu Jue, expose his whereabouts, and trick him into following.

He was a seriously injured patient who had just undergone a craniotomy. If he escaped like this, no gods or Buddhas could protect him.

She was extremely anxious, and without delay, Juntian escorted her to Fufeng County. The half-day of waiting was more like a year.

The man pursed his lips tightly, his cheeks flushed with sickness. He silently looked at the city in front of him, and after a long while he spoke coldly, "Enter the city!"

The author has something to say: Ahhhh, how could this happen.

I'm finishing it, why is it so hard to finish writing?

Is Xiao Pang very loving? I can't help myself

By the way...Liu Liu has laid out deep foreshadowing in these chapters, and you guys didn't seem to notice it. If anything unexpected happens in the future, don't film me!

☆、119 Chapter 119

The distant mountains are like a belt, and the blue-gray city lies quietly in the twilight.

The horses were silent, and the cavalry waited for orders on the spot.

The man pursed his lips tightly, his cheeks were blushing in a sickly way, his eyes were dark, and a faint ink color was surging. After a long while, he spoke coldly, "Go into the city!"

When Huangfu Jue pushed open the door of the inn, Yanzhi was looking at the teacup with a slight distraction. After the initial shock, the latent thoughts in her heart slowly surged up.

She had already made up her mind not to meet Huangfu Jue again.

Snowland had been dormant for nearly a hundred years, and although its hidden power was huge, it had never had any disputes with the royal family. This time, it acted arrogantly and without any concealment.

This has never been Master's style.

The eldest brother's words were mixed. He was always careful and knew the principle of avoiding the key points and making a feint. He loved her and pitied her, maybe, but he had kept it a secret for so long that he would not say it at this absolutely inappropriate time, unless it was just to find an excuse to hide a deeper truth.

And she already knew that the man she fell

in love with had an emperor's heart who regarded everything as chess pieces and weighed the pros and cons.

If it was really caused by her, her leaving quietly might not be the best outcome, but it could avoid greater harm.

But, what has to be faced will have to be faced sooner or later, and I met the burning gaze of the man at the door. I sighed in my heart, that's good, maybe I can be honest with him when I leave.

He leaned against the door, his dark jade eyes slowly moving around the room, as if he was unsure of what he was looking for, before finally focusing on her, and whispered tentatively, "... Yanzhi?"

She was silent for a moment, as if her heart was suddenly clenched. The man in front of her was not the carefree and self-assured Huangfu Jue of the past. His bloodshot eyes concealed irritability and cruelty. His pupils were slightly dilated due to the high fever, and his nostrils were dilated and twitching. She did not feel afraid in her heart. She responded softly and slowly walked forward.

He looked at her without blinking, his voice low and hoarse due to the high fever, "...You promised me that you wouldn't leave." He stretched out his fingers in front of her face, but slowly curled them up and clenched them into fists.

Being so close to him, she could clearly feel his hot breath on her skin.

He was trying his best to restrain himself.
Yanzhi quickly calmed down, met his eyes, and whispered, "No, I'm back." She covered his eyes with her hands, and her calm voice was like a clear spring, "I will never leave until you wake up."

His eyelashes fluttered twice in her palms, and then he fell silent. He put his arms around her waist, hugged her into his hot chest, and let out a long sigh, "Rosacea..."

Haigui left the room quietly.

The quiet inn became lively again, with the owner using the abacus, waiters walking in the hall, and guests speaking with accents from all over the world... Only the bamboo house in the backyard seemed to be isolated in another world.

Huangfu Jue's condition is sometimes better and sometimes worse.

In addition to the persistent high fever, he began to have intermittent headaches. However, as long as Yanzhi was in front of him, he was mostly quiet. Even if beads of sweat covered his face and his body was convulsing uncontrollably, he could still follow her quietly with his eyes.

A faint blue color soon appeared under Yanzhi's eyelids.

He was truly the most cooperative and the most uncooperative patient. No matter how bitter the medicine was, he would drink it without blinking. However, no matter how large the dose was, it would not make him fall asleep for even a moment.

When Yanzhi woke up, she met his open eyes again. He was looking at her sideways, with worry in his eyes, "Why did you wake up again? Did your legs cramp?"

Hearing rustling sounds beside him, he sat up and slowly massaged her legs.

Yanzhi took a few breaths and soon regained consciousness. Very good, the high fever from last night has subsided, and it seems that the headache has not come back.

However, she felt inexplicably upset, and felt that the stone in her chest was getting more and more blocked. She pulled her legs out of his hands, turned sideways, and said lightly, "It's late, go to bed."

In the darkness, she tried her best to open her eyes wide and suppress the urge to grit her teeth.

He passed his arm across her waist and gently turned her over. He said in a low, hoarse voice with a hint of grievance, "Lying on your right side is not good for your heart."

Yanzhi looked at him coldly, with light flowing slowly in her dark and bright phoenix eyes, looking at her tenderly.

He looked very bad, but his eyes were still unusually bright, and his emotions were revealed, as openly as a child.

Yanzhi suddenly softened. Repeated high fever and persistent headaches can make a person lose their mind. He suppressed all the pain and treated her carefully. Even if

it was intentional, she couldn't be cruel.
She lowered her eyelids, her tone a little tired, "Huangfu Jue, what are you doing wrong? You know your body well. If you can't rest well, even if Hua Tuo is alive, I can't save you."

His slightly cool fingertips reached out and rubbed her frowning brows, followed by a gentle kiss on her forehead. He sighed in satisfaction, "...I missed you so much."

Yanzhi's body stiffened and her cheeks felt slightly hot. When she met his black eyes which were full of joy, tenderness and doting, her hands, which had been pushing her away, softly touched his chest.

They had been sleeping on the same bed for the past two days. The moonlight was dim, but he could clearly see the snowy skin under her neck, and the look of anger as she bit her lower lip.

A sweet fragrance floats in the air from the brocade quilt.

With a gurgling sound in his throat, he could not help but lower his head, touching the softness in his memory, and said vaguely, half coquettishly and half willfully: "I just... want to look at you..."

His skin was slightly cool, but his lips were burning hot. There was a bitter medicinal scent between his lips, slowly coming over.

Yanzhi was stunned, and the slight bitterness fermented. The strange yet familiar breath enveloped her, leaving her no room for rejection. The soft lips and tongue had already opened her door and entered her, and even bit her tongue tip as punishment for her slight distraction.

Long-lost touch, long-lost tenderness, the body was hot and cold, Yanzhi soon couldn't think. She still couldn't resist, his kiss was so careful, as if he was protecting a lost treasure. Eyelashes drooped, the bottom of the eyes was a reserved black, but full of tenderness that could overflow. He held her neck, his black hair wrapped around her, and sweet sighs flowed from his lips. His fingers slipped through her clothes and climbed to the top of her soft and smooth vagina. She couldn't help but whimper through her nose and opened her eyes. He looked struggling, as if in pain and happiness, and looked at her expectantly, "...Give it to me...OK..."

Yanzhi stared at him blankly, there was deep hatred and nervousness and restraint in his eyes, and beads of sweat dripped from the tip of his straight nose.

She looked at her for too long, so long that Huangfu Jue had already shown disappointment in his eyes. However, he carefully hid his disappointment, buried his head in her neck, and said softly, "...I won't do that again..."

When Yanzhi touched his face, she found that her fingers were trembling slightly. She took a deep breath.

☆、120 Chapter 120

He soon became weak.

When he was most excited, his fingers tightly grasped the quilt, his slanted eyes widened charmingly, and he looked at her tenderly.

She stared at him intently, panting and thinking vaguely, people only say that beautiful women bring disaster, but I'm afraid that male beauty can also bring disaster to the country.

Even after all these quarrels, she had never seen him so charming and charming.

Gentle, elegant, charming, innocent, forbearing... Such a contradiction intertwined, she never knew how many more faces he had hidden.

He grabbed a handful of her hair and put it in his palm. After all, he was exhausted and his eyes were hazy and blurred. Their foreheads touched each other, and their breaths blended warmly. "The lotus in Taiye Lake is all in bloom... Wait until I wake up... Let's go back to the palace together..."

Yanzhi closed her eyelids and remained silent.

His fingers were still tightly grasping a strand of her hair, and his breathing was no longer ragged but became long and regular.

Yanzhi frowned and looked at the hair in

his hand for a long time, then reached out and took the small silver scissors from the bedside and cut it directly.

The silk shoes stepped on the nanmu wood floor silently.

She added benzoin to the incense burner, smelled the curling fragrant mist, and looked at the man sleeping on the bed.

The lovemaking seemed to have exhausted all his strength, and he fell into a deep sleep like a baby.

Are you really tired, or have you let down your guard and let go of your worries?

The curve of his lips raised up, a hint of self-mockery.

Love and desire are not necessarily inseparable.

Turning around gracefully, there is the swaying shadow of the osmanthus tree outside the window. The crescent moon is like the lonely eyes of a person who has left.

When Huangfu Jue woke up, it was already the evening of the next day. He had a low fever during this period, but it subsided quickly. His limbs felt a little sore, and he tightened the hair in his hands. His facial features were unusually gentle, and he closed his eyes and smiled: "... Yanzhi... I'm so hungry..."

"Your Majesty," Haigui said happily in a low voice, "I will serve the meal right away."

Huangfu Jue suddenly opened his eyes, and

when he saw the broken hair in his hand, his expression froze for a moment. He slowly turned his head to look at Haigui, his eyes cold, "Why is it you?"

Haigui knelt down quickly, gestured to the outside of the curtain, and whispered, "The Queen and Imperial Physician Han are in the hall."

"......If he has internal depression, he will often have headaches. In addition to acupuncture and moxibustion, you can also use massage techniques, such as massaging the liver points, Yanglingquan, Taichong, and Xingjian points, 10 breaths per point, pushing the bridge bow 30 times, and repeating the Zhoutian cycle......"

She was facing him sideways, her black hair tied up with a jade ring, her expression calm and peaceful. Han Lan sat opposite her, frowning and thinking hard as he looked at the fake head full of silver needles.

Huangfu Jue suddenly threw the pearl curtain.

Han Lan quickly knelt down to greet him, but he ignored her and walked around Yan Zhi, put his arms around her waist, put his face against her back, and said sullenly, "...I thought you were gone."

Yanzhi slowly pried his fingers apart, turned around and looked at him, "Awake?"

She looked at him closely with a calm look in her eyes, and said calmly, "The pulse has stabilized. Take good care of it, and there will be no serious problems."

He looked at her stubbornly, with a stubborn light in his eyes, "With you by my side, everything will be fine for me." He frowned, held her hand, and complained softly, "I feel sticky all over, I want to take a shower. I'm also very hungry."

Yanzhi listened to him quietly, with a faint smile on her lips, but the smile was like the mist by the water, floating and uncertain.

"You have been facing bullying from your brothers since you were four years old, and have experienced countless assassination attempts. Without a backer or a mother clan, you ascended to the throne on your own. When have you ever needed to rely on others? When have you ever entrusted your life completely to the hands of others?"

"Huangfu Jue," her voice seemed to be filled with sighs, as soft as the night breeze blowing around the winding corridors, "some things are useless to force. Since there is no problem, go back to the palace."

Huangfu Jue pursed his lips tightly, his face turned pale, but his ten fingers were tightly clasped with hers, refusing to let go. Darkness gradually emerged in his phoenix eyes. He tilted his head to look at her and spoke softly, "I won't let go, not even if I die. If you don't want to go back to the palace, then I won't go back. I don't care about your identity, I don't mind. You are my Yanzhi, you were before and you will be in the future. Whether in life or death."

The color of ink became darker and darker, full of sadness and confusion, "Yanzhi, if you won't forgive me...was last night a dream..."

"The lunch box was a dream," Yanzhi said quickly, her expression no longer calm, but slightly irritated, "Maybe the rise and fall of fate is all a dream. I don't want to guess anymore, what is true and what is false." She paused and looked directly into his eyes, "I'm very tired."

Huangfu Jue's body shook slightly, his eyes showing a mixture of shock and pain. After a long while, he spoke awkwardly, "... Wait for me, let's talk it over, okay?"

His hands were clenched tightly, and his fingertips were extremely cold. He looked at her deeply, then let go and stepped back, striding out.

Yanzhi quietly loosened her left hand that was tightly clenched in her sleeve and found that she had been holding her breath for a long time involuntarily.

As soon as Huangfu Jue entered the bathroom, he waved away the maid who was serving him, restrained his head with his hands, his lips turned purple instantly, and cold sweat dripped down.

Han Lan hurried over and solemnly gave him a few injections on the head. When he began to breathe, he said in a serious tone, "Your Majesty, you need to nourish your energy and calm your mind. If the chronic disease becomes serious, it will haunt you for the rest of your life."

Huangfu Jue closed his eyes and said coldly, "Back off."

He submerged his head under the water and stared at the surface with wide eyes. The pain from the insects biting his head had not completely subsided, but it was far less than the panic in his heart.

Did she know? She must have met Duan Kaiyang. How much would he tell her? No, it was impossible. If she knew everything, how could she still be standing here?

He thought carefully, his eyes gloomy.

Even if you do it, you can't regret it.

She was always soft-hearted towards him. He could definitely win her back.

Huangfu Jue still looked pale and gloomy after taking a bath. Yanzhi knew that he must have had a headache, so she didn't say anything. After he tied his hair, she came behind him and massaged the acupuncture points on the back of his head.

He suddenly held her hand and slowly asked, "Pity or sympathy?"

Yan Zhi was startled and said softly, "The original intention of a doctor."

Huangfu Jue raised his lips with a hint of bitterness. He took her hand and brought her to him, his eyes serious, "I will tell you everything I have hidden. After you listen, you can accuse me of anything, but you can never leave me."

"Yanzhi, I have long been suspicious of your identity. When you were on the western tour, you heard the sound of a flute and looked unusual, so I sent people to track you down. That man should be the heir of the Ye family and the third disciple of Xueshan. When you were kidnapped by Huangfu Fang, I had no clue, but you escaped. Although you were vague, I found traces of Xueyu disciples nearby. I guess you should have a close relationship with Xueyu."

"The first time I admitted that I felt jealous was after I met the young man named Ye Zi. You entered the palace, but you never forgot him. And he actually entered the palace for you."

☆、121 Chapter 121

"This is the first time I admit that I feel jealous after I met that young man named Ye Zi. You entered the palace, but you never forgot him. And he actually entered the palace for you." He looked at her astonished eyes, lowered his eyelids, and said in a light tone, "There are very few things in Shangyuan that can be hidden from me."

"I transferred him to the imperial court, kept an eye on him, and sent him out of the palace to do things. I even often thought about when to make him disappear completely. But I still kept him, wanting to know what about him was worthy of your love. I studied him and hated him. I used some tricks to replace the head of the Hainan Ye family and cut off his roots."

"I'm glad that I didn't take his life. He saved you in Qingping Mansion. You blame me probably because of his death, right?" Her long eyelashes raised and then fell quickly, her expression self-deprecating and lonely.

Without looking at her, he continued, "You were so seriously ill that the doctors were helpless. I hated myself and you. If you wanted to follow him, I would never allow it. Wang Linbo used the late emperor's will to force me. She was a foolish woman who wanted to follow me wholeheartedly. The Yan family also forced me, so I set a plan to kill her and take you back to the palace. I had already made up my mind at that time, whether you live or die, you can't hide from me. I didn't expect that after you returned to the palace, your health actually got better day by day."

"There are still people in this world who can do what I can't do."

"I met the legendary Snow Region Lord Bai Zizai, and finally learned your true identity. He wanted to take you away, otherwise he would investigate Ye Zi's death. I refused him."

He raised the corner of his mouth slightly, a little nonchalantly, "Rejecting the legendary immortal figure always has to pay a price, right?"

He took her hand, his eyes serious and his

expression frank, "Yanzhi, we have both walked on the brink of life and death. The me before the lunchbox is dead, let's start over again, okay?"

Facing his gaze, Yanzhi felt a mixture of worries. For a moment, she was overwhelmed with emotions and was speechless.

Huangfu Jue looked at her, his eyes gradually softened, and whispered: "Yanzhi, I only have you."

He only has her.

He is rich, and all the land under heaven belongs to him, and all the people in the world are his subjects. He has beautiful concubines in the harem and a palace full of civil and military officials, but he can only say to her that he only has her.

His limbs were limp and his expression was tired. He could hear everything that happened around him, but his mind seemed to be floating somewhere far away.

She couldn't say no to his eyes after all.

His words seemed absolutely right, a very complete and reasonable explanation, but I couldn't completely let it go.

Maybe I was hurt too badly and I can no longer trust you wholeheartedly.

I was sleeping in a hazy state and thinking in a hazy state. When the sound of wheels sounded, I sighed softly in my heart. Everything seemed to be returning to the starting point.

Yanzhi has not entered the palace.

She stood at the Xuanwu Gate, with a row of

palace maids kneeling behind her, and said to Huangfu Jue, "I want to go back to the Marquis' Mansion."

Huangfu Jue smiled helplessly, with obvious doting, "The Marquis and Zhishang are both in the palace now, they are also very worried about you. If you miss home, wait for me for a few days, I will go back with you."

Yanzhi frowned. The gate of Wei Wei Palace was a barrier of confinement. If possible, she didn't want to step in at all.

Huangfu Jue smiled and winked. Linglong and Yiyue came forward to pay their respects, both saying, "Your Majesty."

Huangfu Jue smiled and said, "You are not afraid of my worrying about you, but you should also think about them. They must have been sleepless and hungry during the few days you were away from the palace."

Yanzhi saw that both of them had red eyes and pointed chins, and knew that she had dragged them down innocently by leaving. She remained silent.

Huangfu Jue led his men directly to Wuji Palace. When he left Beijing that day, the situation was not stable, so he only left trusted eunuchs to help Huangfu Yu negotiate between his mother's family and the ministers.

Haigui brought Yanzhi to Jiuzhou Qingyan Palace, and Yanzhi looked uneasy.

He bowed repeatedly, "Empress, all your daily necessities are here, there is no need to bother. Besides, you still have to keep an eye on the Emperor, right? I have annoyed you those days, you can just beat and scold me."

In just these few days, Jiuzhou Qingyan Palace has been completely renovated.

The three east rooms inside were replaced with a complete set of furniture decorated with vermilion lacquer, carved with gold-painted flowers, a seven-screen scroll-style armchair, a crabapple-shaped incense table, a landscape green screen, a white marble carved horse, and a painting of a lady by Zhang Zimei.

The emperor's bedroom has become a lady's boudoir.

This arrangement was naturally not completed in a day. Yanzhi had a gloomy face, and Haigui smiled and sent all the capable people around her over, including Shuangli, without missing a single one.

She watched coldly, just waiting to see Huangfu Jue explode.

The wait lasted from noon until the moon rose above the willow trees.

Huangfu Jue looked tired, but when he saw her, he smiled. He walked over and touched her belly, saying softly, "You've been on such a long journey, why don't you rest earlier? Is the child well behaved? Did he bother you?"

Yanzhi had a calm expression and said nothing.

Huangfu Jue looked at her face and suddenly

smiled. He changed his clothes and sat with her. He spoke slowly, "Are you unhappy?"

He was a little hot when he came closer, and Yanzhi's face was a little more annoyed, "Where's my dad?"

Huangfu Jue smiled and said, "My mother-in-law was angry with my father-in-law, so she went to your uncle's house in Yinchuan. My father-in-law met me and he traveled thousands of miles to chase his wife."

He smiled and spoke with a hint of mischief in his expression, as if he shared the same feeling.

Yanzhi shook her hand away and frowned, "Where's Zhishang?"

Her mother was concerned about her and would never leave home easily unless it was something urgent. She was anxious to see her family because she wanted to know where her mother was.

Huangfu Jue stretched out his legs, leaned his head on her shoulder, and whispered: "...Zhi Shang? Well...he went to the Jiang family to pick up his wife. It seems...the family should be reunited tonight..."

Yanzhi closed her eyes dejectedly.

His voice was already unclear. A day in the court must be full of intrigues, exhausting her mind. She didn't take any medicine or drink any water. She just felt angry and bitter in her heart. She wanted to ignore it, but she couldn't bear to do it.

She shook him violently, looked into his half-open eyes, and said through gritted teeth, "Huangfu Jue, tomorrow, I must see my parents."

He smiled at her soothingly, raised his hand and gently scratched the tip of her nose, then closed his eyes peacefully, "Leave it to your husband."

After feeding Huangfu Jue the medicine, Yanzhi was already very tired. Linglong felt sorry for her and hurriedly urged her to sleep in the East Warm Pavilion.

It turned out to be a good night's sleep.

There are some vague dreams, not in fragments, fleeting glimpses, vaguely like pictures without sound.

When I woke up, there was a magnified face in front of me.

Huangfu Jue squeezed onto her bed without her noticing, played with her hair with his fingers, and said with a smile, "Good morning."

Yanzhi was in a trance. Not long ago, he also waited for her to wake up like this with a smile. In just a few dozen days, the world had changed so much that it felt like a lifetime ago.

She lowered her eyelids and whispered, "...Morning."

Tomorrow is like a mountain, and the world is vast and boundless. I am afraid that the human heart is the biggest distance in the world.

☆, 122 Chapter 122

The body has memory.

She rested her head on his arm, with one leg even leaning over his. When they were unconscious, they were so close to each other.

Yanzhi sat up almost in a panic, but the white brocade jacket was still pressing down on his body.

Huangfu Jue chuckled with pleasure, and finally stood up first under her slightly angry gaze.

When Yanzhi was combing her makeup, Huangfu Jue leaned on the couch and watched. Later, he stood up and took the comb from Yiyue.

Her hair was very dense, and she could not comb it all the way through. It was winding down to her knees, which was very pitiful. But it took a lot of effort to tie it up.

After Huang Pujue pulled her hair roots again, Yan Yan snorted softly and stared at him in the mirror, "Are you free today?"

Huang Pujue looked relaxed, and inserted a white jade hairpin into her hair. She smiled and said, "What's the point of looking at a group of old men blowing their beards and glaring?" He swept his finger across the tip of her eyebrows, which were as light as distant mountains. "It's not as fun as drawing eyebrows in the pepper room."

Yan Yan was silent. From a doctor's point of view, he should indeed stay in bed and rest at this moment.

Their eyes met in the mirror.

Huang Pujue's eyes were as black as the finest Hepu jade, glowing with light and overflowing with joy and love. He looked at her quietly.

Yan Yan looked away and said calmly, "What about what you promised me yesterday?"

A gloomy look flashed across his phoenix eyes, and then he acted as if nothing had happened. He picked up a magnolia flower and inserted it into her temple, smiling gently, "But you think that makeup will stain your face. You lightly brush your eyebrows and greet the Supreme. My wife is indeed born with a beautiful appearance."

His tone was naturally intimate, but Yan Yan just looked at him with a slight sneer.

Huang Pujue shook his head and sighed, "It's really hard to please." Then he smiled again. "I was just sending someone to pick up the Marquis of Yan'an and his wife, but Zhishang has already been summoned to the palace for you. Do you want me to accompany you?"

"No." Her voice was light and crisp, like pearls dropping onto a jade plate, with a hint of coldness.

Yan Zhishang was waiting for her at the Linbo Pavilion on the Qujiang Lake. Yan Yan looked at the green umbrella in the lake and smiled softly, "It was also this season when I met you last year. It feels like we have been apart for years."

Yan Zhishang sat with his hands behind his back. There was a hint of displeasure

between his brows. "Why did you come back?"
Yan Yan's smile faded, and she stared at him in a daze. "Zhi Shang. I can't leave. How can I take this child to the snowy mountains?"

Yan Zhishang looked straight at her, with a cold look between his brows. "You can't bear to part with him, right?"

Yanzhi opened her eyes wide, with obvious surprise in them, "Zhishang, you should understand me. I am not desperate for love. I came back, perhaps because of him, but more because I am worried about my parents."

Zhishang paused, his voice gloomy, "If you are fine, then everyone will be fine. If something happens to you, do you think your parents will still send you off?"

Yanzhi shook her head. "I know my own business. Zhishang, why did mother leave home?"

Yan Zhishang said slowly, "There has been a change in the palace. If that person really makes a scene, the Yan family will naturally be purged. Daddy and I have discussed dispersing the female members of the family first. If you miss mother, you will probably be able to return to the capital in two days."

Yanzhi was silent for a while before she said, "I don't know why, but I'm always upset."

Yan Zhishang looked at her, the words were rolling around on the tip of his tongue, he just felt like a fishbone stuck in his throat, he wanted to get it out. Even her smile was shrouded in sadness, the whole person was elusive like the mist in the mountains, it seemed that she could disappear with the wind at any time. He slowly exhaled and said, "Why do you become sentimental when you are pregnant? You don't need to worry about everything, you just need to take good care of yourself."

Yanzhi heard that although his tone was still stiff, he could not hide his concern. She responded softly, her eyes slightly red, and hurriedly lowered her head to pour tea.

Yan Zhishang stroked the teacup and spoke slowly, "Yanzhi, tell my brother what the chances are of both mother and child being saved."

Yan Zhi's movements froze, and some of the tea splashed out of the cup. She lowered her head and drank a sip of tea as if nothing had happened, and smiled gently at Yan Zhishang, "Brother, you are delusional. Life and death are all predetermined, why force it?"

Yan Zhishang frowned, sneered several times, stood up, walked a few steps on the spot, turned back and looked at her with sharp eyes, "We don't accept our fate. Even if it is destined by heaven, brother will fight for you."

Even if it is destined by heaven, I will fight for it for you.

Yanzhi was staring at the lotus leaves in

the pond, unaware that the smile on her lips was bitter.

In the end, she let down those who loved her.

If she hadn't known that she would die, she wouldn't have come back here. She couldn't let her master and Ye Zi see her die, but she could choose to let Huangfu Jue see her off. She wanted to use her blood to make him remember it for the rest of his life.

As long as he still feels guilty, he will not treat the Yan family badly.

Huangfu Jue became very clingy, and except for the morning court, he almost never left Yanzhi's sight.

Yanzhi treated him indifferently, and he was neither angry nor irritated. If she was really anxious, he would just smile and avoid her. After a while, he would come back again.

His presence was not very strong, and he spent most of his time in her room reading memorials. When Yanzhi was taking a nap on the couch, she heard the sound of papers turning, and gradually she fell asleep peacefully.

She received a letter from home from Yinchuan, saying that Ning Yunshu had contracted rheumatism in Yinchuan, and was afraid that he would infect her if he returned to Beijing, so he would stay in Yinchuan for some time. However, he would definitely come back after July.

After hearing the news from her family,

Yanzhi gradually calmed down. When she was in good spirits, she learned needlework from Linglong and embroidered a bellyband for the dolls.

As the adorable doll emerged stitch by stitch, Yanzhi often lost her focus. She was perhaps the only mother who knew clearly that she would never meet her child again, and she wanted more and more to leave some memory for it.

Children always have fantasies about their mothers.

If she was immersed in her own thoughts, she would most likely be interrupted by Huangfu Jue.

He seemed to dislike her needlework, so he asked people to find many rare medical books, which occupied the entire east wall of his imperial study. Whenever he had free time, he would coax her to make tea, play chess and play the piano. He was in an unusually good mood recently, and he could probably coax her to change her mood and temporarily forget her sadness.

He changed to meet the ministers in Wuji Palace. Jiuzhou Qingyan Palace was usually quiet. In the huge palace, there were often only the two of them.

When she looked up from her book, she would sometimes meet his gaze. He looked at her for an unknown amount of time, his expression thoughtful. When he saw her paying attention, his expression would flash by and then return to normal.

Yanzhi never thought deeply, nor did she want to think deeply.

How much idle worry is there? A field of tobacco, a city full of catkins, and rain when the plums are yellow.

As soon as July came, the rain came and went, often for three or two days at a time. The sky was not clear, and people were depressed.

Huangfu Jue seems to be busy these days, and he is often not seen for a whole day. However, Haigui often appears and brings some fruits and snacks. He reminds her from time to time: Madam, it is time to take medicine; Madam, the lilies of the valley are in bloom, you can enjoy the flowers...

Yanzhi knows that he is being instructed by someone, so he does what he wants and ignores him.

That night, Huangfu Jue returned at midnight.

After coming back, he quietly went to Yanzhi's dormitory. He deliberately walked lightly for fear of waking her up, but he heard her unstable breathing, sometimes long and sometimes short.

Huangfu Jue smiled softly.

He loosened his outer robe, walked to the bed, and asked quietly, "Are you still awake? Are you waiting for me?"

Yanzhi lay on her side, eyes closed, silent. She didn't want to admit that she had been paying attention to the movements outside. She had been lying down for a long time but couldn't fall asleep.

She was slightly annoyed by his words and wanted to pretend to sleep. She heard him smile softly, and his warm lips gently touched her forehead, and stayed for a while before leaving. He stroked her belly and whispered, "Good girl, don't bother your mother."

Yan Zhi opened her eyes suddenly and said angrily, "Will you let me sleep?"

Huangfu Jue's eyebrows curved, and he put his middle finger in front of his lips to make a silent gesture. Just as he was about to go to bed, Haigui coughed softly outside the curtain and called softly, "Your Majesty."

Huangfu Jue sighed, quickly touched Yanzhi's face with his fingers, and said softly: "I'll be back soon, wait for me."

When he got to the door, his face had already darkened, and he asked coldly, "What's the matter?"

Haigui closed the door carefully, with a bitter look on his face. Everyone in Jiuzhou Qingyan Palace knew that when the queen was sleeping, no one and nothing could disturb her, but this matter could not be delayed any longer.

"Ou Tingzhou sent someone over again, saying that Concubine Mei might be in trouble."

Huangfu Jue raised his eyebrow and said calmly, "Where is the person?"

His voice was calm, but his expression

became increasingly cold.

Haigui knelt down hurriedly, "Of course, I dare not let anyone get close to me, but the person who came this time... is Ye Liangyuan. She put a knife across her neck, and it is difficult for us servants... to stop her."

Huangfu's eyes flashed with coldness, and he snorted softly. If he hadn't needed Ye Hengrong, Ye Lanyi would have died thousands of times.

A woman who doesn't know what's good for her.

He wanted to turn around and push the door, but his hand didn't even touch the door. He hesitated for a moment and then retracted it. He walked out without hesitation, "Call Han Lan."

The footsteps gradually became quieter.

The glass lamp casts a flickering light, and the hollow incense ball emits a lingering fragrance.

The person in the brocade tent did not move, but his brows were slightly furrowed, revealing a little bit of his thoughts.

☆, Chapter 123

There is a kind of flower that will accumulate all its strength to bloom. Once it blooms, it will be stunningly beautiful. But no one would have thought that this beauty will only last for a moment. While you are amazed, its stems, leaves and branches have already withered silently.

The evening glories and the morning dew bloom only once in their lifetime.

Yanzhi could clearly feel the baby in her belly growing day by day, and it was trying hard to absorb nutrients. The strength she had desperately accumulated was not enough for it to consume, and she seemed to be unable to let it be born safely.

She sat back at the table with a pale face. The aroma of medicine wafted faintly from the dishes. She suppressed the discomfort that was rapidly rising in her chest and abdomen and picked up the chopsticks again.

As soon as the bamboo shoots entered her mouth, a hint of Polygonatum odoratum immediately spread in her mouth. She covered her mouth and Linglong immediately brought the spittoon over.

Another round of overwhelming vomiting.

When she finished washing and picked up the chopsticks again, tears were already in her eyes, "Madam, we don't want to eat anymore. Remove the medicinal food, and I will ask Shuangli to change to something lighter."

Yanzhi took a deep breath and shook her head. This was the best way she could think of, to slightly inhibit its growth without harming her child.

Linglong bit her lower lip and glanced at Yiyue. Yiyue nodded and stepped back.

When Huangfu Jue withdrew from the morning court, Yanzhi was vomiting out the ginseng flower porridge that she had finally eaten.

Her stomach was empty, but she was still retching. Her hands carefully protected her abdomen, and the pale blue blood vessels on her forehead were throbbing, with tiny beads of sweat oozing out.

He suddenly stopped, leaned his hands on the maple flower bed, and watched silently. Yanzhi tried hard to regulate her breathing, her vision was a little blurry, and she closed her eyes tightly.

A silk handkerchief was placed on the forehead, from the corners of the eyes to the lips, with gentle force. The fine and dense Kuilong pattern appeared brightly and dimly in front of the eyes. The embroidery gradually twisted, as if it had stretched out countless tentacles, and slowly tied a knot at the tip of the heart.

Something was roaring and struggling in my heart.

She turned around abruptly and met his eyes which were filled with tenderness and a little annoyance. She snatched the bottle of water from Yiyue's hand, shook her hand, and poured the water out.

"Hiss——" There was an obvious sound of gasping, and it stopped abruptly in the middle.

Everyone in the room knelt on the floor. Linglong opened her mouth to speak, but Haigui pushed her behind him. He knelt and moved quickly, not daring to look up, holding the towel in both hands.

Huangfu Jue narrowed his eyes slightly, and

drops of water rolled down his handsome face one by one, falling into the river and sea cloud patterns, and the auspicious dragon. Yanzhi looked at him hatefully, her eyes were wet, but her lips were extremely bright, a little red.

Darkness slowly rose from his eyes, and without moving his gaze away, he took a towel and wiped it casually, saying in a very light tone, "Get out."

He took a step forward, put his hands under her ribs, and hugged her in his arms, sighing softly, "...It's my fault..." He put his face on top of her head and murmured, "...It's me who made Yanzhi suffer like this."

His voice was calm, but it showed great pain and fatigue.

The hand that was trying to push him away suddenly lost its strength, and the fingertips holding him trembled slightly.

She was afraid, she was finally able to be calm, a deep tremor came out from her bones, she was so scared. It was like struggling on a cliff, escaping death, and finally seeing the top of the mountain, only to find that the rope holding her life was about to break.

She was unwilling, unwilling... She just wanted to be a mother... Why... She couldn't even give up this wish...

The person in my arms was crying through gritted teeth, with broken tears occasionally spilling from his lips. He curled up, protecting his abdomen.

Huangfu Jue held her on the couch, his hands slowly stroking her long hair. His dark eyes looked forward, but his sight seemed very far away.

When Yanzhi calmed down and pried his hands away with a sullen face, he lowered his eyelids and raised the corners of his lips slightly, "Better?"

Yanzhi pursed her lips tightly, with some remaining anger and embarrassment in her eyes.

Huangfu Jue pushed her wet hair behind her ears, held her cheek, put his forehead against hers, looked straight into her eyes, and said in a serious tone, "I will always be here, with you and our child. Yanzhi, forgive me, believe me."

Forgive me, I can't let go: believe me, there will be no more hurt.

Yanzhi quickly lowered her eyelids, her butterfly-winged eyelashes covering her eyes, but her eyebrows were slightly furrowed.

Huangfu Jue quickly kissed her on the lips, "I haven't had my breakfast yet, so accompany me to have some. When you feel better, I have one more thing to apologize to you for."

Yanzhi was angry and cried for a while, and it seemed that all her strength was exhausted, even her picky appetite subsided. The only food served in the kitchen was ginseng flower porridge and black plum lotus root slices, along with a few side dishes. Huangfu Jue used a jasper lotus plate to serve the porridge, and the glutinous rice floated in the jasper, which was surprisingly sweet. Yanzhi drank it slowly, one sip at a time, while Huangfu Jue concentrated on eating, and only picked up the lotus root slices when her plate was empty.

The meal took less than half an hour. Yanzhi put down her chopsticks, and Huangfu Jue also put down his chopsticks. He smiled at Yiyue and said, "The porridge is well made. Here's a reward."

Yanzhi's face was indifferent. She ignored him, took Linglong's hand and stood up.

When her figure turned around the screen, Haigui came up and asked in a low voice: "Your Majesty, the kitchen has prepared some snacks..."

Huangfu Jue's smile faded, and he glanced at Haigui lightly, and Haigui kept silent and retreated.

He sat alone at the table, the corners of his lips curled up, a hint of self-mockery. He slowly spread out his fingers, his palms still sticky with sweat, he wiped them casually with a handkerchief, and stood up and went into the East Pavilion.

The sun had slowly climbed up the flower stand, and the shadows of the roses were spreading all over the floor. Yanzhi was half-leaning on the Xiangfei couch, closing her eyes and pretending to be asleep. Her face was hidden in the light, half bright and half dark.

Huangfu Jue came closer, his breath brushing against her face. She frowned and pulled up her wide sleeves to cover her face.

Huangfu Jue smiled, leaned against her couch, picked up a copy of "Song'an Zhiqu" and read it slowly.

His voice was already gorgeous, and at this moment it was deliberately low, with very long words and a slight rise in the ending tone, which made it somewhat seductive and charming.

"The moss leaves traces of animals, the mountain flowers are bound by green vines, the rice fields are full of green bamboos, and the white buildings are occupied by vacant people. The dead leaves are piled up layer by layer on the bluestones, and the breeze is blowing gently..."

Yanzhi threw down her sleeves and glared at him angrily.

Huangfu Jue put down the book and smiled innocently, "Reading makes people sleep better."

Yan Zhi said calmly, "Your Majesty, you have many military and national affairs to attend to. You should not waste your time with a mere woman."

Huangfu Jue's phoenix eyes were smiling happily, "Yanzhi, if you don't want to sleep, I will accompany you to talk." He held her hand and hesitated, "...Do you still remember Mei Xunyou?"

Yan Zhi looked at him quietly, her eyes were like the light snow in early spring, cold and aloof, with a sense of boredom and loneliness, "What if I remember, what if I don't remember?"

Huangfu Jue held her hand tightly, "When you were not in the palace, her family sent her to the palace, and..."

Looking at her tightly closed eyelids and expressionless face, Huangfu Jue stopped talking and asked suspiciously for a while, "You know everything? Who told you?"

A hand stopped in front of his eyes, making a gesture to send the guest away. Yanzhi closed her eyes and said coldly, "You don't need to ask me for permission for your three palaces and six courtyards. I won't send you off--" The last two words burst out from her lips and teeth, with great strength but almost silently.

He finally spoke out.

For two days in a row, he did not stay in Jiuzhou Qingyan Palace, but would visit her in the middle of the night. There was a strange cold and medicinal smell on his body. He hated her so much, but he couldn't sleep every night, and he was awake to accept the torture in his heart, which almost became a nightmare.

Huangfu Jue suddenly smiled, his eyes tilted upward, leaned close to her ear, and whispered: "Yanzhi, are you jealous?"

He hugged her suddenly stiff body, kissed

her on the cheek quickly, and his tone softened suddenly, "Don't be angry, don't be angry, they are just stopgap measures. I haven't even touched their little fingertips, Ah Lu only wants Yanzhi." His tone gradually became lower, lower to the dust, "There is no one else, only Yanzhi..."

A large tear slowly gathered at the corner of his eye, rolled down, and landed on his slightly parted lips. He sighed softly, "It's bitter... Is Yanzhi's heart bitter too..."

The tall man knelt on one knee in front of her couch and touched her cheek carefully. "It was all my fault before. When Yanzhi gives birth to a child, I will give the throne to Huangfu Yu. Yanzhi will take me to all the places I like. When we both become white-haired old men and women, you can hit me with your cane, okay, okay..."

☆, Chapter 124

Yanzhi takes me to all the places I like... When I am old and gray, you hit me with your cane... Okay... Okay...

The heart seems to be immersed in the deep bottom of the water, the perception is blurred, all the bitterness, sadness, pain and anxiety seem to be separated by the eternal tranquility, only the tears, uncontrollably, flow freely.

The lilac blossoms have ripened, but the tide at the river head has not yet receded.

How could she miss it? She just missed it. After going around in circles in this cycle of life, she finally came to a dead end. What she wanted would never be fulfilled again.

Why... you are so late...

Huangfu Jue placed her hand on his heart, sighed softly, and murmured: "You can cry like this... even the drought can be avoided..." Numerous kisses fell on her face, gradually extending down.

Yanzhi cried in a daze, and only came to her senses when her clothes were untied and someone bit her chest, not lightly or heavily. She was so angry that she raised her hand and swung it out fiercely.

"Pa", Huangfu Jue did not dodge, and his face was thrown to the side. He looked at her, slowly lowered his eyelids, and the corners of his mouth turned downward in a very aggrieved arc, and he muttered softly.

Yanzhi grabbed her collar, her heart in confusion. Thousands of feelings intertwined together, she couldn't tell whether it was bitter or sweet, she just stared at him blankly.

Huangfu Jue glanced at her quickly, pouted, and took her hand, "You've cried enough, you've been beaten enough, you can't be angry anymore."

The clear and elegant eyes looked at him, gradually becoming misty and introverted. "Okay," she said softly, "I won't be angry anymore." As soon as she closed her eyes, fatigue emerged from her brows, like petals falling in the wind in the soft light. "Let me rest for a while, okay?"

When she didn't hear his answer, he carefully lifted her up with his arms, "Don't sleep anymore. If you're lazy now, you won't be able to sleep at night. Besides, you haven't solved my problem yet."

His movements were gentle, and his embrace felt fresh and warm. Yanzhi was a little dazed and let him carry her out.

Huangfu Jue carried her all the way to Qujiang Pond, held her in his arms and sat on the chair together, then grabbed her hand and scattered fish food to her.

There are several new carps in the pond. Their tails are colorful, like dancing flames. They swim in the water, which is very interesting.

Yanzhi was originally not in the mood, but seeing them pushing and shaking their heads for the fish food, she felt a little annoyed and casually threw all the fish food in.

Huangfu Jue looked at her and sighed, "You are not a fish, how do you know the joy of a fish?"

Yan Zhi sneered, "Thunder, lightning, rain and dew are all grace from the emperor. The fish raised by your majesty are naturally happy." Her black and white eyes turned to his face, "If you have anything to say, say it quickly."

Huangfu Juequ tapped her forehead with his middle finger, "You're just trying to choke me. Mei Xunyou and the others won't stay in the palace anymore. I want to send them all out of the palace. First, let them live in a nunnery, and then each family will take them back after a year or two. We can't treat them badly. Who do you think is a good choice?"

Yanzhi sat up from his arms, looking at the vast water, her expression gradually becoming solemn.

He didn't really need her opinion, he was

just making his point. However, she usually disdained it, but now she couldn't.

She was silent for a while before she smiled bitterly, "You don't need to do this."

The army is pressing on Xidian, the court is in turmoil, the Wang family has fallen, the Yan family is alienated, the power is hollow, and new blood must be added. Marrying into the royal family is both a means for the emperor to control his subjects and a guarantee for the subjects to be loyal.

She was already exhausted, so naturally she didn't want him to do anything more for her. Or maybe, she still had a vague thought: if she really left, if he was really left alone, wouldn't the huge Shangyuan be very lonely?

Huangfu Jue smiled, his phoenix eyes sparkling with love, "Yes. From now on, only the queen will stay in my Shangyuan. I wish to have a soulmate and stay with you until the end of our lives."

His expression was playful, but his tone was extremely serious. Yan Zhi couldn't tell what she felt in her heart, she just felt full of resentment, glaring at him, "You know I—"

Huangfu Jue's smile faded, and he put his index and middle fingers on her lips, "What? Yanzhi, have faith in me. You and the child will be fine and stay with me forever."

He spoke slowly, with a hint of determination, as if he was certain.

Yanzhi had thousands of words on her mind, but in the end she could only sigh softly.

Huangfu Jue came back later and later, but no matter how late it was, he would sleep with Yanzhi. If she pretended to sleep, he would wake her up and whisper a few words to the child through her belly. He would also come back on time to have meals with her, and he would enjoy the dishes no matter how much or how little. If Yanzhi vomited, he would clean up without anyone else's help, and he would patiently coax her to finish eating.

Linglong silently watched the two of them get along, and would sigh and cry privately. She had made a vow in front of the Buddha to be a vegetarian for life. She said to Yiyue, "I think the emperor treats the queen like this, and he must love her very much in his heart. If that's the case, why did he do that in the first place... Now it's like this, it hurts to think about it. I just hope that the queen will be relieved and never suffer again."

Yanzhi spends most of her time sleeping and eating. After Huangfu Jue talked with her, the security in Jiuzhou Qingyan Palace was much less guarded, but she no longer likes to go out.

One day, Linglong saw that she had a good breakfast and looked good, so she smiled and snatched the book from her hand: "Madam, don't read anymore. You stay so quiet all day, and the little prince in your belly has lost his temper. Go out for a walk."

So a large group of people came out to admire the lotus flowers in the breeze.

When he arrived at Furong Garden, he met a man, Prince Yu Huangfu Yu.

He seemed to be admiring the lotus alone. Seeing Yan Zhi, he smiled slightly and said, "Greetings, sister-in-law."

It felt like years had passed since we last met. Yanzhi looked at him calmly. This slick and frivolous prince had become much more serious, with a bit more melancholy and vicissitudes between his brows. He must have been going through some pain and torture in his heart. She smiled casually, "Your Highness is here too, what a coincidence."

Huangfu Yu looked at her with a smile, his eyes frank and sincere, "Yu is here to wait for the emperor's sister-in-law."

Yanzhi's expression remained unchanged. Shangyuan was so big, and she rarely came out, so it was impossible to find such a good timing. But I don't know what he did to persuade Linglong.

"My lord, why do you need rouge?" She felt one part guilty and three parts respectful towards this dandy prince.

Huangfu Yu did not speak first. He asked Yanzhi and Yu Jinwu to sit down, and walked around to the other side. After a moment of silence, he said, "I know the health of my sister-in-law. If this matter was not difficult, I would not have violated my brother's taboo to bother my sister-in-law. My sister-in-law lives in seclusion and rarely goes out. I don't think she knows that hundreds of thousands of soldiers from the Eastern Expedition were trapped in Longze by heavy rain. Ye Rongheng forced civilians to build ships and pull boats in Longze. The people suffered terribly and countless people were killed and injured. Xidian could not be conquered and has become useless. All officials urged to withdraw the troops, but my brother insisted on doing it. I have no choice but to ask for help from my sister-in-law. If there is anyone in the world who can dissuade my brother, it can only be you."

Yan Zhi restrained her gaze and remained silent for a long while before suddenly asking, "Did anyone in Prince Yu's mansion pass away?"

Huangfu Yu wore a purple long gown with a cloth belt around his waist and a cloth tassel on his head. As a prince, he should never dress like this, unless... he was in mourning.

Huangfu Yu was startled, with a very strange look in his eyes. He struggled and hesitated, remembering the sorrow, and finally spoke, "The princess... passed away a month ago."

Yanzhi slowly raised her eyes, her eyes were as cold as the moon in the river, and she said slowly: "Wanzhao is dead? How could he die?"

Huangfu Yu's face was pale, his body swayed slightly, and he spoke with difficulty, "Your health is the most important thing, the dead are gone... My brother is afraid that you may have a miscarriage..."

Yan Zhi shouted coldly, "Huangfu Yu!"

Huangfu Yu looked at her miserably, put his five fingers on her cheek, and said in a disordered voice, "He hanged himself... and died..."

Yanzhi closed her eyes, her eye sockets were terribly dry.

Yan Wanzhao, such a proud and beautiful woman.

The sorrow in my heart surged up layer by layer, and my ten fingers tightly grasped the table.

Such love, such determination, could not withstand the iron heart of her lover. She withered at her most beautiful age, and was swallowed up by the imperial power. Not a single drop of her remained. I thought I hated her so much, but at this moment, my heart still felt like a piece of it had been dug out.

The sun was shining brightly above her head, and she felt as if she had fallen into an icy cave.

Huangfu Yu was shocked and shouted in panic: "Sister-in-law... Sister-in-law..."

Yan Zhiqing's eyes stared at his face, slowly raised the corners of her lips, and said softly: "After all, you... betrayed her."

☆, Chapter 125

She knelt in the rich and dark palace, her back straight and proud.
My life before was like the most exquisite mirror, cold and unchanging, maintaining elegance. When he came, the mirror shattered. I finally realized that I am also a woman who can say, laugh and love.
Yanzhi, please help me...
Yanzhi, please help me...
Yan Wanzhao, you dare to love me so much, yet you don't have the courage to go to the end.
The man for whom you betrayed your family and gave up your honor, pushed you to this point. You finally regretted it... you finally made a mistake... you finally felt disappointed...
She didn't hear anything Huangfu Yu said next, and she didn't know when he left.
Linglong came over and hugged her knees and cried, her voice was anxious and uneasy.
She opened her mouth, and a mouthful of sweetness rose to her throat. She smiled at Linglong soothingly, and her voice drifted farther and farther away, "...Don't cry...Don't tell the emperor..."
A very long dream.
The girl in the dream had her hair tied up in two braids, a purple mattress, and a goose-yellow skirt. She looked cold and

arrogant. She said to the fat girl with a bun-like hairdo, "My mother only has me as her daughter. I don't have a sister. Get out of my house."

She pushed the fat girl hard, and she fell into the lake. The water was deep and cold, rushing into her mouth and nose like crazy...

Yanzhi suddenly opened her eyes, still feeling suffocated by the lake water pouring into her throat.

A warm hand immediately reached out to her. Huangfu Jue's voice was faintly hoarse, "Don't be afraid, I'm here." He stroked her cheek and paused when he felt the wetness. "Are you feeling unwell?"

Yanzhi stared at him in a daze. He was only wearing a single layer of clothes, with his black hair loose. His phoenix eyes showed undisguised worry, and he looked at her intently. She stared at him intently, held his hand with her backhand, and slowly leaned over. When she felt the real warmth, she closed her eyes again.

"Rosacea?" he asked hurriedly, tightening and unclenching his arms, trying to search her face.

Yanzhi stopped his hand and asked softly, "Why didn't you tell me?"

Huangfu Jue rested his forehead on hers and hummed softly, "It's just an irrelevant person."

Yan Zhi's mouth corners slowly rose, and her smile was bitter and sarcastic. What an irrelevant person. Although she didn't say what Yan Wanzhao did, he must have doubts in his heart. Yan Wanzhao was at a dead end, and he watched coldly, which was kindness. His hand slipped into his clothes, touched his chest, and asked faintly: "If I die, will this place... be sad?"

His breathing gradually became heavier, and his slightly hoarse voice was unusually calm, "If you die, I won't let you be lonely in the underworld, so I will definitely send all the things you like to accompany you."

Yanzhi listened quietly, and suddenly smiled, "What if I only like you?"

His chin was grabbed by someone, and his hot lips pressed down. In the breath of the air, he whispered softly, "...Then don't want anyone else. I will accompany you, to the azure sky and the underworld."

After the kiss, both of them were breathing unsteadily. Yan Zhi put her hand on his chest and smiled slightly: "It's beating so fast, Huangfu Jue, you will also be upset."

Huangfu Jue looked at her with a smile in silence, his phoenix eyes gentle and reserved.

Yanzhi sighed softly and looked up at him, "You don't want me to die, but it's because I can fill a part of your loneliness. If everyone is like you, those wives whose husbands have died, children whose fathers have lost, and mothers whose sons have lost, wouldn't they all be unable to live and die to vent their anger?"

Huangfu Jue suppressed his smile and twisted a strand of her hair around his finger. "Sometimes, I wish your heart was small, so small that it only held me, but no, my queen also has a compassionate heart." He put his lips on her hair and kissed it gently. "Don't worry, I know how to handle the affairs of the court. You just need to take care of yourself."

Wait for me, wait for me to conquer Xidian and get what I want.

Huangfu Yu never appeared in Shangyuan again, but Linglong regretted it. When Yanzhi left the palace, Weiyang Palace was basically protected by Huangfu Yu. She was extremely grateful to this prince. She never thought that complying with his request would make Yanzhi vomit blood and faint.

Huangfu Jue did not punish her, but she was already heartbroken, and knelt in the small Buddhist temple with Yanzhi on her back for a day and a night. From then on, she was extremely careful in taking care of Yanzhi's daily life.

Yanzhi was very confident in her heart, knowing that given her current situation, Huangfu Jue would never touch the people around her, so she just found an opportunity to gently counsel Linglong.

She was already seven months pregnant, and was becoming more and more exhausted. In the second half of the night, her meridians often became blocked. Huangfu Jue stayed up all night to relieve them with his inner strength. When the two of them were together, it was as if they had returned to the time when there was no barrier between them. Yanzhi knew that she didn't have much time left, so she threw away all the entanglements in her heart.

She resented him, but also loved him. Since love could not last forever, why should she resent him?

The only thing she was worried about was her mother and father, who had not yet left Xiaoyinchuan. Huangfu Jue saw her looking at the pigeons gloomily again, put down the memorial in his hand and walked over, hugged her from behind, and said with a smile: "It has long been rumored that Lady Ning has a bad temper. The Marquis is a military god, but his skills in coaxing women are not necessarily better than mine. After half a lifetime of military service, it is rare for him to coax his lovely wife. Why do you have to force them to come back?"

Yanzhi leaned into his arms, feeling a little depressed, "Is face more important than my daughter?"

Huangfu Jue told her that her mother forced Yan Wanzhao to drink a sterilizing drug when she left the house. Her father found out about this, and after Yan Wanzhao committed suicide, the two had a big fight. Her mother left home in anger, and her father waited until the situation calmed down before chasing after her.

When she first heard about it, she was indeed stunned for a while. She didn't know that her mother had done this, but she didn't feel surprised. She felt that if her child was hurt in the future, her means of revenge might be more tragic than this. On the contrary, it was difficult for her father to be caught in the middle.

Huangfu Jue smiled with a relaxed expression, "Of course they are worried about you, but don't worry about me. You know I will take good care of you."

Yanzhi snorted coldly, and her depressed mood was slightly cheered up, "It's better to trust a ghost than to trust you."

Huangfu Jue flicked her forehead and said, "Nonsense. What do you want to eat for lunch? Shuangli and the others have picked a lot of fresh lotus pods. Do you want to peel them and make lotus seed soup?"

Yanzhi rubbed his forehead and thought for a while, then said with a smile: "Lotus can be picked in Jiangnan, and the lotus leaves are so lush. Let's go pick lotus too."

Her expression was unusually bright in recent days. Huangfu Jue looked at her with eyes full of doting, but said, "It can't be too long. You have to consult Imperial Doctor Jiang to check her pulse when you come back." Although she was an expert in medicine, she was extremely lazy about herself and made people feel uneasy.

Yanzhi glanced at him and hummed in a long nasal tone.

Green waves, green shirt, and beauty.

Yanzhi lay on the boat, squinting her eyes at Huangfu Jue who was rowing the boat, feeling comfortable and relaxed. Huangfu Jue rowed the boat into the depths of the lotus, then put down the prize, broke off a lotus leaf as green as a canopy, and lay down next to Yanzhi, using the lotus leaf to cover their faces.

Everything is silent and the years are peaceful.

Her ears could hear his long, steady breathing, her nose could smell the refreshing fragrance of lotus, and there was a well-behaved baby in her belly. She relaxed her limbs and the corners of her mouth naturally turned up.

Huangfu Jue's hands slowly drew circles on her belly. Occasionally, her belly would bulge, and his black eyes would light up. He smiled softly and said, "Little guy, don't bully your mother."

The boat rocked along the waves, rocking out rhythms and dreams. Yanzhi pillowed on the lotus fragrance, hugged Huangfu Jue's arm, and let sleepiness drag her into dreamland.

How nice it would be if time could stand still.

The author has something to say: No matter how slow the tortoise is, it will eventually reach the finish line. Comrades,

Liuliu can finally say that the final moment has finally arrived! The next chapter will be the ending.

☆、Chapter 111 Ending (Part 1)

Huangfu Jue seemed to be in a good mood these days, and he spent more and more time in Jiuzhou Qingyan Palace during the day. It should be because the plum rain had passed and the war in the front was no longer stalemate. Yanzhi felt lazy and did not ask.

Her appetite was still not very good. She barely ate half a bowl of ginseng flower porridge for dinner. She woke up in the middle of the night with an empty heart.

When she turned her head, she touched Huangfu Jue's hand. There was a strand of black hair wrapped around his fingertips. There was no sleepiness in his narrow and long phoenix eyes. He was looking at her with his chin tilted. There seemed to be a strange and dark light flowing faintly.

Yanzhi was still confused and blinked subconsciously.

The next moment, he turned sideways and said in a low voice, "Are you awake? Are you thirsty?"

He was covering her with his hands beside her face, restricting her movements. Yanzhi frowned and tried to push him away.

His body was tense, and the skin under his fingers was as hard as iron, trembling slightly when she covered it.

The alarm bells in his heart rang quietly, and he stared at her without blinking. His pupils were a dark shade of black, and something was stirring inside, like a beast that had been imprisoned for a thousand years. Desire, excitement, and impulse.

She immediately stopped moving and stammered, "I'm hungry."

His fingers gently stroked her face, then immediately moved away, and a lingering sigh rang out beside her ear.

He stood up.

Yanzhi let out a breath quietly, and before she could relax her body, he had turned around. Without any pause, he still held her face with one hand and kissed her lips.

Her lips and tongue, which were forcefully pried open, were forced to carry the scent of warm tea and a faint loquat aroma. When she swallowed, she heard his sigh of satisfaction and joy.

His lips were like dense spring rain, dripping on the tip of her nose, ears, and neck... Her heart was like peach blossoms in March, the sound of rain urged the buds to open, the colors were just right, and the beauty was dazzling.

The spring rain is silent, and the spring is in full swing.

He didn't even give her a chance to speak. A long kiss had already made her eyes sparkle. He held her in his arms, his clothes open in the moonlight, and pulled her hand against her naked skin, grinding her lips with his lips and teeth, and murmured: "... I'm hungry too..."

The skin under her palm was burning hot, and the texture was like jade. The slightest movement would cause large areas of trembling. His phoenix eyes were full of mystery, and the peach-red charm on his face seemed to be reflected in the bottom of his eyes and eyebrows. The slightest movement was difficult to describe.

He was in her hands, and he was tossing and turning for her.

She could not resist pressing her face against his warm skin and wrapping her arms around his waist. He was the knot in her heart that could never be untied. She was greedy for him, just because of this love.

I listened to the spring rain in the small building all night.

When she got off him, Yanzhi was already limp and her legs were still trembling. Huangfu Jue carried her to wash up, and when he returned to bed, he slowly massaged her waist and legs.

He had internal strength in his hands, and the soreness gradually faded away. Yanzhi yawned slightly, trying to suppress her sleepiness. The man beside her was refreshed, still with a languid charm. He leaned to the side, letting her rest her head on his shoulder more comfortably, and smiled softly, "Want to sleep? I asked them to prepare a midnight snack."

Yanzhi shook her head and reached her hand under his clothes. She knew he was not satisfied yet.

Huangfu Jue smiled and grabbed her hand, saying jokingly, "Do you want more?" The emotions that had been pent up for many days finally had a release point today. Even though she was a little carried away, she still knew how to restrain herself.

Yanzhi's face turned red, and she pressed hard on that hard spot with her hand, listening to the man beside her gasp with satisfaction.

Huangfu Jue hugged her neck tightly, gnashing his teeth and said angrily: "Pull the ladder out after climbing over the wall, huh? Want to ruin your happiness for the rest of your life?"

Yanzhi was laughing secretly, but the smile gradually faded. She listened to his deep and shallow breathing beside her ear and said after a while, "Is the war in Xidian over? You seem very happy today."

Huangfu Jue stared at her with his dark eyes, and suddenly bit her shoulder, shouting with some accusations in his voice, "You don't believe me."

At the same time, the little guy in her belly kicked her in unison. Yanzhi was startled, and felt that the man's mood changes tonight were really inexplicable. She stared at him fiercely, "What do you believe in?"

Huangfu Jue looked down at me and said

slowly, "Believe me, you will stay with me forever."

"Trust me, you and the baby will be fine."

"Trust me to be truly free with you."

He looked straight into her eyes, word by word, and every word seemed to hit the ice and snow, like a piece of flowing beads and broken jade. Every point, every piece, reflected her unfathomable and unbearable thoughts.

A sigh lingered in my heart.

She softened her expression, and her eyes were a little misty and wet. "Okay, I believe you."

He was not relieved, and snorted softly, pressed the round teeth maliciously with his fingers, and said slowly: "You say one thing and mean another."

After being tormented by him for half the night, her mind became duller and duller. Only a little intuition reminded her that this man must be worried about something tonight, and this worry was probably related to her. She vaguely wanted to escape.

Her body felt a little weak, and her hands and feet were limp. She thought for a moment, "Send me some food." It looked like he wouldn't let her sleep peacefully.

Yiyue brought over a soup of coix seed, lotus root, rice and black chicken. Huangfu Jue held her in his arms and fed her spoonful by spoonful. If he stayed overnight in Yanzhi's room, he would never invite anyone to stay. He would bring water and tea himself.

There was some warmth in her belly, and her head became more and more dizzy, her eyebrows and eyes were dim, her mind was lazy, and she felt a heaviness in her belly, as if a huge rock was pressing on her. She woke up suddenly, her heart pounding.

Huangfu Jue placed his hands on her abdomen, pressing down slowly with his fingers and palms.

Yanzhi was shocked and angry, and grabbed his hand, "What are you doing?"

He raised his head, his eyes were as clear as ice and snow, with real hatred, his tone was soft and cold, "Yanzhi, I hate it. I lied to you, I never liked children. For you, I am willing to try to like it. But if it weren't for you, if you were to... Yanzhi, I'm afraid, I'm afraid of what I would do to it." Yanzhi grabbed his hand and felt cold sweat on both of their palms. Her heart beat too fast, and there was a brief blank in front of her eyes. She said in a trembling voice: "What... are you going to do?"

Huangfu Jue stared at her for a long time, his eyes flickering countless times, and finally became empty. He said softly, "I want you to live."

Yanzhi glared at him angrily, trying hard to hold back the dizziness, her nails digging into his flesh, "You clearly knew it, you clearly knew it! If it weren't for you... if it weren't for you... if you had treated it badly, I would not let you go even if I became a ghost!"

She struggled hard, her body swaying, her lips turning purple, but her eyes were fixed on him.

Huangfu Juefeng's eyes were slowly filled with deep sorrow. With a slight movement of his hands, he broke free from Yanzhi's grip, held her face, and pressed his forehead against hers. "I only have you. No matter who wants to snatch you from me, I will not let you go. Yanzhi, for me and for the child, try to survive, okay?"

It was clearly June, with flowers in full bloom and the scent of musk flowing, but she felt so cold that her teeth were chattering. She felt as if she was in the snowy plains of the far north and her heart was in the abyss.

There is murderous intent in his eyes!

She was totally wrong!

How could she forget that this man's blood was cold. Being in the royal family, where brothers and sisters had been killing each other since childhood, how could he still care about blood ties? If he wanted a child, how could such a large harem be empty? It was ridiculous that she actually believed it. He was calculating against her, using her child to calculate against her, and her child was a chess piece that he could only use before it was born.

His tears, his surprise... were all fake.

He was a cold-blooded liar. It was ridiculous that she actually believed them. Her teeth were clenched so tightly that they made a clattering sound, and her eyes were terribly empty. Huangfu Jue kept staring at her, and with lightning speed, he pinched her jaw, forced her to open her mouth, and fed her a fragrant pill. His fingers kept pressing on her tanzhong, and when he saw that her eyes had regained some spirit, his tense back slowly relaxed.

Yanzhi only had time to say one word, "You..." before something was quickly stuffed into her hand. He held her hand and pushed it forward, just against his left chest.

"Hate me?" The softest tone and the coldest words, "If you hate me so much, just use some strength and it will end. No one will let anyone go. You, me, and our child will be together forever."

The sheath is made of black shark, the blade is made of hardened steel, and the blade is slightly blue, like the light of dawn. The famous sword Jiang Li is the king of short blades. It can cut hair without being stained by blood. At this moment, it is in her hand, against his chest.

Yanzhi's trembling hands suddenly calmed down, her eyes were dim, and her voice was as soft as a dream that was about to wake up, "You forced me, you actually... forced me to this point!"

When the first drop of blood splashed on

her hand, she was actually thinking in a trance that the famous sword and precious weapon were indeed worthy of their reputation, and it could cut through human flesh as easily as cutting white paper.

Huangfu Jue gasped for air, his face instantly turned pale, his dark eyes still smiling at her. He held her hand, which trembled slightly, and suddenly pushed it forward again.

One inch, two inches... one more inch, and the sword tip would penetrate into the atrium, cutting the blood vessels. When it was pulled out, blood would spurt out and splash three steps away.

His face, smiling eyes, constantly changing, dismantling and reassembling before her eyes, overlapping and circling. This night, it was like a nightmare beast, swallowing her into its belly, without seeing the sun, tightly bound, and tortured.

His soul seemed to rise into the air, and he watched her withdraw her hand and pull out the hairpin with a cold and sober look. In almost the blink of an eye, she had pressed thirteen acupoints on his chest.

She hated him, but even when she hated him to the point of being unable to sleep or eat... she never thought of killing him.

Huangfu Jue suddenly grabbed her hand and panted, "I broke your heart, you... give me back a sword, and we'll be even, okay?" The warmth in his palm was dissipating, but his eyes were still as soft as spring water,

"Yanzhi, will you forgive me? Will you stay with me, okay?"

Yanzhi tilted her head to look at him, her eyes blank, tears unknowingly covering her face, "I don't have it," she quickly repeated softly, "I don't have what you want. I can't give it to you." Her voice was light and cold, and strangely empty.

She had given him everything she could give, and it was in vain for him to try anything to possess what she could not possess.

Huangfu Jue held her hand tightly, with a faint light in his eyes, "If I give you... three points of hope, will you try your best... to stay?"

His blood seeped slowly, leaving dots of red on his plain clothes. He looked at her stubbornly, making a bet with his life.

Who can watch the flowers bloom and fall with a smile, who can hold hands and look at each other in the world of mortals, who can love each other, and be together for life and death, this is all the warmth she wants.

I don't want to let go, I can't bear to let go.

☆、Chapter 112 Ending (Part 2)

Who can watch the flowers bloom and fall with a smile, who can hold hands and look at each other in the world of mortals, who can love each other, and be committed to each other for life and death, this is all the warmth she wants.

He took a long breath, his lips as pale as brocade, the temperature in his palms gradually became colder, and his slanted phoenix eyes were like the twilight outside the window, as desolate and mournful.

After being together for such a long time, she thought she had understood him, but she still couldn't figure it out. He was clearly cold, but his blood could be so hot. I dipped my hands in the warm blood and smeared it on his lips, turning the dark lip color into a crimson, bewitching beauty. He is such a man. The sincerity in the world is nothing but using and being used. Why is he so obsessed, why is he so forced? Why, why...

My chest felt tight, as if something was stirring again after being silent for a long time.

He felt a pain at his fingertips, and he suddenly opened his mouth and bit her finger, as if he was ruthless, and it was sharply painful.

Huangfu Jue took a breath and forced his eyelids open again. After months of planning, sleepless nights, and a serious injury, his body had reached its limit. With this desperate gamble, he had no way back.

Yanzhi could stay beside him peacefully, not because of forgiveness or forgetfulness. She knew she would die, so she was willing to let go.

But he didn't want to let go, he wanted her to live. Now, he realized that he couldn't let her go no matter what.

His pupils were slowly dilating, and his teeth were still clenched. Looking at him, Yan Zhi suddenly curled the corners of her lips, stroked his forced eyelids, and sighed softly, "You bully me like this, just relying on my..." love.

The last two words were too light, too faint, like an illusion in a lake or a swamp, and he didn't hear them. Her compromise was the last straw that completely crushed his will and dragged him into darkness.

I fell into a deep sleep and when I woke up, the sun was setting.

Several layers of curtains and shadows cannot hide her fair complexion and beauty.

Yanzhi sat at the side of the table, supporting her chin with her hand, her clothes flowing out from below her knees, with a faint light flowing through them.

He looked at her almost greedily, but she didn't look at him. Her whole attention was on the white jade ice sculpture in front of her.

The ice sculpture has a bird's beak, a phoenix crown, three legs and a long tail. Hot flames are flowing in its transparent body. It raises its head towards the sky. Although it is a dead object, it has an arrogant and domineering aura that comes towards you.

Yanzhi looked a bit infatuated, and slowly reached out her hand. Huangfu Jue hurriedly shouted, "Don't touch!" He stood up too quickly and couldn't help but groan.

When Yanzhi came over to support him, Huangfu Jue half leaned on her, still frowning, "That's thousand-year-old black ice, how can you touch it so easily?"

Yanzhi remained silent. Blood smeared out of the bandage again. She felt his pulse, reapplied medicine, and then spoke calmly, "You had a head injury before, and now your lungs are damaged. Even if you have a good foundation, you will eventually become weak. If you don't take care of yourself, even the Golden Immortal can't do anything to you."

Huangfu Jue looked lazy and hummed softly with a nasal tone, "As long as you are watching over me, I will naturally cherish you."

His face was still pale, his eye sockets were sunken, and there was a new beard on his cheeks. He looked haggard, but handsome in a different way. It was not the first time I saw him in pain, but this time was particularly difficult.

Is it because the damage was caused by her own hands?

"The three-legged golden crow is only seen occasionally. How can you find it?"

How? Use the whole nation's strength and all its troops.

Huangfu Jue took her hand and kissed it

gently, then said with a smile: "God has pity on my deep love for him and couldn't bear to see me sad, so he specially gave me this great opportunity."

He half-closed his eyes, smiled and spoke, his brows calm and composed. He didn't look at her, but tilted his head towards her abdomen and said softly, "Baby, Daddy scared you yesterday. Daddy was wrong. Don't disturb your mother. When you come out, Daddy will apologize to you."

She tightened her hands hanging at her sides, and after a while she held his hand. Her fingertips were slightly cold, but he held it tightly without saying a word.

I can't tell whether my heart is bitter or astringent, and all the mixed feelings finally turn into a sigh.

Forget it, forget it.

With the depth of Snow Region's background and the ability of the master, they still couldn't find any information about the Three-legged Golden Crow. How much effort he put in, how could she not guess.

She is not a cowardly person. Since she is already so bound, why shouldn't she dare to start over?

Yanzhi held his hand and placed it on her abdomen, and spoke softly, "The Three-legged Golden Crow has been frozen. Although the Fire Spirit is still there, I don't know how much of its efficacy is left. It is also a legendary item and has never been used as medicine. I have not yet figured out its use. Huangfu Jue, I will give it a try as you wish. But... I am only 30% sure."

Huangfu Jue pulled her close, his phoenix eyes looked straight into hers, and said softly but firmly, "I will bet on these three points with you."

Yanzhi was silent for a long while before she said, "Okay. You swear that no matter what happens in the future, you will treat my son well."

Huangfu Jue blinked, feeling a little aggrieved, "If I didn't scare you, how could you come out of your shell?"

"……swear."

"I, Huangfu Jue, the 28th generation grandson of the Huangfu family, now swear by my ancestors and the country: I will treat Yanzhi and her son well..."

"Be kind to my son!"

"…Bad rouge…"

Yanzhi's body became heavier day by day, but her complexion improved day by day. Almost the entire Imperial Medical Bureau moved to the Ouxiangting Pavilion near Jiuzhou Qingyan Palace, and worked hard to study the Three-legged Golden Crow under Yanzhi's command. Huangfu Jue only stayed in bed for three days, and then returned to the former court to handle government affairs. Jiuzhou Qingyan Palace returned to its usual tranquility.

Yanzhi got up from the bed with great difficulty and looked at her swollen legs with a frown.

Linglong knelt on the ground, holding her feet and massaging them slowly, and said with a smile: "The maids said that women who are about to give birth are all like this. The medicine that the emperor found is really a miracle medicine. I see that the queen's complexion is getting better and better."

Yanzhi waited until the numbness subsided, put on her silk shoes, and walked slowly for two steps. The nap was not peaceful, the fetus was moving violently, and she felt a little irritated, "Has the emperor been here?"

Linglong wrung out the handkerchief and helped her clean her face while answering, "The Emperor came this morning, but he was afraid of disturbing the Empress's nap, so he just sat quietly for a while."

After burning incense and washing hands, she played the Qingping tune. Outside the window, banana leaves were thick, and a pair of orioles were chirping and jumping around, pecking each other's feathers. Their lively figures were reflected on the smoky window screen. Yanzhi stared at them quietly for a while, with the corners of her lips slightly raised.

"Send a message and ask my sister-in-law to come to the palace."

Her parents finally got up and returned to Beijing. The Marquis's Mansion was sealed off once, and most of the servants in the mansion were dismissed. She was powerless to do many things in the palace, so she had to ask her sister-in-law for help.

My mother is finally coming back, and I feel a little relieved. When the birth is imminent, I always hope that my loved ones can be with me.

Linglong paused slightly while tying the black Ruyi silk ribbon, and then she spoke as if nothing had happened, "Lord Jiang is ill, and the wife of the Marquis of Changning has returned home to take care of him. Besides, she is a new bride, and I am afraid she is still unclear about the preferences of the Marquis and the wife. If the queen is worried, I will go back to the mansion tomorrow to check."

"Is he sick?" Yan Zhi frowned slightly, "Is it serious? Why didn't you tell me earlier?"

"The day before yesterday, the young marquis sent someone to deliver something. He mentioned it briefly, saying it was an old illness and it was nothing serious. If the majesty hadn't asked, I would have forgotten about it."

Yanzhi thought for a moment and said, "Send someone to deliver some medicinal herbs and bring back the imperial physician's prescription." He was her brother's father-in-law, so he was considered a family member. She paused and said, "Report to the emperor. I will go back with you tomorrow."

Tomorrow we will be separated by mountains

and the world will be vast and boundless. I don't know if I will have the chance to spend time with my family at home again.

Linglong hurriedly smiled and said, "My lady, please pity me. If you go, the emperor will definitely follow you. The whole family is busy serving him, so how can I work?"

When Huangfu Jue came back, Yanzhi was leaning on the chaise longue, fiddling with the nine-ring chain in her hand without even raising her head.

Huangfu Jue changed his outer clothes, came close to her and took a look, then said with a smile, "Why did the situation suddenly change?" Then he squeezed in and sat down next to her, tapping her belly, "Little brat, did you offend your mother?"

Yanzhi slapped his hand with a cold face, "It can't hear or see, it's deaf and blind, how could it provoke you?"

Huangfu Jue was startled when he heard this, and then he narrowed his eyes and slowly glanced at everyone in the hall. He looked stern, then lowered his head and smiled, "Well, let me think, if it's not the younger one who caused the trouble, then it must be the older one. No new concubines, no beauties to see, no drinking, but do you think I came back too late today?"

Yanzhi threw the nine linked rings in her hand at him and said, "You don't need to talk nonsense to fool people. Inform the Ministry of Internal Affairs to arrange the ceremonial guard. I will leave the palace tomorrow."

Huangfu Jue smiled and embraced her, "Yanzhi is bored, the day after tomorrow, Marquis Yan and his wife will be here, we will hold a banquet in the palace, is it okay for you to stay in the palace?"

Her eyebrows raised, but before she could speak, Huangfu Jue hugged her and shook her, begging, "My dear queen, please spare us two. Can we just play in this palace? I will play the piano with you, watch the opera, sing songs, play finger-guessing games and play dice, okay?"

Yanzhi was originally slightly angry. Since she returned to the palace, he had guarded Jiuzhou Qingyan Palace like an iron barrel. No matter how big the storm was outside, it was just a gentle breeze and drizzle in Jiuzhou Qingyan Palace. She also knew that her body was indeed better for rest. But he was too defensive and refused to tell her even the bad news at home. He was being coquettish and clingy, and gradually she couldn't stand it anymore. With a slightly embarrassed face, she secretly pinched his waist and spat, "Do you still look like the Supreme?"

Huangfu Jue quickly kissed her on the cheek and wiped her forehead exaggeratedly, "Finally the sky cleared up after the rain." He stood up and pulled her down from the bed, "Today, Li Zhiqing dragged me to listen to the saint's way of governing the country for a long time. I haven't had dinner yet, but I'm starving. What else can I eat?"

Yanzhi's small kitchen was kept busy all day, and soon a table of food was ready. Huangfu Jue held her hand tightly and ate with one hand.

He had not been injured for long, so his diet was still mainly nutritious. Yanzhi saw that he was eating in a hurry, frowned, and served him the food personally, "Slow down."

Huangfu Jue tightened his grip and smiled at her, "I have an appointment with Pei Zhongqing and Meng Shifan tonight. Don't wait for me and go to bed early. I'll send a southern opera troupe to entertain you tomorrow."

There was still a light blue color under his eyes, and there was a well-hidden weariness in the depths of his eyes. Yanzhi felt bitter in her heart. He was responsible for the country of Kyushu, and she could not bear to add to his troubles, so she nodded slightly.

Huangfu Jue looked at her, his eyes filled with a soft light, "Good girl."

Huangfu Jue waited until she rested before leaving.

Before leaving, Huangfu Jue gave her a deep kiss on the lips. The fresh scent on her lips was mixed with the slightly sweet benzoin, and her breath was disordered. He gave her delicate kisses on her blushing cheeks, and with his eyes rolling, he murmured, "I really don't want to leave."

Yanzhi's hand slid down from his forehead, with a soft light in her eyes, and she spoke softly, "Come over tomorrow morning, I have something to tell you."

Huangfu Jue looked at her deeply, rubbing his cheek in her palm, "Okay, go to bed early."

The steps were very light, and they went farther and farther away.

Her consciousness gradually blurred in the brocade and red candlelight of the tent. Let's talk about it tomorrow, she thought. She was not a canary in a cage, nor a cold-hearted clay figure. He couldn't protect her like this for the rest of her life.

This kind of love is close to being imprisoned. Only honesty can make it last.

That's what she thought at the time.

What happened later··· Time passed, the fragrance faded, my heart struggled under the rock, and then I realized how naive I was.

The emperor's intentions are unfathomable; the emperor's heart is out of reach; the emperor's desires are endless.

As expected, a stage was built in Shangyuan Liuyunpu, with green lotuses holding up and a faint fragrance floating in the air. A wisp of flute music sounded like weeping and complaining. The person on the stage softened his posture, his eyes were as soft as water waves, and a piece of southern music lingered in his mouth.

The short couch in the shade of the drunken flowers, the purple and charming lady, could not hide her natural charm. The sunlight leaked through the phoenix tail tung tree, occasionally skipping over Yanzhi's eyes, she squinted slightly, her expression comfortable and relaxed. She leaned on the couch, under the wide gauze dress, a pair of jade feet were exposed, even though she was nine months pregnant, she was still extremely pure and beautiful, only her every move was more tender.

Tianpin sat slightly behind Yanzhi, and from the blind spot on the right, she looked at Yanzhi with unbridled eyes. Beauty brings disaster to the country, and a smile can conquer the city. These are not made up in ancient books. Tianpin smiled, picked up the teacup, and thought leisurely, but she didn't know if this beauty would also be doomed in the end.

On the stage, the actor's sleeves were fluttering to the fullest, rolling up slowly, shaking off a blue lotus. He bent his waist, his black hair falling to the ground, but the lingering sound from his mouth was still soft and clear, like a wisp of love slowly entwining people's hearts.

Yanzhi suddenly turned sideways and looked at Concubine Tian, who was obviously startled. Her expression remained unchanged, her pupils were clear and she smiled and said, "Sister, don't you like this play?"

Concubine Tian took a sip of tea and pursed her lips as she said, "The Emperor has been eager to find this actor for you. He is a famous actor in southern opera. He sings very well, but I don't like this kind of opera."

Yanzhi held her chin with one hand and looked at her for a long while, only to see that Tianpin was slightly panicked. She avoided her gaze by looking at herself, "Your Majesty, why do you look at me like this? But what's wrong with me?"

Yanzhi's eyes were full of meaning. "No, you are fine. All these years are thanks to you. You are the only old man left in the palace these years. If you have any request, the emperor and I will not refuse it."

Concubine Tian was slightly stunned, then she chuckled, "I have experienced a lot in these years, I just want to live a quiet life like this, I dare not have any more extravagant demands."

Yanzhi looked at her, the smile in his eyes gradually deepened, and then gradually dimmed. He turned his gaze to the dazzling phoenix flowers not far away, as if frozen, and sighed for a long while, "It's so colorful, but it will be blown away by the rain and wind in an instant. The flowers are too short-lived."

Concubine Tian listened with a smile, the tea in her hand moved slightly, and a few drops of water seeped into the sleeves of Zi Yanluo's embroidered clothes.

Yanzhi was indeed wary of Concubine Tian. Huangfu Jue once told her that Concubine Tian was a chess piece she could trust in the harem. She was not his, but she was tied to Huangfu Yu. He kept Concubine Tian in the palace, initially to monitor the concubines, and later to serve as a shield for her.

She trusted Huangfu Jue, but until now, she was subconsciously a little reserved when dealing with people. Today was the first time she stepped out of Jiuzhou Qingyan Hall without Huangfu Jue's company. Almost as soon as he sat down, Haigui whispered a few words in his ear, and he looked uneasy. While he was still hesitating, she spoke.

"Go and do your thing. I have so many people to keep me company. If you're not here, everyone will be more at peace."

His smile didn't reach his eyes at that time, but he didn't insist. After giving a few instructions, he got up and left. If it wasn't an extremely difficult matter, he would never do this. But the timing of the difficult matter was so coincidental that she felt a little confused.

Concubine Tian's expression today was not right.

She was tentative when she spoke, and she did have the intention of making the decision for her. If she stayed in the harem, the best outcome would be obscurity. For a woman, the twenties are like a flower that blooms to its fullest, and will soon wither and fall to the ground, consigning her body to the soil. However, she clearly hesitated, but still perfunctorily passed it over.

She was unmoved even though she had her own agenda. She thought at the time that the inducement was not big enough. But she didn't expect that what she wanted was indeed something she couldn't afford.

Concubine Tian was right behind her, her slender jade fingers were lightly pressing on her qi points, her voice was a little panicked, "Your Majesty, I will accompany you back to the palace first."

Yanzhi slowly turned sideways and looked into her dark eyes that pretended to be flustered. Suddenly, she reached out and held her hand on her waist. It was cold and smooth. She said lightly, "Tianpin is too timid. You must be steady and don't hurt my son."

Concubine Tian's face turned extremely pale, but she tightened her grip and spoke calmly, "Don't panic, Your Majesty. The prince will be fine."

What a mess.

When the song "The Story of the Purple Hairpin" reached its climax, Qingyi took out a little child in her hand and began to sing in a very serious manner, with a hint of childishness in her singing. Yanzhi was surprised at first, but she immediately laughed and raised her hand to wave to Yiyue, "Why is Tianyou here?"

The Queen Mother forced the emperor to abdicate, and Huangfu Fang changed sides at the last minute. When Huangfu realized what was going on, she released Tianyou from the palace, but rejected Huangfu Fang's request to return to the Northern Frontier, and kept him in Beijing. It had been a long time since she last saw this little man.

Yiyue was also very surprised and said with a smile: "It must be a surprise from the Emperor for the Empress."

It's enough to be surprised, but not necessarily happy.

The girl in green had a charming look in her eyes and lovingly called Tianyou "My son——". Before she finished her words, the actress dressed as a maid who had just come on stage suddenly jumped up, knocked the girl in green away, and slapped Tianyou on the top of his head.

At the same time, a shadow appeared beside Yanzhi, and a gray-clothed figure appeared in the air, condensing energy into a blade, slashing towards the back of the little maid. The little maid twisted in the air, changed her palm into a blade, and slashed directly at Tianyou's waist.

The little child's body was thrown hard towards a person-high exquisite stone three meters away.

Two figures suddenly appeared in the inner prison. One of them swept out a palm, causing Tianyou to deviate from the rocks, while the other rolled on the ground and hugged him before he hit the ground. The two figures in mid-air were already fighting with each other.

At this time, Yanzhi screamed, "Tianyou——" She grabbed Yiyue's hand, her fingertips trembling, "Quick, help me over!"

The palace servants and eunuchs beside her, whose faces had long turned pale, knelt down and cried, "Master, you can't do this."

Yiyue also knelt down and begged, "Your Majesty is in a dangerous position. You cannot go to dangerous places lightly. I beg you to return to the palace."

Yanzhi's face darkened, "Shut up! Who wants to stop me--" The two eunuchs exchanged glances quickly, one of them picked up Tianyou and left, and the other knelt down and kowtowed to Yanzhi, saying, "Your Majesty, please return to the palace."

They had already received the emperor's oral instructions that they had the power to make arbitrary decisions on matters, and the safety of the Empress was the top priority.

Yanzhi pursed her lips tightly, her face extremely ugly. She stared at him for a long while before speaking coldly, "I will leave the affairs of this place to you. You must protect the prince and catch the thief." She held Yiyue's hand tightly, "There is definitely no suitable person to take care of the prince. You take your people with you."

The assassination was extremely strange, but Tianyou was still a child, and she had to protect him at all costs.

Yiyue hesitated for a moment, but seeing that Yanzhi was determined, he had to wave to a few people and left in a hurry.

Concubine Tian took a step forward and got very close to her, "Your Majesty, the baby is the most important. This place is dangerous. I will accompany you back to the palace."

The author has something to say: Hahahaha, I, Hu Hansan, am finally back!

☆、Chapter 113 Ending (Part 3)

Tianyou's position is very delicate, he is the eldest son of Huangfu Fang. Although Huangfu Fang is detained in the capital, he has not given up his military power. He is also deeply loved by Yanzhi. She watched this child leave his biological mother and enter the palace. With pity for her, she felt a little more responsibility.

If Tianyou really got into trouble in front of her, she couldn't stand it. She understood it, and so did others. So when Tianyou got into trouble, the secret guards around her moved, and Yiyue went even though she didn't want to. Tianpin stood beside her naturally, smiled and blocked Zhenyue's step, and supported her hand.

She remained calm, but her heart was in turmoil. It was not until Tianpin's hand suddenly rested on her waist and the people she brought quickly separated her and restrained her that she realized what was going on.

Entered the hub again.

She stopped. Her hair lingered around her ears, causing the white jade pendant to rustle. Her eyes, which used to be calm, were now surprisingly bright, with a rare hint of worldly air. "Princess Tian, please keep your hands steady, don't startle my prince."

Concubine Tian's face was pale but she was still smiling, "Don't worry, Madam, I will definitely support you." She pushed her forward without losing any strength. Yanzhi sneered slightly, and although she looked arrogant, she moved forward as she wished.

There were originally only four people around her, and four more people joined in from Liuyunpu to Cuizhang Pavilion.

They walked very quickly, four in front and four behind, with her in the middle. They didn't even have a sedan chair ready. They walked along a secluded and quiet path without any hesitation.

Along the way, if we occasionally saw people, they would just kneel down to greet us from afar.

Although her face was calm, there was a ripple in her heart.

There were no sentries, no patrols, and someone had secretly deployed the imperial guards!

Although the road they chose was remote, it was heading southeast and gradually approached the Guanju Palace where Concubine Qi once lived.

Tianpin's hands had changed to half holding and half hugging, but Yanzhi's face was getting paler and paler, and sweat was seeping out from her temples. Tianpin looked at Yanzhi's face with anxiety in her eyes, but she never urged her. Their pace inevitably slowed down.

The white stone path was surrounded by bamboos on all sides. Yanzhi staggered slightly, and the hem of her gauze dress swirled slightly, hooking onto a clump of bamboos. Her center of gravity was unstable, and her left foot tripped over her right foot, and her body fell forward.

"Be careful!" Concubine Tian changed from dragging to hugging, and leaned forward with her elbows, barely holding Yanzhi. Before she could breathe a sigh of relief, she met Yanzhi's eyes - very calm eyes, without a trace of panic. She was startled and her hand loosened.

Yanzhi felt a little relieved at this moment. She brushed her hand away with her sleeve and leaned slightly against the corridor wood behind her. "I'm tired and don't want to walk anymore." Although her tone was light, it left no room for her to turn back.

Concubine Tian's face darkened, her eyes swept forward, and she immediately frowned and said, "Your Majesty, you can't help it at this moment."

Yanzhi smiled, but there was a bit of weariness and disgust in her eyes, "Even if it's not up to me, I don't want it to be up to you." Her hand slid to her abdomen, "Rather than letting it become a prey and worrying all day, why not let me end it today."

One of the two eunuchs in front turned around. He had an ordinary face, but his skin was darker. He looked at Yanzhi coldly and said, "The Queen is a smart person, so she won't do stupid things. We only want you, and it doesn't matter whether you have children or not."

As soon as he finished speaking, he stretched out his five fingers and grabbed her wrist, with his right index finger slightly bent, ready to press her fainting point. When it was close to the back of her neck, his pupils slightly opened, and his fingers were only a hair's breadth away, but suddenly froze.

Yanzhi held a hairpin in her free hand, and she didn't know when the tip of the hairpin had pressed against her temple. Her eyes were cold and infinite. Seeing him stop, she spoke softly, "Since I decided to be a mother, I have secretly vowed that I will never be manipulated by others in this life. You can tell me your purpose. If I can do it, I will directly agree to it. If you insist on using me as a pawn, then I might

as well perish together with you."
He raised his eyebrows, and his eyebrows slowly twisted into a "川" shape. He looked at her for a long while, and seeing that she was unmoved and her expression was still indifferent, he slowly put his hand down.
His expression was quite complicated. "Would you rather die with honor than live in dishonor? Such a hot temper is really a headache." When he said the word "ah", his tone suddenly changed, just like gorgeous silk suddenly appeared under the old-fashioned gray robe, and cheerful spring water suddenly burst out from the barren yellow soil, with a little bit of laziness and a little bit of pampering.
Yanzhi raised her eyes and scanned his face. She had always suspected the origins of this group of people. They seemed to have no ill will towards her. She deliberately tripped them to force them to the bottom line. She heard it clearly, and it was also his low cry just now.
She was sure that he had changed his appearance. His tone... was strangely familiar. He was an old friend!
"Who are you?"
He raised the corners of his lips, and his dull face was like a spring water that suddenly broke, with slight ripples. He blinked, "Guess?"
Concubine Tian snorted coldly and inserted herself between the two of them. "Your

Majesty, we are also following orders. You should not delay. Someone asked me to tell you about 'Snow on Tianshan Mountain, Flowers Without Death'. You will understand it after you go out."

Snow on Tianshan Mountain, flowers without sorrow, snow on Tianshan Mountain, flowers without sorrow, Tianshan Mountain... without sorrow...

Yanzhi's complexion remained calm, her posture still elegant, but her face turned uncontrollably pale. In an instant, confusion, weakness, desire, enlightenment, hesitation... all kinds of emotions intertwined and finally disappeared.

She spoke, and facing the ordinary eunuch, her voice was still clear and pure, "Tell me, who are you."

He looked at her, stretched out his hand, as if to touch her hair, but stopped a little away. Something in his eyes was slowly dissolving, a bit of struggle, a bit of pity.

"Come with me." When he spoke again, his voice was a little hoarse.

Yanzhi looked at him silently, and suddenly took a step forward. His hand touched her face, and her hand also touched her face.

Yanzhi pursed her lips tightly, and her fingers slowly moved around, feeling the real face under the human skin mask. Long eyebrows, sunken eyes, straight nose bridge...

The uncertainty that has long existed in my

heart, the subtle ripples that have long existed under the calm, the warmth that has long seemed unbreakable... It has always been there in the awakening when I wake up from my dreams at midnight, it has always been surrounded by clouds and mists, and the mountains and rivers are heavy. Just one step away, just one step away, and today I will be able to see the real truth...

My body is cold, my heart is beating fast, but my mind is clear. I would rather come and go naked without any worries than be bound by a cage surrounded by brocade and jade, covering the ground with pus and blood.

He curled his fingers and brushed them across her cheek. He seemed to pause, met her stubborn gaze, sighed softly, and held her shoulders tightly, "Yanzhi, don't be afraid. Come with us. You don't belong here anyway."

Yanzhi's hand had slid to his chin, her eyelashes trembled, and her eyes were mixed with sadness and joy, "Why? Pang Tong, you left here, why do you come back here?" There was no joy of reunion, only desolation and confusion in his eyes.

He opened his mouth, and Concubine Tian scolded in a low voice, "Are you crazy? What are you doing? This is not the time for you to be gentle and considerate! It doesn't matter if you die, but don't implicate others. Things over there can't be delayed for long, leave quickly!" Given the Queen's temperament, she might still consider the baby in her belly. But if she saw through even the slightest bit of it, how could she follow them obediently?

The eunuch glanced at her and said coldly, "Shut up." After a moment's hesitation, he squatted down and picked up Yanzhi horizontally, saying softly, "Yanzhi, I'll take you away first."

Yanzhi did not struggle, but her calm eyes contained a heat that could burn everything. She smiled gently, "Pang Tong, long time no see. It's a pity that I still won't go with you." Her smile was too light and too faint, as if it still had some of the lightness of a young girl, but more of it was like wisps of clouds on the mountains and thin mist in the fog, as if it would be dispersed by the wind.

"Put me down."

Pang Tong was stunned, then smiled bitterly, "This is not the time for you to be willful. Young Marquis Yan and your senior brother are waiting for you outside. You will understand everything when you meet them."

"No, send me back to Jiuzhou Qingyan Palace. The emperor will be worried if he loses me."

The tenderness from yesterday was still there, the tenderness between her brows was still there, but her mind was in a state of confusion. A small baby animal crawled out of her body, gnawing at her tendons and bones with its sharp teeth, chewing her flesh and blood. Unspeakable pain, unspeakable fear, unspeakable disappointment. But she couldn't do anything. This embrace was not the warmth she was familiar with, and she didn't know how the outside world had turned upside down.

Huangfu Jue, Huangfu Jue, what did you do to force Master to break the iron rule of Snow Region not involving the royal family, to force your virtuous ministers to join forces with outsiders, and to force the person who loved me the most to commit fraud and take me away from the palace on the eve of my delivery.

What on earth did you... do?

The rouge eyelids are half closed, and the curled eyelashes and narrow corners of the eyes have a smooth curve, which sets off the clear black and white pupils with a cold and distant beauty.

She just lay quietly in his arms, her fingers even casually crossed on her abdomen. If you didn't observe carefully, it would be difficult to see the panic, anger and paranoia in her eyes. Pang Tong seemed to have a crazy look in his eyes. He was stunned for a moment, and then slowly loosened his hand.

"Someone is here." One of the eunuchs suddenly said in a deep voice.

Pang Tong's face turned grim, and he immediately became alert. He tightened his grip and said, "Go!"

"No!" Yanzhi frowned and said coldly. As her fingers closed, the carefully maintained fingertips on her left little finger broke off.

At the same time, a loud laugh rose up, "The Queen wants to stay, who dares to leave?" On the rockery, beside the pond, and on the ivy racks, more than a dozen human figures suddenly appeared, holding black gold crossbows, with the sharp crossbow tips quietly pointing at them. A man came out from behind the screen wall, with black hair and black clothes, bright eyes, and a cold smile. It was Prince Gong Huangfu Fang.

His smiling eyes wandered over Pang Tong, he closed the folding fan in his hand and pointed at Pang Tong, "Hey, you bold traitor, why don't you put the queen down quickly."

Pang Tong narrowed his eyes and said with a smile, "Your Highness Prince Gong, what are you doing?" As he spoke, eight eunuchs and palace maids moved and surrounded Pang Tong and Yanzhi.

Huangfu let go and raised his bowstring, twisting it, and said with a smile: "The palace is deep and it is inconvenient to travel by car, so I came here to keep you for a while."

Pang Tong's phoenix eyes flashed with cold light. With a wave of his hand, the formation changed to a one-two-two-one assault cone. He shouted, "Huangfu Fang, don't you want the hundreds of people in Prince Gong's Mansion?"

The crossbow arrow broke through the air, and the strong force brought a hot wave in the air. Huangfu Fang laughed: "I have to thank the Queen for protecting Tianyou. The others died."

The black gold crossbow can fire five arrows in a row at a very fast speed. More than a dozen black gold crossbows occupied the commanding heights and fired indiscriminately over a large area. The people brought by Pang Tong were all good fighters, but they had no weapons in their hands. They took off their long gowns and swept the crossbows. In an instant, two people were injured. The rest of the people kept silent, replaced the injured behind them, and the group did not hesitate to go straight to the southeast corner.

Pang Tong's face was as gloomy as water. Since Huangfu Fang dared to attack, he was prepared to kill him. The most urgent thing now was to break out and meet up with the other side. Maybe there would be a chance for a turnaround.

"Fuck that old man." He cursed softly, turned sideways and flashed the sword. He kicked hard with his left leg, kicking the man who attacked from the left side away. Several arrows flew from the air, and a streak of blood appeared.

In just a few steps, they had already lost

six people. Except for him and Concubine Tian, the remaining two were injured.

Yanzhi was still in his arms, his expression solemn.

Pang Tong took a breath and put her down. He brought all the assassins with him. Two of them sacrificed their lives as arrows, and only then could they escape from Huangfu Fang's encirclement. However, he was still biting at them.

He wiped the blood off Yanzhi's face with his sleeve and grinned at her, "It's okay. The emperor will be here in a moment at most. It's just..." But I can't take you away with me.

He pushed Yanzhi to Concubine Tian and said, "We can't leave now. Let's find a place to hide first."

He glanced at Yanzhi and turned to meet the enemy without hesitation. He had a soft sword wrapped around his waist, so he freed his hand and drew his sword quickly, saving the remaining two people and barely resisting the attack.

Concubine Tian's face was pale and her eyes were frighteningly cold. She went over and held Yanzhi's arm, "Go!" Her hands were so strong that she pulled Yanzhi and walked two or three steps.

Yanzhi frowned and used some skill to pull her hand out. Ignoring Concubine Tian's angry look, she stood there and watched the battle silently.

"Empress, you can't keep losing your temper.

If you don't leave, he will die here in vain." Concubine Tian sneered.

Yanzhi suddenly removed the hairpin from her head, shook her head, and her black hair flowed down. She tilted her head slightly, inserted her left hand into the thick roots of her hair, and used her fingers as a comb, slowly sliding it down.

Very strange picture.

Whether the killer or the killed, they all tried their best to suppress their voices. Amid the riot of flowers, there was a strong smell of blood. But there was a woman, wearing a light silk shirt, with a light makeup, and a delicate demeanor. Her fingers gently stroked her hair, and where her long hair curled, a snow lotus slowly bloomed on the Shura field.

Time stopped for a moment.

Concubine Tian had a cold face and stepped forward to grab Yanzhi. The uncontrollable turn of events was really a bit weird. She couldn't think too much, but she couldn't give up.

Yanzhi did not move, but slightly tilted her palm and placed her fingertips just against Tianbin's wrist. She moved her hand closer and placed her knuckles just against her nails.

At first, Concubine Tian felt only a slight pain, and then it became numb and itchy. She was startled and quickly withdrew her hand. Although it was only a shallow red mark, there was a faint blue light on the

edge. She was shocked and angry, "You..."
Yanzhi ignored her and focused only on the battle situation. She shouted, "Pang Tong."
Pang Tong was about to stab his opponent's ribs with his sword, but he pulled it out with his backhand and chopped the other man's waist. He shouted loudly, and the tip of the sword lifted up the six-foot body and spun in a circle, blocking a wave of arrows. Fang Shun retreated.

"Why aren't you leaving yet?"

When he got close to her, he could smell a special fragrance, light but not scattered, sweet but not greasy, and even a bit lazy. He frowned and said, "Why are you still messing around with these things when you're about to give birth?"

Yanzhi smiled, but her smile was a little sad. She said nothing, but scratched his palm with her broken nails in the same way, and then said, "Be careful."

Pang Tong raised his eyebrows, his eyes still showing the old romantic style, and kicked the person who attacked from behind with a side kick, and gently pushed Yanzhi towards Tianpin with his backhand, "Let's go."

Yanzhi took a few steps back and opened her lips silently.

He could see clearly the blood splashed by the sword tip.

Take care, she said.

The world is so small, but the mountains are high and the water is long. Tomorrow is a mountain away, and the world is so vast. Life and death are irrelevant, and life and death are invisible.

A vague sense of heroism suddenly surged in his chest. He let out a long roar, and with his sword waving like a meteor, he pounced towards the crowd.

The author has something to say: Looking back, it seems like a dream. Looking back, my heart remains the same.

☆、Chapter 114 Ending (Part 4)

Concubine Tian took a deep breath, brushed her sweaty hair, and randomly pulled the vines at the entrance of the cave a few times, then said to Yanzhi, "What should we do?"

They were only a few hundred steps away from Pang Tong when they encountered three waves of pursuers. It was all thanks to Yan Zhi's pretending to be unaware and luring them to death with poison.

Concubine Tian looked at the woman in front of her with a complicated expression. Her long rouge hair was disheveled, her face was pale, she placed one hand on her abdomen, and leaned slightly against the stone. In such a situation, she still did not look embarrassed. The meaning of her existence in the deep palace was this woman. She had wasted her best years. She thought she could leave the deep palace this time and fulfill her long-cherished wish, but who knew that her life was hanging by a thread. She might blame her, but now she had some admiration for her.

In such a world of upheaval and life and death, she never felt sad or desperate, screamed or cried, and was not panicked or afraid. She seemed to have understood everything. But if she really understood, how could she not be hurt?

Yanzhi adjusted her breathing and tried to relax her body. She lowered her eyelids and looked at her rising and falling belly. Her eyes were very soft, and they only focused on this point. She only responded nonchalantly, "Wait."

The person they lured to death at the end did not have strong murderous intent, but was very wild and familiar. She guessed that he must be Huangfu Jue's man. If she couldn't leave, she would just wait, wait for Huangfu Jue, or Huangfu Fang, or... someone else.

Concubine Tian gritted her teeth and said, "I'll go outside and guard. If anyone comes, I might be able to lead them away." Yanzhi definitely couldn't leave. She might not be able to give birth to the child safely without tossing her body. Although she didn't say anything, the cold sweat on the tip of her nose and the trembling fingertips showed how bad the situation was. Their original plan was to prevent her from thinking too much, so they kidnapped her and took her out of the palace. Who knew that Huangfu Fang turned against them at the last minute, and the situation was out of control.

Yanzhi slowly stroked her abdomen with her palm, and smiled slightly when she heard it. "I should have let you go. If you could escape, you might still have a chance of survival. If you stay, no matter who comes, I'm afraid the ending will not be too good. But..." She raised her head. Although her hair was messy and her face was pale, her eyes were shiny black without any impurities, like star diamonds, with a compelling aura, "I need you, can you stay?"

Concubine Tian was stunned for a moment, then immediately looked at her belly. Seeing a stain on the hem of her phoenix-tail skirt, she spoke in panic, "...You...you are going to give birth? Now...now?"

She turned around twice in confusion. How could she give birth? How could she give birth? She could give birth in Fengque, where there were good medicines and a group of great doctors from the Imperial Hospital. She could also give birth outside the palace, where her loved ones were, and there were all the necessary preparations.

The whole country's strength and wealth have been used to carefully prepare for her for such a long time. Everyone has made careful plans and calculated the worst possible situation, fearing that something might happen to her. In the end, she ended up giving birth here, with no one, no medicine, and not even a basin of hot water? Concubine Tian staggered to kneel in front of her, stretched out her hands helplessly in the air, opened her mouth, and uttered after a long time, "How are you...ah...can't you wait...aren't you a good doctor...let it...let it not come first..." By the end, she was already crying.

She was afraid that if Yanzhi and the child were in trouble, the world would be in chaos in an instant. What about Huangfu Yu? She had waited for so long, hoped for so long, even if she got nothing, but Huangfu Yu, the obsession that she had kept in her heart for so many years, she could not give up, absolutely could not give up.

Under the green wutong tree, he looked at her, his eyes full of emotions, and he sighed slowly after a while, and his fingers fell on her hairline, like a butterfly flapping its wings, but it stirred up huge waves in her heart. She didn't care about the pity and love in his eyes, the struggle and relief in his expression. She only knew that this man with a noble face finally stopped joking and could finally look at her as a woman.

He is a prince and she is the daughter of a household general.

For thirteen years, the difference between the monarch and his subject could not be bridged, and he never showed any sympathy for her emotions other than loyalty.

"...After you finish this... then stay with me..."

I can't let go of the hope that I finally grasped after such a long period of loneliness.

Concubine Tian looked at her bulging belly in despair. She heard a chuckle and a pair of cold, wet hands held hers and pressed them down on her bulging belly. Yanzhi's voice was still clear, "Shh, don't panic. It's healthy. It's moving. It's okay. Believe me."

It was true. Her belly felt so tight under the thin clothes that she even felt like she was touching the child's clenched fist.

Her calmness seemed to be contagious. Concubine Tian tried her best to suppress her trembling and spoke stiffly, "I...what should I do..."

The smile on her rouge lips faded, but never disappeared. She said slowly, "Don't be afraid, it will be quick. Help me take off my clothes first."

She tried her best to collect dry grass and put her clothes on top. When she saw the belly that was particularly high compared to the slender legs, Concubine Tian's mouth was dry and cold sweat was pouring down. When she saw Yanzhi twist off the hairpin, revealing a sharp and shiny tip with a faint white luster, she almost screamed out, "What are you doing?"

"Shh." He placed two fingers on her lips. "We don't have much time. Please listen to me."

The cold tip of the hairpin was pointing at the light brown midline of pregnancy on her abdomen. Concubine Tian was horrified to discover that there was a hint of relief in her smile. She held her breath and watched the tip of the hairpin gradually slide down and stop just above the Shenque point.

Yanzhi said, "I can only hold out for so long. It's up to you. Don't be afraid. It's very simple. Take the child out and leave. If you meet someone, take him hostage." She closed her eyes, with a bit of laziness and fatigue between her eyebrows. She laughed at herself, "If I die, this child can still be used. This is your chance. If you can escape, give it to my mother to raise."

She suddenly leaned forward, her eyes fixed on Concubine Tian, "I can only give it to my mother. Can you promise me?"

Her pupils were so deep and so bright that Concubine Tian couldn't look away and nodded involuntarily.

"You swear that if you send this child to someone else, the one you love will not live as he wishes, will die without a supporter, will be alone and miserable, and will be destitute for half his life. He will not be allowed to enter the imperial temple, will not be worshipped, and will be removed from the family tree."

Concubine Tian hesitated, but could not

think. She only felt that the eyes were getting brighter and brighter, like fireworks bursting out, with blurred colors, and like countless whirlpools of light, flickering. She stared at them, unable to turn away, and only heard herself saying, "I swear..."

There was a sudden burning pain between her brows, and her expression became clear. She saw Yan Zhi remove the bloody index finger from her brows and said in shock and anger, "You...what did you do!"

Yanzhi's face became paler and her lips were pale. She leaned against the stone and took a few breaths before she said, "Don't be afraid. It's the 'Three Lives Gu'. As long as your feelings remain unchanged, and you remain faithful to it no matter whether you live or die, it will sleep forever."

Three lives and three worlds, this love will never change. When love is deep, we only hope it will last forever, but how can we know that even the most beautiful woman can't stand the passing of time? It's better for me to be with you in this life, and I will always be by your side wherever you go or wherever you sit.

"Sansheng... Gu?" Concubine Tian covered her forehead with her hands. There was no abnormality between her eyebrows. It seemed that the pain just now was just an illusion. She asked suspiciously, "Why do you carry Gu with you? Are you... kidding me?"

"Of course it's not specially prepared for

you." It has been sleeping on her fingertips for several months. The person it was prepared for will probably never see it again. "When you become a mother, you will forgive me."

She bit a strand of hair and let the tip of the hairpin slowly fall down towards her abdomen. Her black hair and red lips made her look extremely charming.

"Don't forget your oath, otherwise, the Three Lives Gu will come out, and the sufferings of three lives will accumulate in one person."

Concubine Tian looked pale as she watched the scene in horror. Her blood poured down her snow-white belly. Suddenly, she heard a voice saying, "Wait a minute."

Chapter 130 Finale

When you become a mother, you will understand.

All the suffering can be borne for him, all the principles can be abandoned for him, all the back roads are paved for him. Pour all the love of this life into this moment.

A line of blood meandered down the snow-white belly, strangely sad, but also strangely charming. Concubine Tian had a dry mouth and watched all this almost like a madman.

Only with this sound did the spell of the almost stagnant air be broken.

The vines at the entrance of the cave were picked apart, and Huangfu strode in. He glanced inside and fixed his eyes on Yanzhi. He was stunned for a moment, then sneered. He pushed Concubine Tian aside with the sharp tip of his sword and stood beside Yanzhi, looking down at her.

"Stupid woman."

Yanzhi spat out the hair in her mouth. Her lips were almost the same color as her clothes. Her hair on her forehead was wet with sweat, but her face showed almost no pain. A cold look flashed in her eyes. Her eyelids were half closed, and her tone was cold, "Don't look at anything inappropriate."

Huangfu Fang was speechless for a moment, looking at her abdomen with a gloomy expression.

The sallow skirt had been untied, and the breath was disordered due to anger, so the blade could not go down. Pulling the clothes over, breathing slowly, he smiled coldly, "Prince Gong is a smart man, why do we have to kill him all?"

Huangfu Fang's gaze shifted to her face, his eyes filled with emotions that were difficult to discern, "...Is it worth it for a man like this?"

"Prince Gong is plotting to conquer the world, so he naturally doesn't care about this little bit of love." The invisible left hand curled up and grasped inside the clothes, nails piercing into the palm,

"This child can't hinder Prince Gong, he won't stay in the palace. Take his life in exchange for yours."

Printed in Great Britain
by Amazon